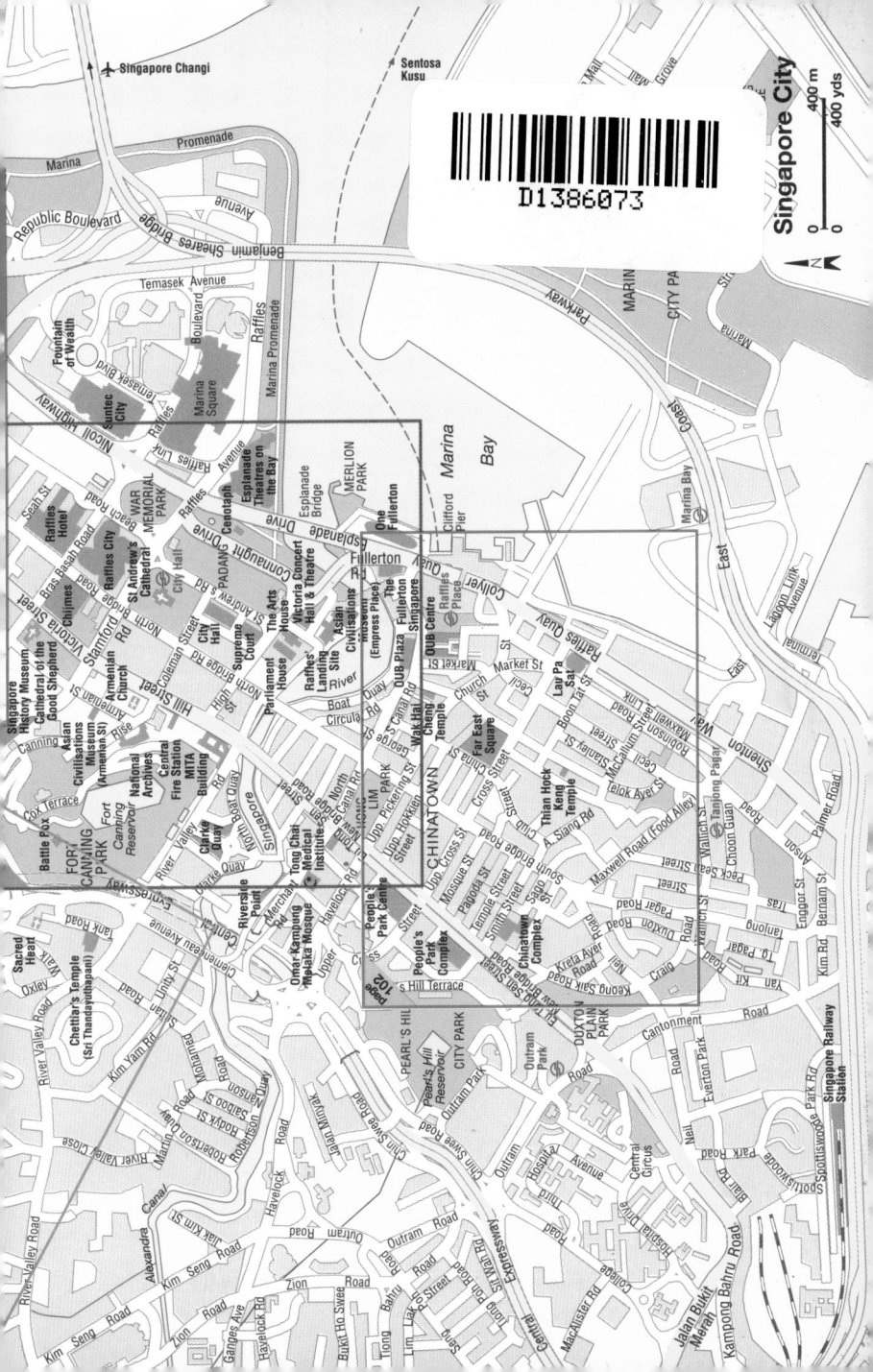

INSIGHT CITYGUIDE

SINGAPORE

Discovery CHANNEL

APA PUBLICATIONS L
Part of the Langenscheidt Publishing Group

INSIGHT GUIDE
SINGAPORE

Editor
Francis Dorai
Art Director
Klaus Geisler
Picture Editor
Hilary Genin
Cartography Editor
Zoë Goodwin
Editorial Director
Brian Bell

Distribution

UK & Ireland
GeoCenter International Ltd
The Viables Centre, Harrow Way
Basingstoke, Hants RG22 4BJ
Fax: (44) 1256 817988

United States
Langenscheidt Publishers, Inc.
46–35 54th Road, Maspeth, NY 11378
Fax: (1) 718 784 0640

Canada
Thomas Allen & Son Ltd
390 Steelcase Road East
Markham, Ontario L3R 1G2
Fax: (1) 905 475 6747

Australia
Universal Publishers
1 Waterloo Road
Macquarie Park, NSW 2113
Fax: (61) 2 9888 9074

New Zealand
Hema Maps New Zealand Ltd (HNZ)
Unit D, 24 Ra ORA Drive
East Tamaki, Auckland
Fax: (64) 9 273 6479

Worldwide
**Apa Publications GmbH & Co.
Verlag KG (Singapore branch)**
38 Joo Koon Road, Singapore 628990
Tel: (65) 6865 1600. Fax: (65) 6861 6438

Printing

Insight Print Services (Pte) Ltd
38 Joo Koon Road, Singapore 628990
Tel: (65) 6865 1600. Fax: (65) 6861 6438

©2005 Apa Publications GmbH & Co.
Verlag KG (Singapore branch)
All Rights Reserved

*First Edition 1972
Eleventh Edition 2004
(Reprinted 2005)*

ABOUT THIS BOOK

This guidebook combines the interests and enthusiasms of two of the world's best-known information providers: Insight Guides, whose titles have set the standard for visual travel guides since 1970, and Discovery Channel, the world's premier source of nonfiction television programming.

The editors of Insight Guides provide both practical advice and general understanding about a destination. Discovery Channel and its website, www.discovery.com, help millions of viewers explore the world from the comfort of their own homes.

How to use this book

The book is carefully structured both to convey an understanding of the city and its culture and to guide readers through its sights and activities:

◆ The Best of Singapore section at the front of the guide helps you to prioritise what you want to see: top family attractions, the best walks, parks and shopping as well as uniquely Singaporean attractions and useful money-saving tips.

◆ To understand Singapore today, you need to know both about its past as well as what makes the city tick today. The first section covers the city's history and culture in lively, authoritative essays written by specialist writers with intimate knowledge of the city-state.

◆ The main Places section provides a full run-down of all the attractions worth seeing. The main places of interest are coordinated by number with full-colour maps.

◆ A list of recommended restaurants and cafés is included at the

The contributors

This new edition was edited by Insight's Singapore-based managing editor **Francis Dorai**, who restructured the book into its current practical and reader-friendly format. Assisting him in this task was Singapore writer **Joan Koh**, who specialises in travel, food and lifestyle topics. She not only updated all of the places chapters but also wrote the insightful restaurant listings and the feature on shopping. As a keen food enthusiast (who happens to cook to relieve stress!) Koh is well acquainted with Singapore's ever-changing restaurant scene.

Audrey Perera, a former newspaper journalist and correspondent for the Asia-Pacific edition of *Business Traveller* wrote Singapore After Dark. Another Singapore freelance writer, **Wyn-Lyn Tan**, wrote the fact-packed Travel Tips section. The incisive social campaigns essay was the work of political activist **James Gomez** while Singapore English was penned by humorist **Sylvia Toh**. Past contributors whose work remains in condensed form in this edition include **Tan Chung Lee, Chua Chong Jin, Tisa Ng, Robert Powell, Shamira Bhanu, Kenneth Wong, Joseph Yogerst, Rachel Farnay, Ilsa Sharp, David Pickell, Julia Clerk, Marcus Brooke, Star Black** and **Eric Oey**.

Most of the striking images were taken by **Jonathan Koh, Alain Evrard, Jack Hollingsworth** and **David Henley**.

end of each chapter in the Places section. The best of these are also described and plotted on the pull-out restaurant map that is provided with this guide.

◆ Photographs throughout the book are chosen not only to illustrate geography and architecture but also to convey the different moods of the city and the pulse of its people.

◆ The Travel Tips section includes all the practical information you will need, divided into four key sections: transport, accommodation, activities (including nightlife, shopping and sport) and an A–Z listing of practical tips. Information may be located quickly by using the index printed on the back cover flap.

◆ A detailed street atlas is included at the back of the book, complete with a full index.

CONTACTING THE EDITORS

We would appreciate it if readers would alert us to errors or outdated information by writing to:

Insight Guides, P.O. Box 7910, London SE1 1WE, England. Fax: (44) 20 7403 0290. insight@apaguide.co.uk

NO part of this book may be reproduced, stored in a retrieval system or transmitted in any form or means electronic, mechanical, photocopying, recording or otherwise, without prior written permission of *Apa Publications.* Brief text quotations with use of photographs are exempted for book review purposes only. Information has been obtained from sources believed to be reliable, but its accuracy and completeness, and the opinions based thereon, are not guaranteed.

www.insightguides.com

Maps

Travel Tips

TRANSPORT

ACCOMMODATION

ACTIVITIES

A–Z: PRACTICAL INFORMATION

THE BEST OF SINGAPORE

Setting priorities, saving money, unique attractions...
here, at a glance, are our recommendations, plus some
tips and tricks even locals don't always know

SINGAPORE FOR FAMILIES

These 10 attractions are popular with children though
not all will suit every age group.

- **Duck Tours**. A wacky amphibious craft will take you around the Civic District before splashing into the Singapore River. *See pages 85 and 230.*
- **Escape Theme Park** and **Wild Wild Wet**. Thrilling adrenalin-pumping rides for the fearless and young-at-heart. *See page 182.*
- **Forum The Shopping Mall**. Children's clothing and speciality toy stores are found at this kid-friendly mall. *See page 128.*

- **Jurong Bird Park**. The region's leading bird park has some 600 species of birds. Don't miss the four walk-in free flight aviaries. *See page 169.*

- **Night Safari**. Clever lighting and realistic recreation of habitats will make you feel as though you're in a tropical jungle at night. *See page 193.*
- **Singapore Science Centre**. Everything you need to know about science is found here in its over 1,000 exhibits. Kids will have fun with the interactive galleries. *See page 166.*
- **Singapore Zoological Gardens**. Over 300 species of wildlife are presented in their natural environments. Not to be missed are the animal shows and Children's World. *See page 192.*
- **Sentosa**. An island retreat that has everything for the family: museums, an aquarium, an old fort, a musical fountain, beaches, and more. Plan to spend a full day. *See page 151.*
- **Igors**. If you have an affinity for things that go bump in the night, don't miss this hilariously funny horror-theatre dinner show. *See pages 57, 173 and 184.*

ABOVE: the massive Fountain of Wealth at Suntec City.
BELOW LEFT: kids are well catered for at Sentosa island.
BELOW: the Singapore Sling was invented at the Long Bar.

ONLY IN SINGAPORE

- **Durians**. You either love or hate this pungent fruit. Stalls in Geylang sell them year round. *See page 174.*
- **Breakfast with Wildlife**. Fancy having toast and scrambled eggs with unusual company? *See page 192.*
- **Chilli Crabs**. You cannot leave Singapore without tucking into this wonderfully robust dish. Everyone raves about it. *See pages 61, 64, 179 and 185.*
- **Fortune Tellers**. Have your fortune told by a parrot (with the aid of his human assistant) in Little India. *See pages 137 and 138.*
- **Fountain of Wealth**. Touching the waters of

the world's largest fountain is said to bring one good luck and prosperity. *See pages 84 and 118.*
- **Singapore Sling**. Order one at Raffles Hotel's Long Bar, where the drink originated. *See pages 86 and 87.*

BEST WALKS

- **Chinatown**. Explore Trengganu, Pagoda, Smith and Sago streets and soak in the Singapore of yesteryear. Don't miss the Chinatown Night Market. *See pages 101–14.*

- **Civic District**. The city's colonial past is well preserved in the old churches, hotels and museums of this charming district. *See pages 79–94.*
- **Peranakan Place and Emerald Hill**. Be enthralled by quaint shophouse and terrace house architecture in this little enclave. *See pages 124–25.*
- **Little India**. Be prepared for a sensory overload. Start at Little India Arcade and walk down Serangoon Road. *See pages 135–41.*

BEST FESTIVALS AND EVENTS

- **Chingay Parade**. Celebrated as part of Chinese New Year, the city's biggest street procession sees decorated floats and acrobats parading down the street. Exact day is dependent on Chinese New Year.
- **Great Singapore Sale**. A retail blowout that offers steep discounts all over the island. From late May till early July.
- **Singapore Arts Festival**. Three weeks worth of dance, music and theatre by some of the world's best and most innovative performers. From late May till June.
- **Singapore Food Festival**. Eat till you drop. This month-long festival celebrates Singaporeans' favourite pastime – eating – with

food tours and food-related events. July.
- **Thaipusam**. Male devotees bear the *kavadi*, a heavy metal arch with spikes, and walk from Sri Srinivasa Perumal Temple on Serangoon Road to Sri Thandayuthapani Temple on Tank Road. The exact date is dependent on the lunar calendar. Usually in January.
- **Thimithi**. Hindu devotees demonstrate their faith, courage and endurance by walking across a bed of burning coals at the Sri Mariamman Temple. Usually in October or November.
- **World Gourmet Summit**. Some of the world's best chefs cook up a storm at top restaurants during this two-week event. Mid April.

ABOVE: Chinatown is full of interesting souvenirs, like these handmade Chinese fans, for instance.
LEFT: trishaws provide rides around the streets of Little India.

BEST MARKETS

- **Campbell Lane**. Fresh produce, jasmine garlands, aromatic incense, Bollywood CDs and statues of Hindu gods are all found here. It becomes especially lively in the evening. *See page 138.*
- **Clarke Quay Flea Market**. Rummage through a pile of curios, old stamps, bronze statues and other trinkets at this Sunday market. *See page 93.*

- **Chinatown Complex**. Start early morning and head to the basement to see a "wet" produce market. The fishmongers at work make for great photography. *See page 105.*
- **Chinatown Night Market**. Every evening Trengganu, Pagoda and Sago streets close to traffic and vendors set up carts selling souvenirs and gifts. *See page 105.*

BELOW: a Hindu penitent, spiked and skewered with steel rods and carrying a *kavadi*, at the annual Thaipusam festival.

BEST BARS AND CLUBS

● **Attica**. This ultra-hip bar / lounge / disco at Clarke Quay is currently one of the hottest nightspots in town. *See page 220.*
● **Bar Opiume**. It's so hip, poseurs often stand

in line to see and be seen. Its location, by the riverfront side of the Asian Civilisations Museum, is stunning. *See pages 81 and 220.*
● **Harry's Bar**. One of Boat Quay's stalwarts

is still the city's best jazz bar. On Friday and Saturday nights, the crowds often spill out into the streets. *See pages 113 and 220.*
● **New Asia Bar**. The drinks are easily overshadowed by the stunning floor-to-ceiling views of the city from its 71st-floor perch at the Swissôtel The Stamford hotel. *See pages 86 and 221.*
● **Post Bar**. This predinner spot at the Fullerton hotel – with its wide martini selection – exudes both style and casual elegance. *See pages 82 and 221.*
● **Zouk**. Where serious clubbers head to for cutting-edge dance music and a wild party atmosphere. High on the "be-seen" scale. *See pages 57, 94 and 222.*

TOP PARKS

● **Bukit Timah Nature Reserve**. The number of plant species here exceeds that found in the whole of North America, says conservationist Dr David Bellamy. *See page 191.*
● **East Coast Park**. You can be as active as you want to – cycle, kayak, rollerblade – or just work on your tan by the beach. *See page 178.*
● **MacRitchie Reservoir Park**. Several trails, taking from one to five hours, offer a good workout; signboards in the

reserve offer an insight into its flora and fauna. *See pages 190 and 191.*
● **Singapore Botanic Gardens**. Singapore's oldest national park is a living museum of tropical plants. Picnickers, *tai chi* and yoga practitioners are a common sight. *See page 128.*
● **Sungei Buloh Wetland Reserve**. Noted for its diversity of bird life, the park has hides to allow you to birdwatch. Don't miss the walk through the mangrove forest. *See page 195.*

ABOVE: Thian Hock Keng Temple in Telok Ayer Street is one of Chinatown's most visited temples.
LEFT: barman in action at Fullerton Hotel's Post Bar.

MOST IMPORTANT PLACES OF WORSHIP

● **Kong Meng San Phor Kark Temple**. Singapore's largest (and busiest) Buddhist temple is also an important Vesak Day place of worship. *See page 190.*
● **Sri Mariamman Temple**. The city's oldest Hindu temple is dedicated to the Goddess Mariamman – who cures people of serious illnesses. *See page 103.*
● **Sri Srinivasa Perumal Temple**. This Hindu temple in the heart of Little India is a hive of activity on most days. Its busiest time of the year, however, is during the annual Thaipusam festival. *See page 140.*

● **Sultan Mosque**. Singapore's largest mosque, with its striking golden dome, is a familar landmark in the Malay-dominated enclave of Kampung Glam. *See page 143.*
● **St Andrew's Cathedral**. This colonial-era monument, completed in 1862, is where Singapore's Anglican community worships. *See page 85.*
● **Thian Hock Keng Temple**. Dedicated to Ma Cho Po, Goddess of the Sea, this ornate temple, dating back to 1842, is always thronged with devotees burning joss sticks. *See page 110.*

BELOW: bronze sculpture at the Singapore Botanic Gardens.

FREE SINGAPORE

on the Bay on Fri–Sun evenings for free music performances. *See pages 82–3.* Singapore Botanic Gardens has outdoor concerts at least once a month. *See page 128.*

- **Nature Reserves.** Entry to most nature reserves – Bukit Timah, Pierce, Seletar and MacRitchie – are all free. *See pages 190–92.*

- **Museums.** Both Asian Civilisations Museums, Singapore Art Museum and Singapore History Museum all have free entry on Friday evenings from 7pm onwards. *See pages 80, 89 and 94.*

- **Music.** Head to the Outdoor Theatre at Esplanade – Theatres

- **Newspapers and Magazines.** Pick up free copies of *Streats* and *Today* newspapers from MRT and bus stations. Free *I-S*, *Juice* and *Where* magazines, with the latest on dining and clubbing, are found at selected eateries and bars.

- **Temples.** Entry to all churches, temples (both Chinese and Hindu) and mosques are free.

ABOVE: woven baskets of every shape and size at Arab Street.
LEFT: statuary at Asian Civilisations Museum, Empress Place.
BELOW: *Streats* and *Today* tabloids are free.

BEST SHOPPING EXPERIENCES

- **Arab Street.** The one-stop street for all kinds of fabrics – silk, satin, linen, cotton – as well as glittering crystals, sequins and beads. *See page 142.*

- **Serangoon Road.** This main street which runs down Little India and its sidestreets all vie for attention with shops selling incense, silks, flowers, jewellery and arts and crafts. *See pages 135–40.*

- **Funan The IT Mall.** Computer and electronics buffs will find everything they need at this specialist mall. *See page 224.*

- **Ngee Ann City.** Japanese retailer Takashimaya and

Singapore's largest bookstore Kinokuniya are here. Shop till you drop at over 130 stores. *See page 125.*

- **Tanglin Shopping Centre.** Asian furniture, antiques, rare prints and Persian carpets are the mainstays of this mall. *See page 128.*

- **Tangs.** This homegrown department store has funky electronic gadgets for the home and top local fashion labels. *See page 126.*

- **Thow Kwang Industry.** Home to a giant "dragon" kiln and a great place to buy all sorts of pottery and earthernware. *See page 170.*

MONEY-SAVING TIPS

Discounted Tickets. Avoid watching movies on Fridays and weekends when ticket prices are at their highest. (S$8.50). Cinema tickets cost only S$6.50 from Monday to Thursday. Similarly, at the theatre, watch a matinee instead of an evening performance – you'll shave 20 percent off prices.

Save on GST If you plan to shop a lot in Singapore be sure to claim your GST

refund, which amounts to 5 percent off your total cost. *See page 224.* Also, smart shoppers know the best time to shop is during the annual Great Singapore Sale from end May to early July (www.singaporesale.com.sg).

Cheap Drinks Import taxes on alcohol are high, so a martini at a top end bar can cost as much as S$18 a pop. Savvy drinkers can get their money's worth during "happy hour" when

prices can be discounted as much as 50 percent. At some bars, "happy hours" can stretch from 3–9pm (hic!).

Pay What You Want Unbelievable but true. At Annnalakshmi, an Indian restaurant serving vegetarian meals, you pay what you want after your meal. *See page 96.* At some Buddhist temples, vegetarian meals on the 1st and 15th of every month are free; it's polite to give a small donation.

SAVVY SINGAPORE

Even its fervent admirers used to admit that the city-state was bland and boring. But a surprising transformation is taking place, as the city learns to take itself less seriously – and have fun

Who would have thought a decade ago that Singapore's thriving arts and entertainment scene would make the cover of *Time* magazine? Journalists used to focus on the city as a model of efficiency and its economic prowess, or on its draconian rules (remember the American teen who was caned for vandalising a car?). But suddenly Singapore has become hip and happening: *Time*'s eight-page article was called Singapore Swings. And a few days later, the *New York Times*, in its arts and leisure section, chimed in by praising the city's explosive arts scene.

Arts in the city

True, the city-state's economy, which seemed unstoppable, has been dented by the continuing global recession, yet walk down Singapore's streets and the energy remains palpable. The economy is being liberalised, whizz-kid foreigners are being hired as top management in Singapore companies, homegrown entrepreneurs are aiming to become world-class names, and e-commerce is alive and kicking. As years of affluence have created a society desiring things less tangible than housing or a decent income, censorship laws have gradually been eased to pave the way for greater artistic freedom. Films which would previously have been banned are now given a Restricted (Artistic) rating, allowing even full frontal nudity. On stage, this has led to a flourishing of the arts scene; the play *M. Butterfly* exposed the bare buttocks of the lead transvestite character to an audience who didn't bat an eyelid. For better or worse, actors are showing more skin than ever, shedding their clothes, along with other inhibitions on stage without qualm. Not only was the local play *Shopping and F***ing* given the nod by the usually straight-laced censors, it also won the Best Director prize.

And when the Esplanade – Theatres on the Bay was unveiled, the authorities unashamedly proclaimed Singapore's intention to be the region's arts hub. The theatre venue, dubbed the "durian" – as its facade resembles the pungent, spiky tropical fruit – had earlier raised a stink because of its controversial design. Detractors may argue that the Esplanade has some way to go before it becomes Asia's answer to Sydney's Opera House, but no one can deny it has created some ripples in international arts circles.

PRECEDING PAGES: CBD skyline framed by a travellers' palm; the old world Raffles Hotel.
LEFT: Stamford Raffles (founder of modern Singapore) statue at the Raffles Landing Site.

This liberalisation is not confined to the arts alone. The call for an open society saw former Prime Minister Goh Chok Tong announcing that homosexuals would be accepted in the civil service. The call to embrace diversity was no longer confined to religion and race. Though the minister's liberal views raised eyebrows among the more conservative, it was a sign that Singapore was ready to swing. And swinging it is today: nubile young things routinely clamber onto bar tops to dance, youngsters are skyrocketed into the air in Singapore's first reverse bungy jump, and gay bars make no bones about who they court – all sanctioned by the authorities, of course.

Smart orderliness

On a map of any scale, Singapore is just a dot at the tip of Peninsular Malaysia. Despite fears for its survival, the tiny 682-sq km (263-sq mile) island has blossomed into one of Asia's success stories. Much of this has to do with its obsession with cleanliness, orderliness and a healthy *kiasu* ("afraid to lose" in the Hokkien dialect) attitude. Not content with consistently bagging the world's best airport, port and airline titles, and as if to compensate for its lack of size, Singapore relentlessly builds the biggest and tallest something. Never mind the Swissôtel The Stamford is no longer the world's tallest hotel, Singapore has the world's biggest fountain (at Suntec City) and when the Singapore Flyer is ready by the end of 2005, it will supersede the London Eye as the world's highest observation wheel.

There is no doubt Singaporeans are laughably methodical even when it comes to fun and leisurely pursuits. The matchmaking aspirations of the Romancing Singapore festival led to jokes about the Lion City turning into the Loin City. Sanitised Chinatown is ironically trying to recreate its former bustle with the street markets it was once famous for (but without the attendant chaos). Contrived as it may be, many have to come appreciate how everything works with a systematic clockwork precision. After all, predictability makes for safety – and good, clean fun is Singapore's forte.

A melting pot

Asian and Western cultures and values mesh in this dynamic, cosmopolitan city, giving rise to eclectic lifestyles, a heavenly range of cuisines – many Singaporeans count eating as a pastime – and a funky, but still wholesome, nightlife scene. There are few places in the world where different cultures, religions and races co-exist so peacefully. The lingua franca is English but on the streets you will see Chinese, Malay, Indian and Eurasian as well as Caucasian faces. Mosques, churches, and Hindu and Chinese temples often stand side by side, and local cuisines borrow ideas and ingredients from one another.

On the surface, the island-state may appear Western in its outlook, but in reality, Confucian precepts still temper ideals of personal freedom, and respect for one's elders ranks high. Society and public discourse are kept on a tight rein compared to the West, and there are fines for littering, spitting and other social misdemeanours. The result, however, is an uncommonly efficient city, with the cleanest streets outside of Switzerland.

Singapore is Asia with all its exotica and colour but without the slog sometimes associated with travelling in the region. It is, as its tourism advertising has claimed, Uniquely Singapore.   ❑

RIGHT: Esplanade – Theatres on the Bay, Singapore's new cultural landmark.

GROWTH OF A LION CITY

Singapore's role as a 21st-century hub for global
growth is a throwback to its earliest days
as a pivotal East–West trading post and
rendezvous point for merchants and sailors

The story of how Singapore got its name reads rather like a fairy tale. The earliest (and most racy) of Malay histories, the 17th-century *Sejarah Melayu*, tells of the exploits of Sang Nila Utama, who assumed the title of Sri Tri Buana as ruler of Palembang, heart of the great Malay seafaring empire of Srivijaya. He was out searching for a place to establish a city one day when his ship was struck by a sudden and ferocious storm. The ruler reputedly saved the day by casting his crown into the waves. Ashore on an uncharted island, he was intrigued by the sight of a strange creature with a red body, black head and white breast. On inquiring of its name and told it was a lion, he decided to name the place Singapura, which means "Lion City" in Sanskrit.

Merchants and pirates

Singapore owes its reputation as a trading centre to the bustling activity in the region. Even before the birth of Christ, Tamil seamen from southern India were plying heavy ships through the Straits of Melaka (Malacca). Later, the Greeks and then the Romans sought tortoise shell, spices and sandalwood from the Malay archipelago. By the 5th century, Chinese junks were sailing into peninsular waters, braving "huge turtles, sea-lizards and such-like monsters of the deep". The Arabs and Persians traded in the region too.

By the 14th century, Singapore was well-established on this East–West trade route.

Though its various rulers exacted duties from the passing ships, what most worried traders were the so-called "freelancers": pirates.

According to the 1350 Chinese text, *Description of the Barbarians of the Isles*, the traders were unmolested as they sailed west. But on the way back, loaded with goods, "the junk people get out their armour and padded screens against arrow fire to protect themselves, for a certainty two or three hundred pirate junks will come out to attack them. Sometimes they have good luck and a favouring wind and they may not catch up with them; if not, then the crews are butchered and the merchandise made off with in short order."

LEFT: contrasting faces of early Chinese businessmen.
RIGHT: 17th-century map of the Malay Peninsula.

FORGOTTEN OUTPOST

On arrival in 1819, Raffles found "all along the beach… hundreds of human skulls, some of them old but some fresh with the hair still remaining, some with the teeth still sharp, and some without teeth."

The scale of the pirate fleet seems inflated, but there is no doubt the threat was real.

Singapura, often called "Temasek" in the literature of that period, was most likely founded around 1390 by the Palembang ruler Parameswara. A scion of the former Srivijaya empire, he had fled Palembang after an abortive attempt to cast off allegiance to the

great Javanese Majapahit Empire (1292–1398). His Temasek settlement was short-lived, however. Towards the end of the 14th century, it came under attack, possibly by the Majapahits but more probably by the Thai state of Ayutthya or one of its Malay vassals.

Temasek came under the authority of the newly founded Melaka sultanate, and later devolved into an insignificant fishing settlement, becoming little more than an overgrown jungle. When Sir Thomas Stamford Raffles, the founder of modern Singapore, landed here on 29 January 1819, he found swamps, jungle and a lone village of some 100 Malay huts by the mouth of the Singapore river. Upriver

lived 30 or so Orang Laut sea nomad families. It was, to put it mildly, a pretty bleak picture.

The island was controlled by the Temenggong, the Malay chief of the southern Malay Peninsula, and the land was owned by Johor.

The Sultan of Johor had four wives but no clear heir, though he had two sons by two different commoners. When the sultan died, the younger of the two sons was placed on the throne, with the legitimacy of his rule recognised by both the British and the Dutch. The elder son, Hussein, who was away at the time, subsequently went into exile.

Raffles' shrewd move

Raffles knew the younger son would never permit the establishment of a British presence in Singapore and concocted his own plan. He invited the elder son Hussein to Singapore and proclaimed him heir to the throne of Johor. On 6 February 1819, Raffles signed a treaty with the Temenggong and the new sultan, giving the British East India Company permission to establish a trading post in Singapore. In return, the company would pay the Temenggong 5,000 Spanish dollars a year and the sultan 3,000 dollars. Raffles returned to Bencoolen, leaving Major William Farquhar in charge as the island's first Resident while retaining ultimate control as lieutenant-governor of Bencoolen.

Farquhar cleared the jungle, constructed buildings and dealt with the rat problem. The first settlers were traders and itinerants, mostly Chinese, with others from the Middle East, Europe and Melaka. The population topped 5,000 by June 1819, from 1,000 in January.

When Raffles returned to Singapore in 1822, he drew up a detailed plan for its development. Among other things, he abolished gambling, going so far as to order that all keepers of gaming houses be flogged in public. Two years later, the British, having traded off other regions to the Dutch, took formal control of Singapore. Payments to Sultan Hussein and the Temenggong were increased in exchange for outright cessation of the island.

His health ailing, Raffles returned to England in 1823 and died three years later of a suspected brain tumour. The British put Singapore under the Indian colonial government, appointing a new Resident, John Crawfurd.

By 1824, the island was home to 11,000

people, mostly Malays, with a large number of Chinese and Bugis, and fewer Indians, Europeans, Armenians and Arabs. Under Crawfurd, Singapore began to make money for the British. He ran a tight ship and his strict adherence to the bottom line alienated many locals. He made no friends among the Europeans either when he re-opened the gaming houses.

As Resident, Crawfurd had his work cut out. In the early 1830s, much of the town area was still swampland. Floods and fires were major hazards, while the filth and bad drainage, and the resulting water pollution, caused cholera outbreaks. Violent crime was another problem; gangs of robbers raided the town almost every

From India and Britain came cloth, opium, whisky and haberdashery for the expatriates.

A sense of permanence had been established by this period; three banks had been set up and elaborate houses of worship built. Wealthy Europeans constructed Palladian-style houses. A writer described the charming city with its bustling harbour, lush greenery and fine houses as "the Queen of the Further East".

Immigrant entrepreneurs

By this time, the Chinese population had swelled to 61 percent of the total and showed no signs of slowing down. Most Chinese immigrants (*sinkeh*) came as indentured

night. Added to these were poverty, malnutrition, overcrowding and excessive opium smoking, the last of which exacted the heaviest toll. Tigers were a menace, devouring as many as 300 citizens a year during the mid-19th century. The imposition of a government bounty led to the last tiger being shot in 1904.

By 1860, Singapore's trade had reached £10 million a year. Among the goods traded were Chinese tea and silk, ebony, ivory, antimony and sage from across the archipelago, and nutmeg, pepper and rattan from Borneo.

labourers and later struck out on their own. The number of Malays also increased, though less rapidly. Immigrants from South India came as well, some as merchants and labourers, others as convicts brought in by the British to build roads, buildings and other public works.

In these early days, Chinese men outnumbered the women 15 to 1, and the social lives of young bachelors revolved around secret societies. These societies used coercive tactics to run criminal rackets and secure territory. To control the situation, in 1877, the government installed a Chinese protectorate headed by W. A. Pickering, the first European who could read and speak Chinese.

LEFT: portrait of Sir Stamford Raffles, *c.* 1820s.
ABOVE: most Chinese came as indentured labourers.

Literary Greats

For more than 100 years, Singapore has been kind to the travelling scribe. Many stayed at the Raffles Hotel, a home away from home for scores of authors including Hermann Hesse and James Michener. But above all, Singapore played host to the literary lions of the British empire such as Conrad, Kipling and Maugham.

Joseph Conrad spent 16 years (1878–94) as a seaman in the Far East, with Singapore as his most frequent port

of call. *Lord Jim* (1902) was inspired by a real-life incident in which a ship called the *Jeddah* – with 950 Muslim pilgrims aboard – was abandoned by her British crew when the vessel began taking on water after leaving Singapore. Conrad also drew material from his own life. He was first mate on the *Vidar*, a schooner circuiting between Singapore and Borneo. A few of his works can be traced to these trips, including his first novel, *Almayer's Folly*, as well as *An Outcast of the Islands*, *The Rescue* and *Victory*.

Rudyard Kipling came to Singapore at an interesting time in his career. It was

1889, he was 24, and he had just left his beloved India on a journey that would change his life forever. Kipling's seven years in India were spent writing for English-language newspapers, including the *Pioneer* in Allahabad. Clever dispatches earned him a reputation as a rising star of British journalism.

He was surprised by the pervasive Asian atmosphere of Singapore. "England is by the uninformed supposed to own the island," he quipped. Kipling was fond of strolling along the waterfront and seemed to have stumbled upon Raffles Hotel by chance, describing it as a place "where the food is as excellent as the rooms are bad. Let the traveller take note. Feed at Raffles and sleep at the Hotel de l'Europe." The latter was demolished in 1900.

When **Hermann Hesse** reached Singapore in 1911, he was already well-known in Germany for works such as *Peter Camenzind* (1904) and *Gertrude* (1910). He observed the English, and penned ascerbic descriptions of tipsy Englishmen who "played around in the hall with the brutality of football players" and "fought with each other half the night like pigs".

Somerset Maugham, more than any other novelist, is often linked with Singapore. From his three visits to the island between 1921 and 1925, Maugham collected material for magazine articles that later went into his collection of short stories, *The Casuarina Tree*.

In it, Maugham's descriptions of Singapore's inhabitants are perceptive: "The Malays, though natives of the soil, dwell uneasily in the towns, and are few. It is the Chinese, supple, alert, and industrious, who throng the streets; the dark-skinned Tamils walk on their silent, naked feet, as though they were but brief sojourners in a strange land... and the English in their topees and white ducks, speeding past in motor-cars or at leisure in their rickshaws, wear a nonchalant and careless air." ❑

LEFT: Somerset Maugham was a frequent visitor.

PRISONERS OF WAR

Japanese prison camps were tropical hell-holes of rats, disease and malnutrition. Many of the prisoners sent to work camps in the jungles of Southeast Asia died, victims of disease and starvation.

In 1867, the Straits Settlements were made a Crown Colony under London's direct control, and a governor was appointed. In its early days, as sailing ships gave way to steam vessels, Singapore became a coal station for ships travelling to Europe through the Suez Canal, which opened in 1869. Singapore's trade expanded eight-fold between 1873 and 1913

eating Western food shipped in at great cost, and barring other races from their social clubs and prestigious civil service posts. Roland Braddell's *The Lights of Singapore* (1934) described life as "so very George the Fifth… if you are English, you get an impression of a kind of tropical cross between Manchester and Liverpool." With the building of its airport a few years later, Singapore was headed towards modernisation. Then came World War II.

Britain, a firm Japanese ally during World War I, severed her treaty with Japan in 1921 at the suggestion of the US. As war tensions in the Pacific increased, Singapore was groomed as a regional base for British war-

as a result, securing its permanent status as a major entrepot on the leading east-west trade route, and a most vital commercial link in the chain of the British Empire. By 1903, the little island had become the world's seventh-largest port in terms of shipping tonnage.

In 1911, the population stood at 312,000 and included 48 races speaking 54 languages, according to census takers. During this period, a large number of Europeans migrated here, marking perhaps the nadir of colonial snobbery. They distanced themselves from the "locals",

ABOVE: view of the waterfront in front of Fort Canning at the turn of the 19th century.

ships in the event of an outbreak of hostilities. In 1927, Japan invaded China, occupying Manchuria by 1931 and withdrawing from the League of Nations. Six years later, the Japanese formally declared war on China. Airfields and dry dock facilities for the British fleet were completed in Singapore in 1938. The substantial-looking defences earned the island the moniker "the Gibraltar of the East".

Defence debacle

The only problem was that Singapore had all its defences pointing out to sea, while the Japanese, in a legendary manoeuvre, chose to invade it by land from the north, via Malaya.

The Japanese 25th Army was led by Tomoyuki Yamashita, whose well-known discipline was said to be "rigorous as the autumn frost".

Japanese aircraft raided Singapore on 8 December 1941, the same day they devastated US ships and airfields in Pearl Harbor. When informed, Governor Shenton Thomas told Lieutenant-General A. E. Percival, "Well, I suppose you'll shove the little men off."

His nonchalance proved misplaced. The Japanese quickly established land and air supremacy, taking two British Royal Navy battleships. They pushed southwards through the Malayan jungle paths. Percival, realising his northern border was unprotected, grouped the

last of his troops along the northeast coast. The Japanese, in collapsible boats and other makeshift vessels, cut around the northwest flank and invaded Singapore on 8 February 1942.

Reign of terror

After days of heavy shelling by the Japanese, Percival surrendered unconditionally. Prime Minister Winston Churchill called it "the largest capitulation in British history", while Yamashita, as he later wrote, attributed his success to "a bluff that worked". In fact, the Japanese troops were outnumbered more than three to one by the island's defenders.

The Japanese reign of terror began with the renaming of Singapore to "Syonan" – Light of the South. The Chinese were singled out for brutal treatment, with many killed, imprisoned or tortured for the flimsiest of reasons. The Europeans were classified as military prisoners or civilian detainees, while the Malays and Indians were urged to transfer their allegiance to Japan or be killed. Syonan's economy deteriorated. Inflation skyrocketed, food was scarce and corpses were a common sight on the streets.

On 21 August 1945, the Japanese surrendered and the British returned in September. But Communist resistance to the Japanese had changed the political climate. The people had plans for their own destiny and the British would no longer write the rules.

"Neither the Japanese nor the British had the right to push and kick us around," recalled Singapore's former prime minister, now senior minister, Lee Kuan Yew in 1961. "We determined that we could govern ourselves and bring up our children in a country where we can be a self-respecting people."

The nationalistic itch among Singapore's population was not ignored by the British. One year after their return, the British ended their military rule of the Straits Settlements and set up separate Crown Colonies in Singapore and Malaya. The new governor instituted a measure of self-government on the island by allowing for the popular election of six members to a new 22-member Legislative Council. Elections were set for 1948.

Independence

Even before the war had ended, political activity had begun in Singapore. In 1945, the Malayan Democratic Union was formed with the goal of ending colonial rule, and merging Singapore with Malaya. *Merdeka* – Malay for independence – was the rallying cry. The first election in 1948 was a lacklustre affair, with a slim turnout and only 13,000 votes cast. The Chinese majority was sidelined in favour of the English-speaking minority, an unequal state of affairs that would later steamroll the Communist insurrection known as the Emergency (*see text box on page 25*).

LEFT: formal British surrender to the Japanese, 1942.
RIGHT: David Marshall, Singapore's first Chief Minister, negotiating with Malaya's Tunku Abdul Rahman.

A British review recommended that all citizens be automatically registered to vote and that a Legislative Assembly with 32 members – 25 elected – be established with broadened powers. The constitution was enacted in early 1955 and, later that year, Labour Front member David Marshall was elected Singapore's first Chief Minister. He led an all-party delegation to London the following year to negotiate complete independence from the Crown. He returned home empty-handed and resigned as he had failed to keep his *merdeka* promise.

Lim Yew Hock of the Singapore Labour Party took over as Chief Minister and made another bid in London in March 1957. The second delegation – which included a People's Action Party (PAP) member and a young Cambridge-educated lawyer named Lee Kuan Yew – accepted roughly the same terms Marshall had been offered: a fully-elected Assembly of 51 members, no power over external affairs and representation on – but not control of – an internal security council.

Back home, the Legislative Assembly ratified the terms and, in 1959, the British Parliament passed an act approving the new constitution. The general election was set for May. The PAP won a sweeping victory and Lee Kuan Yew became Singapore's first prime minister, a position he would hold until 1990.

THE EMERGENCY

The Japanese defeat and the restoration of British colonial rule to Malaya and Singapore did not go unchallenged, particularly by Communism. The Communist Party of Malaya (CPM) had emerged from World War II with newfound strength, having built up its prestige as a patriotic resistance movement during the Occupation. It now sought to infiltrate the labour movement by inciting unrest to overthrow British imperialism and establishing a Communist state. This organised insurrection of the CPM from 1948 onwards was termed the "Emergency".

The CPM had its headquarters in Singapore, with branches in other Malayan towns. It operated through its General Labour Union cells to mobilise support among the workers and to gear the trade unions to its political ends. Attacks were launched in 1948 against European and local managers in tin mines and rubber estates to disrupt the economy and instil a climate of fear. In response, the British promulgated Emergency regulations in June 1948 that sanctioned arrest and detention without trial. They also initiated a campaign to win over the civilian population to erode the CPM's base among the populace, particularly the Chinese. The Communist insurgency began to lose steam by 1953, but it was only in 1960 that the Emergency officially ended.

The PAP takes charge

The new government immediately set about reviving the economy, which had been suffering from a steady decline in entrepot trade, as Singapore's Asian neighbours increasingly took charge of their own trade. The PAP aimed for diversification: it beckoned multinationals with tax breaks, promises of protection against nationalisation of private enterprise and other attractive terms. A push on manufacturing also began.

The PAP's main concern was the abolition of colonialism. Exactly what form this would take caused a bitter split in the party. The PAP was divided into two wings – the relatively moderate, English-speaking social democrats (Lee Kuan Yew's wing) and the fiery, Chinese-educated Communists. The moderates were eager to join up with Malaya for independence – an approach approved by the electorate, which in a referendum in 1962 voted overwhelmingly for a merger.

Merger offered both raw materials and a wider market for Singapore's industrial products. An independent Singapore, Lee said at the time, with no raw materials and no appreciable internal market, was "a political, economic and geographic absurdity". The right-wing Malayan government would support the moderate Lee in his struggle with Sin-

CONFRONTATION

The merger with Malaysia caused faultlines to appear not only on the domestic front but also on the international scene, with Indonesia. As leader of Southeast Asia's largest Muslim state, President Sukarno was opposed to the Malaysian Federation.

To destabilise it, he initiated a policy of coercive diplomacy from 1963–6 that amounted to an undeclared war against Malaysia. Although Confrontation was fought along the Indonesia-Malaysia border, it spilled over into Singapore, with Indonesian saboteurs infiltrating the island in 1964. Confrontation ended with Sukarno's downfall in 1966.

gapore's leftist opposition Barisan Socialis. However, Malaya feared that absorbing Singapore's one million Chinese would adversely affect the balance of power in its Malay-dominant territory. But the greater evil of an "Asian Cuba" at its doorstep persuaded the anti-Communist Malayan prime minister Tunku Abdul Rahman to offer unification.

The merger took place on 16 September 1963. To balance the influx of Chinese from Singapore, the British colonial states of Sarawak and Northern Borneo (Sabah), with their largely indigenous Malay populations, also joined the Federation of Malaysia.

Within a week, the PAP held a general

election, catching the opposition by surprise. Riding on the fresh success of the merger, the PAP won 37 seats against 13 for the Barisan Socialis. Almost immediately, the PAP arrested and detained 15 opposition leaders. This move decimated the Barisan Socialis, and was explained away by the PAP as necessary to wipe out the "Communist plot to create tension and unrest in the state".

The PAP entered the Malaysian political scene aggressively by insisting on an immediate common market, meeting head-on with Malaysian resistance. This was just one example of the tension-ridden differences between Singapore and its federation partners.

Divisive differences

But far worse was the racial tension. The PAP's foray into federal politics was viewed by Malaysia's Malays as a Chinese bid to challenge Malay supremacy. The discord culminated in two major race riots in Singapore between Malays and Chinese in July and September 1964, setting the stage for a split. On 9 August 1965, Singapore was expelled from the federation, and became independent. The next month, the island nation became a full-fledged member of the United Nations.

For Singaporeans, independence was a matter of worry, not joy. How could this tiny state survive, surrounded as it were by giant unfriendly neighbours? Britain was to vacate its Singapore base – part of a general withdrawal of troops from east of Suez. For Singapore, this prompted economic concerns as much as security worries: the British bases accounted for some 20 percent of its GNP and employed a good chunk of the labour force. When the British left in 1971, Singapore introduced compulsory two-year national service for all 18-year-old males. Today, it has all the trappings of a modern-day fighting force, including an arsenal of sophisticated weaponry.

The newly-independent country was also faced with high unemployment rates, inadequate housing, no natural resources and little cash. It also lacked national cohesion, being essentially a disparate group of immigrants comprising the majority Chinese, and Malays,

Indians and Eurasians. However, the fledgling state had a few aces up its sleeve.

Its strategic location made it an established trading hub and it had inherited British rule of law. The other ace was the pragmatic – some would say ruthless – Lee Kuan Yew, who provided vision and the necessary drive. His government took to heart the basic economic premise that to attract foreign investment, a developing country had to offer political stability, cheap labour, a good location, and few or no restrictions on currency movement. As a result of his efforts, Singapore's industrial sector grew 23 percent a year from 1968 to 1972 – one of the highest rates the world has seen.

Nimble economic strategies

This growth was spurred by careful and far-sighted economic planning. Singapore has always adhered to an open market economy with a global network and perspective. Each decade threw up its challenges, which the country effectively fended against. In the late 1960s and 70s, its capital and skill-intensive industries laid the groundwork for the entry of electronics giants such as Sony and Matsushita.

When the 1980s demanded knowledge-intensive industries, Singapore had in place by the decade's end a base of manufacturing capabilities. Companies undertook research and development, engineering design and

LEFT: Lee Kuan Yew at a 1984 election rally.
RIGHT: people are the island's greatest resource.

software development. The 1990s, characterised by buzzwords such as "globalisation", "borderless world" and "knowledge-based economy", saw forays into Vietnam, India and China. Realising that it cannot compete with other Asian countries in labour-intensive industries, Singapore aimed to be a world-class information technology hub and Southeast Asia's banking and financial centre. At the turn of the 21st century, life sciences was identified as the new engine of growth.

Along with economic growth, public housing was a top priority *(see page 168)*. Today, more than 87 percent of the population live in comfortable government-built Housing and Development Board (HDB) flats which they own, using funds from a compulsory retirement savings programme called the Central Provident Fund (CPF) to finance most of the mortgage.

The PAP at the helm

Over the decades, the PAP has proved itself a sturdy government able to deal decisively and competently with crises of different shapes and sizes: the 1970s oil crisis, the 1985 economic recession, the economic downturn of the late 1990s and the 2003 SARS epidemic.

If its increasingly sophisticated people chafe under a paternalistic style of government, such sentiments have hardly been reflected in the

POLITICIANS' BIG PAY PACKETS

Singapore may be a small country, but when it comes to paying its leaders, it's in the big league. Prime Minister Goh Chok Tong earns more than US$1 million a year, while a top cabinet minister in Singapore earns close to US$800,000. Compare that to the paltry US$10,000 that the Philippine president pulls in, or even the US president's mere US$200,000. Such high wages are due to Singapore's free-market philosophy of paying its ministers salaries competitive with top executives in the private sector. Only in this way does it expect the best brains to join the civil service. Needless to say, this is an area of much contention.

polls. The PAP, re-elected continuously since 1959, has only suffered a tiny hiccup in its history of political dominance – at the 1991 general election it lost four seats to the opposition, instead of the customary one or two.

Prime Minister Goh Chok Tong, whose rule has seen some political and social liberalisation in the last decade, retired in 2004, giving way to his deputy, Lee Hsien Loong, the eldest son of former prime minister Lee Kuan Yew *(see opposite)*. There are fears that the younger Lee may return to the more autocratic style of his father, but the critics may be proven wrong. ❏

ABOVE: Singapore's stock exchange in action.

Lee Kuan Yew

He stepped down more than 10 years ago as Singapore's first prime minister but Lee Kuan Yew very much remains a political force to be reckoned with. The Cambridge-educated, fourth-generation Singaporean is widely credited with shaping a tiny island comprising a disparate group of immigrants into a gleaming model of efficiency that enjoys the second-highest standard of living in Asia after Japan.

Lee's family origins reflect the migrant nature of the country: Chinese forefathers of hardy Hakka stock who moved to the area and married local Malays. Lee was born on 16 September 1923, when Singapore was still a British colonial outpost, to a father who worked for oil giant Shell before retiring to sell watches and jewellery. The eldest of five children, Lee topped candidates from the Straits Settlement and Malaya in the Senior Cambridge School Certificate examination in 1939 to win a scholarship.

A strong legacy

This political whizz helped found the People's Action Party (PAP) in 1954, shrewdly representing its moderate faction while the party itself courted the Chinese majority on an anti-colonial left-wing ticket. He was prime minister for 31 years until late 1990, when he handed the reins over to Goh Chok Tong's more consensus-oriented style of governance. While widely admired for his grasp of a wide range of issues and especially for his social and economic vision, Lee's uncompromising attitude and his critical, and often intimidating personal style, is not always well-received.

He has been described as autocratic, high-handed and authoritarian, with foreign critics describing Singapore's political system as intolerant. Whatever one's opinion, it is undeniably a system that works, and the country's rise to affluence remains the greatest testament to Lee's personal beliefs.

The story of how Lee transformed Singapore is fascinating because no other leader in the modern world has had such a hand in influencing and directing his country's progress from independence to developed nation status. It is said none has straddled the two worlds with as much success: the revolutionary world in the first half of the 20th century for independence from a colonial empire, and the development world in the second half for wealth and progress.

Lee instilled good governance and

bureaucratic efficiency and dealt harshly with corruption while building modern ports, a top world airport and other infrastructure to lure foreign investors. To compensate for the lack of local manpower, he implemented a policy of attracting foreign workers, including top corporate managers and professionals.

Today, Lee is a well-respected statesman, an octogenarian whose views on Asia's emerging role in the world economy are sought by other world leaders. At home, in his advisory role as mentor minister, he continues to have a say in what goes on in Singapore's affairs. ❑

RIGHT: the much respected Lee Kuan Yew.

Decisive Dates

The early years

2nd century AD: Sabara, a trading emporium, is identified in Ptolemy's *Geographic Huphegesis* as being at the southern tip of the "Golden Chersonese", possibly Singapore.

3rd century: Chinese are said to have given the the island the name P'u Luo Chung.

1292: Marco Polo mentions a large and noble city where Singapore now stands.

1365: The Javanese *Nagarakretagama* records a settlement called Temasek – the old name that used to refer to Singapore.

1390s: Temasek is settled by a scion of the Srivijaya empire, Parameswara (also known as Iskandar Shah).

14–15th centuries: Siam (Thailand), followed by Java's Majapahit empire, seizes Temasek but shows little interest in it. Temasek exists as a vassal of the Malay kingdom of Melaka and is governed by a Temenggong (chief) from Johor.

1511: The Portuguese capture Melaka, then an important centre in east-west trade.

17th century: Singapore is forgotten and left to the Orang Laut (sea nomads).

1786–1824: The British East India Company opens a trading post in Penang and assumes possession of Melaka from the Dutch.

British colonial rule

1819: Sir Thomas Stamford Raffles arrives in Singapore. He is convinced the island, located at the crossroads of the South China Sea, will become an important port. The Temenggong and Sultan Hussein allow Raffles to open a trading post in Singapore in exchange for money.

1822: Raffles returns to Singapore and draws up plans for the island's development.

1823: Raffles issues regulations outlawing gambling and slavery. Leaves Singapore in June.

1824: The British agree to withdraw from Indonesia, in return for Dutch recognition of British rights over Singapore. Singapore in ceded in perpetuity to the British.

1826: The trading stations at Penang, Melaka and Singapore are named the Straits Settlements, under the control of British India.

1839: The first Singapore-built ship is launched.

1846: Chinese funeral riots. First major secret society trouble begins.

1851: Straits Settlements placed directly under the rule of the Governor-General of India.

1867: Straits Settlements become a Crown Colony, controlled by Colonial Office in London.

1870s: Suez Canal opens and number of ships calling at Singapore increases. Trade flourishes.

1880s: Henry Ridley, director of the Botanical Gardens, succeeds in growing rubber trees. The Malaysian peninsula and Singapore develop into the world's main rubber exporters.

World wars

1911: Population of Singapore grows to 250,000 and the census records 48 races on the island, speaking 54 languages.

1920s: The Great Depression's reverberations are felt in Singapore as prices of commodities such as rubber collapse. But it is still the greatest naval base of the British empire east of Suez.

1923: Singapore is linked to Malaysia by a 1-km (⅝-mile) causeway.

1941: Japan invades Malaysia, landing at Kota Bahru. Singapore is bombed on 8 December.

1942: British troops surrender to Japan. The Japanese rename Singapore Syonan, "Light of the South". During their occupation, many civilians, particularly the Chinese, are killed and suffer hardships.

1945: Three-and-a-half years of Japanese rule end in August, with the landing of Allied troops. The British declare Singapore a Crown Colony.

Independence and federation

1948: The British allow limited elections to the Legislative Council. A state of emergency is declared in June following the Communist Party of Malaya's uprising against imperialism.

1951: Legislative Council election. Singapore formally proclaimed a city with a royal charter.

1955: Rendel Commission granted by the British leads to elections and David Marshall becomes chief minister. A Legislative Assembly consisting of 32 members, 25 elected, is established. The Labour Front has a majority, but the People's Action Party (PAP) forms a powerful opposition.

1956: PAP Central Executive Committee election in which Communists decline to run. Chinese student riots; PAP leaders are arrested.

1958: A constitutional agreement for partial independence for Singapore is signed in London.

1959: PAP wins elections with 43 of 51 seats, with 53 percent of the popular vote. Lee Kuan Yew becomes the country's first prime minister.

1962: A referendum is held on merger with Malaya. 71 percent vote in favour.

1963: Malaysia agreement signed in which Singapore, Sarawak and North Borneo (Sabah) are joined with the existing states of Malaya to form Malaysia. PAP wins Singapore general election.

1964: PAP wins only one seat in Malaysian general election. Communal riots ensue.

The Republic of Singapore

1965: PAP wins Hong Lim constituency by-election. Singapore leaves Malaysian federation, becoming an independent nation. Joins the UN and the Commonwealth.

1967: Singapore, Malaysia, Thailand, Indonesia and the Philippines form the Association of Southeast Asian Nations (ASEAN).

1968: PAP sweeps first parliamentary general election, winning all 58 seats.

1971: British Far East Command ceases.

1972: PAP wins all seats in general election.

1981: In a by-election, J.B. Jeyaretnam of the Workers' Party wins the first seat to be held by a member of an opposition party.

1984: PAP loses two of 79 seats in the general election, its first loss of a seat since 1964.

1990: Lee Kuan Yew steps down as Prime Min-

ister and is replaced by Goh Chok Tong. The constitution is amended to provide for an elected president.

1991: PAP wins the general election again but loses four seats to the opposition. In addition, its share of the vote fell from 61.8 to 59.7 percent, the lowest since it has been in power.

1995: Singapore ranks second in the *World Competitive Report 1995*.

1996: Singapore is no longer regarded as a "developing nation" by the OECD.

1998: Singapore's economy is affected by the regional economic chaos in Southeast Asia.

1999: The economy makes a dramatic turnaround, growing 4–5 percent. Ong Teng Cheong

steps down as President. S.R. Nathan from the minority Indian race is appointed President.

2000: Economic growth hits 10.1 percent.

2001: PAP wins 75.3 percent of votes in general elections. A global downturn leads to a 4.7 percent unemployment rate, a 15-year high.

2002: Al-Qaeda-linked terrorist plot to bomb the US embassy uncovered. Some 15 suspects are arrested and jailed without trial.

2003: Outbreak of Severe Acute Respiratory Syndrome (SARS) in April, but quickly controlled. North-East Line extension of the MRT opens.

2004: Prime Minister Goh Chok Tong retires and his deputy Lee Hsien Loong takes office. The economy shows positive signs of recovery. ❑

LEFT: harbour with Fort Canning in the distance, *c.*1840.
RIGHT: guard-of-honour at a National Day parade.

THE PEOPLE

Ethnically diverse but racially tolerant, Singaporeans have managed to combine time-honoured traditions with modern ways of life. Their traditional Asian hospitality, too, has helped to create a multi-cultural society that is both gracious and warm

ramed against a backdrop of skyscrapers, a Singaporean in shirtsleeves and tie steps out of his Mercedes, phone plugged to his ear. Likely as not, he's on the line with his stockbroker, checking the latest share market gyrations as he heads for his favourite lunch spot, a tiny noodle stall in Chinatown.

In another vignette of tradition amid modernity, a *feng shui* (geomancy) expert is called in when things do not go well at a luxury hotel on Orchard Road. He recommends that the main doors be re-angled, and profits magically soar. Why? Because the cashier's desk was previously placed opposite the main door, so money and luck had "flown out into the streets".

These two faces of Singapore are no contradiction. A Singaporean may be sophisticated and completely at home with Western ways, but he is not above hedging his bets with the gods of fortune. A Hindu penitent may walk on glowing coals in supplication to his god, and a Chinese may light paper effigies of household items, intended for a deceased relative in the expectation of reciprocity.

Singapore's Asian aspect manifests itself in other ways as well. Agreeing with elders and superiors is important to help preserve "face", and the government's paternalistic rule is not as resented as might be expected. There is a sense of practicality behind this: as long as their material welfare remains secure, few question the role of the government in their private lives.

Singaporean imperatives

A multi-ethnic melting pot of Chinese, Malays, Indians, Eurasians and Caucasians, Singaporeans have been socialised over the years by official policies of multi-racialism and meritocracy to think of themselves as Singaporeans first.

Still, it would be myopic to take the view that the different races live together as one big happy family. There are underlying tensions which may not be noticeable to the first-time visitor *(see also page 144)*. The Muslim community for instance, like elsewhere in the world following 9/11, has suffered. An Al-Qaeda-linked plot by a group of local Muslims

---

PRECEDING PAGES: Tamil devotees at a Hindu temple.
LEFT: barman at the funky Post Bar, Fullerton Hotel.
RIGHT: joss sticks offerings at Thian Hock Keng Temple.

OFFICIAL LANGUAGES

There are four official languages: English, Mandarin, Malay and Tamil. The language of administration is English, which is also the lingua franca.

to bomb the US embassy was uncovered in January 2002 leading to some tension among the different communities. A few months later, four Muslim schoolgirls who insisted on wearing the *tudung* (head scarf) to school were suspended. The government's line is that schools need to maintain a certain uniformity in dress.

Likewise, some Malays and Indians too feel that they are disadvantaged, especially when

(see page 59). Talk to a Singaporean about culinary matters and you're on the right track. Singaporeans put in long hours at the office, but unless exceptionally hard-pressed, they'd prefer a decent cooked meal (even if served on styrofoam) to grabbing a sandwich at the desk.

Having long since left their *kampung* (village) lifestyles behind, Singaporeans are now city slickers, as adept with computers and the Internet as any Silicon Valley whizzkid. They live in highrises and are just as horrified at the sight of cockroaches and lizards as any tourist.

Constantly urged to strive for excellence, Singaporeans are only happy with straight "A"s, They have become afraid to lose out to

they seek employment in Chinese-dominated companies. Racial differences do remain under a veneer of modernism, but tolerance is always the watchword. Most people, if cornered and asked, would place their nationality first and their ethnic identity second.

Locals tend to be reserved in conversation, but they will immediately ask " How much you pay, ah?" when you've bought anything from a new BMW to a bowl of noodles. Part of this stems from the money-driven society they live in and visitors should not see this as an intrusion of privacy. It's just the way Singaporeans are.

The one thing which unites Singaporeans, Chinese and Malay, old and young, is food

the next fellow. This trait is now humorously termed the "*kiasu* syndrome" *(see page 38)* and is often the subject of social comment. For example, parents, anxious not to lose out in their children's education, queue up overnight to get them into a school of choice. Getting a bargain is more than mere monetary satisfaction for the Singaporean, it is almost a moral victory.

That they can laugh about all this is a refreshing thing. Satirical and even critical books written by locals are nudging for space where once they were proscribed, and censor-

ABOVE: Chinese couple at Trengganu Street, Chinatown.
RIGHT: Peranakan wedding couple.

ship has been eased. Things are changing slowly, paving the way for more original thought and a more open society.

Increasingly, racial differences are submerged beneath shared experiences and Western influence. Young singles want their own apartments, and married couples (an increasing number of which are inter-racial) prefer not to live with their in-laws. Marriage and starting a family have taken a back seat as getting ahead in one's career takes priority. Yet family ties remain strong and it is not unusual for married offspring to visit their parents every weekend.

Singaporeans have left their immigrant and post-colonial struggles behind and are finding their place in the international community. Sandwiched between East and West, they attempt to combine the best of both worlds.

The Chinese

The Chinese comprise 77 percent of its 4.131 million population (as of June 2001). This is no recent phenomenon. When Stamford Raffles founded modern Singapore in 1819, Chinese planters, pirates, fishermen and traders were already present. Five years after its establishment, Singapore had 3,000 Chinese and more were arriving weekly. Most were either traders from southern and eastern China fleeing the turmoil and corruption of 19th-century Chinese politics. By 1836 Chinese were the numerical majority, a pattern of racial demographics that exists till today.

Singapore's Chinese population can be broken down into several linguistic groups. Hokkiens from the southern Fujian province form the largest subgroup (42 percent) followed by Teochews (23 percent) from the Shantou region in Guangdong, Cantonese (17 percent), who hailed from Hong Kong and the lowlands of central Guangdong, Hakkas (7 percent) from central China and Hainanese (6 percent) from Hainan Island.

The Chinese speak a variety of dialects but their common link is Mandarin, or *Hua-Yue*, the language of the Beijing area, which is taught in Singapore schools as the official mother tongue of the Chinese. The long-standing Speak Mandarin Campaign, held annually, is an attempt to promote the use of Mandarin in place of native Chinese dialects.

THE PERANAKAN PEOPLE

Singapore's Chinese population has an interesting subgroup known as the Peranakans. They are the descendants of intermarriages between Chinese men and Malay women that took place from the 17th century onwards in the Malayan Straits Settlement colonies of Melaka, Penang and Singapore.

Male Peranakans are called *baba* and the women *nonya*. Their lingua franca is a Chinese-Malay patois. "Inside Chinese, outside Malay" was one description applied to the Peranakans, although increasingly they are becoming less distinct as a racial group, having intermarried with other races. The Peranakans were the first locals to speak English and to adopt Western customs. In fact, their loyalty to the British led some to describe them cynically as the "King's Chinese".

The often wealthy Peranakan families in Singapore, at Emerald Hill *(see pages 123–24)* and also in Katong *(page 177)* on the east coast, left behind a rich culinary heritage blending Malay and Chinese cooking styles and ingredients, clothing and also quaint houses with a distinctive architectural style. To learn more about the Peranakan culture, be sure to visit the Asian Civilisations Museum, Armenian Street *(see page 89)*. Or visit the Peranakan Association website at www.peranakan.org.sg.

A further unifying bond between many Chinese is a belief in superstition. Fortune tellers and geomancers figure largely in the Chinese world, their advice meticulously followed to bring luck and prosperity. The older generation also place their trust in the old ways, eschewing modern medicine for herbal cures. Acupuncturists continue to practise an ancient science, which is only now recognised in the West.

Food occupies a preeminent place in Chinese culture. A minister once quipped: "If a Chinese sees a snake in the grass, he'll think of a way to eat it." Not surprisingly, restaurants offering every conceivable Chinese dish are found in Singapore.

The Malays

Like the Chinese and Indians, Singapore's Malays are largely descendants of immigrants, although their arrival most certainly predates that of the other races. For this reason the Malays are considered the indigenous people of Singapore. Today, they make up 14 percent of Singaporeans, and comprise several sub-ethnic groups who trace their origins to the Javanese, Sumatrans, Bugis, Boyanese, Arabs and local Malays, among others.

Singapore's Malay origins are enshrined in the symbolic trappings of statehood – the national anthem is sung in Malay, the national language is Malay and the island's first presi-

KIASU-ISM

Kiasu is a common Singlish word made popular through the army and taken from two Chinese Hokkien dialect words *kia* (afraid) and *su* (to lose). Its early usage in the army was innocent enough; a recruit over-zealously putting in an extra minute or doing a centimetre more was guilty of being *kiasu*. But in the last decade, *kiasu* has become a Singaporean preoccupation.

Fuelled by global recognition in just about every quarter, Best Airport, Best Airline, Best Economy, Best Students, Best Hotel, you name it, Singapore bests it. Once a term used of a person, "why are you so *kiasu*?", it is now tagged to the nation: "Singapore is so *kiasu*".

dent after independence was a Malay. Today, despite Singapore's overt Chineseness, given its dominant Chinese population, it retains in many ways its Malay core: graceful *baju-kurung*-clad girls, or the more traditional *tudung*-attired females, are as much a part of the cityscape as their Western-attired compatriots; the *surau*, or community mosque, lies at the heart of every Malay neighbourhood; and *satay* – skewered pieces of grilled meat dipped in spicy peanut sauce – is as much a symbol of Singapore as Hokkien noodles.

Until as late as the 1970s, everyday Malay life centred on the *kampung* or village – with wooden slat houses built on stilts and where food was grown to feed the community. Such *kampung* are now almost non-existent as most Malays have moved to government apartments and adapted to high-rise living. Having imbibed the government's ambitious approach, a good number have merged into the landscape as professionals and entrepreneurs.

Historically, however, the Malay community has always been socio-economically weaker than the Chinese and Indians. This is partly because of its rural roots and partly due to Malay education, which closely follows a religious syllabus and has a reputation of lagging behind the English school system. The government, aware of the social and educational problems of the Malay community – including drug abuse and school dropouts – set up a self-help organisation called Mendaki to promote the progress of the Malay community. Today, Malay youths are successfully entering the mainstream, slowly improving the negative perceptions attached to their community.

The Malays are deeply religious and follow Islam. Orthodox Malays save hard for holy pilgrimages to Mecca as their status increases with the title Haji and the use of the white skull cap earned from a pilgrimage.

The Indians

Although Indians constitute only 7 percent of the population, they are a vital component of Singapore. Their documented habitation of the island goes back to the days of Raffles' arrival, when he was accompanied by sepoys (soldiers) from the East India Company brought along to guard Britain's imperial interests. This trickle soon enlarged to include Indian merchants, with a larger flow arriving in the 1820s in the form of convicts from Britain's penal colony in Bencoolen.

These Indians were a polyglot mix, and came from all over India and Sri Lanka. Reflective of the original inflow, Singapore's Indian population today consists of numerous sub-ethnic and ethnic divisions, ranging from Tamils, Malayalees and Bengalis to Punjabis, Telegus, Gujuratis, Sikhs and Sindhis. The majority (60 percent) are Tamils, with Malayalees the next largest group (8 percent). Religion-wise, they comprise a colourful mix of Hindus (53 percent), Muslims (27 percent), Christians (12 percent) and Buddhists (1 percent), as well as smaller groups of Sikhs, Jains and Parsis.

The Indian population of early Singapore tended to group together according to region of origin, religion and occupation type. Today, certain traditional Indian trades still occupy specific locations in Singapore. Sindhi, Sikh and Gujurati textile and electronic goods merchants are still located along High Street, while the Tamil Muslims still predominate in the money-changing trade, in areas such as Arab, Chulia and Market streets.

Although the first-generation Indians who

settled in Singapore in search of a better life still maintain sentimental ties to their homeland, their offspring lack such attachments and consider themselves Singaporeans first.

Nevertheless, in the late 1980s and early 90s, a significant number of well-educated Indians left Singapore for greener pastures in Australia, Canada and the US. This outflow from the professional class was partly due to an unease over state policies promoting the increasing "sinicisation" of Singapore, and uncertainty over equal opportunities in the job market.

Like the Malays, the Indians too have a socially and educationally disadvantaged segment that has been left behind in the rush to

LEFT: Malay boys at a cultural performance.
RIGHT: Tamil women in colourful saris.

progress. The Singapore Indian Development Association (SINDA) was set up in 1990 to assist these elements re-enter the mainstream.

Others races

Singapore's census shows an enigmatic category called "Others", which includes all those who are not Chinese, Malay and Indian. The most numerous "Others" are the Eurasians, who form about 1.4 percent of Singaporeans. Most are the offspring of mixed marriages, dating back to the times when the region was occupied by the Portuguese and Dutch. Eurasians are often half English, half Dutch or half Portuguese. Some are immigrant Eurasians who

came from Indonesia, Malaya, Thailand and other places. The Eurasians carry family names such as D'Souza, Pereira, (Portuguese), Westerhout (Dutch), Scully (Irish) and Young (British). Many are also part Filipino, Chinese, Malay, Indian, Sri Lankan or Thai.

Although a sense of alienation in the 1970s caused sizeable numbers to migrate, Eurasians today fit well into the society. They are a close-knit group and there is even an Eurasian Association to promote the interests of the community. Patois Portuguese (or Cristao) is still spoken among the older generation. Many Eurasians still profess a sentimental attachment to Katong in the eastern part of Singa-

pore, as the community congregated in this area before urban development caused habitation patterns to shift.

There are very few Armenian families remaining in Singapore. The Jews, once a thriving community that occupied the Sophia Road, Queen Street, Wilkie Road and Waterloo Street areas, are now scattered through urban renewal; only the old Hebrew lettering on some of the shophouses in these localities bears testimony to their once vibrant presence.

Foreigners

Roughly, every one in four people (or one million) living in Singapore is a foreigner, many of whom have acquired Permanent Residency status. They come from literally all corners of the world. In the past, expatriates were mainly Westerners, often sent to Singapore by their home companies to oversee local or regional operations. They mostly came on expatriate packages that included a generous salary, a fairly luxurious residence, company car and maid. Today, that picture has undergone a transformation. Expatriates are as likely to hail from India and China as from the West, and most are offered employment packages that are no different from those given to local workers.

Referred to in the local media as "foreign talent", these professionals are mostly employed in the high-tech sectors and finance. Their presence is the result of an open-door policy by the Singapore government to recruit qualified workers from abroad to redress the dearth of local talent in high-growth sectors.

Apart from a large pool of expatriates in the white-collar professions, there is a noticeable blue-collar element, made up mostly of South Indians and Southeast Asians, who work in construction and environment maintenance as well as women who work as live-in domestic maids. They generally undertake jobs that hold little appeal for Singaporeans.

Foreign workers are especially visible on Sundays. The Indians and Bangladeshis congregate in Little India, the Filipinos at Lucky Plaza, and the Thais and Burmese at Golden Mile Tower at Beach Road. This is their weekly opportunity to catch up on home news and relax in the company of compatriots. ❏

LEFT: a mixed race couple.

Singlish-speak

If ever a language can be described as relaxed and animated, malleable, frank and affectionate, it is Singlish. Singlish is English peculiar to Singapore, hence the term – the agglutination of the "head" of Singapore and the "tail" of English. And, at a wild guess, your Funk & Wagnalls is unlikely to have it listed.

Singlish does not pretend to have its origins steeped in the history of language. Quite simply put – and Singlish says it most simply – it is an oral language that was only given a spelling as recently as 1982.

As earliest memories of Singapore's baby boomers will testify, the rich vernacular used in daily life then was a linguistic mix of schoolboy English, Chinese dialects, slang popular to the time and Malay. A command like "*Siapa tidak dancing kee lowteng*!" ("Those who are not going to dance go upstairs!") ordered in a sentence combination of Malay, English and the Chinese Hokkien dialect would, not surprisingly, be understood by almost everyone (at the party certainly).

Once shunned by the print and broadcast authorities as "broken English", which it is not, 21st-century Singlish is no longer a major language issue. It has gained currency islandwide, as evidenced by the occasional spoken and written example on radio and television, and in newspapers and magazines. Curiously, having at first won notoriety, it now wins respect as Singapore's unofficial lingua franca.

However, Singlish is not championed in the corridors of academia. Students know not to offer Singlish in their exam papers, just as any white-collar worker knows not to employ it on office stationery. Yet both student and office worker would likely use it readily in the canteen and at home. It is at heart a "homey" language that departs from English in structure and syntax, grammar and punctuation, but it is still English, and not broken English at that. Well, maybe a slight fracture – which is not

at all helped by the fact that it's often spoken at such breakneck speed that visitors often mistake Singlish for a foreign language altogether.

Singlish is from the gut and to the point, often taking short cuts by losing the article. "Hurry lah!" is "Can you please hurry up!". Sentences often end with the words "lah" or "meh" – derived from the Hokkien dialect – the first to drive a point home, and the second an expression of incredulity.

Singlish is distinct from say the pidgin and Creole patois of New Guinea and New Orleans in that it is a patois which

has no rank in the social stratum, having taken root among the masses and continued to change with its people.

You know you're in Singapore as a visitor when you try to but cannot understand the following phrases:
• toast bread – toast
• plain water – water
• don't have – we do not have
• wait first – hold on/later
• check for you – I'll try to find out
• see how – undecided/not sure
• can I hepchew? – may I be of assistance?
• got nets card? – I prefer cash
• any udders? – will there be anything else?

RIGHT: quirky Singlish on a t-shirt.

SOCIAL CAMPAIGNS

No other nation in the civilised world is as obsessed
with spoon-feeding its people with social guidelines,
covering everything from courtesy and, incredibly,
toilet behaviour to marriage and childbirth

Singapore's earnest social campaigns, organised with much fanfare by its government, often draws mirth and scepticism from visitors who are used to more intrinsic behavioural values. While outsiders may find it strange for a country to spend millions of dollars on countless campaigns to tell people the seemingly obvious – be courteous; keep the country clean; flush public toilets – the majority of Singaporeans do dutifully follow such exhortations on social behaviour.

Indeed, from the smiling immigration officer at a Changi Airport checkpoint to the helpful – and also smiling – taxi driver whisking visitors to their hotels in downtown Orchard Road, Singapore's social campaigns appear, on first impression, to have been successful. Non-Singaporeans may be puzzled by such an apparently socialist approach by a government that is a proponent of a free-market economy.

But it has a spin-off more in tune with capitalism – behind those smiles there is a dollar sign. Take the on-going Courtesy Campaign for instance, which costs the government the rather serious sum of S$2 million annually. The fact is, it is simply good business to smile at tourists and visiting businessmen, to encourage them to return. Government-sponsored advertisements often feature a mix of Singaporeans flashing rows of perfect pearly whites.

And look at the message on why Singaporeans should smile. One advertisement says: "Just one thing to keep in mind when you next see our visitors. Simply smile and be gracious. Make our guests feel welcome. It will mean a better tomorrow for ourselves." So zealously was this campaign taken up that government agencies in 1996 went as far as installing smile "mirrors" on their computer terminals to prompt staff to project a more courteous corporate image. However, not all campaigns owe their origins to purely mercenary concerns.

Socialist influences

Part of the answer can be found in the socialist politics of the country. Singapore, with its majority Chinese population, like many parts

LEFT: Singapore is a "fine" city.
RIGHT: a campaign that has since lost favour.
FAR RIGHT: heed the sign or pay the fine.

of Southeast Asia was rife with Communist fervour in its early days. In the political struggle after World War II, democratic socialism emerged as the dominant ideology. Given this historical connection it is no wonder that social campaigns are an important part of the psyche of the Singapore government and its people. Over the years social campaigns have evolved from a Communist backdrop to take new meaning in modern Singapore.

Indeed, it seems there has been a campaign at every turn to match the needs of the day, from the perennial Courtesy Campaign to one which persuaded Singaporeans (not very successfully) to be punctual for wedding dinners.

One of the earliest campaigns was the Family Planning Campaign. Launched in 1966, just after Singapore was asked to leave Malaysia because of political differences, it was the government's knee-jerk response to a desperate situation: insufficient housing, unemployment and a declining trade economy. The solution: check the population growth.

To execute this the Singapore Family Planning and Population Board was set up in 1966, to introduce population control and family planning. Many baby boomers will remember that they are the products of a nationwide campaign that exhorted their parents to "Stop at Two". It was an aggressive drive that empha-

HOW TO TOILET TRAIN A NATION

You may be fined if you are caught not flushing a public toilet after use. To drive home this point, the local paper did a daily review of the various "Toilets of Shame" in the 1990s, complete with pictures of urine and excreta splattered public loos. However, to date, the campaign has not successfully admonished people into peeing straight.

Thankfully, though, no one has ever been convicted of this "crime". It shows how difficult, if not ludicrous, it is to enforce such a rule – short of appointing toilet rangers in every loo. But the situation is different in elevators. Ask any Singaporean who has lived in public housing in the 1970s and the 80s and they will tell you that people

mistaking elevators for toilets used to be commonplace.

But Singapore's civil servants have found a solution. Using high-tech gadgets, elevators identified as being frequently abused are fitted with urine detectors and labelled with a sign which caricatures a young naked boy with pants at his ankles and cuffed at the wrists. The gadget, when it senses the offending fluid, jams the elevator mid-journey and remains so until the doors are forcibly opened by officials. This has proven so effective that people now suspect that many elevators with urine detector signs are in fact fakes. However, no one wants to risk being caught with his (or her) pants down.

sised the restriction of incentives in housing, education, tax and health care benefits – if families had a third child or more. In true socialist fashion, women were called on to be sterilised after the second child. Medical assistance for sterilisation was made affordable and quick. However, the goverment was to realise the folly of this campaign two decades later.

The Keep Singapore Clean Campaign is another early campaign in post-independent Singapore. First launched by the former prime minister Lee Kuan Yew in October 1968, its aim is to educate all Singaporeans on the importance of maintaining a clean environment. Slogans such as "Keep Singapore

Litter-Free" and "Clean and Green City" were generously articulated.

To ensure that the collective efforts were effective, fines were introduced by the government to punish those who spit and littered in public. Fines are such a commonplace feature of the country that Singapore is often infamously known as the world's "finest" city. Some snicker that the phrase "have a fine day" takes on new meaning in this island-state.

By the 1970s, unemployment was wiped out and adequate housing was provided, accompanied by spectacular economic growth. It testified that such campaigns were successful in achieving policy outcomes. The PAP, which enjoyed a monopoly over national politics and achieved political support from the majority, embarked on more social campaigns.

Campaign follies

By the 1980s, a decade of successful campaigning had resulted in fewer children. Singapore now suffered from a shortage of workers and the spectre of an ageing population had raised its ugly head: it has been estimated that by 2020 about one-fifth of Singaporeans would be aged 65 and above.

The government could now afford to be less heavy-handed. Rather than wave the stick of disincentives, it dangled carrots in the form of tax incentives. Never one to be cowed, the government launched a counter campaign, this time calling the people to "Have Three or More if You Can Afford it".

The Graduate Mothers' Priority Scheme was also introduced to offer incentives to female university grads who were mothers. They were encouraged to have more children and in return enjoyed hefty tax incentives. In contrast, the lowest educated women were encouraged to stop at one or two children in return for a cash grant of S$10,000 in their social security funds, which could be drawn upon to purchase public housing.

The move sparked a furore among Singaporeans and led to lengthy debates on the topic of "nature" versus "nurture". The PAP provoked considerable public criticism over its attempt at genetic engineering. The loss of two seats in Parliament to the opposition in the 1984 general elections – for the first time since 1963 – and loss of nearly 13 percent of the votes cast from the election in 1980, showed the unpopularity of such a misguided policy. In 1985, the priority scheme for graduate mothers was terminated. Shortly after, the Singapore Family Planning and Population Board was closed.

To skirt around the issue, the government set up the Social Development Unit (SDU), conceived as a matchmaker for university-educated singles. Dubbed "Single, Desperate and Ugly" by its detractors, the SDU's mission is to bring singles together for the purpose of marriage. Its programmes include subsidised outings and get-to-know-you sessions. The scheme was later expanded and separate units were set up for those with more basic qualifications. The government's unofficial policy of pairing off singles of similar educational backgrounds may raise hackles elsewhere in the world but the success rate of the SDU and its sister organisations speaks volumes.

Social campaigns today

In today's Singapore, more and more campaigns are merged with technology. The nature of campaigns is changing its shape from written form to electronic transmission through the the Internet. Phrases such as "Cyber Courtesy" have emerged to help tone down the language in chat groups. In 1998, the Courtesy Campaign was further narrowed down to mobile phone users as technological changes brought about new areas of concern. Campaigns are also changing to a less indirect or discreet format. The government is now more concerned with policy making and launching social campaigns that are not directly related to racial, ethnic and religious issues.

Another change is that social campaigns today are supported by foreign investors. Most campaigns launched in the past few years secured large amounts of sponsorship from multinationals. Many have forgotten, it seems, the campaigns' original links to socialism.

What has been the effect of these campaigns on the life of Singaporeans? On the socio-cultural plane, the Speak Mandarin Campaign has, for instance, reinforced racial differences in the community. Some think the millions of dollars contributed by taxpayers towards these campaigns promote the interests of the ruling party. For example, one journalist wrote in *The Straits Times* some years ago: "Here is what's really scary: what if a campaign like Smile Singapore actually works? I mean, what will that tell you about our people? Do you really want such a pliant population, even if the message it is absorbing seems to be a harmless one?" Others, meanwhile, think that social campaigns bring a positive benefit to society, and that is reason enough to continue them.

However, many people will agree that some of the campaigns have been successful. The Keep Singapore Green campaign has kept the tiny island, for all its concrete, fairly green. As a result of another campaign, Tree Planting Day, many more trees have sprung up, especially in the public housing estates. The PAP takes it so seriously all its ministers are out in full force at this annual event to plant trees, assisted by numerous gardeners of course.

Another campaign was the Great River Clean-Up, initiated by Lee Kuan Yew, to clean the once filthy Singapore River. Coupled with river activities throughout the year and the redevelopment of buildings along Boat and Clarke quays, the riverside is now a big draw for tourists and residents alike. From this perspective at least, some of the campaigns have been a resounding success. ❏

SPEAK MANDARIN

The Speak Mandarin Campaign was launched in 1979 to get dialect-speaking Singapore Chinese to adopt Mandarin as a common "mother tongue" language. The campaign has worked: a 1999 study by *The Straits Times* found that six out of ten Chinese students speak more Mandarin than English, despite Singapore's English-dominated environment. But detractors claim this has been at the expense of English-language learning and that Singaporeans will have trouble communicating with the rest of the English-speaking world. In addition, the Malay and Indian minorities have felt left out by a campaign aimed exclusively at the Chinese.

LEFT: marriage is encouraged. **RIGHT:** the Mandarin campaign is viewed with suspicion by minority races.

EVENTS AND FESTIVALS

Almost every month of the year, Singapore's streets, temples and ethnic enclaves come alive with a motley assortment of religious and cultural celebrations. A growing list of contemporary events now adds to the jam-packed calendar

With its multi-racial character, it's no surprise that Singapore is a constant hive of activity, celebrating one cultural festival after another. The following festivals are among the most important in the calendar, and offer the most interest to the visitor.

January to March

Chinese New Year: As the name suggests, Chinese New Year symbolises a new beginning and is the most widely celebrated festival among the Chinese. It falls on the first day of the lunar calendar, usually between mid-January and mid-February. Chinese custom decrees that the previous year's debts be paid, the home

cleaned and new clothing purchased. It is also a time for reaffirming ties at the family reunion dinner that takes place on the eve. The 15-day festival, beginning with a two-day holiday, is commemorated by feasting and the giving of *hong bao*, red packets of "lucky money".

A good place to catch the festive spirit is Chinatown where the streets are all lit up and chock-a-block with people jostling for festive goods. Dragon and lion dancers throng the streets, making plenty of noise to keep the mythical monsters traditionally associated with Chinese New Year at bay. A riverside carnival called River Hongbao usually takes place at the Marina Promenade with all sorts of entertainment and food stalls. The celebrations end on a high note with the Chingay parade – an exuberant procession which is held on the Sunday following the New Year. Lavish floats, stilt-walkers, martial arts troupes and mini-dramas illustrating classical Chinese myths are some of the parade's best-loved features.

Thaipusam: This Hindu festival is observed between January and February, in the Tamil month of *Thai*. Devotees honour Lord Muruga, god of bravery, power and virtue, by performing feats of mind over spirit. The festival begins at dawn at the Sri Srinivasa Perumal Temple *(see page 140)* in Serangoon Road. Here, devotees who have entered a trance have their bodies pierced with metal hooks or spikes attached to a *kavadi*, a cage-like steel contraption which is carried on their shoulders. The procession makes its way to the Sri Thandayuthapani Temple *(see page 123)* at Tank Road, accompanied by chanting supporters.

April to June

Singapore International Film Festival: A varied diet of art-house films from various countries are showcased during this two-week period, which usually falls in April. Locally made films are also screened, and are attracting an increasing following for their insightful vignettes of Singapore life. Fringe events include retrospectives, tributes, seminars and film-appreciation workshops.

World Gourmet Summit: A two-week long gastronomic event with workshops and seminars on fine food and wines. Singapore's best chefs and restaurants are feted with awards while guest chefs from around the world play

SUMMER SHOPPING

Held island-wide from end May to early July, the Great Singapore Sale indulges those with a passion for shopping — with goods at shopping malls all over slashed down to bargain basement prices.

believed to purify negative actions of the past and is an act of homage to Lord Buddha.

Singapore Arts Festival: This annual event in June showcases a bonanza of Asian and Western performing arts. Past performers have included the Washington Ballet and the London Philharmonic Orchestra, and also less commercial and cutting-edge ventures like a Lithuanian

host at selected restaurants with special menus.

Vesak Day: Usually celebrated in May, this is the most important event in the Buddhist calendar for it honours the birth, death and enlightenment of Buddha. Temple celebrations begin at dawn with a candlelight procession. As part of the celebrations, caged birds are released and free meals are distributed to the poor.

On the eve of Vesak, monks at the Kong Meng San Phor Kark See Temple *(see page 190)* lead devotees through a three-step-one-bow ritual around the temple grounds. This is

adaptation of Shakespeare's *Othello*. The festival also features an eclectic fringe segment and workshops by visiting companies.

Dragon Boat Festival: Every June, colourful longboats with prows carved to represent dragons and birds crest the waves of Marina Bay, propelled by dozens of pairs of strong arms. The Dragon Boat Race is an international-class event that draws teams from Australia, Europe and the US, among others.

The festival honours a Chinese patriot, Qu Yuan, who drowned himself in 278 BC to protest the corruption at court. Fishermen tried to rescue him but failed. Small packages of rice were then thrown into the water to distract

LEFT: Chinese New Year celebrations at the Marina Promenade. **ABOVE:** Chingay street entertainers.

fishes from his body. Drums and gongs were sounded to frighten away predators, and villagers decorated their boats with dragon heads and tails with the same purpose in mind. Today, several varieties of these rice dumplings are available throughout the year.

July to September

Singapore Food Festival: The island celebrates another favourite past-time – eating – with a month-long food fiesta in July. Various food-tasting events and unique dining experiences which cover a gamut of cuisines are held.

National Day: At least a month before 9 August, you'll hear children practising

appease these wayward spirits, joss sticks and paper money are burned and feasts whipped up as offerings. Neighbourhood banquets, including *wayang* (Chinese opera) or increasingly these days to cater to a younger crowd, *getai* (mini pop concerts), are held, climaxing in a lively auction. After the ghosts have had their fill, the food is eaten by the celebrants.

Monkey God's Birthday: The Monkey God is a character from the Chinese classic *Journey to the West*, celebrated for protecting his master, a monk of the Tang dynasty, dispatched to India to collect the Buddhist *sutras* (holy books). During this festival in September, acrobats perform at various temples.

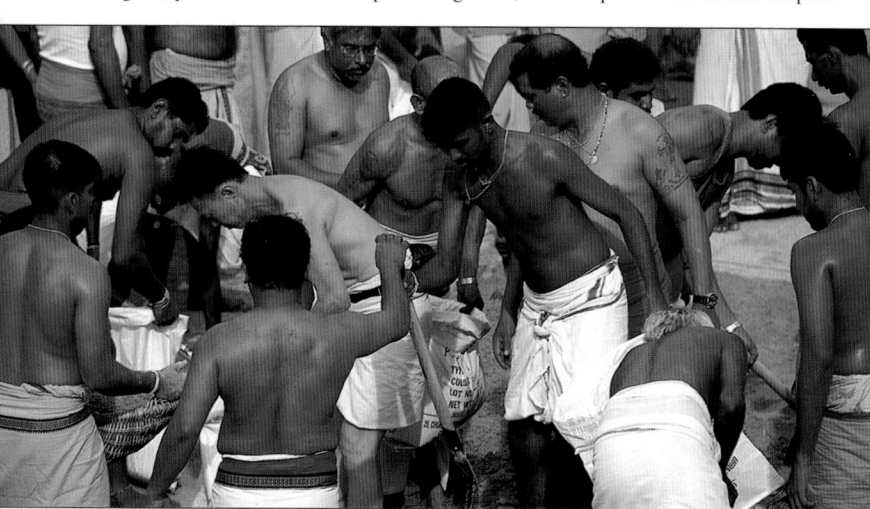

anthems of nationhood, and see military bands, acrobats and dragon dancers working to perfect the National Day Parade. This takes place at either the National Stadium or Padang *(see page 84)* and marks the anniversary of the island's independence in 1965. At the parade, which becomes more spectacular with each passing year, performers with torches, flags and flashcards form intricate patterns for cheering spectators. The pomp and pageantry culminates in a stunning firework display.

Festival of the Hungry Ghosts: Taoists believe the gates of hell are opened throughout the seventh lunar month, usually August/September, to allow ghosts to wander the earth. To

October to December

Mid-Autumn Festival: On the 15th day of the eighth lunar month, usually in October, Chinese celebrate the 14th-century revolution that overthrew the Mongol dynasty. Mooncakes – rich pastries filled with lotus seed or red bean paste and salted egg yolks – are eaten. The cakes, as the legend goes, were used by rebel forces to smuggle revolutionary messages to the people, while lanterns were used to signal the start of the civilian uprising. Today, the festival is marked by an impressive display of lanterns at the Chinese Garden *(see page 167)* in Jurong.

Navarathri: Tamil for "nine nights", Navarathri pays homage to the three consorts of the Hindu gods, with nine days of traditional Indian music and dancing at all Hindu temples. The festival concludes with a procession. This October event provides a rare opportunity to experience Indian arts; elaborate performances are held at the Sri Thandayuthapani Temple *(see page 123)* and other Hindu temples.

Thimithi Festival: Thimithi is a breathtaking fire-walking ceremony that occurs in October at the Sri Mariamman Temple *(see page 103)* at South Bridge Road. Male devotees sprint barefoot across glowing coals, without any apparent injury to their feet, in honour of Draupathi, a legendary heroine deified by South Indian Tamils. On the eve of the festival a magnificent silver chariot honouring Draupathi makes its way from this temple to the Sri Srinavasa Temple in Little India.

Pilgrimage to Kusu Island: During this month-long festival falling between the 1st and 15th day of the Chinese ninth lunar month (usually Oct/Nov), Taoists take the ferry to Kusu Island to make offerings at the Tua Pek Kong Temple and at a Malay shrine. The legend behind the pilgrimage tells of a turtle *(kusu)* that turned itself into an island in order to save two shipwrecked sailors, a Malay and a Chinese.

Deepavali: Also known as the Festival of Lights, to symbolise the conquest of good over evil, this is the most important festival in the Hindu calendar. Usually occurring in October or November, it is celebrated by the traditional lighting of oil lamps at homes and in Little India, which is turned into a fairyland of twinkling lights. Prayers are recited in temples and statues of deities carried around the grounds.

Christmas: A sizeable percentage of the population is Christian but almost everyone, regardless of religious affliation, gets into the spirit and exchanges gifts come Christmas time. The festive season is given an official fillip with a yuletide light-up that transforms Orchard Road into a riot of lights and glitzy displays. Shopping malls and hotels try to outdo each other with the most imaginative decorations and vie for the "best decorated award". Nevertheless, as with all things Singaporean, Christmas here is celebrated with a difference – just tuck into a tandoori turkey and you'll see!

LEFT: Thimithi fire-walking celebrants at Sri Mariamman Temple. **RIGHT:** inflated Santa at Orchard Road.

Variable dates

Hari Raya Puasa: This Muslim celebration falls on the first day of the 10th Muslim month; the date varies from year to year. During Ramadan, the month preceding Hari Raya Puasa, all able Muslims observe a strict fast from sunrise to sunset – so that they are better able to commiserate with the less fortunate. On Hari Raya Puasa, celebrants ask for forgiveness from family members, make new resolutions and feast on traditional food.

The other Muslim festival celebrated with a holiday is **Hari Raya Haji**, which marks the sacrifices made by Muslims who undertake the pilgrimage to Mecca. ❏

CONTEMPORARY EVENTS

A boom in world-class venues plus a growing population of fun-seeking city-dwellers has led to a significant increase in events, from the Singapore Fashion Festival and the New Year Countdown Party to the International Comedy Festival and world music extravaganza WOMAD. Recent additions to the calendar include the fun Singapore River Buskers Festival.

For the most current list of events and celebrations, check the Singapore Tourism Board website at www.visitsingapore.com or go to any of its Visitor Centres. *The Straits Times* and free tourist magazines like *I-S* and *Where* also provide details.

A POTPOURRI OF FESTIVALS

Where else can you see snow in a tropical island, watch bodies being pierced and skewered without bleeding, and burn money for the dead?

Singapore is a fascinating melting pot of Chinese, Malays, Indians, Eurasians and expatriates from around the region and the West. Add to this a diversity of religions and you have a virtual kaleidoscope of rituals and ceremonies – some seemingly strange to the foreign eye. The Chinese make up the majority, and their distinctive cultural identity is manifested in many customary and religious practices, both Buddhist and Taoist, and often a combination of both. Despite the city's outward modernity, Chinese temples are bustling and noisy places thronged with devotees going about their rituals. Most Hindu temples and Muslim mosques also welcome visitors, but make sure that you're modestly attired (no shorts and revealing tops) and remember to remove your footwear before entering. There is always something going on at these places – all of which provide ample fodder for avid photographers.

ABOVE: in accordance with Chinese tradition, devotees burn paper money as offerings to both long dead ancestors and recently deceased loved ones. It is believed that these burnt offerings – supposedly legal tender in the afterlife – will give the dead money to spend. Besides money, cars, houses and other items (even credit cards and mobile phones) made of paper are added to the bonfire.

LEFT: *wayang* or Chinese opera is a colourful stage entertainment that combines mime, dance, songs and dialogue, and is often performed during the Festival of the Hungry Ghosts. Shrill voices punctuated by loud gongs, clashing cymbals and droning stringed instruments may seem quite alien, but the plot is usually a familiar story of heroes fighting against evil and lovers escaping from disapproving parents.

FESTIVAL LIGHT-UPS AND DECORATIONS

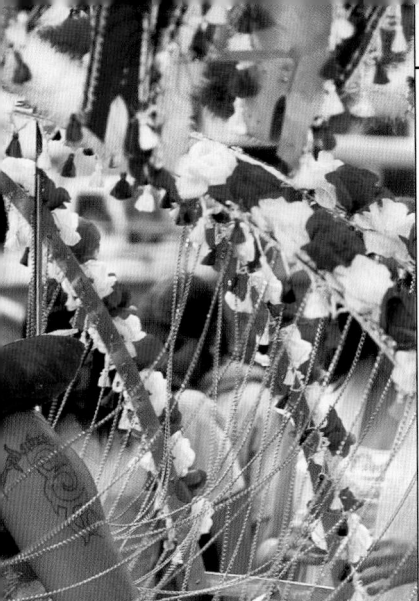

ABOVE: in an intense and dramatic demonstration of belief and devotion, the body of a Hindu devotee is pierced with spikes and skewers as he carries a heavy steel *kavadi* decorated with peacock feathers and flowers during a Thaipusam festival procession. This almost inhuman feat requires devotees to undergo weeks of rigorous spiritual preparation before they can take part in this ritualistic journey. During their tranced state, no blood is shed even with steel rods pierced into their tongues, cheeks and other parts of the body – definitely not a sight for the squeamish. The procession also sees some devotees walking on a bed of nails.

ABOVE: the Mid-Autumn or Mooncake Festival is a time when lanterns are lit and mooncakes stuffed with lotus bean paste are eaten.
The cultural significance may be lost in modern society, but children still gleefully mark this occasion by carrying lanterns on the night of the festival – which these days come in an array of forms, from traditional cellophane to battery-operated plastic.

Believe it or not, you can see snow in Singapore come December – artificial snow, that is. The Christmas light-up on Orchard Road is a yearly tradition; the street is set ablaze with thousands of fairy lights, and shopping malls deck their facades with decorations in the spirit of the season. From snowmen to log houses and larger-than-life Santa Claus figures, almost every Yuletide cliche is played out – never mind that it's alien to local culture. Another colourful festival to look out for is the Chinese Lunar New Year. In the days leading up to it, the streets of Chinatown are decorated with lights and lined with bazaar stalls selling festive food like waxed duck and barbecued meats. The excitement culminates on the eve when revellers congregate to ring in the Lunar New Year and watch a dramatic fireworks display. Likewise, Deepavali sees a riot of neon lights on the streets in Little India at Serangoon Road, while Geylang Serai is all abuzz during the Muslim festival of Hari Raya Puasa.

LEFT: apart from the street decorations and festival light-up at Geylang Serai, another hub of activity during the Muslim Hari Raya Puasa is Bussorah Street.

SINGAPORE AFTER DARK

The city rocks after dark. Come dusk, pubs shift gears, clubs rev up their music, and theatre and dance come alive on stage. There's something for just about everyone, whether they prefer a night at the opera or a pub crawl

When the government announced in 2003 that bar-top dancing would be allowed in Singapore, there was much sniggering among the island's more vocal detractors. Trust over-regulated officials to make such a big deal about activities that are passé anywhere else. But wait. Official go-ahead or not, there has been a recent and visible opening up of Singapore's social life. Once decried as a sterile place with no soul, Singapore has, over the past five years, completely transformed itself into a lively arts and entertainment city.

Not only is the Lion City increasingly creative, it is learning to take itself less seriously. Bar-top dancing has been given the nod, gay bars are increasingly open about their inclination, clubs at designated districts can operate 24/7, a reverse bungy jump outfit has been given the licence to take the plunge, and busking is no longer frowned upon. Though sticky issues still exist – sugar-free chewing gum is only available with a prescription – Asia's economic powerhouse is having a fine time playing hard and still working as hard.

So whether it's being moved to tears at the opera, having a chuckle at a stand-up comedy act, tossing back a Singapore Sling at a dimly-lit karaoke lounge, or shooting pool at 3am, you will find it in Singapore. And if you reach down deep enough, you'll hit the underbelly of Singapore society – as vibrant and decadent as the best of them.

LEFT: al fresco dining and drinking at One Fullerton.
RIGHT: BQ Bar, the latest hotspot in Boat Quay.

The art of entertainment

Every year, the month of June is taken over and saturated by the Singapore Arts Festival, which features acts from all over the world, from dance and theatre to music. To give you an idea of its quality, its 2004 presentation included performances by luminaries such as Yo-Yo Ma, the Count Basie Orchestra, Soweto Gospel Choir and an award-winning Lithuanian adaptation of Shakespeare's *Othello*. The festival also offers a Kidsfest and a fringe with free performances in public spaces.

Festival aside, there is an incredible number of arts and entertainment events throughout the year for a tiny city like Singapore. Arts venues such as the stunning Esplanade – Theatres on the Bay offer a year-round calendar of events, both free and ticketed. The country's newest arts venue, The Arts House at the historic Old Parliament Building was transformed in early 2004 into a performing arts venue overlooking the Singapore River.

The National Arts Council, the government body that looks after Singapore's cultural soul, organises year-round free concerts at lush Singapore parks. Other annual fixtures are the world music festival WOMAD, the International Comedy Festival, the Singapore Buskers Festival and the Singapore Dance Theatre's Ballet Under the Stars series.

The Singapore Repertory Theatre is most associated with Broadway-scale productions which bring together the world's most talented Asian stars – like David Henry Hwang, Lea Salonga, Pat Morita, Tsai Chin and Shabana Azmi – along with award-winning directors, playwrights, lighting, set and costume designers. Most recently, SRT's musical *Forbidden City: Portrait of an Empress* returned for a second sell-out season to audiences fascinated with the story of the scheming Empress Dowager, Cixi, and her transformation from ingenuous concubine into ruthless ruler.

Hot on the heels of this hugely successful production came another tale from the annals

The theatre scene

New Broadway-destined shows with an Asian focus occasionally premiere in Singapore while long-running shows like *Les Misérables, Oliver!* and *Cats* frequently make an appearance here. All these alongside a very healthy Singapore theatre scene, which features both locally-written and produced works as well as international collaborations. Wild Rice, a theatre company that creates "glocal" works inspired by Singapore society and universal issues, recently played to sell-out crowds at the New Zealand International Festival, with a distinctly and disturbingly Singaporean adaptation of Orwell's *Animal Farm*.

of Asian history – the world premiere of *I La Galigo*, an epic-length theatre, music and dance production based on the Bugis people of South Sulawesi in Indonesia. Directed by international theatre visionary Robert Wilson, it opened in Singapore in 2004 before touring New York, Amsterdam, Spain, France and Italy.

Dance and music

Classical music in Singapore revolves around the Singapore Symphony Orchestra, which traces its history back to 1979. The critically acclaimed orchestra gives more than 100 concerts a year at Esplanade – Theatres on the Bay. Its repertoire tends to be mainstream, most concerts comprise the standard overture, concerto and symphony, but it also performs more accessible classical and contemporary music, to build new audiences. Big names that have performed with the SSO include percussionist Evelyn Glennie and tenor Jose Carreras.

Dance in Singapore is dynamic, with a corps of dancers and choreographers moving between projects and ensembles. The most important is the Singapore Dance Theatre. Hailed as an "Asian jewel", its repertoire ranges from *The Nutcracker* and *Sleeping Beauty* to contemporary dance. Choreographer Jamaludin Jalil's *Juxtamotion*, and Paul Ocampo's *Who Cares?* set to the music of the pop group Queen have all entered into its repertoire, and some have been included in overseas tours.

Film fare

Recent years have seen the local film industry grow at an unprecedented rate, with a slew of high-grossing films tackling social issues with both humour and style. Local directors such as Jack Neo, Eric Khoo, Tan Pin Pin and Royston Tan are increasingly enjoying the limelight at home and overseas with their award-winning movies and short films. Singapore's young film industry has far outstripped its sister, the television industry, in terms of quality and depth.

For the visitor, it's a matter of luck and timing as to whether you catch a well-produced local film, but one thing that you can count on are the excellent year-round foreign film festivals. One highlight is the Singapore International Film Festival in April – now into its 17th year – which showcases some of the world's (and Singapore's) best.

The movie-goer here is spoilt for choice. Virtually every shopping mall in Singapore boasts a multi-theatre cineplex, albeit screening mainly Hollywood pulp fare, up to six times a day. Midnight shows in the past were confined only to weekends, but today, movie-lovers can watch all-night movie marathons. At Cathay Cineleisure on Orchard Road, for instance, movies on Fridays, Saturdays and the eves of holidays run overnight until the crack of dawn. Golden Village Cineplex in Great World City on Kim Seng Road offers – for a price – plush sofa-style seats for two, with the option to enjoy a meal as you watch the movie.

Favourite nighttime haunts

If you don't have much time, and want a definitive Singapore pub experience, don't take the first piece of advice you get. Think about what you want – there is a pub to suit every taste and quirk, and some are better than others. Make the wrong choice and you'll wonder where you were when techno, house and rave replaced music.

One long-standing favourite with locals and expats who want to listen to a great cover band

LEFT: Singapore Repertory Theatre's *Forbidden City: Portrait of an Empress*, was a qualified success.
RIGHT: Singapore Dance Theatre's *pas de deux*.

is Anywhere at Tanglin Shopping Centre. This is the absolute "comfort food" of pubs, unpretentious and welcoming, where everyone sings along with the band when a well-loved song comes on. The band Tania has been around for more than 20 years, and still rocks, with gender-confused frontman Alban batting spider-leg fake eyelashes and pouts to kill.

Stand-up comedian and local gay icon Kumar is another must-see, for a true slice of Singapore humour. Dressed in slinky gowns, Kumar holds forth on a variety of issues, while poking fun at audience members and bemoaning the local singles scene. He performs at Hard Rock Café on Monday nights, and at the Boom

Boom Room in Far East Square on weekends.

Another favourite – with blues lovers – is Crazy Elephant at Clarke Quay, where you can jam with the best or worst, and get cheered on or booed off the stage accordingly.

Nightlife hubs

One neighbourhood worth a leisurely trawl is Mohamed Sultan Road. Rows of old shophouses have been transformed into Singapore's most happening chill-out (or warm-up) precinct. Among the most enduring are places like Next Page, Siam Supper Club, The Liquid Room and Madam Wong's. A couple of wee hours local-style coffeeshops along River Valley Road are

COURTING THE PINK DOLLAR

Singapore, like other large international cities, has wised up to the increasingly large and cash-rich international pink dollar market. While not openly offering welcome banners, efforts are well underway to put out the word – through the right channels – that the gay and lesbian community can comfortably enjoy a vacation in Singapore, without fear for personal safety or persecution.

In fact, Singapore's former Prime Minister Goh Chok Tong may have inadvertently sparked this change in official mindset when he remarked in 2003 that the civil service did not discriminate against the hiring of gay people. Taking the cue, the local and international press

ran several articles on Singapore's gay community. These days, gay-themed plays have become commonplace along with a rash of gay-friendly bars and saunas, especially in the Chinatown area. Gay-cruising spots too have emerged from the shadows. Local gay rights advocacy group People Like Us (www.plu-singapore.com) seek to champion the cause of the community but have so far failed in lifting regulations in Singapore which outlaw homosexual sex. And it looks like it has a long way to go in still-conservative Singapore. Community-specific platforms on the Internet (like www.fridae.com) advise gay and lesbian travellers on what's out there for them.

a stone's throw away if you need sustenance to take the edge off that alcohol-induced high.

A short distance away at Jiak Kim Road is Zouk – the ultimate in cool and well known in international clubbing circles. It plays a diet of edgy underground and house music, and has hosted in the past DJ luminaries like Paul Oakenfold, John Digweed and Sasha. Also high on the "be-seen" scale are the New Asia Bar and City Space at the Equinox, Balaclava at Suntec City, China Jump at Chijmes, Harry's and BQ Bar at Boat Quay, Post Bar at the Fullerton and Bar None at the Marriott.

If jazz is your thing, there are a handful of places worth a visit. For international acts, head to Blue at the Shangri-La Hotel, while local jazz veterans can be found at Jazz @ South Bridge on Boat Quay, and J Bar at the M Hotel.

Theme pubs

Theme pubs are popular, and among the long-standing favourites are Hooters at Clarke Quay with its well-endowed waitresses (enough said), Devil's Bar (Orchard Parade Hotel), aimed at die-hard Man U fans, and Ice Cold Beer on Emerald Hill for 9-inch hotdogs and 30 varieties of ice-cold beer. Paulaner Brauhaus at Millenia Walk is a German microbrewery specialising in freshly brewed light and dark lagers, while Que Pasa at Emerald Hill is an old shophouse converted into a Spanish-inspired bar serving tapas, sangria and cigars. Penny Black at Boat Quay will do nicely if you want a taste of old England, while the Irish pub Muddy Murphy's at the Orchard Hotel was reportedly built in Dublin, taken apart, shipped to Singapore and reconstructed painstakingly.

Speaking of pain, Igor's at Stadium Boulevard is a horror-themed theatre dining experience – expect ghoulish-looking wait staff to serve your "last supper" amid blood-curdling screams and zombies who suddenly lurch out at you in the dark. Dinner is served between the two-act rib-tickling show.

Karaoke

Karaoke lounges are everywhere, with membership clubs offering private rooms for rowdy sessions without punishing other patrons. K-Box Karaoke Lounge has about a dozen outlets in Singapore, and is open till 3am – when no one cares any longer who's singing what.

Tanjong Pagar, once home to a rash of pubs, has seen its fortunes dwindle, and the district is now home to a more lucrative slice of the entertainment pie. Behind gaudy, neon-lit facades, drunken off-key renditions of Chinese and English classics are rendered, with hostesses who ply their groping male customers with drinks – and whatever else takes their customers' fancy.

Red-tinted pursuits

Smack in Orchard Road is yet another underworld. Claymore Rise, near Orchard Towers,

and nearby streets are packed with "working girls" and their agents on weekend nights. If you are female and alone, don't choose this as a meeting place – unless getting the sleazy-eye from agents on the prowl for fresh talent or shifty-eyed men making unwanted overtures don't faze you. Inside Orchard Towers are well-known pick-up joints like Crazy Horse, Ipanema and Peyton Place.

All-you-can-drink alcohol buffets, drag nights, sex-for-sale joints disguised as health clubs and gyms, it's all here in Singapore, if you know where to look and who to ask. ❏

● *Individual nightlife spots are listed in the Travel Tips section (see pages 220–23).*

LEFT: the heaving crowds at a nightspot.
RIGHT: "pink" is hip in the Lion City.

CUISINE

Singapore's extraordinary cultural diversity has given the island-state an explosion of flavours – Chinese, Malay, Indian – and a delicious hybrid Peranakan cuisine that is entirely its own. Add to this the world's major cuisines and you have a city that never stops eating

There are few places in the world where life revolves around food like it does in Singapore. Singaporeans talk about food all the time just like the English talk of the weather. People from all walks of life display remarkable critical abilities in matters culinary. They can debate on where to get the freshest seafood, the hottest chilli sauce, the best chicken rice or *satay* for hours on end – preferably over a meal. Whether served on polystyrene in a rough and ready food centre or on bone china in a chi chi restaurant, food is a major focus in Singapore.

The racial mix of Chinese, Malays and Indians, as well as an expatriate population from the world over, has led to a range of cuisines which is nothing less than incredible. These immigrants brought their favourite dishes, ingredients and techniques, resulting in a variety of food which has merged then re-emerged as unique, and available today in venues ranging from hawker stalls to world-class restaurants.

There are few cuisines which aren't represented in Singapore, so much so that the choice is wonderfully daunting. For most Singaporeans, however, nothing beats hawker-style Indian, Chinese, Malay and Peranakan specialities – and homegrown favourite dishes like fish head curry and chilli crab.

Peranakan

The combination which really has its own identity and provides Singapore with its most indigenous cuisine is Peranakan or Nonya

food. Peranakans (*see page 37*) are descendants of early migrants from China who settled in Penang, Melaka and Singapore, and married local Malay lasses. The product of this union is the unique Peranakan culture and a cuisine which deftly blends Chinese ingredients with Malay spices and herbs – resulting in a cuisine that is both imaginative and tasty.

Central to Peranakan cuisine is the *rempah*: a mixture of spices such as chillies, shallots, lemon grass, candlenuts, turmeric and *belacan*, or prawn paste, ground by hand in a stone pestle and mortar (*batu tumbuk*). It is this nose-tickling mixture which imparts a distinctive flavour and aroma to Peranakan cuisine.

LEFT: *dim sum* at Chinatown's Yum Cha Restaurant.
RIGHT: proud chef at Fullerton Hotel's Town Café.

Although best eaten in a Peranakan home, the food can be enjoyed at a small number of restaurants. Look out for dishes such *otak otak*, a blend of fish, coconut milk, chilli paste, galangal and herbs wrapped in banana leaf. Another is *ayam buah keluak*, which combines chicken with Indonesian black nuts (the American *Gourmet* magazine once likened *buah keluak* to chocolates slathered in mud!) to produce a rich gravy. Be sure to leave room for desserts – colourful cakes and sticky sweet delicacies.

Chinese cuisine

The Chinese have a way with food. Whether it's fresh fish and pork, produce like mush-

helping oneself with chopsticks (or more likely these days, spoon and fork) from a selection of dishes shared by all the diners.

The adaptation to regional and climatic demands, as well as the absorption of foreign influence, has led to a fascinating variety of tastes from all over China. In Singapore you don't just say you'll eat Chinese; you say you'll eat Sichuan (for Szechuan), Cantonese, Teochew or any of a dozen distinct types of food from China's various regions.

There is more than ample opportunity to sample crispy Peking duck (from Beijing), piquant hot and sour soup (Sichuan); sizzling hotplate barbecue and wholesome steamboat

rooms and vegetables, or exotic abalone or bird's nest, Chinese cooks will whip up the tastiest of dishes in a flash. In recent years, Chinese food has also taken a turn for the healthy; increasingly cooks make do without lard and fatty cuts of meat, preferring instead slivers of lean meat or fresh seafood, accompanied by a range of fresh vegetables quickly stir-fried to preserve their flavours.

Chinese cuisine is also incredibly inventive: while there are uniquely Singapore-inspired Chinese dishes like chilli or pepper crabs, the large Chinese population here generally ensures the authenticity of the cuisine. The meal is always eaten in traditional style – by

(Mongolia), or the most famous and lightest of Chinese cuisines, Cantonese.

An ancient Chinese proverb advises to live in Suzhou (noted for its refined manners and beautiful women), die in Liuzhou (where teakwood coffins are made), but eat in Guangzhou (Canton). As more Cantonese than any other Chinese from other regions settled in the West, their cuisine is perhaps the best known of all, with its stir-fried fresh ingredients and light sauces. Although the Cantonese form only a fraction of the Chinese population in Singapore, they are still the most prolific restaurateurs here.

Cantonese dishes are simply flavoured, and cooked using a variety of methods: steaming, frying in a wok, roasting, poaching and deep frying. A perennial Cantonese favourite is *dim sum* (little heart), small steamed or fried buns, pastries and dumplings served in bamboo containers. These little delicacies are usually stuffed with a variety of meat, prawns, minced vegetables and herbs, and are available at most restaurants during lunchtime.

Less common but equally good is Hakka food, simple and hearty fare that often features beancurd as one of the main ingredients. The guest people, as the Hakkas were known when they came from the western border of Kwantung, use their ingenuity to make the most of every scrap of food. Homemade wine is used to make heady soups such as beefball soup, while *yong tau foo*, beancurd stuffed with minced fish and vegetables and served with a dark sweet sauce, is another speciality.

Seafood with well-flavoured sauces is typical of Hokkien cuisine. But perhaps most popular of all is *Hokkien mee*, thick egg noodles sauteed with pork, squid, prawns and vegetables in a rich sauce, usually served with half a fresh lime and a dollop of chilli paste. Also worth trying are *popiah* or fried spring rolls, thin crepes filled with shredded turnip, prawns, sausage and eggs seasoned with garlic, chilli paste and sweet bean sauce.

Then there is Hainanese food: the most famous dish of all is Hainanese chicken rice, a combination of boiled or roasted chicken, splashed with a touch of sesame oil and soy sauce, and served with rice cooked in chicken stock and a side dish of spicy chilli-garlic sauce.

Vegetarians need not despair: tofu (soya beancurd), widely used in Chinese cuisine, makes a protein-packed meal for non-meat eaters, and there are endless ways of preparing and flavouring it. Chinese vegetarian restaurants also use wheat gluten to create dishes that resemble meat and poultry.

Seafood

Surrounded by tropical waters, Singapore is assured of a plentiful supply of fresh fish and seafood. Succulent prawns, crayfish, lobster, crab, pomfret, *ikan merah* (red snapper) and *tenggiri* (mackerel) are featured in many local dishes. Next to Peranakan food, seafood-based cuisine is perhaps the closest there is to a homegrown culinary art. Asian spices combined with Chinese cooking methods make for concoctions like chilli or pepper crab, steamed prawns and crispy fried *sotong* (baby squid).

Singaporeans adore seafood and will happily make the pilgrimage to the east coast to find the best seafood restaurants (although there are smaller numbers scattered in other parts of Singapore as well).

Chilli crab, sometimes said to be Singapore's national dish, are stir-fried in their shells with a thick sauce of garlic, sugar, soy sauce, tomato sauce, eggs and of course, lots of chilli.

SPICY FISH HEAD CURRY

Another leading contender for the national dish is fish-head curry, which comes in spicy Indian, Malay and Peranakan variations. Despite the somewhat unappealing sight of a giant fish head floating in a thick sea of gravy, the succulent flesh and the accompanying hot and sour gravy flavoured with curry powder and tamarind juice is a delicious and satisfying taste sensation.

Fans of the dish wax lyrical about the eyeballs and the cheeks of the fish head; true blue aficionados even resort to tossing a coin to see who gets to eat the choice parts. Most people, thankfully, are happy just slurping the gravy.

LEFT: smiling Bugis Street hawker.
RIGHT: fish head curry may be an acquired taste.

The result is a pile of bright-red crustaceans to be savoured, no attacked, with a hammer and fingers, an utterly delicious experience made even better when crusty French bread is used to mop up the sauce. Devilish looking black pepper crabs, coated in a tongue-tingling sauce, some say, are even better. Whichever you choose, be prepared to get messy.

Malay cuisine

Malay food in Singapore is an amalgam of traditional dishes from Peninsular Malaysia, with strong influences from the Indonesian islands of Sumatra and Java. Rice is the staple that counterbalances the spiciness of the food.

Coconut is also important, with the flesh grated and squeezed for the rich milk used in countless gravies, as well as cakes, desserts and drinks. Malay dishes are flavoured with a startling array of spices and herbs: lemon grass, kaffir lime leaves, shallots, galangal, coriander, tamarind, turmeric, cumin, ginger and garlic. Another vital ingredient is *belacan*, a pungent dried shrimp paste often combined with pounded fresh chillies to make *sambal belacan*.

Nasi padang, originally from the Padang area of West Sumatra, is a perennial favourite, combining a variety of spicy meat, chicken and vegetable dishes served with rice and placed in the centre of the table. A typical meal would include beef *rendang*, a thick and spicy curry made from coconut milk, spices and herbs, served with a fragrant rice dish, *nasi minyak*, to which cardamom and cinnamon have been added, a vegetable curry called *sayur lodeh* (mixed vegetables in coconut) and *sambal goreng* (an aromatic dish of tofu, *tempeh*, a preserved soya bean cake, and long beans).

One of Singapore's all-time Malay favourites is *satay*. These are small bamboo skewers of marinated beef, mutton or chicken which are grilled over coals and served with sliced onion, cucumber, *ketupat* (compressed rice cakes) and peanut sauce. Not to be outdone, the Chinese have come up with their own version, made with either pork (which is taboo for Malays) or chicken, and served with a sweeter version of the traditional peanut sauce.

Indian cuisine

Indian food, characterised by its complex use of spices to make its staple curries, is not always spicy. Northern Indian cuisine is more aromatic than spicy, its rich flavour resulting from a complex use of spices tempered by yoghurt. Food cooked in a *tandoor* or clay oven is one of the highlights of northern Indian cuisine. It is used for baking leavened *roti* (bread) or *naan*, and to produce delicious marinated fish or chicken dishes, using either whole (*tandoori*) or small pieces (*tikka*) of meat. The bread is perfect for sopping up the yoghurt-based gravies, an influence of the nomadic tribes and their hill-grazing cattle.

In the south of India, fiery curries are a speciality and coconut milk is often used in the gravy instead of yoghurt. Southern food is also

listinctive for its use of mustard seeds and fra-
gran mint, curry and coriander leaves. *Korma*
lishes are generally mild, although anything
prefixed by the word *masala* is likely to be hot
and will be reddish in colour. The so-called
"banana leaf" restaurants of Serangoon Road
are well-known for their spicy fare served on
banana leaves. Ice-cold beer or lime juice is the
perfect accompaniment to douse the fire.

Indian Muslim food is very popular in Singapore. One speciality is *murtabak*, which is
a fluffy pan-fried bread stuffed with minced
lamb or chicken. When the bread is served
plain, it is called *prata*. Another is *nasi
briyani*, a fragrant rice dish redolent of saffron

Dutch, Malay, Javanese and Indian ancestry –
is typically multi-cultural. Malay herbs spice
up pork, further enhanced by Indian mustard
seeds and chillies. Typical is Devil Curry, a
fire-and-brimstone name for a spicy dish of
chicken pepped up with vinegar, mustard and
chillies. Similarly, English dishes such as stews
and roasts are transformed with the addition of
soy sauce, green chillies or sour tamarind juice.

International and fusion fare

If local fare doesn't grab you, take your pick
from any number of French, Italian, Mediterranean and Greek or Thai, Japanese, Korean
and Vietnamese restaurants. Some of the best

and cooked with seasoned mutton or chicken.

A variety of vegetarian dishes, savoury
snacks, lentils and breads have been created,
as well as cloyingly sweet milk-based desserts.
Vegetarian meals are often served on a banana
leaf, or on a *thali*, a large tray holding a mound
of rice, on which smaller bowls or *katori* are
placed, filled with the accompanying dishes.

Eurasian food

Eurasian cuisine – which hails from Singapore's minority community of Portuguese,

chefs in the world have been drawn to Singapore's shores and have set up restaurants here.

Whether you call it Pacific Rim, Modern
Australian or Modern French, Californian or
New Asian – or whatever fancy name bandied
by international culinary gurus – the hallmark
of this emerging trend is the clever combination of Asian flavours with Continental methods of preparation. While the results may be hit
or miss, the fare is always interesting – imagine
a soy- and wasabe-flavoured salad dressing
over crisp Romaine lettuce, or grilled Chilean
cod drenched in Japanese miso sauce. ❏

LEFT: barbecued sticks of *satay* are heavenly.
ABOVE: spicy South Indian fare eaten off banana leaves.

● *Individual restaurant recommendations are listed at
the end of each chapter in the Places section.*

SINGAPORE-STYLE HAWKER FOOD

A visit to the city-state is incomplete without a meal at one of its food centres, where an astonishing variety of dishes are cooked on the spot

The hawker centre offers multi-ethnic Singapore cooking at its best. Whether it's a simple dish of noodles for S$3 or a S$20 three-course meal of barbecued fish, chilli prawns and fried vegetables with rice, the cost is a fraction of what you would pay for a similar meal in a restaurant. Prices apart, the experience is unique, and a pleasant reminder of your stay in this food-crazy city. When celebrity chef Anthony Bourdain visited Singapore, he proclaimed, "...I love the hawker centres. The whole style of casual eating here is sensational."

For the uninitiated, here's how you order a meal at a hawker centre. If there's a group of you, have one person sit at a table to *chope* (meaning reserve in local parlance) seats for the rest of the party. Don't be surprised if you see seats with bags or packets of tissue paper on them; it's a sign that they have been taken. The others, having noted the table number, should order their food and tell the stall owner the table number they are seated at, unless of course it's a self-service operation. If you're on your own, you can share a table with strangers. As you savour your meal, you will realise why true-blue local gourmets will head for their favourite food stall at every opportunity.

ABOVE AND LEFT: hawker centres vary in ambience. Lau Pa Sat *(above)* offers one of the most attractive settings in a Victorian cast-iron structure *(see page 114)*. These days, hawker centres have also gone upmarket and global in their offerings. Instead of open-air surroundings, you now find them in the air-conditioned environs of shopping centres. Called food courts *(left)*, these places may offer Vietnamese, Thai, Turkish and even Italian dishes in addition to Singapore food – albeit at slightly higher prices.

ABOVE: plate-sized and bright-red crabs smothered in a piquant chilli and tomato sauce is a typical Singapore dish that you'll find at hawker stalls that specialise in seafood. The dish isn't as robustly spicy as it looks but if you're not feeling particularly adventurous, order black pepper crabs instead, which is just as yummy.

CHANGING TIMES FOR THE HAWKERS

In the old days, there was no such thing as a hawker centre. Instead, the sound of an ice-cream bell, or the clacking of a bamboo stick against a wooden block, or the chant of the *mua chee* man selling sticky nougat-like candy, would send children – and their parents – scrambling from their homes into the streets to buy their favourite snack. The fare on offer was amazing. From bread and bowls of steaming noodle soups to peanuts and *poh piah* (spring rolls), the roving hawker was a familiar fixture in the neighbourhood.

Then came the roadside hawkers, who set up their makeshift stalls on the streets after dark, when parking lots were emptied of cars and replaced by wooden tables and stools, and a pushcart which doubled as a mobile kitchen. By 1987, with creeping urbanisation and an obsession with cleanliness, the last of the roadside hawkers were cleared. The only place where you can find roadside hawkers today is Chinatown's Smith Street *(see page 105)*. This sanitised recreation of yesteryear does its best to resemble the city's once bustling and colourful street life.

If you're sufficiently enamoured of hawker food after reading this, pick up the leaflet called *Makan Delights* from any of the STB's Visitor Centres. It tells you all you need to know about hawker *makan* (food) in the city.

ABOVE: flaky *roti prata* – plain or stuffed with onions or an egg – and eaten with curry is an Indian bread that is enjoyed by many for breakfast. Try and catch the *roti prata* man in action, twirling pieces of dough in ever increasing circles until it becomes a flat bread that is pan-fried on a griddle.

LEFT: *mee rebus*, literally "boiled noodles" is a Malay dish that tastes much better than it sounds. Yellow wheat noodles are dunked in a spicy-sweet brown gravy and topped with chopped tofu, spring onions, green chillies, a hard-boiled egg and a dash of dark soya sauce.

SHOPPING

It's not for nothing that Singapore is renowned the world over as a shopping haven. The range is stupendous with malls so huge one could get lost in them. If retail therapy is your idea of heaven, you'll find bliss in Singapore

The notion seems implausible, even laughable – that shopping, along with eating, are serious pastimes for many Singaporeans. People in Singapore shop all the time – during lunchtime, after work and on weekends. Call it retail therapy, or a necessary evil, the buying culture is so firmly embedded that Singaporeans are easily spotted – by like-minded Singaporeans when they shop outside the country.

The result? Every neighbourhood on the island has at least one mall, never mind that they retail similar offerings. The guiding principle appears to be, if there's an empty plot of land, let's build a shopping centre. If a historical building is falling apart, let's give it a lick of paint, and put in some shops and restaurants (as opposed to a museum).

Is there such a thing as too much of a good thing? Not if you look at shopping mecca Orchard Road *(see page 121)*. It is *the* place for all things hot, trendy and newly minted. With over 30 malls stretching along a tree-fringed road, it's truly a testimony of the country's number one passion.

Admittedly, except at a handful of high-end boutiques, service levels can be erratic. You might encounter the occasional surly sales person who scowls and snipes "Everything is on display" when asked for alternative sizes or colours. Thankfully, most usually oblige and make an effort to follow up on requests.

Astounding diversity

The joy of shopping in Singapore lies in its diversity. From swanky air-conditioned malls to steamy bazaars, sleepy ethnic neighbourhoods to buzzing department stores, it's up to you to decide how to vary your shopping experiences. Singapore is also a city of duty-free luxury goods, of cutting-edge technology and high fashion, as well as a centre for traditional Asian exotica such as tea, silk, porcelain, traditional medicine and spices.

Despite keen competition from up-and-coming shopping destinations in the region, shopping in Singapore is a pleasure. It's easy to buy because English is the lingua franca. With the efficient transportation network, zipping around with your shopping bags in tow is a breeze. Some malls are so well connected by pathways and underground tunnels, you can easily walk from one to another without getting wet on a rainy day, or see the light of day.

An even greater delight is how hassle-free it is. Touting is virtually absent along the main shopping districts – and most stores accept major credit cards. ATMs are plentiful and stores are open from about 10am–9pm daily. It's highly likely you could shop till you drop.

The best times to shop

The Great Singapore Sale, from late May to early July, has become a much anticipated annual shopping bonanza for both locals and visitors. The generous discounts – sometimes up to 70 percent – see even the most tightfisted

Expect chi chi fashion runway shows, fashion-related exhibitions and glamorous parties.

The mall, the merrier

Tip for shopping in Singapore: temptations are everywhere – everything and anything money can buy and you can possibly want – lustrous pearls, age-old *huanghuali* (golden rosewood) desks, vintage handbags and the latest digi-cams – are found along the prime shopping districts of Orchard Road and Marina Bay.

On the surface, Orchard Road looks like a relentless stretch of gleaming five-star hotels and unremarkable malls. For shopaholics in the know, however, every shopping centre is

parting with some cash. If there's one time to max out on your credit card, it would be during this retail blowout.

Fashionistas would consider another important event on the local fashion calendar. The star-studded Singapore Fashion Festival, an annual event in April, aims to position the city as the region's fashion capital. Young and talented Asian designers share the limelight with international fashion powerhouses and cutting-edge couture designers from the world's most renowned fashion capitals.

LEFT: expect bargains during the Great Singapore Sale.
ABOVE: palace to conspicuous consumerism.

TOYS FOR BOYS

Observe any flight leaving for India at Changi Airport and you will see long queues of Indians carting home bulky flat-screen TVs, stereo equipment and even the odd washing machine. It's no secret that Singapore is one of the world's best places to shop for gadgets and all things electronic. You name it, PDAs, computer hardware and software, the latest cameras and MP3 players, you'll find them at speciality malls such as Funan The IT Mall and Sim Lim Square. Electronic stores like Harvey Norman and Best Denki have outlets all over town and merchandise is very competitively priced. Be sure to ask for an international guarantee though.

a shrine replete with inimitable finds. Tangs at the corner of Scotts Road and Orchard Road, for example, has an illustrious history dating back to the 1930s. Despite a traditional architecture that's modelled after the Imperial Palace in Beijing's Forbidden City, its Beauty Hall is *the* place for cult cosmetic and skincare labels; the Home department in the basement has extraordinary gadgets for modern homes.

Just down the street, the formidable Ngee Ann City is one of the few places with a good balance of high-end retailers and mid-priced stores. The mother of all malls, however, is the colossal 3,000-sq metre (1 million-sq ft) Suntec City Mall just five minutes' drive away, at the Marina Bay area. Going through the 300 or so shops is an exercise on both feet and patience.

What's also worth your time are the shopping carts parked at the ground floor of Raffles City Shopping Centre and Parco Bugis Junction. Young entrepreneurs often peddle one-of-a-kind wares sourced from all over the world. This relaxed, everything-goes type of shopping seems to be catching on. Shoppers love browsing the wares, chatting with stall owners and perhaps knocking off a few dollars off the price.

There are also shoping malls with attitude: for the rebellious young, a section of The Heeren Shops on Orchard Road, called The Annex, is modelled after the trendy youth urban

BUY BUY SINGAPORE

Singapore's multi-cultural heritage has given birth to uniquely local gifts. Here are a few worth carting home.
● **RISIS**, known for its orchid accessories in 24K gold also has other nature-inspired jewellery (01-084 Suntec City Mall, tel: 6338 8250, www.risis.com.sg).
● Purple gold jewellery by **Lee Hwa** is a unique amalgam of yellow gold and aluminum, purportedly a world's first (B1-30 Wisma Atria, tel: 6736 0266; www.leehwa.com.sg).
● The ground floor of **MITA Building** is the best one-stop shop for sculptures and paintings by local and Asian artists. There are several galleries here but of note is Art-2 (01-03 MITA Building, 140 Hill Street, tel: 6338 8713).

● **Boon's Pottery** has vases, teapots and crockery – all crafted by local potters (01-30 Tanglin Mall, tel: 6836 3978).
● **Museum Shop** at Asian Civilisations Museum, Empress Place, managed by Banyan Tree, is a treasure house for repros of precious treasures and trinkets (1 Empress Place Road, tel: 6336 9050; www.museumshop.com.sg).
● Fresh, handmade pralines, including durian and mango ones, are found at **SINS Choc Shoppe** (B1-05 The Heeren, tel: 6735 1678; www.sinschocs.com).
● Take home ready-to-cook versions of spicy *laksa* or *satay* by **Prima Taste** (www.prima taste.com.sg) available at Cold Storage or NTUC supermarkets.

centres of Asia – Tokyo's Harajuku, Taipei's Ximending and Bangkok's Siam Square. So is Level One at Far East Plaza at Scotts Road. The manufactured grittiness even comes complete with thumping techno pop and graffiti-filled walls. They may not have replicated their ediginess – this is after all squeaky-clean Singapore – but many young, bold and very talented Singaporean designers have their fashion boutiques here. Definitely worth a peruse if you're planning to bring home more than Chanel and Prada.

Uniquely Singapore

Being at the crossroads of the East and West have also inspired local fashion designers. Whether it's a modern cut on a cheongsam or a subtle addition of beads to an elegant evening dress, the designs show off the edge cosmopolitan Singapore has. The best places to seek out homegrown fashions are at The Heeren Shops (iS/f.w.d Forward Statement, X:odus and Fourskin boutiques), Far East Plaza (Womb and Ming stores) and Hemispheres Designers' Gallery (Orchard Point). Plenty of inspired designed-in-Singapore ready-to-wear can be found at independent boutiques such as projectshopBLOODbros (Paragon), M)Phosis (Ngee Ann City), Song+Kelly21 (Forum The Shopping Mall) and Woods & Woods (Raffles City Shopping Centre).

For a slice of everyday Singapore life, hop onto the train and head to the heartlands. There is always a mall to lose yourself in – if you haven't had enough in the city. Tampines Mall (Tampines MRT) and Junction 8 (Bishan MRT) will give you a good idea of what people in the suburbs buy. Fendi and Gucci may not be represented there, but prices tend to be lower and bargaining is acceptable at some shops. If you're lucky, you may chance upon a *pasar malam*, a makeshift nightmarket selling all manner of food and goods – some of it unsavoury like pornographic VCDs – and occupying empty space near MRT stations.

If it's colour and atmostphere you're after, the city's ethnic pockets – Chinatown, Little India and Kampung Glam – are flush with quirky finds. Hit Chinatown for Chinese silk, exotic herbal cures and antique furniture; Kam-

pung Glam for handmade perfume bottles, basket ware and fabrics; and Little India for henna tattoos, incense and Bollywood VCDs.

Oddly, though Singaporeans fervently embrace the concept of market shopping outside Singapore, the culture has not caught on back home. Unlike Bangkok's Chatuchak, London's Camden and Sydney's Paddington, such markets in Singapore are dismal and sometimes contrived affairs. If, however, you are looking a little adventure, flea markets make interesting detours.

Among the remaining handful, Sungei Road's Thieves' Market is the oldest. Broken radios, chipped crockery and used clothing

spread haphazardly on the floor is hardly the sort of thing you would want to buy, but it's an insight into the city's underbelly.

Serious shoppers are better off at Clarke Quay's Sunday Market. The day-long affair sees street performers and artists showing off their skills alongside 60 stalls peddling rare stamps, curios and handmade wares. The weekend afternoon bazaar outside Chinatown Complex hawks a stash of treasures – antique bronze ware, Chairman Mao memorabilia and handmade beaded handbags – mementoes from a fast disappearing side of Singapore. ❏

● *See also Orchard Road (pages 121–28) and Travel Tips (pages 223–27) for more information on shopping.*

LEFT: teapots for sale at Chinatown.
RIGHT: international brands are well represented.

PLACES

A detailed guide to the city, with the principal sites
clearly cross-referenced by number to the maps

Singaporeans used to joke that if they left the city-state for more than three months, they wouldn't be able to recognise many familiar places on their return, so relentless was the pace of urbanisation. Some things have changed, thankfully, and today, conservation has become a buzzword. If a building is of architectural or historical significance, the tendency is to restore it rather than replace it with a new-fangled one.

The results are apparent everywhere – in Chinatown, the Civic District, Kampung Glam, Little India and the old residential neighbourhoods. The gentrification of these places, apart from giving the city added charm, has also help develop among Singaporeans a sense of their own history and a link with the past of their forefathers. This is appropriate, for Singapore remains largely carved up according to Stamford Raffles' plans for the layout which he implemented in June 1819.

The colonial hub of the city, today's Civic District, is still the heart of administration, as it was in Raffles' time. The clamour of Chinatown and the hum of business in the Central Business District around Raffles Place have not diminished. The Muslim area of Kampung Glam, and the predominantly Hindu Little India, which developed around the kilns and cattle pens near Serangoon Road, retain their ethnic feel and laid-back air. Chic Orchard Road has come to be identified as one of Asia's premier shopping areas, and, befittingly, has been compared to the Champs-Élysées in Paris. All these places are more than amply covered in this guide.

Singapore packs in quite a bit given its tiny size. Once you've covered the city centre, venture out to the suburbs, where residential boundaries have been pushed even further as former farming land and fishing villages have been replaced with suburban towns linked by highways. Here you'll find tiny pockets of Singapore where time has stood still and where there is precious space for its people to take in the fresh air. Parks and beaches provide opportunity to unwind and there are nature reserves to explore and discover local flora and fauna. The average visitor, say the statistics, spends three days in Singapore. This book is filled with ideas on how to extend your stay to a week – and still be sufficiently enthralled at the end of it. ❏

PRECEDING PAGES: CBD area with the Singapore River snaking alongside; Esplanade – Theatres on the Bay at night. **LEFT:** Merlion statue with the Fullerton Hotel in background.

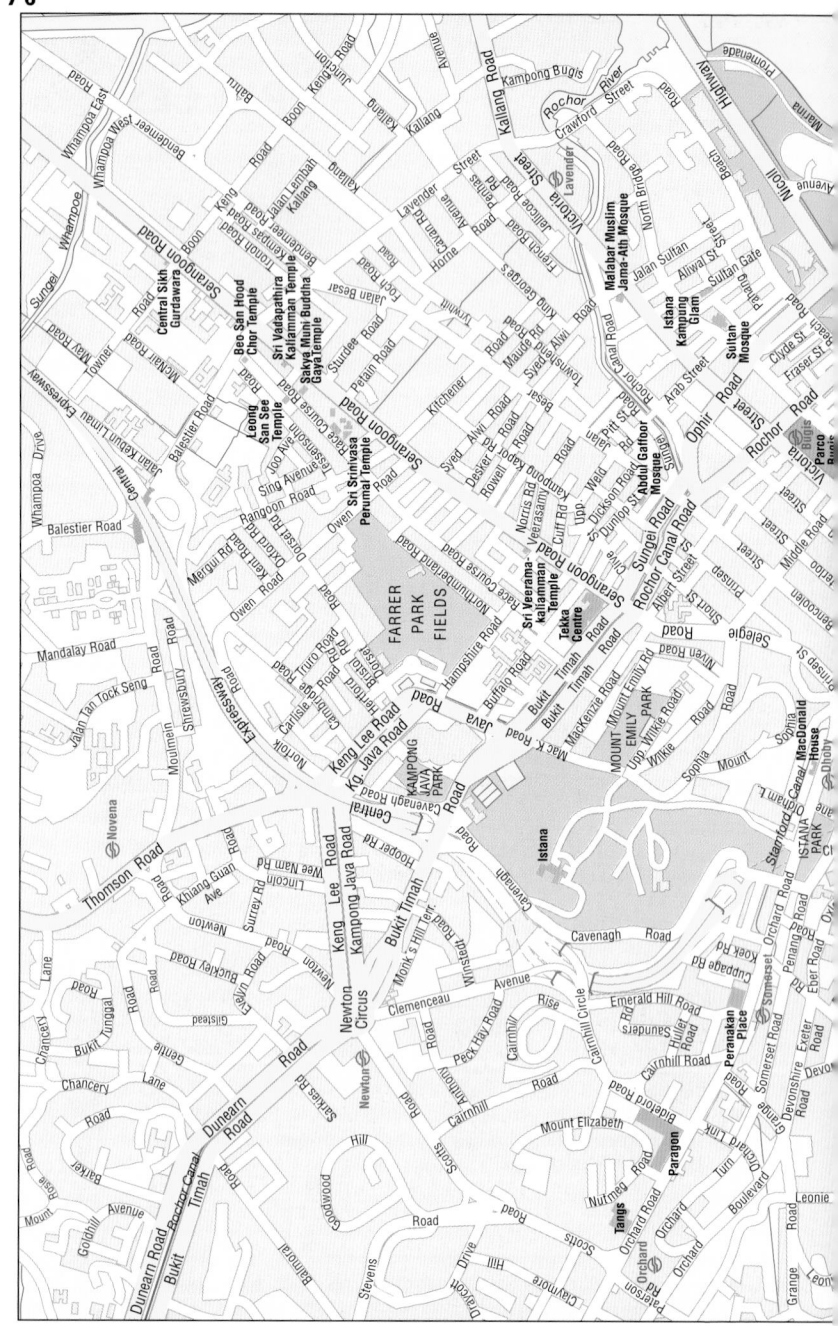

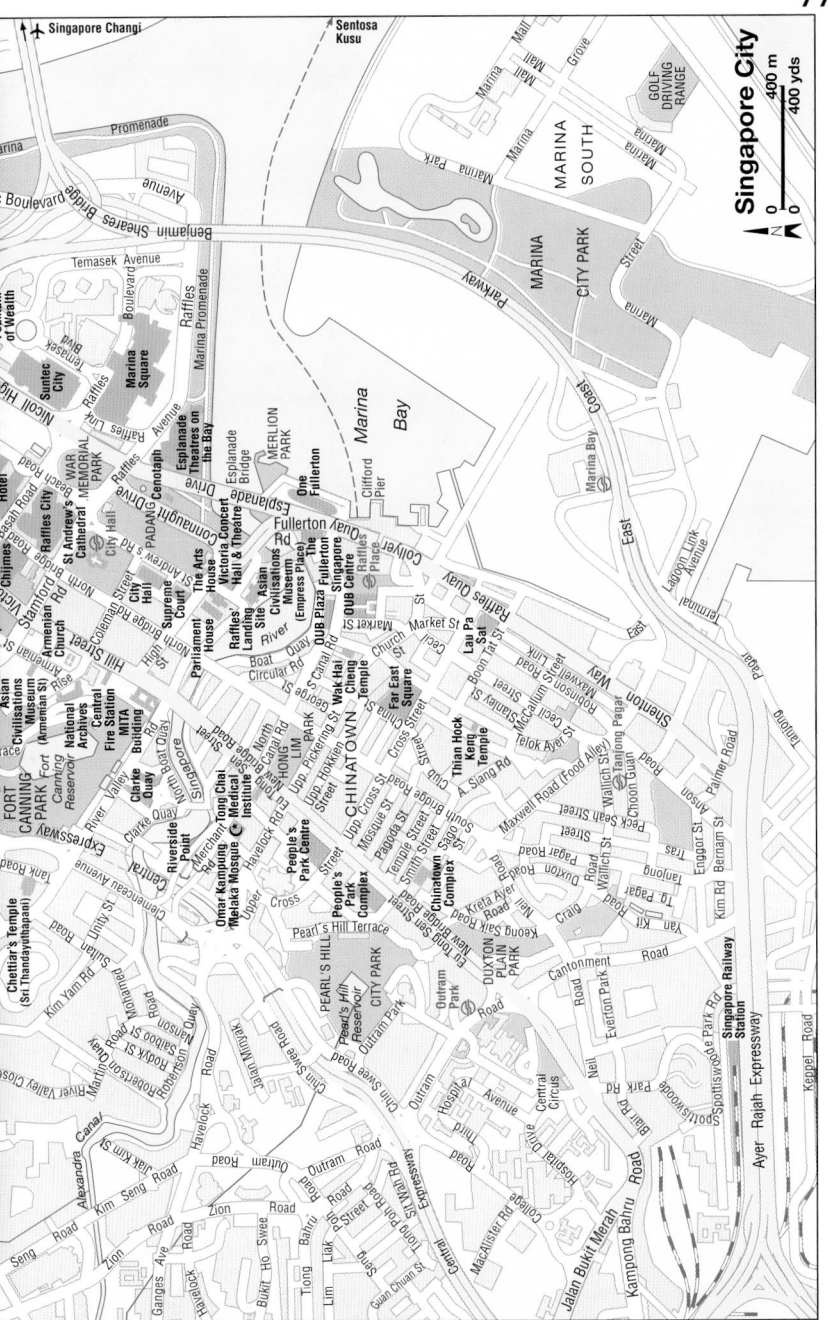

Singapore City

0   400 m
0   400 yds

THE CIVIC DISTRICT

From the site where Raffles first landed in 1819, you can explore the heart of Singapore, speckled with stately colonial buildings and majestic churches, and a mix of lively quays, theatres and museums

Nearly two centuries after Stamford Raffles first set foot in Singapore, the island is still governed from the colonial nucleus he established on the east bank of the Singapore River. A walk in this **Civic District** – the heart of colonial Singapore – is essentially a stroll down memory lane, featuring sights and monuments that reflect the city-state's rich historical past.

Raffles Landing Site

It's appropriate to start this walk from where it all began – at **Raffles' Landing Site ❶** on the left bank of the **Singapore River**, the commercial lifeline of Singapore for more than a century. It was here, on the very spot where a replica white marble statue of Sir Thomas Stamford Raffles stands, that the founder of modern Singapore stepped ashore on 28 January 1819. The view of the skyline on the opposite side of the river from the landing site is stunning: an arc of beautifully restored shophouses above the steps of **Boat Quay** set against the dramatic backdrop of soaring towers in **Raffles Place** *(see page 113)* – a wonderful contrast of the old and the new.

The Arts House

Just behind is **The Arts House ❷**, a new performing arts centre that took

over the premises of the Old Parliament House, Singapore's oldest state building (box office tel: 6332 6919, www.theartshouse.com.sg). Refurbished but still retaining its original spaces, the most significant feature is the 152-seat Chamber for music and drama performances – previously used by Members of Parliament to debate bills and laws.

The original building was the work of George Dromgold Coleman, the architect responsible for shaping colonial Singapore, and was built

Map on page 80

LEFT:
main entrance,
Esplanade – Theatres
on the Bay.
BELOW:
Raffles Landing
site, with CBD in the
background.

Statue of a Ming general standing guard outside the Asian Civilisations Museum, Empress Place.

in 1827 as the private home of a British merchant. Due to land lease problems, however, it was turned into a courthouse and later became the Parliament House for the incumbent government.

In 1999, the new **Parliament House**, just next door, was completed – five times larger than the old building but still retaining the colonial architectural style to preserve a sense of history. Porcelain dating back to the Ming and Yuan dynasties were found on the site during construction and these are displayed in the new complex.

Asian Civilisations Museum

Just adjacent is the stately **Asian Civilisations Museum, Empress Place ❸** (Mon 1–7pm, Tues–Sun 9am–7pm, Fri 9am–9pm; admission charge; tel: 6332 7798; www.nhb. gov.sg). Housed in the neo-classical **Empress Place Building**, this is one of the oldest structures in Singapore. Built by Indian convicts between 1864–67 and designed by J.F.A. McNair, it was first unveiled as a courthouse for the colonial government and later housed Singapore's legislative assembly. By the early 1980s, the building had seen

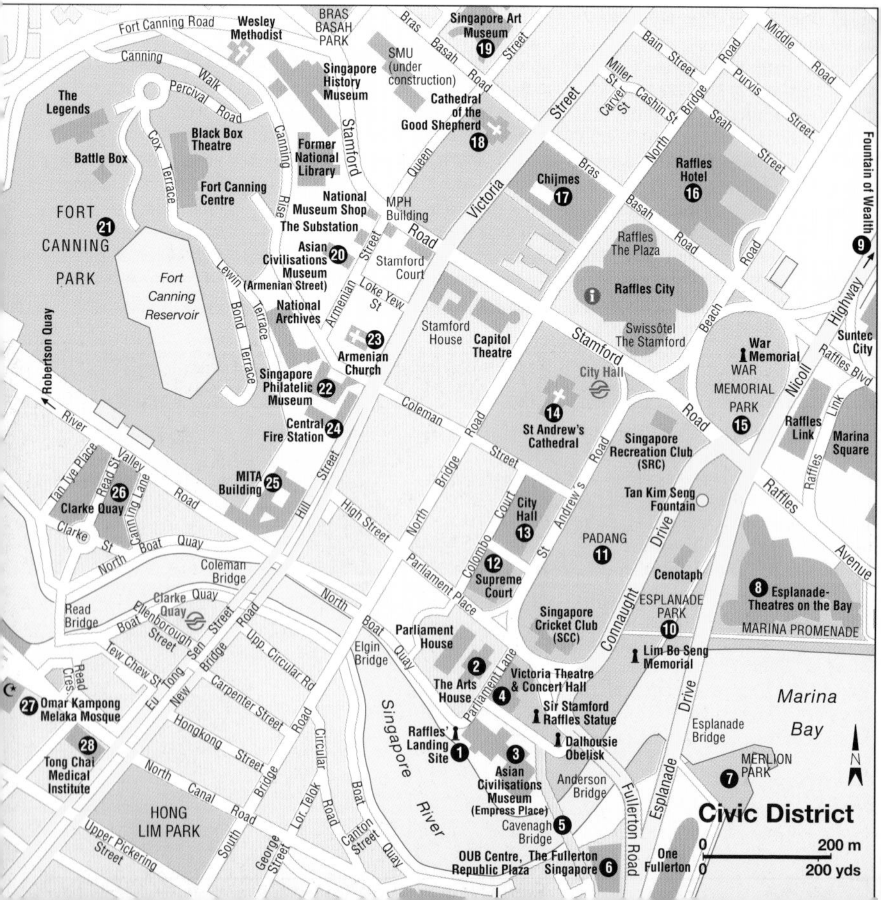

THE CIVIC DISTRICT ◆ 81

better days, and there was talk of demolition. Fortunately, the Singapore Tourism Board came to the rescue and spent millions renovating it. It engaged the services of a French Gothic and neo-classsical conservationist, Didier Repellin, who helped restore the building to its original splendour. In 1989, it re-opened as a museum showcasing Chinese artefacts but it closed after some years.

More restoration work followed and in March 2003, it became home to the Asian Civilisations Museum (a smaller wing of the museum is found along Armenian Street – *see page 89*). At 14,000 sq m (151,000 sq ft), this outstanding museum *(see also pages 98–9)* provides generous space to display its sizeable collections on the civilisations of East, Southeast, South and West Asia.

With 11 galleries spread over three levels, each of the four regions has its own thematic storyline and permanent displays integrated with interactive kiosks and discovery corners, along with a centre specially dedicated to younger visitors.

The building's river-facing wing is often abuzz with people at **Siem Reap II** (tel: 6338 7596), a restaurant serving Indochinese specialties, and the trendy **Bar Opiume** next door.

Victoria Theatre and Hall

Facing the side of Empress Place Building are two distinctive structures well known to local drama fans and concert lovers: the **Victoria Theatre and Concert Hall ❹** (originally known as Victoria Memorial Hall). Both were built in the 1880s to commemorate Queen Victoria's Diamond Jubilee. Victoria Theatre was originally built as Singapore's Town Hall in 1862 before it was converted into a theatre in 1905. It features a distinctive clock tower with a Westminster chime that has never stopped pealing on the hour since its installation in 1906.

The original 1887 bronze statue of Stamford Raffles, a replica of which stands at Raffles Landing Site *(see page 79)*, graces the front of Victoria Theatre and Concert Hall, where it was placed in 1919.

The concert hall stages opera, ballet and classical music while the

Map on page 80

Bronze statue of Stamford Raffles outside the Victoria Theatre and Concert Hall. Crafted by Thomas Woolner, it was first unveiled in 1887 and moved to its present site in 1919.

BELOW:
Victoria Theatre is a well-loved icon.

Locals refer to the Esplanade – Theatres on the Bay as the Durian. The spiky facades of the twin domes of the theatre and concert hall resemble the thorny exterior of the tropical fruit – universally loved by Singaporeans.

BELOW:
the Fullerton hotel once housed the city's Post Office.

theatre is a principal performance venue for dance and plays.

Just opposite is the **Dalhousie Obelisk**, a memorial dedicated to Marquis Dalhousie, India's governor-general from 1848–56, who visited Singapore in 1850.

Cavenagh/Anderson bridges

A walk along the riverside from Empress Place Building leads to **Cavenagh Bridge ❺** first, followed by **Anderson Bridge**. The latter bridge was built in 1910 when the Cavenagh, constructed in Scotland and assembled in Singapore by Indian convict labour in 1868, could not cope with increasing traffic.

Cross Cavenagh Bridge, and on the left are whimsical bronze statues of five boys leaping into the river. Tucked away on the right are tiny brass sculptures of *Kucinta* cats, indigenous to this part of the world *(see text box page 83)*.

The Fullerton Singapore

The grand Palladian-style building across Cavenagh Bridge is Singapore's former General Post Office, restored to its current reincarnation as the five-star hotel, **The Fullerton Singapore ❻**. Originally built in 1928 and named after Sir Robert Fullerton, the first governor of the Straits Settlements, the building is a wonderful example of the neo-classical style that once dominated the district. Artfully renovated for an astounding S$340 million and re-opened in 2000, the hotel is deceptively contemporary within its stately walls – best described as modern art deco. The historical landmark offers 400 broadband-ready rooms, two restaurants and the stylish **Post Bar** which attracts an equally well-heeled crowd. Enter by the massive revolving main door and see the central atrium, created by punching out several floors and the old ceiling.

Merlion Park

For a study in architectural contrast, take the underpass beneath The Fullerton to the glass-and-steel **One Fullerton** structure, a new restaurant and nightlife hub by the waterfront. There are swanky restaurants and bars, most with floor-to-ceiling windows offering stunning views of **Marina Bay**.

At the northern end of One Fullerton is the **Merlion Park ❼** with the Merlion statue anchoring it, the rather kitschy half-fish, half-lion creature that has been adopted as the city's tourism mascot. Visitors, however, seem to fall for it, given the crowds here at any time of the day. The Merlion was inspired by the creature that Prince Sang Nila Utama *(see page 19)* saw when he arrived in Temasek in the 13th century. Believing it to be a *singa* (lion), he renamed Temasek *Singapura* (Lion City).

The Esplanade Theatres

Looming acoss the waters of Marina Bay is the prickly hedgehog-like outline of **Esplanade – Theatres on the Bay ❽**, a S$600 million performing arts centre with the equally grandiose aim of establishing itself as a cultural landmark akin to Australia's Sydney Opera House (check www.esplanade.com for the schedule of programmes). The massive complex, which seems a little hemmed in by its waterfront location, is a realisation of Singapore's aspiration to be Asia's hub for the arts.

Opened with much fanfare in October 2002, the 6-hectare (15-acre) site houses a concert hall for an audience of 1,600, a 2,000-seat theatre, smaller recital and theatre studios, an open-air theatre, a practice studio, outdoor spaces for informal performances and sculpted gardens by the waterfront. The design of this landmark icon – which people either love or hate – with its distinctive facade of sharp-edged metal sunshades, has been mired in controversy since the model was first unveiled in 1992. Designed by Michael Wilford, the British architect quit the project in 1995 over unexplained differences, leaving homegrown company DP Architects to complete the job.

Design controversies aside, the Esplanade, trying its best to live up to the hype generated, has so far played host to top names like Jose Carerras, Dee Dee Bridgewater and Lincoln Center Jazz Orchestra. The concert hall is especially lauded for the acoustics designed by celebrated American sound scientist Russell Johnson. Its attempt to bring arts to the masses sees free performances on Friday and weekend evenings at the Outdoor Theatre by Marina Bay. Avant-garde installation art is also a regular feature at the concourse level.

The adjoining **Esplanade Mall** houses an interesting array of shops and restaurants – performance nights are especially busy.

Suntec City

Rising behind the Esplanade Theatres is the outline of Marina Square and Suntec City – all built on reclaimed land. This area is virtually a self-contained city. **Marina Square** is a huge American-style mall linked to the trio of John Portman-designed hotels, the **Marina Mandarin**, **Oriental** and the **Pan Pacific**, and

Map on page 80

TIP

Take a half-hour tour of the Singapore River on a "bumboat". Departures are from the jetties at the Raffles Landing Site and Merlion Park. Tickets cost S$12 (daily 9am–11pm). Contact Singapore River Cruises, tel: 6336 6119, or check www.rivercruise.com.sg

BELOW: bronze sculptures, titled *First Generation*, outside the Fullerton hotel.

Riverside Sculptures

Start your art trail from Colombian sculptor Fernando Botero's lovably fat *Bird* outside UOB Plaza. Walking along the Singapore River towards The Fullerton hotel, local sculptor Aw Tee Hong's *The River Merchant* depicts Alexander Johnston, one of Singapore's early merchants. Just before Cavenagh Bridge, the lifelike bronze *Kucinta* cats on the left often attract real stray cats. Outside The Fullerton, the scene of five playful, naked boys leaping into the river is the work of Chong Fah Cheong. Across the bridge two sets of sculptures tell the story of Singapore's development from port to financial centre: *The Great Emporium* and *From Chettiars To Financiers* .

Cenotaph memorial at the Esplanade Park honours "Our Glorious Dead" – the soldiers who died in the two World Wars.

the swanky **Ritz-Carlton Millenia** designed by Kevin Roche.

Across Raffles Boulevard is a massive convention and shopping development called **Suntec City**, noted for its gigantic water-spewing **Fountain of Wealth** . The purportedly auspicious bronze structure was inspired by the Hindu *mandala* but in fact looks more like an alien mothership about to take off. Interestingly, Suntec City's design was closely governed by the principles of Chinese geomancy or *feng shui* (*see pages 118–19*).

Shopping options abound here – both at the massive **Suntec City Mall**, Singapore's largest, as well as nearby **Millenia Walk**, where there are many stores to empty the most padded of wallets. Oscar's Café at the adjacent **Conrad Centennial** hotel or the myriad pubs and restaurants in this area are perfect for flopping out.

Esplanade Park

Flanking Esplanade Theatres and the Esplanade Bridge is **Esplanade Park** and the tree-lined **Queen Elizabeth Walk**, formerly a seafront promenade where colonial-day Europeans spent their leisure time strolling or playing cricket.

At the park's southern end is the **Lim Bo Seng Memorial**, with its four bronze lions. It is dedicated to a local hero and martyr, Lim Bo Seng (1909–44), an active member of an underground resistance movement against the Japanese during World War II. Further along is the **Cenotaph**, built to remember the soldiers who died fighting in the World Wars. At the park's northern end is **Tan Kim Seng Fountain**, built in gratitude of a donation "towards the cost of the Singapore Water Works" given in 1857 by the trader and public benefactor, Tan Kim Seng (1805–64). His £13,000 contribution to the water works was a princely sum in those days.

The Padang

Adjacent to the Esplanade Park across Connaught Drive is an expanse of green called **Padang** ("field" in Malay), the venue of Singapore's annual National Day celebrations on 9 August. Known as the

BELOW: National Day Parade at the Padang (with City Hall in background).

Esplanade in colonial times, this is where the British took a turn in the cool of the evening in their horse-drawn carriages, exchanging the latest gossip at the so-called Scandal Point. After the Japanese captured Singapore in 1942, European civilians were rounded up on the Padang and marched to Changi Prison. The Padang, flanked by two of the city's oldest leisure clubs – the **Singapore Recreation Club** (1883), now rebuilt on its original site, and the **Singapore Cricket Club** (1852) – is also the venue for cricket and rugby matches on weekends.

Supreme Court/City Hall

Adjacent to the Cricket Club, across St Andrews Road, is the **Supreme Court ⓬**, with its stout Corinthian columns and green dome. It sits on the site of several earlier structures: the first was a private house designed by Coleman, the same colonial architect who built the Old Parliament House (*see page 79*). This made way for the Hotel de l'Europe, which was demolished in 1900 to make room for the Grand Hotel. This in turn was replaced by the present building in 1927. Just behind Supreme Court, construction has already begun on a new Supreme Court building, slated for completion in late 2005.

Next to the Supreme Court and facing the Padang is Singapore's most important government building, **City Hall ⓭**. Completed in 1929, with a facade of Greek columns and a grand staircase, it was on these steps that Lord Louis Mountbatten accepted the surrender of Singapore by the Japanese General Itagaki in September 1945. Singapore's former Prime Minister Lee Kuan Yew declared the island's independence from Britain on the same spot 14 years later, in 1959. Today, the grand staircase suffers from the ignominy of being a favourite picture backdrop for wedding couples.

St Andrew's Cathedral

Across Coleman Street amid an expanse of greenery rises the spire of **St Andrew's Cathedral ⓮** (daily 6am–6pm; tel: 6337 6104; www. livingstreams.org.sg/sac). The church, a gazetted monument, owes its smooth white surface to the strange plaster used by the Indian convict labourers. Called Madras *chunam*, the plaster was made of egg white, eggshell, lime, sugar, coconut husk and water, and gave the building a smooth polished finish.

Interestingly, this is the second place of worship on the premises. The original, designed in Palladian style by Coleman, was twice struck by lightning and demolished in 1852. The present cathedral, in the style of an early Gothic abbey and designed by Ronald MacPherson, was consecrated in 1862.

The gleaming white exterior contrasts with the dark pews inside, with sunlight gently filtering through the coloured stained-glass windows in the mornings. The cathedral served as an emergency hospital just before the fall of Singapore in 1942.

Map on page 80

TIP

The zany Duck Tour is a great way to see Singapore. The amphibious craft drives past key landmarks in the Civic District before splashing into Kallang River for a scenic ride around Singapore River. Call tel: 6333 3825, or check www.ducktours.com.sg

BELOW: St Andrew's Cathedral with Swissôtel The Stamford rising behind it.

Enjoy a Singapore Sling at the Long Bar of the Raffles Hotel, where it was first concocted in 1910 by barman Ngiam Tong Boon. The gin-based drink packs a punch even though it tastes so delightfully fruity.

BELOW:
Raffles Hotel's old-world interior.
RIGHT:
monument at War Memorial Park.

Capitol Theatre

Across the church, at the junction of North Bridge and Stamford roads lies the neo-classical **Capitol Theatre**. When it was completed in 1931, this popular icon was one of the first air-conditioned theatres in Singapore. Anti-Japanese locals bombed the building during World War II but it was rebuilt and turned into a cinema, before it eventually closed in the late 1990s. Plans to convert it into an entertainment venue have been shelved and it now lies vacant.

Next door is the resplendent **Stamford House**, with history dating back to 1904. Designed by colonial architect R.A.J. Bidwell of Swan and Maclaren (who also designed Raffles Hotel and Goodwood Park Hotel), the elegant Venetian Renaissance-style structure once housed the Oranjie Hotel.

Raffles City

Towering over St Andrew's Cathedral is **Raffles City**, a silver monolith with shops, offices and hotels within as well as the busy City Hall MRT Interchange. The I.M. Pei-designed tower stands on the former site of Singapore's first school, Raffles Institution, built in 1823 and now relocated to the suburbs. The complex connects to both the 72-storey **Swissôtel The Stamford** (formerly Westin Stamford), Southeast Asia's tallest hotel, with panoramic views from its **New Asia Bar** on the 71st floor, as well as the 26-storey and more plush **Raffles The Plaza** hotel.

Linking Raffles City and its MRT station to Suntec City *(see page 84)* is the subterranean **CityLink Mall**. The underground shopping strip houses over 50 stores, including restaurants and cafés, and makes for a great rainy day route.

War Memorial Park

To the right of Raffles City and opposite Singapore Recreation Club is the **War Memorial Park ⑮**, dedicated to 50,000 civilians from the four main ethnic groups who suffered and died in Singapore during World War II. Popularly known as the "Chopsticks Monument", the war memorial consists of four interlinked tapering columns representing each ethnic

group. Beneath the 67-metre (220-ft) columns are urns containing the remains of some of those who died.

Raffles Hotel

The Civic District is also the location of Singapore's most famous landmark, **Raffles Hotel** ⑯, at the corner of Bras Basah Road and Beach Road. Nearly everyone who comes to Singapore ends up at Raffles Hotel at one point or another, usually to try the world famous Singapore Sling at the Long Bar (invented here in 1910) or to walk through the lush gardens. Enter via its cast-iron porticoed entrance along Beach Road – the hotel originally faced the beach before it fell victim to reclamation– which leads into the lobby, its marbled floors embellished with plush Persian carpets.

Opened in 1887 by the Sarkies Brothers, the "Grand Old Lady of the East" has seen its fair share of kings and queens, presidents and prime ministers, movie actors and lions of literature, as well as ordinary people attracted to this icon of tropical elegance and style.

Having survived a chequered history – it was briefly used by the Japanese Occupation forces when it was renamed Syonan Ryokan (Light of the South Hotel) – the Raffles underwent a major facelift in the early 1990s. Whether or not the restoration was sensitively done is contentious but it did involve years of work, tracking down original plans and finding skilled craftsmen to repair and recreate the original fittings. For most people, the result is a resounding success and Raffles can once again take her place among the great hotels of the world.

The hotel also houses the **Raffles Hotel Museum** (daily 10am–6pm; free), a museum of Raffles memorabilia – some of which were found during renovation work – a shopping arcade and the **Jubilee Hall Theatre**.

Chijmes

Beside Raffles City at the corner of North Bridge and Bras Basah roads is **Chijmes** ⑰, the former Gothic-style Convent of the Holy Infant Jesus (CHIJ), painstakingly restored with the help of Didier Repellin, the same conservationist who worked on the Empress Place Building. The name Chijmes (pronounced "chimes") was adopted to incorporate the initials of the convent, church and school that had stood here since its founding in 1840 by the Sisters on the Seine from France. The convent also ran an orphanage; its Gate of Hope on Bras Basah Road was where babies would be left by their unmarried mothers.

Chijmes is today a collection of restaurants (outdoor dining in its softly-lit courtyards is a delight), pubs and art and handicraft shops. Don't miss the Belgian-crafted stained glass windows of the Chapel, renamed **Chijmes Hall** and a venue for concerts and weddings. The **Fountain Court**, flanked by pubs and restaurants with alfresco dining areas, reverberates with life when there are

Map on page 80

TIP

Keen to learn how to cook from some of Singapore's finest chefs? The Raffles Culinary Academy runs cookery classes, Tues–Fri. Each session lasts up to 4 hours. For details, call tel: 6412 1256, or visit www. raffleshotel.com

BELOW:
the Gothic-inspired Chijmes is now a nightlife venue.

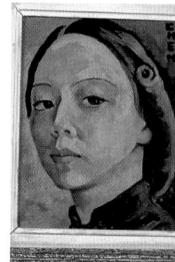

Self portrait of Georgette Chen, one of Singapore's pioneer artists. Her works are part of the permanent collection of the Singapore Art Museum.

free outdoor concerts. Make time for the interesting guided tour (Mon–Fri 11am–3pm; tel: 6338 2529; admission charge; www.chijmes.com.sg).

Good Shepherd Cathedral

Adjacent to Chijmes is the Roman Catholic **Cathedral of the Good Shepherd** ⓲ (Mon–Fri 7am–5.30pm, Sat 7am–7.30pm, Sun 7.30am–7pm; tel: 6337 2036). Built in 1846 in the design of a crucifix, the cathedral was the second Roman Catholic church in Singapore. It has Roman Doric pillars and a marble pavement from Antwerp.

Singapore Art Museum

Like Chijmes, the **Singapore Art Museum** ⓳ further down Bras Basah Road, and diagonally opposite the cathedral, was a mission school (daily 10am–7pm, Fri 10am–9pm; admission charge; tel: 6332 3222; www.nhb.gov.sg). Formerly known as St Joseph's Institution, it was founded by the French De La Salle Order in 1867. The 19th-century school building was renovated and opened as a multi-cultural arts museum in 1996. Apart from its permanent collection of some 4,000 Southeast Asian artworks, the museum also offers rotating exhibitions from around the world. A post-prandial coffee at **Dome**, its outdoor terrace café bordering Queen Street, is quite pleasant.

Along Stamford Road

The area in front of the Singapore Art Museum and the Cathedral of the Good Shepherd is currently the site of some major reconstruction with the building of the new Singapore Management University and the Circle Line MRT, due to open in 2006. As some of the surrounding roads like Waterloo Street and Queen Street may be closed because of construction work, head left along Bencoolen Street towards the **Singapore History Museum** at 93 Stamford Road. Until 2006, however, be content to gaze at the historic neo-classical building, topped with a gleaming dome, from the outside. First opened in 1887 as the Raffles Museum, the building is currently closed for major expansion

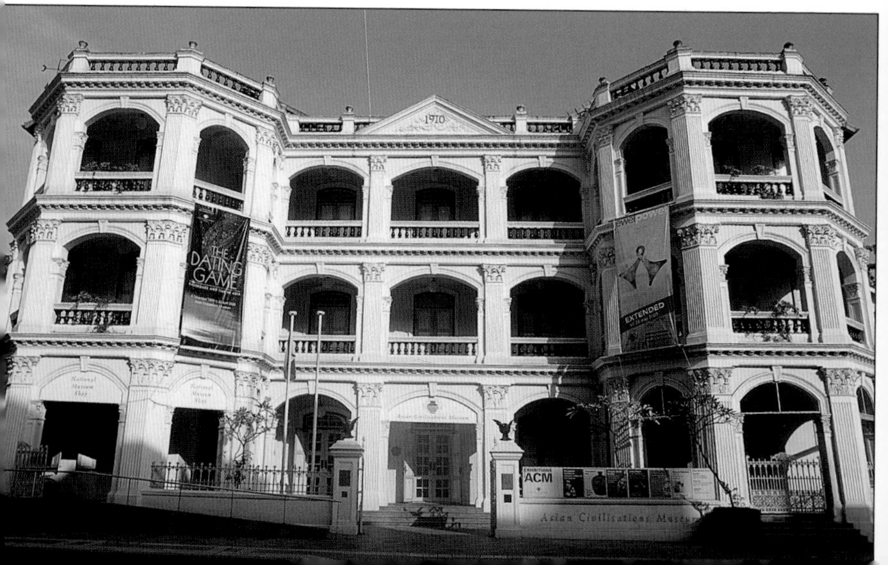

BELOW: the Singapore Art Museum occupies the premises of an old school.

and renovations. Meanwhile the museum's collections are temporarily housed at **Riverside Point** opposite Clarke Quay *(see page 94)*.

Past the Singapore History Museum along Stamford Road lies the red-brick **National Library**, which closed in March 2004 when the Singapore Management University took over its site. The library will move to a new building on Victoria Street, when it is completed in 2005.

Asian Civilisations Museum

Further down at the corner of Stamford Road and Armenian Street, is the striking red and white Edwardian-style building that was once the Methodist Publishing House, or **MPH Building** as it was affectionately known. It now houses the tertiary institute **AIT Unicampus**. It was built in 1908 by the colonial architects Swan and Maclaren.

At 45 Armenian Street is **The Substation**. With its active contemporary arts and drama calendar, it regularly attracts Singapore's young artistic talents (tel: 6337 7535; www.substation.org). The Substation also houses an art gallery, an art shop selling paintings and ceramics, and a delightful Balinese-style courtyard café called **Fat Frog**.

Further down Armenian Street and housed in the former Tao Nan School is the second wing of the **Asian Civilisations Museum, Armenian Street** ⑳ (Mon 1–7pm, Tues–Sun 9am–7pm, Fri 9am–9pm; admission charge; tel: 6332 3015; www.nhb.gov.sg).

Opened in 1997 in an elegantly restored school building that dates back to 1910, more than half of the museum – which houses 10 galleries on three levels – is dedicated to the unique culture of the Peranakan people of Singapore, Malaysia and Indonesia. The Peranakan *(see page 37)* is a unique hybrid culture evolved through intermarriage between Chinese men and Malay women from the 17th century onwards. Interesting thematic exhibitions are held from time to time, so call the museum for more details.

Fort Canning Park

Rising behind Stamford Road and Hill Street is a tree-covered bluff, on which sits **Fort Canning Park** ㉑. It was once known as Bukit Larangan (Forbidden Hill) because no commoner was allowed to come up here. During the early years of Singapore's history, this strategic location was the site of grand palaces protected by high walls and swamps. The Majapahit princes who ruled Singapura in the 14th century were buried there – archaeological excavations in the area have uncovered remains from the period – and it was rumoured that royal spirits haunted the place. Undeterred by such superstition, the practical Raffles built his residence there in 1823 and renamed it Government Hill. He had chosen the site for the same reasons as Singapore's early rulers – it had a good vantage

Map on page 80

TIP

Here's a novel way to spend your Friday night – museum-hop for free. The Singapore History Museum (SHM), Singapore Art Museum (SAM) and Asian Civilisations Museum (ACM) waive admission fees on Friday evenings – The ACM and SHM from 7pm and SAM from 6pm. For details, visit www.nhb.gov.sg

BELOW: remains of the old walls at Fort Canning Park.

Cruise Control

A tiny island filled with too many people with high disposable incomes poses a potential problem: too many cars choking up the roads. While traffic in the rest of Asia crawls at a snail's pace during rush hour, in Singapore it whizzes past at a reasonable 50–60 kph (about 35 mph) on the expressways during peak hours – barring traffic accidents jamming up the roads, of course. Despite having one of the highest car densities in the world, Singapore has found a solution, through a combination of regulation and technology, to a problem that has stumped traffic authorities elsewhere.

The guiding principle behind traffic management in Singapore is a simple one: by government decree, the population of cars cannot grow faster than roads being built. And with the land available for road infrastructure being so limited in Singapore, curbs on car ownership are considerable.

For starters, cars here are probably the most expensive in the world: after a hefty 45 percent tax on car imports, a registration fee of 150 percent, and an annual road tax pegged to the engine capacity of the car, a 1,600cc saloon can easily cost in excess of

S$50,000. But that's not all; in 1990, the Certificate of Entitlement (COE) was introduced, without which one cannot purchase a new car. In April 2002, the cost of a COE for a 1,600cc saloon was S$37,000, jacking up the eventual price of the car to a whopping S$87,000.

Only limited numbers of COEs are available each month and these are sold through a complex bidding system. The COE is valid for 10 years – the theory is that fewer old cars reduce breakdowns and traffic congestion – after which a new COE must be purchased. Instead of paying inflated road taxes to keep a car beyond 10 years, people would rather turn it into scrap metal and buy a new car instead, or at least a second-hand car with a few years left on its COE.

To encourage more people to commute by bus and train (and also those who don't want to pay through their noses for cars), the authorities have poured millions of dollars into building, and constantly upgrading, an excellent public transportation system.

Not content to leave things as they were, the authorities tried out various area licensing schemes over the years – which were mainly cumbersome and labour-intensive – to restrict car usage. Then in 1999, they struck a brainwave in the form of the Electronic Road Pricing (ERP) system. With the S$200-million-dollar system in place, ERP overhead gantries stategically located in the Central Business District and expressways automatically deduct a fixed toll throughout the day from cash cards inserted in the special in-vehicle units (IU) installed in cars. Sensors on the gantries are connected to a central computer system which logs all vehicles passing under them. Motorists without IUs or insufficient cash cards will have their licence plates photographed. A few days later a summons to pay a fine arrives in the mail.

While this new system has drawn a mixed response – government coffers have swelled from the fees collected via the ERP – it has succeeded in reducing traffic during peak hours. Traffic during ERP operating hours has dropped by 15 percent as motorists either pool cars or take the bus or train to work. ❏

LEFT: ERP gantry along North Bridge Road.

point for spotting enemy movements at sea. Later, it was renamed Fort Canning Hill after Viceroy Canning of India.

In 1860, the British built a fort atop the hill, from where dawn, noon and dusk were announced each day by cannon fire. The cannons have since been removed to Fort Siloso on Sentosa Island *(see page 154)*. Apart from being the first home of Singapore's rulers and the site of the first fortress, Fort Canning had the island's first lighthouse, the oldest cemetery and the island's first Botanic Garden – now the **Spice Garden**.

Today, this lovely oasis of green has been designated as a historical and cultural park. An underpass up a flight of steps beside the old National Library car park leads to the Spice Garden and through one of two Gothic-style gates to the old cemetery. The cemetery, which was use from 1820 to 1864, was exhumed in 1970 to make way for the park, and its tombstones were embedded in its boundary wall. They contain many names associated with Singapore's

history such as Coleman, Napier, the first law agent and Major Farquhar, Raffles' assistant. The park also contains an older tomb purported to contain the remains of Parameswara, the last king of Singapura. This has been consecrated as a Muslim *keramat* (shrine).

Mid-way up the park is the entrance to the World War II underground bunkers, now known as the **Battle Box**, used by the British military to plan strategies against the Japanese enemy (daily 10am–6pm, admission charge, tel: 6333 0510). The 9-metre (30-ft) deep bunkers, led to the former Far East Command Building (now The Legends Fort Canning Park). It was here that Lieutenant-General A.E. Percival, commander of the British forces, decided to surrender to the Japanese on 15 February 1942 when he realised that Singapore was running short of food and ammunition. An exhibition inside the maze of tunnels details the desperate battle against the Japanese.

Fort Canning Centre is also a hub of the arts in Singapore, with

Map on page 80

In the middle of Fort Canning Park is is an underground reservoir built in 1926 to feed water pipes connecting to homes in the area. The reservoir was the site of a natural spring used as baths by 14th-century Malay royalty.

BELOW: Battle Box wax figure exhibit.

BELOW:
Armenian Church
dates back to 1835.

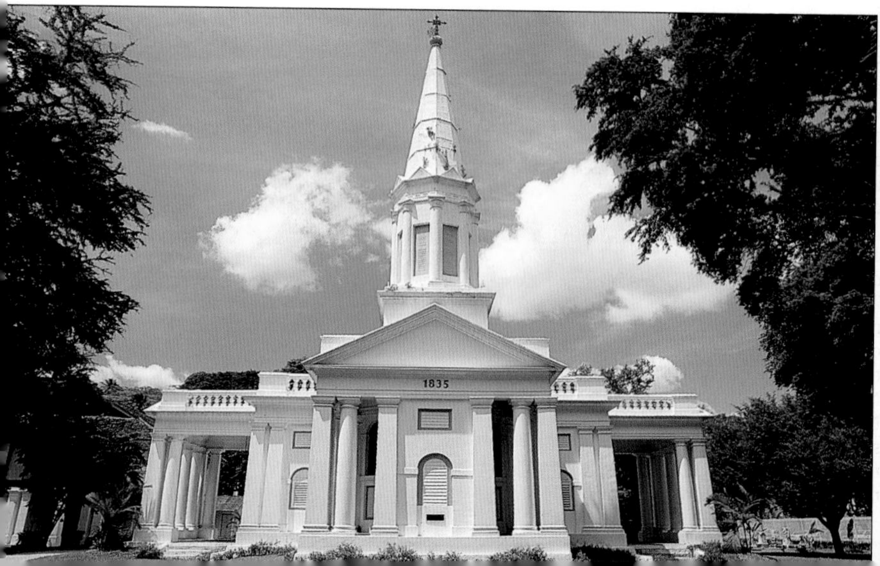

productions at both the nearby Sub-station and the Black Box Theatre by local arts groups. It also houses the practice studios of the Singapore Dance Theatre and a culinary academy called **at-sunrice**. Sign up for a guided tour through the lovely Spice Garden followed by a hands-on gourmet cooking class (bookings required; tel: 6336 3307; www.at-sunrice.com). The academy also houses a café and shop offering Asian spice mixes and handicrafts.

Philatelic Museum

At the foot of Fort Canning Hill along Canning Rise is the **National Archives** where written and oral records of Singapore's history are kept. Its rich archival holdings date back to the early 1800s. Further down at the corner of Armenian and Coleman streets is the **Singapore Philatelic Museum ㉒**. Completed in 1907, it was formerly part of the Anglo Chinese School before it was restored in 1995 (Mon 1–7pm, Tues–Sun 9am–7pm; admission charge; tel: 6337 3888; www.spm.org.sg). Although tiny, the interactive museum is a delightful treasure trove of stamps, first-day covers and postcards, and has regular exhibitions.

Armenian Church

At the corner of Coleman and Hill streets is the tiny but atmospheric **Armenian Church ㉓**, also called St Gregory the Illuminator (Mon–Fri 9am–5pm, Sat 9am–noon; tel: 6334 0141). Built in 1835 and designed by Coleman, this exquisite church is the oldest in Singapore.

A cemetery in the church grounds is where the tombstones of some eminent Singaporeans are found, among them the Sarkies brothers who founded Raffles Hotel and Agnes Joaquim (1864–99), after whom Singapore's national flower, *Vanda* Miss Joaquim, is named. Agnes discovered a purple bloom (later named *Vanda* Miss Joaquim) in 1893 in a bamboo grove behind her home in Tanjong Pagar. She took the orchid to Henry Ridley, the director of the Botanic Gardens at the time, who identified the plant as a rare natural hybrid, and the rest, as they say, is history.

Central Fire Station

At No. 62 Hill Street is another architectural gem of a building, the old **Central Fire Station 24**, headquarters of the Singapore Fire Brigade and the oldest existing fire station in Singapore. This distinctive red and white "blood and bandage" building was completed in 1909 and is typical of the architecture of Edwardian England, a departure from the usual Palladian and classical styles prevailing in Singapore at the time. The "blood" is exposed brick while the "bandage" refers to brick that has been covered in whitewashed plaster.

The **Civil Defence Heritage Gallery** on the ground level traces Singapore's civil defence developments from the 1900s (Tues–Sun 10am–5pm; tel: 6332 2996; free; www.scdf.gov.sg). Register for a guided tour and you get to climb up the hose tower, the lookout point for fire fighters in early Singapore.

The MITA Building

Also along Hill Street, near Coleman Bridge, is the MITA **Building 25**, which formerly housed the Old Hill Street Police Station. The more delicate features of this classical Renaissance-style building with horseshoe arches are rather overwhelmed by its startling multicoloured shutters – there are 911 altogether – but experts agree that it is one of the city's premier examples of British colonial architecture.

Built in 1934, the building was once occupied by the Japanese army during World War II. It re-opened in 2000 after undergoing extensive restoration, and today houses the offices of the Ministry of Information and the Arts (MITA), the National Arts Council and the National Heritage Board. Be sure to stop by the **ARTrium** courtyard on the ground level, occupied by a number of interesting art galleries.

Clarke Quay

Clarke Quay 26 lies opposite MITA Building, across River Valley Road. The **G-Max** bungy outfit at the junction of Hill Street and River Valley Road marks the entrance to this old warehouse district along Singapore River, now a thriving shopping, eating and entertainment area.

Bounded by Tan Tye Place and Canning Lane are five buildings comprising 60 warehouses and shophouses, restored to their original 19th-century style, and now occupied by retail outlets, bars and restaurants. Clarke Quay's attractions are more varied than Boat Quay's *(see page 113)*, and at night, a festive atmosphere prevails when cool breezes provide ideal conditions for riverfront wining and dining, and stalls offer traditional *satay* (skewers of meat cooked over a charcoal fire) drenched in a peanut sauce. On Sundays, Clarke Quay becomes the venue for a flea market with some 60 stalls offering trinkets and collectibles, including Coca-Cola paraphernalia.

Read Bridge spans the Singapore River and connects Clarke Quay with

Map on page 80

Thrill seekers should check out Clarke Quay's G-Max reverse bungy, which propels you 60 metres (200 ft) into the air (daily noon till late). tel: 6338 1146; www.gmax.co.nz

BELOW: old fire engine at the Civil Defence Heritage Gallery.

Map
on page
80

TIP

At nearby Magazine Road is the ornate Tan Si Chong Su Temple, a Hokkien place of worship with well-preserved carvings, ancestral tablets and a delightful rooftop of dancing dragons and ceramic flowers (daily 7.30am–5.30pm). The temple was built in 1878 as a gathering place for the Tan clan.

BELOW: Next Page pub at Mohamed Sultan Road.

Riverside Point, a complex of shops and restaurants that bears no hint of its seedier past when it was a gathering place for secret societies, opium smokers and ladies of the night. The **Singapore History Museum** on level three hosts the interactive exhibit, *Rivertales*, while its Stamford Road building is closed for refurbishment (Mon 1–7pm, Tues–Sun 9am–7pm, Fri 9am–9pm; admission charge; tel: 6332 5642; www.nhb.gov.sg).

Robertson Quay

The quiet residential enclave known as **Robertson Quay** lies upriver west of Clarke Quay. In the old days, European and Chinese merchants used this part of the river mostly for storage of goods. Although a few warehouses still exist along **Rodyk Street**, Robertson Quay has been taken over by some of Singapore's most exclusive riverside apartments. Several arts companies have also made this quay their home base. Among them are **Singapore Repertory Theatre** at the junction of Merbau Road and Unity Street and the **Singapore Tyler Print Institute** on Mohamed Sultan Road.

The latter, housed in a restored 19th-century warehouse, is dedicated to printmaking, paper making, and paper-based art (Tues–Sat 9.30am–8pm, Sun–Mon 1–5pm; free; tel 6336 3663; www.stpi.com.sg).

Robertson Quay is perhaps better known as the locale of **Mohamed Sultan Road**, a rowdy strip flanked by pubs and bars on both sides. Equally well known is the ultra trendy **Zouk** club, further west at Jiak Kim Street. Early settlers to Singapore would never have dreamt that their lifeline could be turned into a thriving entertainment hub.

Omar Melaka Mosque

Across the river from Clarke Quay and past Merchant Road on Keng Cheow Street is the gilded minaret of **Omar Kampung Melaka Mosque** ㉗. It stands proudly on the site as Singapore's first mosque. Built in 1820 by wealthy Arab merchant Syed Omar Ali Aljunied, the original basic wooden structure made way for the present brick building in 1855.

Thong Chai Medical Institute

One block east across New Market Road, at the corner of of Eu Tong Sen Street and Merchant Road, stands the former **Thong Chai Medical Institute** ㉘ with its distinctive green-tiled gabled roofs shaped after clouds on the sides and ornately decorated ridges. It was built in 1892 to serve as a free hospital and its architecture is reminiscent of the Chinese southern-style, similar to Tan Yeok Nee's house on Clemenceau Avenue *(see page 123)*. The medical institute was designed after a southern Chinese palace and has two inner courts. The institute, now restored and preserved as a national monument, served in the recent past as a nightclub and later a restaurant. Neither took off and today the building stands empty. ❑

RESTAURANTS

Restaurants

American

Brewerkz
01-05/06 Riverside
Point, 30 Merchant Rd.
Tel: 6438 7438. Open:
Mon–Thur noon–1am,
Fri–Sat noon–3am, Sun
11–1am. $$$
www.brewerkz.com
Handcrafted beer fresh
from its on-site micro-
brewery and hearty
American cuisine in an
industrial-like setting.
Brew master Scott
Robertson has at least
seven varieties of beer,
including his best-selling
India Pale Ale. Try the
mussels with beer sauce.

Morton's of Chicago
4/F, The Oriental Singa-
pore, 5 Raffles Ave. Tel:
6339 3740. Open: D
daily. $$$$
www.mortons.com
The dark wood interiors,
knowledgeable and
attentive waiters, 24-
ounce Porterhouse and
premium wine list are all
part of the Morton
experience. Start the
evening with a martini at
the bar, with filet mignon
steak sandwiches.

Chinese

Golden Peony
3/F, Conrad Centennial
Singapore, 2 Temasek
Blvd. Tel: 6432 7488.
Open: L and D daily.
$$$ (set lunch) $$$
(à la carte)
www.conradhotels.com
Refined Cantonese
cuisine is complemented
by good service and an
elegant dining room
furnished in golden
pinewood. Superb *dim
sum* is available at
lunchtime (try the
beancurd skin rolled with
cheese). There's also a
special set menu paired
with choice wines.

Hai Tien Lo
37/F, Pan Pacific Hotel,
7 Raffles Blvd. Tel: 6434
8338. Open: L and D
daily. $$ (set lunch)
$$$$ (à la carte)
www.singapore.panpacific.com
It's *dim sum* and classic
Cantonese dishes in the
sky. When you're dining
37 floors up, your *dim
sum* seems especially
delicious. Its seafood
dishes are always
special – order the wok-
fried lobster with chilli
sauce and baked cod
with champagne sauce.

**Imperial Herbal
Restaurant**
3/F, Metropole Hotel, 41
Seah St. Tel: 6337
0491. Open: L and D
daily. $$$ (set lunch)
$$$ (à la carte)
From ministers and
visiting VIPs to celebri-
ties, the who's who of
Singapore have all dined
here. Why? Perhaps the
presence of a Chinese
herbal doctor helps.
Consult him before you
tuck into curative double-
boiled soups. If you're
feeling adventurous, try
black ants on shredded
potato or deep-fried
scorpions.

Jade
The Fullerton, 1 Fuller-
ton Sq. Tel: 6877 8188.
Open: L and D daily.
$$$ (set lunch) $$$$
(à la carte)
www.tunglok.com
Bill Clinton was so
smitten by Sam Leong's
creations he likened his
meal here to an art
gallery. It's not just the
Riedel and Wedgwood
wares resting on every
table or the artistic
presentation. Cantonese
haute cuisine imbued
with creative touches –
cocoa pork ribs and
pan-seared scallops
skewered with lemon
grass – and a world-class
wine list draw highbrow
business professionals.

Lei Garden
01-24 Chijmes, 30
Victoria St. Tel: 6339
3822. Open: L and D
daily. $$ (set lunch) $$$
(à la carte)
One of Singapore's best
dim sum and Cantonese
cuisine spots is still *the*
place to impress. The
dim sum and healthful
double-boiled soups,
seafood dishes and
various bird's nest con-
coctions are wonderful.

My Humble House
02-27/29 Esplanade
Mall, 8 Raffles Ave. Tel:
6423 1881. Open: L and
D daily. $$$ (set lunch)
$$$$ (à la carte)
www.tunglok.com
What can you expect
when the creative direc-
tor is an artist-turned-
restaurateur? The result:
a Chinese restaurant so
wonderfully sensuous
even the soft shell crabs
are named *Asleep in the
Petals*, the poetic menu
reads like a work of art,
the designer decor is
both sexy and dramatic
and the Modern Chinese
cuisine is just splendid.

Royal China at Raffles
3/F, Raffles Hotel
Arcade, 328 North
Bridge Rd. Tel: 6412
1330. Open: L and D
daily. $$ (set lunch) $$$
(à la carte)
www.raffleshotel.com
London's most notable
Cantonese restaurant is
one of Singapore's best
places for *dim sum*, plus
wholesome double-
boiled soups, lobster
noodles fit for royalty
and creative Chinese
desserts that will leave
you begging for more.
Food shares the lime-
light with Helen Wong,
the restaurant manager
who makes you feel at
home in no time.

PRICE CATEGORIES

Prices for a three-course
dinner per person without
drinks and taxes:
$ = under S$20
$$ = S$20–$30
$$$ = S$30–$50
$$$$ = more than S$50

European

Equinox

68-72/F, Swissôtel The Stamford, 2 Stamford Rd. Tel: 6431 5669. Open: Sun–Thur 11–1am, Fri–Sat 11–3am. $$$ (set lunch) $$$$ (à la carte)

www.equinoxcomplex.com

A complex of five restaurants and bars sits atop Southeast Asia's tallest hotel. Start with drinks at the **New Asia Bar** on the 71st level while taking in stunning city views from its floor-to-ceiling windows, then descend one level to swanky French-Cambodian restaurant **Jaan**, decorated with Murano crystal and shimmering Cambodian silk.

Pierside Kitchen & Bar

01-01 One Fullerton. Tel: 6438 0400. Open: L Mon–Fri, D Mon–Sat. $$$ (set lunch) $$$$ (à la carte)

www.marmaladergroup.com

Seafood never looked so smart in the pared-down, quiet sophistication of this waterfront restaurant. By day stylish and by night intimate and relaxed, the Modern European menu is served alongside great views of the marina. Must haves: Robin Ho's oven-roasted miso cod and Valrhona choc fondant.

French

Amuse Bouche

01-03, 1 Raffles Link. Tel: 6338 9414. Open: L Mon–Fri, D Mon–Sat. $$$ (set lunch) $$$$ (à la carte)

www.lesamis.com.sg

It's a Modern French restaurant, tapas bar and wine shop all rolled into one elegant space. In a hurry or want something light? Resident chef Freddie Lee has a tapas menu featuring about 20 hot and cold tapas. Try the Chilean seabass on toast, tomato tart tartin and chicken cannelloni.

Raffles Grill

Raffles Hotel, 1 Beach Rd. Tel: 6331 1611. Open: L Mon–Fri. D Mon–Sat. $$$ (set lunch) $$$$ (à la carte)

www.raffleshotel.com

The timeless grace of the Raffles Hotel is captured in this handsome French restaurant, also one of the city's finest. Waiters are attentive but discreet, and chefs spare no expense when it comes to quality – French truffles, fresh Scottish King scallops and the best olive oils are flown in regularly.

Saint Julien

3 Fullerton Rd. Tel: 6534 5947. Open: L Mon–Fri, D Mon–Sat. $$$ (set lunch) $$$$ (à la carte)

www.saintjulien.com.sg

Frenchman Julien Bompard's resume includes Michelin-starred restaurants, though aficionados will probably remember him from his days at Gaddi's at Peninsula Hong Kong. Now the commander of his own place, Bompard does what he does best: classical French cuisine complemented by a fine French wine list – in a quaint old boat house by the waterfront.

Saint Pierre

01-01 Central Mall, 3 Magazine Rd. Tel: 6438 0887. Open: L Mon–Fri, D Mon–Sat. $$–$$$ (set lunch) $$$$ (à la carte)

www.saintpierre.com.sg

Belgian owner-chef Emmanuel Stroobant is as dishy as the foie gras, braised black cod and flourless choc cake he dishes up in his smart, award-winning Modern French restaurant. There are at least six varieties of foie gras on the menu and his pan-fried version with caramelized green apple and old port sauce is simply divine.

Fusion

Coriander Leaf

02-12, Clarke Quay, 3A River Valley Road. Tel: 6732 3354. Open: L Mon–Fri, D Mon-Sat. $$ (set lunch) $$$ (à la carte).

www.corianderleaf.com

Chef-owner Samia Ahad's food defies all categories: calling it fusion does it no justice. Prepare to be bowled over at its new location in atmospheric Clarke Quay, where its brilliant pan-Asian and Mediterranean menu given a Western spin (or is it the other way around?) continues to hold court; try the mezze plate followed by the spice-rubbed rack of lamb or snapper with chilli-crabmeat crust.

Doc Cheng's

02-20 Raffles Hotel, 1 Beach Rd. Tel: 6331 1761. Open: L Mon–Fri, D daily. $$$ (set lunch) $$$$ (à la carte)

www.raffleshotel.com

Why fusion works here: exuberant wait staff, Western dishes with a bold, flavourful Asian twist, and a contemporary Asian setting. Despite a couple of misses, such as the Chinese sausage pizza with Italian smoked cheese, fans return for the fresh-from-the-tandoor naans, the wholesome five spice duck broth and melt-in-the-mouth miso butterfish.

Indian

Annalakshmi

02-10 Excelsior Hotel, 5 Coleman St. Tel: 6339 9993. Open: L daily, D Mon–Sat. $–$$$$

www.annalakshmi.com.sg

Few restaurants manage to look stately yet remain unpretentious. Annalakshmi is one of those. Exquisite Indian vegetarian cuisine is served by friendly staff members who are volunteers. The menu has no prices and diners pay as they wish – the money funds artistic and charitable activities.

Rang Mahal

3/F, Pan Pacific Singapore, 7 Raffles Blvd. Tel: 6333 1788. Open: L Mon–Fri and Sun, D daily. $$$ (buffet lunch) $$$$ (à la carte)

The modern interiors hint of understated sophistication, befitting the classical northern, southern and coastal Indian specialties. Whether it's a new twist to a traditional dish (tandoori oyster) or a classic favourite (*murg hazari*, or stuffed chicken), rest assured of a memorable meal.

Italian
Capella
01-29 Chijmes, 30 Victoria St. Tel: 6334 9928. Open: L and D daily $$–$$$ (set lunch and dinner) $$$$ (à la carte) Expect an Italian menu with some subtle Asian accents at this sleek new restaurant. Try the antipasti platter of goose liver, salmon and garlic prawns or the carpacio of Wagyu beef as starters. The chef is equally deft at the main courses of fish, lamb and beef or pastas.
Ristorante Bologna
4/F, Marina Mandarin, 6 Raffles Blvd. Tel: 6845 1113. Open: L Mon–Fri, D Mon–Sat. $$$ (semi-buffet lunch) $$$$ (à la carte)
www.marina-mandarin.com.sg
Excellent, from the attentive wait staff and smart dining room to the perfectly starched tablecloths. Signature dishes include the pan-fried goose liver in cognac and morel sauce, and spaghetti with baby lobster in white wine sauce.

international
Max Brenner
Chocolate Bar
01-06/08 Esplanade Mall, 8 Raffles Ave. Tel: 6235 9556. Open: Sun–Thur 11am–11pm, Fri–Sat 11am–midnight. $$
The Chocolate Bar that took Harrods London by storm is a fantasy come true for chocoholics. Don't be distracted by the sandwiches, tapas and home-baked muffins. This ultimate temple for chocolate worshippers has chocolate in every imaginable form and some, like the signature Max's Suckao, may even sound deliciously obscene.

Japanese
Keyaki
4/F, Pan Pacific Hotel, 7 Raffles Blvd. Tel: 6434 8335. Open: L and D daily. $$$ (set lunch) $$$$ (à la carte)
www.singapore.panpacific.com
To get to the restaurant, you stroll past a zen garden and fish pond before smiling, soft-spoken waitresses greet you at the entrance. Take your pick from *kaiseki, robatayaki, sashimi, teppanyaki* and *shabu-shabu*. Round off with *sake* in the garden.
Wasabi Bistro
4/F, The Oriental, 5 Raffles Ave. Tel: 6885 3091. Open: L and D Mon–Sat. $$$ (set lunch) $$$$ (à la carte)
www.mandarinoriental.com
Hawaii's most famous Japanese bistro sets tongues wagging (and on fire) with its fiery *sushi* rolls. This is California-influenced Japanese cuisine. Traditional favourites are interpreted in a refreshing manner – the rainbow roll is a visual feast and the exquisite Philadelphia roll is a clever take on American culture.

Local
Clarke Quay Satay Club
Clarke Quay, Read St. Open: Sun–Thur 6pm–1:30am, Fri–Sat 6pm–2:30am. $
www.clarkequay.com.sg
Dress light, order sticks of *satay*, mutton soup, Indian fried noodles and local tea from the nine street stalls, then tuck in under the stars.
Kopi Tiam
2/F, Swissôtel The Stamford, 2 Stamford Rd. Tel: 6431 6221. Open: daily, 11:30am–11pm. $$$
It's air-conditioned and the local dishes are lip-smacking delicious. No wonder Singaporeans make a beeline for the Hainanese chicken rice, Indonesian fried rice and tom yam soup. Catch the chef flip *roti prata*, an Indian bread, on a griddle, on weekends.
Soul Kitchen
7 Purvis St. Tel: 6333 0676. Open: L and D Mon–Sat. $$
The name says it. It's soul food in a tiny but funky lime green space. Chef-owner Damian de Silva's Eurasian recipes are three generations old and many are painstakingly prepared. Must-haves include Devil Curry, *singgang* (Eurasian fish stew with wolf herring) and *ayam buah keluak* (chicken stewed with black Indonesian nuts).

Mediterranean
Esmirada
01-07 Chijmes, 30 Victoria St. Tel: 6336 3684. Open: Sun–Thurs, 6–10.30pm, Fri–Sat 6–11pm. $$$
www.esmirada.com.sg
Great, somewhat pseudo-Mediterranean atmosphere in this lively (read: extremely boisterous) tavern with rustic wooden tables and dripping candles. Well loved for its garlic baguette, hearty Caesar salad, soups, moussaka and lasagna, paella, bouillabaisse, skewered meats and other staples.

Thai
Yhing Thai Palace
36 Purvis St. Tel: 6337 1161. Open: L and D daily. $$
There's nothing palatial about this place; In fact, the decor is uninspiring and it can be noisy. But it pleases with a bill of Thai-Chinese fare at reasonable prices. The olive fried rice and Thai fish cakes are particular favourites as is the grilled squid salad drenched in a piquant sauce.

PRICE CATEGORIES
Prices for a three-course dinner per person without drinks and taxes:
$ = under S$20
$$= S$20–$30
$$$ = S$30–$50
$$$$ = more than S$50

THE ASIAN CIVILISATIONS MUSEUM

Religious statuary, calligraphic art, textiles and architecture that span several centuries are all housed in the equally historic Empress Place Building

ABOVE: over 1,300 artefacts from the ancient civilisations of Asia are housed within the Empress Place Building, a grand national monument whose history dates back to 1864 *(see page 80)*. With hands-on activities for children, ongoing talks and work-shops, and changing special exhibitions, a trip here is no boring history excursion. There is even a restaurant, café and bar to rest your feet and satisfy more prosaic needs after your cultural jaunt.

LEFT: Chinese society is strongly rooted in ancestral and religious worship. Taoism is commonly practised and fused with various beliefs that worship a pantheon of gods. These two life-sized demonic-looking figures in the China gallery are Thousand-Li Eyes and Wind-Favouring Ears, guardians of the Sea Goddess. They are former demons that the goddess had tamed, and this explains their monstrous appearance.

BELOW: this late 19th-century batik piece from Java is part of the fabric collection of the Southeast Asia gallery. The patterns and motifs are inspired by various rituals and taboos, and the ideas are said to come to the weavers in dreams sent by the gods. The gallery displays mainly textiles from the Malay-Indonesian world.

If you're wondering how the multi-ethnic culture of Singapore originated, this museum holds the key. Even visitors who are not history buffs will find the interactive zones, innovative virtual hosts and in-gallery videos highly entertaining. With 11 galleries spread out over three floors, you can easily spend half-a-day at this excellent museum.

Your tour starts with the Southeast Asia collection on level two. From prehistoric agricultural tools to fabric displays and artefacts, the exhibits reveal the diversity of Southeast Asia. On the same level is the China and West Asia galleries. Learn about the Middle Kingdom from the displays – the Chinese deities and fragile Dehua porcelain are highlights – before continuing to the West Asia gallery with its Koran-inspired calligraphic art.

On level three are more Southeast Asia and West Asia galleries, after which head down the central staircase to level one, the South Asia galleries, dominated by religious statuary and architectural motifs. To fully appreciate the museum, take the free one-hour guided tour (Tues–Fri 11am and 2pm; Sat–Sun 11am, 2pm and

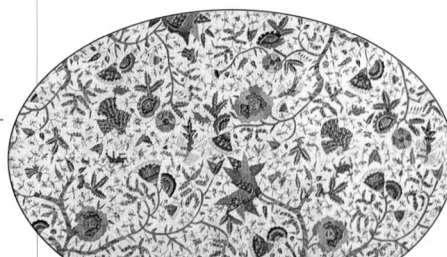

ABOVE: this impressive gateway, constructed from blocks of sandstone, is characteristic of provincial Mughal architecture and is likely to have come from a mansion of a Hindu nobleman from the Vraja region. The Mughals liked to surround themselves with objects of beauty which had a distinct decorative and architectural style. The gateway leads to the gallery of Medieval India (located within the South Asia gallery), where another collection of exhibits from the 13th to 19th century showcases the period's culture spanning the arts, architecture, textiles and paintings.

BELOW RIGHT: the main subject of the West Asia galleries is Islam, with a section focusing on the Qur'an. The Qur'an is the holy book that forms the foundation of any Islamic education, and it means "to read" or "to recite". It is also admired as a calligraphic art form, and the various styles of calligraphy can be seen in these galleries – on paper, textiles, metalwork and even ceramics. Look out for a quaint mosque-like setting where images of mosque architecture from around the world are projected for viewing.

ABOVE: in this re-created scholar's studio are a traditional 19th-century wooden couch bed from Fujian, and on it, a string instrument called the zither. Painting and music were some of the main pursuits of the Chinese literati. These intellectual leaders belonged to a higher class of society in China, and were seen as having the ideal

RIGHT: Naga Muchalinda, the King of Mythical Serpents, shelters a sandstone figure of Buddha from the floods. This 11th- to 12th-century artefact from Cambodia is similar to stone images that were placed in Khmer temples for worship. Theravada Buddhism is the main religion in Cambodia, Burma, Thailand and Laos.

CHINATOWN AND THE CENTRAL BUSINESS DISTRICT

Beneath the gleaming glass and steel skyscrapers of Singapore's financial district lies the colourful hubbub of Chinatown, where old temples, restored shophouses and quaint markets provide a fascinating contrast

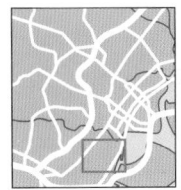

The area south of the Singapore River comprises two distinct neighbourhoods – Chinatown and the Central Business District. For the most part Chinatown comprises low-rise shophouses set against a backdrop of towering banks and office buildings, one of the tallest skylines in Southeast Asia.

It may seem strange to have a Chinatown in a place that has a predominantly Chinese population, but the oddity can be traced back to Raffles who subdivided his new town into various districts and according to racial lines in the early 1820s. He used two rivers as dividing lines. The marshy area at the mouth of the Singapore River was designated a commercial area while the area directly west was given to Chinese immigrants who did much of the manual labour. Kampung Glam between Rochor River and the sea was zoned off for Arab traders and Malay merchants.

Despite urbanisation, Chinatown, huddled on the south bank of the Singapore River and stretching inland as far as Cantonment Road, still has pockets of narrow streets and shophouses. In the past, it was divided into different dialect-speaking quarters as the early immigrants tended to congregate in certain neighbourhoods according to the dialect they

spoke and their village origins. This distinction is blurred today.

The entire quarter may be hemmed in by soaring high-rises today but Chinatown, thankfully, is still dominated by exotic sights and smells, albeit amid mountains of gaudy tourist junk. Frogs await skinning in the local wet markets, while in the medical halls there are pearls to be ground and ginseng roots to rejuvenate the tired. At certain times of year the pungent aroma of the seasonal durian fruit permeates the air.

Map on page 102

LEFT AND BELOW: candlestick detail and worshippers at Chinatown's Thian Hock Keng Temple.

Shops specialising in traditional Chinese medicinal herbs can be found around Sago Street and South Bridge Road.

Past and present

A S$97.5 million project, driven by the Singapore Tourism Board (and slated for completion at the end of 2005), aims to evoke a sense of the past and to recreate Chinatown's rich heritage, lost through urban renewal. Part of the plan is to revive traditional trades, street hawkers and performers, and also encourage people to live in Chinatown again. Critics, however, fear that this new Chinatown might turn into an artificial theme park for visitors, losing its gritty edge and ambience in the process.

But even without such deliberate planning, a stroll in Chinatown still reveals contrasting vignettes that make the district a fascinating blend of the past and the present. It is not uncommon to see executives toting briefcase in one hand and mobile phone on the other pass temples where elderly women in *samfoo* (Chinese traditional blouse and trousers) toss wooden sticks from a tin can at temples as they pray for "lucky numbers" in the lottery.

Beautifully refurbished shophouses that are now home to trendy advertising agencies and funky bars stand shoulder to shoulder with decaying shophouses selling antiques and bric-a-brac. And in the shopping centres and on the streets that thread through Chinatown, handmade puppets, opera masks, silk clothing, herbs and traditional Chinese furniture are sold alongside computers and other electronic goods.

Chinatown has its fair share of Buddhist and Taoist temples. But one of the most curious things about the neighbourhood is that it harbours some of the island's best known Hindu and Muslim shrines. Chinatown, like Singapore's other ethnic enclaves, reflected a healthy eclecticism that has survived to this day.

The Chinatown MRT station at New Bridge Road/Eu Tong Sen Street allows easy access to this area.

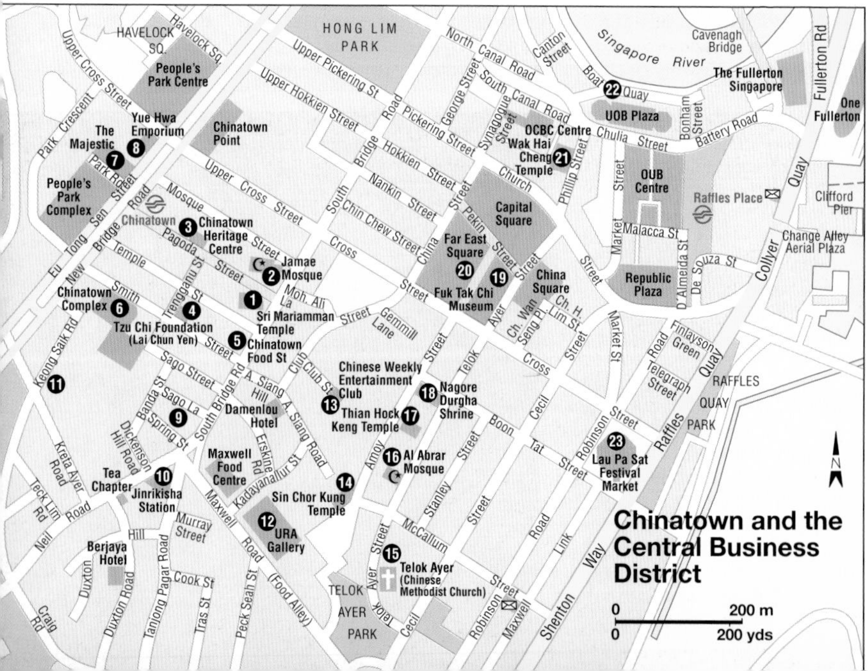

Chinatown and the Central Business District

0 — 200 m
0 — 200 yds

Sri Mariamman Temple

Towering above the shophouses along South Bridge Road are the brightly painted figures on the *gopuram* (tower) entrance of the **Sri Mariamman Temple ❶** (daily 5.30am–9.30pm; tel: 6223 4064). Dedicated to goddess Mariamman – who is known for curing serious illnesses – it's the oldest and most important Hindu shrine in Singapore. Here, devotees perform *pujas* (prayers) amid gaudy statues and vivid ceiling frescoes.

Built during the 1820s, this is the annual site of Thimiti *(see page 49)*, the Hindu fire walking festival that takes place in October. In an elaborate ceremony that honours the goddess Draupathi, the faithful work themselves into a frenzied trance and walk over burning embers to fulfil their vows. Curiously, it's a ritual that also draws participation from a small number of Chinese devotees.

Eu Yan Sang Medical Shop

Across the same street at No. 269 is **Eu Yan Sang**, a traditional Chinese medicine shop with over 70 branches in the region (tel: 6223 6333; www. euyansang.com). The original shop was founded in Malaysia over a century ago by Eu Kong, a Chinese immigrant who used traditional Chinese medicine, instead of opium, to alleviate the pains tin miners suffered from. Today, you can walk into its Chinatown store and consult a *sinseh*, or Chinese doctor, who will prescribe the correct herb for your ailment. But even if you are in the pink of health, the bottled bird's nest, herbal candies and ginseng wines make interesting souvenirs.

Jamae Mosque

Adjacent to Sri Mariamman Temple across Pagoda Street is the lovely **Jamae Mosque ❷**, with its distinctive pagoda-like minarets rarely seen in Muslim mosque architecture (daily 5am–8.30pm; tel: 6221 4165). Its unique design was perhaps a gesture of deference to the predominantly Chinese neighbourhood. The mosque was constructed in 1827 by Muslim Chulia immigrants who came from South India's Coromandel Coast.

Map on page 102

TIP

Beijing Tong Ren Tang Chinese Medical Hall, founded in China in 1669 by an imperial medical official, is best known for its niu huang qing xin wan (211 South Bridge Road; tel: 6223 7386). The pill, with a recipe written during the Song dynasty, purportedly keeps the liver, spleen, stomach and muscles healthy.

BELOW: close-up of the entrance tower at Sri Mariamman.

Stop at No. 5 Smith Street and sip tea while admiring the traditional Chinese opera costumes on display at the Chinese Opera Teahouse. Opera excerpts, with dinner provided, are performed on Friday and Saturday nights, tel: 6323 4862; www.ctcopera.com.sg.

BELOW: display at the Chinatown Heritage Centre.

Chinatown Heritage Centre

Chinatown, like most old areas in Singapore, is in danger of losing its character. Temple Street's old tradesmen for instance – the pavement barber, idol carver and calligrapher – have all gone, their places taken up by sometimes nondescript restaurants, pubs and offices.

For this reason the **Chinatown Heritage Centre ❸** was opened in 2002 to give Chinatown a sense of history (daily 10am–7pm; admission charge; tel: 6325 2878; www.chinatownheritage.com.sg). Occupying three restored shophouses on Pagoda Street, the museum showcases the lifestyles, traditions and rituals of the people who lived and worked there. The dark and cramped living quarters of 1950s Chinatown are realistically recreated and one of the centre's highlights is the home of a Chinatown tailor and his family. Using authentic furniture, utensils and other paraphernalia, the living conditions of the Chinatown of yesteryear are brought to life.

In addition, there are 15 exhibition galleries which take visitors through a journey to discover the evolution of Chinatown. There are depictions of Chinese clan associations and gambling dens, festivals, food and culture as well as multimedia displays of famous Chinatown personalities.

Trengganu Street

The heart of Chinatown is an area off South Bridge Road that embraces Pagoda, Temple, Trengganu and Sago streets. Linking Pagoda Street is atmospheric **Trengganu Street**, which, not so long ago, was lined with street stalls selling live snakes, turtles and other exotic wildlife destined for the dinner table. The only exotica to be found these days are arts and crafts from Asia and wild herbs from China. Trengganu Street is in fact Chinatown's main hub because it's the neighbourhood's only full cross street.

Many of the elegantly restored shophouses in the area now play host to a colourful assortment of restaurants, cafés and teahouses as well as Chinese "medical halls", antiques and handicrafts stores.

Chinatown Night Market

In the evenings, Pagoda, Trengganu and Sago (*see page 106*) streets are closed off to traffic and transformed into the lively **Chinatown Night Market** (Sun–Thurs 5–11pm, Fri–Sat 5pm–1am). With over 200 stores selling both traditional Chinese goods like calligraphy, masks and lanterns as well as contemporary items like funky jewellery and bags, the market deserves a leisurely trawl.

Tzu Chi Foundation

At the corner of Trengganu Street and Smith Street is the Buddhist **Tzu Chi Foundation ❹** (daily 10am–7pm, tel: 6324 6889). The restored building, with gleaming wooden floors and carved banisters – look up at the balcony running along its upper level – was formerly called **Lai Chun Yuen**, a Cantonese opera house that packed in fans in its heyday. Famous opera stars performed here in the 1920s. If there is a faint similarity between the facade of the theatre and that of the Raffles Hotel, it's because both were designed by R.A.J. Bidwell. The Buddhist association occupies the upper floor while along its ground floor is a string of antiques shops.

Along Smith Street

Smith Street is home to several arts associations. Often, in the afternoons, you can follow the sound of a Chinese fiddle, wander up a narrow staircase and find old folks honing their art. They are always delighted to play to an appreciative audience – but it's polite to ask first.

This is also a chance to relieve the hustle and bustle of 1960s street hawking – with 21st century sanitation standards – when the street is closed to traffic in the evenings and weekends. A lively mix of 18 hawker stalls ply a range of local culinary staples at **Chinatown Food Street ❺** (Mon–Fri 6pm–midnight,

Sat, Sun and holidays 11am–midnight). Tuck into barbecued seafood drenched in *sambal* (chilli gravy), *wonton* noodles and mutton soup, which are all to be recommended.

Chinatown's streets are a gourmet's paradise. You can pop into any restaurant and the worse thing that can happen is a mediocre meal – it's unlikely to be bad. **Yum Cha** allows you to tuck into *dim sum* in a traditional setting (02-01, 20 Trengganu Street; tel: 6372 1717). Or make time for a Chinatown institution – **Da Dong** at 39 Smith Street (tel: 6221 3822) – which has survived stormy periods during the war and independence since its founding in 1928.

Along Smith Street, the higher floors of **Chinatown Complex ❻** have stalls offering a tempting array of local food. The basement is also worth exploring for the unusual ingredients on sale – from live fish and poultry to bean curd, fresh fruit, flowers and vegetables. The best time to visit this "wet" market is in the morning. Be privy to the constant banter between housewives and fishmongers, although the faint-hearted

Map on page 102

TIP

Apart from shopping for souvenirs at the Chinatown Night Market, look out for the occasional cultural performance, either lion and dragon dances, Chinese opera, stilt walkers or *wushu* Chinese martial arts displays. These events provide fascinating fodder for photographers.

BELOW: Trengganu Street, the heart of Chinatown.

Yue Hwa Emporium at the corner of Eu Tong Sen and Upper Cross streets is a treasure trove of Chinese arts and crafts.

BELOW: Sago Street shophouses.

may just find the sight of skinned frogs a tad too grisly. On weekend afternoons, old folks spread their treasures – old stamps, dusty crockery, bronze Buddhist statues – on blankets. If something catches your fancy, remember to bargain.

Eu Tong Sen Street

The pedestrian bridge (also known as Garden Bridge) across New Bridge Road and Eu Tong Sen Street leads to **People's Park Complex**, a local favourite for its mix of shops, offices and cinemas. If looking for Chinese silk and textiles, be sure to visit this place. Next door is **The Majestic ❼**. Once known as Tin Yin Dance Stage, a venue for Cantonese opera, this former art deco-style cinema hall was recently restored and converted into another sterile shopping mall. The facade has been kept intact but the interior is almost unrecognisable in its new reincarnation – filled with mostly ho-hum clothing shops and beauty salons.

Yue Hwa Emporium ❽ is adjacent, a good one-stop shop for all things Chinese. The emporium occupies the building of the former Great Southern Hotel, once considered the grand old lady of Chinatown.

Across the street is **People's Park Centre** with a motley assortment of shops while opposite, at the corner of New Bridge Road and Upper Cross Street, is **Chinatown Point**, a good place to shop for Chinese arts and crafts and trinkets.

Sago Street and Lane

Returning to the heart of Chinatown proper, Trengganu Street meanders left into **Sago Street**, named after the numerous sago (a pearl-like starch) factories that used to operate here. These days you are more likely to find restored shophouses that have been turned into Chinese bakeries, restaurants and herbal shops. Drop in at **Fong Moon Kee** at No. 16 (tel: 6223 0940), where traditional healing oils are sold as cures for asthma, colds and other common ailments. Citronella oil, for instance, a fragrant oil made from lemon grass repels mosquitoes when rubbed on the skin. Traditional, too, are the delicious Chinese pastries such as the walnut biscuits you'll find at **Leung Sang Hong Kong Pastries** at No. 18 (tel: 6221 1344).

Opposite is **Sago Lane ❾**, once known as the "Street of the Dead" as it was here that Chinese families brought their aged to die. Beds were rented out in macabre death-houses for the elderly to wait out their last days. The lane also had shops selling coffins, joss sticks and miniature houses and cars made of paper, which were routinely burnt for the dead to serve them in their after-life. The street in the old days resounded to a constant cacophony of sounds from funeral bands and chanting from priests performing the last rites. The death-houses of Sago Lane are long gone, replaced by an empty field that is now used for religious festivals and Chinese opera performances.

Tanjong Pagar district

From Sago Street (or Lane), turn right and walk to the corner of Tanjong Pagar and Neil roads, where the stately **Jinrikisha Station ⑩** stands. Rickshaw coolies once parked their two-wheeled vehicles here. The station, built in 1903 in the classical style, is crowned by a dome. The first *jinriks* (rickshaws) arrived in Singapore in the 1880s from Shanghai. They were the main means of transport in Singapore in the early 1900s before they were replaced by the three-wheeled trishaws in the 1940s. The rickshaw coolies found it convenient to live around the station, renting bed-space in tiny Chinatown cubicles. Sometimes, the same bed-space was rented out to two coolies working different shifts.

Once a decrepit part of town, the **Tanjong Pagar** district has been restored into a haven for all kinds of arts and crafts, as well as cosy restaurants and pubs. Recently, a number of discreet gay and lesbian clubs and saunas have also proliferated here.

The area has a long and interest- ing history. Once a Malay fishing village known as Tanjong Pagar (Cape of Stakes), legend has it that this part of the coast was afflicted by schools of sharp-toothed garfish which attacked people on shore. As a result, a barricade of plantain stems was erected along the coast to trap the fish. In the 1830s, the land around Tanjong Pagar was turned into a nutmeg plantation. The area became a thriving commercial hub, but by the 1960s, the neighbourhood fell into disrepair and would have met the wrecker's ball if the government had not started its big conservation drive. Tanjong Pagar soon became an archetype and a testing ground for how the remainder of historic Singapore would be restored.

The 200 shophouses were reno-vated for "adaptive reuse", in architectural-speak, as restaurants, shops and offices. The first units were put up for tender in 1987 and almost overnight Tanjong Pagar became a drawcard for creative people in search of office and restaurant space. The area takes on a magical glow at night when the lights come on and

Map on page 102

Hop onto a trishaw to explore Chinatown. To book, visit the Chinatown Trishaw Tour kiosk at Kreta Ayer Square, opposite No. 30 Sago Street, or call 6339 6833.

BELOW: you can learn about Chinese tea at Neil Road's Tea Chapter.

Chinese Teahouses

The appearance of traditional tea-houses in Chinatown and Tanjong Pagar goes along with a recent quest by local Chinese to discover their roots. **Tea Chapter** at 9/11 Neil Road offers a wide range – over 50 varieties – that may be savoured in tiny teacups (daily 11am–11pm; tel: 6226 3026; www.tea-chapter.com.sg). It also offers tea appreciation workshops, which include tips on how to brew that perfect, fragrant cup. **Yixing Xuan Teahouse** at 30/32 Tanjong Pagar Road pampers its regulars by storing their tea leaves in containers with the customers' names written on the sides (daily 11am–11pm; tel: 62261646; www.yixingxuan-teahouse.com).

Window detail from a Keong Saik Road shophouse.

people unwind in the numerous pubs and restaurants lining Tanjong Pagar, Craig, Neil and Duxton roads.

The two-storey structures – narrow yet deep – lend themselves perfectly to romantic dining with their ornate plaster facades and wooden window shutters, pastel hues, teak floors, wooden stairways, high-beamed ceilings and red-tiled roofs.

Tanjong Pagar also has its own luxury boutique hotel, the **Berjaya** at No. 83 Duxton Road, which rambles through eight Victorian shophouses and blends traditional Singaporean and European decor.

Keong Saik Road

Further down along Neil Road past Kreta Ayer Road is the once notorious **Keong Saik Road** ⓫, a red-light district that has now been gentrified. Many of its splendid examples of shophouses in the Chinese Baroque architectural style *(see pages 148–49)* have been restored and converted into boutique hotels such as the Royal Peacock and Regal Inn, and Chinatown Hotel in the adjoining Teck Lim Road.

BELOW: the URA Gallery gives visitors a useful overview of the city.

Joining these older hotels is the the über-cool **Hotel 1929**, which opened its doors in 2003 and is partly responsible for making this once seedy strip hip. Holistic centres, bars, a yoga studio and an art gallery now jostle for space with brothels and scruffy coffeeshops.

URA Gallery

Returning to the Jinriksha Station, Tanjong Pagar Road forks right into Maxwell Road. At the corner with Kadayanallur Street lies the recently renovated **Maxwell Food Centre**. One of Singapore's oldest hawker centres, snaking queues are a regular sight at lunchtime.

Across Kadayanallur Street is the Urban Redevelopment Authority's **URA Gallery** ⓬ where the key attraction is a massive model of the city (Mon–Fri 9am–4.30pm, Sat 9am–12.30pm; free; tel: 6321 8321; www.ura.gov.sg). Spread over two storeys are permanent exhibits, interactive displays and touch-screen terminals, as well as video and audio-visual programmes that offer an insight into the workings of this

THE ROYAL PEACOCK HOTEL

efficient city. The displays succinctly tell how Singapore grew from a fishing village into the thriving modern metropolis it is today. You can also read all about URA's ambitious Concept Plan, a long-range blueprint for the physical development of the city in the 21st century.

Club and Amoy streets

Kadayanallur Street leads uphill into Ann Siang Road, which joins up with **Club Street**. This street and the one down the hillside, **Amoy Street**, were once the strongholds of the Hokkien community whose members lodged here once they got off the boat from China. These streets used to hum with the activities of various *kongsi* (clan associations), which catered to the needs of immigrants who came from the same village in China, shared the same surnames, dialects and often occupations.

Camaraderie still thrives on Club Street but present-day clans include trendy professionals from nearby advertising and design firms who convene in the numerous restaurants and bars lining the street.

At the corner of Ann Siang Road and Club Street is unpretentious **Damenlou Hotel**, one of many small hotels that have capitalised on their location and architectural character to offer visitors a slice of old Chinatown. At its adjoining **Damenlou (Swee Kee) Restaurant**, the Hokkien speciality of fish-head noodle soup is worth trying.

A dead-end road to the right of Club Street leads to the members-only **Chinese Weekly Entertainment Club ⓭** after which the street took its name. This Victorian-style mansion was the social club for prominent members of the Chinese community who met here for regular card games. Founded by a wealthy Peranakan in 1891, a number of the club's members later went on to establish some of Singapore's leading banks.

Returning to Ann Siang Road, past Damenlou Hotel and Batey House is a dead-end, occupied by a little oasis called **Ann Siang Hill Park**. A staircase leads downhill to Amoy Street and the tiny but atmospheric **Sin Chor Kung Temple ⓮**

Map on page 102

TIP

Browse among stalls in the makeshift afternoon flea market tucked in a corner of a small park on Club Street, leading towards Cross Street. You may chance upon some good finds among the old porcelain plates, religious figurines, semi-precious stones and old posters.

BELOW: streetside calligrapher at work – a rare Chinatown sight.

(daily 7.30am–5.30pm). Just next door is the Amoy Street Food Centre. Built in 1869 and dedicated to the Tua Pek Kong deity, the temple is popular with the Teochews. Despite its diminutive size, the temple is always thronged with people and filled with smoke from the joss sticks burnt by worshippers.

Telok Ayer Methodist Church

Parallel to Amoy Street is **Telok Ayer Street**, where the red and white **Telok Ayer Chinese Methodist Church** ⓯ stands diagonally opposite the Amoy Street Food Centre (Mon–Fri 9am–5pm, Sat 9am–1pm; tel: 6324 4001). Its unusual architecture is a blend of East and West – a flat-roofed Chinese pavilion and a ground floor graced by European-style columns – and a testament to the British Protestant missionary effort in Singapore. The national monument was once a refugee shelter during World War II.

Al Abrar Mosque

Heading north along Telok Ayer Street, past McCallum Street, is the brown and white concrete building known as the **Al Abrar Mosque** ⓰. It was constructed between 1850 and 1855 by the Muslim Chulia community from South India (daily 5–7am, 11.30am–9pm; tel: 6220 6306). The earlier mosque that used to sit here in the 1830s was a mere thatched structure known as Kuchu Palli (hut mosque).

Thian Hock Keng Temple

Telok Ayer Street, meaning "Water Bay" in the Malay language, once bordered Singapore's original shoreline. Today the reclaimed land is blocked from the sea by a wall of gleaming skyscrapers. It was here that seafarers and immigrants from the Fukien Province set up a joss house in the 1820s in gratitude for their safe arrival after their long voyage from China. The joss house eventually became the **Thian Hock Keng Temple** ⓱, or Temple of Heavenly Happiness (daily 7.30am–5.30pm; tel: 6423 4616). Dedicated to Ma Cho Po, Goddess of the Sea, she reputedly could calm rough waters and rescue those in danger of drowning.

The little joss house gave way to a visually extravagant temple in 1842, built without the use of a single nail and with materials imported from China. Dragons, venerated for protection on sea voyages, leap along the roof and curl around solid granite pillars. Incense wafts from great brass urns in front of altars laden with fruit offerings. During renovations in 1999, a silk scroll bearing the handwriting of Qing Emperor Guang Xu (1871–1908) was found in the temple. The scroll, inscribed with four large Chinese characters saying *bo jing nan ming* ("the wave is calm in the South Seas") was a gift from the emperor to the Thian Hock Keng Temple in 1906 to mark the completion of its first major restoration. It is considered a rare

TIP

If there is time for a diversion, just behind Telok Ayer Methodist Church across Cecil Street at Capital Tower lies the arresting *Shimmering Pearls* sculpture. The 36 coloured glass globes, inspired by the movement of water, are the work of Singaporean sculptor Han Sai Por.

BELOW: ornate painted doors at the entrance of Thian Hock Keng Temple.

piece of calligraphy by the emperor who gave similar pieces only to two other temples in the region – the Wak Hai Cheng Temple on Phillip Street *(see page 112)* and a temple in Malaysia's Penang island.

Nagore Durgha Shrine

Further down, past **Telok Ayer Green** on the same street is the **Nagore Durgha Shrine** ⑱, also called Masjid Chulia, an architectural companion to Jamae Mosque on South Bridge Road. The Muslim shrine, built in 1830, is an interesting marriage of the classical style typified by moulded arches with Indian-Muslim motifs such as the perforated grilles at roof level. The shrine, which also combines Western architectural elements like Doric columns and Palladian doors, is currently closed for renovations.

Far East Square

North along Telok Ayer Street, past Cross Street, on the left is **Ying Fo Fui Kun** at No. 98, the first Hakka Clan Association founded in 1822 by the Hakka people from China.

Further down at No. 76 is **Fuk Tak Chi Museum** ⑲, previously the Fuk Tak Chi Temple, dedicated to Tua Pek Kong the Earth God (daily 10am–10pm; free; tel: 6532 7868). Dating from 1824, Singapore's oldest temple was set up by the Hakkas and Cantonese. The museum has a collection of 200 artefacts, including a Chinese gold belt, abacus board and even a rental expiry notice, from early Chinatown residents.

Opposite is **China Square**, a sprawling food court spread over four floors. The entire third floor is occupied by the **Teahouse**, where Chinese *dim sum* is sold the traditional way – in parading trolleys piled high with treats like century-egg porridge, fried radish cake and various steamed dumplings.

Far East Square ⑳, opposite China Square, is a conservation area bounded by three roads: Cross Street, Telok Ayer Street and China Street. The square blends the new with the old to provide 16,550 sq metres (178,000 sq ft) of commercial space taken up by offices, restaurants, bars and shops. The area

Map on page 102

Ornate painted doors mark the entrance to Fuk Tak Chi Museum at Far East Square.

BELOW: Far East Square has gates dedicated to each of the five elements.

The courtyard of Wak Hai Cheng Temple is hung with numerous burning spirals of incense, filling the air with its slightly acrid smell. The large ones can take up to 10 days to burn.

BELOW: Wak Hai Cheng Temple.

encompasses the four kinds of shophouse styles prevalent in Chinatown (Early, First Transitional, Late and Second Transitional) from the 1840s to the 1960s *(see pages 148–49)*.

Look out for the five gates that mark the main entrances into Far East Square, each one representing the five elements that make up the Chinese universe: metal, wood, water, fire and earth. Its buildings of historical significance include the aforementioned Fu Tak Chi Museum and **Chui Eng Free School**, one of Singapore's first Chinese schools and established in 1854 to give the poor a chance to be educated. In its current form as the **Bamboo Court Restaurant** (tel: 6536 3771) it doles out delicious Thai-Chinese cuisine.

At Pekin Street – now closed to traffic – noted for its remittance houses where the early immigrants sent money back to their families in China, look out for the plaster relief signs on the columns of No. 42. It once belonged to Seng Huat Sign maker who made similar signs for his clients in Chinatown to advertise their businesses.

Wak Hai Cheng Temple

Opposite **Capital Square**, a modern office block with a sheet of water cascading off a wall on its side, is the dark and incense-filled **Wak Hai Cheng Temple** ㉑ (daily 7am–5.30pm; tel: 6533 8537). Tucked away at the corner of Church and Phillip streets, it huddles beneath the shadow of the towering I.M. Pei-designed **OCBC Centre**.

The temple was built in the 1850s by the local Teochew community for the protection of traders traveling between Singapore and China. The temple, which combines the worship of both Buddhism and Taoism, has an ornately decorated roof that depicts scenes from Chinese village life, including an opera stage and houses. In the courtyard is a large terracotta furnace where paper money is burned to assist the deceased in their journey to the "west".

Central Business District

The core of "Singapore Inc" runs along the waterfront from the Singapore River to Keppel Road and the massive Tanjong Pagar Container

Chinatown Spas

Boutique spas have sprouted all over Chinatown faster than you can say essential oils. **Red Peach Boutique Spa** at 66 Pagoda Street (tel: 6324 1250) offers Chinese-style foot reflexology in a Chinese-inspired space. At 83A Club Street, **Qi Mantra** dispenses traditional Chinese acupressure massage (tel: 6221 5691; www.qimantra.com). More Chinese-inspired therapies can be had at **Rustic Nirvana**, 25 Cantonment Road (tel: 6227 9193; www.rustic nirvana.com). Staff dispense chopsticks and kung fu massages (ouch!). **Spa Haven**, 45/46 Amoy Street, is best known for its chocolate massage (tel: 62212203; www.spahaven.com.sg).

Terminal. The commercial area centres on **Raffles Place**, which has been transformed into an open-air plaza with the busy Raffles Place MRT interchange station below.

The two main thoroughfares are Shenton Way and Robinson Road, but Cecil Street and Battery Road also brim with skyscrapers. Many more buildings are being constructed, especially on the reclaimed **Marina Bay** area bordering the sea. Named Downtown @ Marina Bay, this seamless extension of the CBD is being built in phases and is expected to be ready in 2020. The financial hub is supported by a range of shopping, dining and entertainment activities. Also under construction in the area is the **Singapore Flyer**, Singapore's answer to the London Eye. When completed in the last quarter of 2005, it will be the world's highest observation wheel.

For the moment, the tallest buildings are centred in the Raffles Place area, which adjoins the neighbouring **Civic District** *(see page 79)*: **OUB Centre**, **UOB Plaza** – both designed by Japanese architectural maestro Kenzo Tange – and **Republic Plaza** (by famous Japanese counterpart Kisho Kurokawa) all reach a height of 280 metres (919 ft) – the maximum allowed by local aviation rules. The atrium outside UOB Plaza, with its large bronze statue of Salvador Dali's *Homage to Newton*, is always filled with smartly dressed executives with ears permanently plugged to their mobile phones. The buzz, and the seething mass of humanity, especially at lunchtime, is quite incredible.

Boat Quay

On one side of UOB Plaza is the Singapore River, with **Boat Quay ㉒** sitting immediately left of the building. For a century until the late 1960s, Boat Quay reverberated to the clamour of coolies loading and unloading sacks of rice, coal and other cargo between lighter-boats huddled at the bottom of the steps and shophouses connected precariously by narrow gangplanks. When the fervour of urban renewal gripped Singapore in the 1970s, this crammed south side of the river was deemed unsightly.

Map on page 102

TIP

Chinatown is located close to the financial district, which means that office staff from the surrounding office towers descend on food centres in droves at lunchtime. For a leisurely meal, avoid the peak hours of noon–1.30pm.

BELOW: Boat Quay riverside dining with CBD skyline in the background.

Map on page 102

The lighter-boats were banned from the river, flotsam and jetsam resulting from the loading activities were cleared from the waters and the shophouses of Boat Quay were refurbished and converted to a Latin Quarter of sorts with bars and restaurants. Today, Boat Quay echoes to the clink of wine glasses at dusk when executives descend from surrounding office towers to unwind at drinking holes like Penny Black, Molly Malone's Irish Pub and Harry's Bar with their open-air terraces overlooking the river. Although recent competition from similar waterfront areas have taken its toll on this entertainment district, dining options are still plentiful – all the world's cuisine can be found along this riverfront strip, from Italian to Indian, Thai and Japanese.

Lau Pa Sat

In the CBD's maze of steel and glass, the distinctive **Lau Pa Sat Festival Market** ㉓ (whose Hokkien name translates into "old market") stands out (daily 24 hours). Bounded by Shenton Way, Robinson Road, Cross Street and Boon Tat Street, this Victorian octagonal-shaped structure was built from cast iron in Glasgow and shipped in 1894 to Singapore where it was reassembled on the waterfront. The national monument, once a wet market, underwent massive restoration in 1986 and re-opened with some 60 food stalls selling a variety of hawker fare. In the evenings, **Boon Tat Street** on one side is closed to traffic and transformed into an al fresco dining area.

Collyer Quay

The waterfront along **Collyer Quay** once bustled with the comings and goings of clipper ships, lighter-boats and junks. But most of the activity has moved to Keppel Harbour and the container terminals. The best views are found at the northern end of **Clifford Pier**, where **One Fullerton** (see page 82) building is located. Settle down with a drink at one of its bars with outdoor terrace areas, and watch little "bumboats" bobbing in Marina Bay and sleek modern craft heading in from the Southern Islands. ❑

BELOW: Boon Tat Street hawkers.
RIGHT: Molly Malone's pub at Boat Quay.

RESTAURANTS

Australian

Broth
21 Duxton Hill. Tel: 6323 3353. Open: L Mon–Fri, D Mon–Sat. $$$
Tucked at the end of a cobblestoned path between a row of shophouses, you feel like you're a world away from everything else. Chef-owner Steven Hansen makes scrumptious salads and lamb loin in mint sauce. Check out the old and rare vintages of boutique Australian reds.

Moomba
52 Circular Rd. Tel: 6438 0141. Open: L Mon–Fri, D Mon–Sat. $$$ (set lunch) $$$$ (à la carte)
www.themoomba.com
The city's first Australian restaurant is still among the best. Expect good service, an extensive collection of boutique Australian wines and excellent contemporary Australian cuisine. Over 90 percent of the produce it uses is imported from Australia.

Chinese

Damenlou (Swee Kee) Restaurant
12 Ann Siang Rd. Tel: 6222 8926. Open: L and D daily. $$
www.damenlou.com
The robust home-style Chinese cuisine and atmosphere would have you thinking you're dining

with an extended family at grandma's house. Sit outside so you can watch the creative hub of Chinatown in action, order chrysanthemum tea, or if you desire, wine, to complement the superb deep-fried prawn sauce chicken and fish head noodles.

Da Pal Dang
267 New Bridge Rd. Tel: 6325 4897. Open: Tues–Sun noon–11pm. $
www.mouth.com.sg
Hong Kong street food is transplanted to Singapore's Chinatown. The din, efficient but somewhat loud waitstaff, noodles and *dim sum* are all an authentic Hong Kong experience. The melt-in-your-mouth steamed rice rolls with prawns or pork are freshly prepared when you place your order.

Qun Zhong Eating House
21 Neil Rd. Tel: 6221 3060. Open: L and D daily; closed on Wed. $
A queue forms outside the restaurant even before mealtimes. Disregard the surly staff and drab decor, and order the reasonably priced Beijing fare – simple yet satisfying. Do what the rest do, order the *xiao long bao* (steamed pork dumplings), noodles and red bean pancake.

Silk Road
2/F, Amara Hotel, 165 Tanjong Pagar Rd. Tel: 6227 3848. Open: L and

D daily. $$ (set lunch) $$$$ (à la carte)
www.silkroadrestaurants.com
Everything about Silk Road is so refined, be it the poem by Tang poet Li Bai carved onto the entrance floor, the warm, contemporary decor, the delicious Chinese provincial cuisine – Beijing, Liaoning, Shanxi and Sichuan – prepared by the bevy of chefs, or the tea master who pours the aromatic Eight Treasure Tea from a copper kettle with a metre-long spout.

Soup
25 Smith St. Tel: 6222 9923. Open: L and D daily.$$ (à la carte)
Its nutritious double-boiled soups are superb and always recommended by the waitresses here. The Samsui Ginger Chicken, once consumed by impoverished *samsui* women (who worked as construction workers) purportedly banishes the "chills". Served with lettuce and a ginger sauce, it's amazing something so simple can be so satisfying.

Swee Kee Fishhead Noodle House
96 Amoy St. Tel: 6224 9920. Open: L and D daily. $$
www.ka-soh.com.sg
The stern-looking waitresses will tell you their menu has not changed since the 1940s. So reliable it is that celebrities

and politicians are known to drop by regularly for its wholesome and creamy fish head soup, prawn paste chicken and pork ribs in "secret" sauce.

Teahouse
3/F, China Square Food Ctr, 51 Telok Ayer St. Tel: 6533 0660. Open: L and D daily. $–$$$ (set lunch) $$ (à la carte)
www.tunglok.com
Dim sum the old-fashioned way means trolleys groaning with dainty *dim sum* are rolled before your table and you pick what you want. Favourites are the barbecued pork buns and *har gau* (shrimp dumplings). Round off the meal with the nutritious double-boiled soup of the day and superior stock crab vermicelli.

French

L'Aigle d'or
Berjaya Hotel, 83 Duxton Rd. Tel: 6227 7678. Open: B, L and D daily. $$$ (set lunch) $$$$ (à la carte)
It would be very difficult to decide which you would love best: the

PRICE CATEGORIES

Prices for a three-course dinner per person without drinks and taxes:
$ = under S$20
$$= S$20–$30
$$$ = S$30–$45
$$$$ = more than S$45

well-dressed dining room that's conducive for both a romantic rendezvous and important business lunch, or the exquisite French cuisine. Devotees swear it's both.

L'Angelus
85 Club St. Tel: 6225 6897. Open: L Mon–Fri, D Mon–Sat. $$$ (set lunch) $$$$ (à la carte)
Just what you would expect a typical, small, Parisian restaurant to look like. Bistro-type menu – which changes monthly – with dishes like chicken liver pate with onion marmalade, duck confit, grilled lamb fillet with cream of garlic and white wine sauce, and an assortment of cheeses.

Indian

Kinara
57 Boat Quay. Tel: 6533 0412. Open: L and D daily. $$$
www.valley.com.sg
Warm, friendly staff serve hearty Punjabi cuisine by the Singapore River in a beautiful space decorated with antique furniture from Rajasthan. It's one of the few places in Boat Quay where you'll happily dine indoors. The roasted leg of lamb, marinated for over 24 hours, is a must-try.

Indonesian

House of Sundanese Food
55 Boat Quay. Tel: 6534 3775. Open: L Mon–Fri, D daily. $ (set lunch) $$ (à la carte)
Busy but charming place with delicious West Java-

inspired fare such as spicy prawns, grilled chicken and *sayur lodeh* (vegetables in coconut milk). Their charcoal-grilled fish is legendary; the secret lies in the traditional Sundanese sauce.

Italian

Buko Nero
126 Tanjong Pagar Rd. Tel: 6324 6225. Open: L and D Tues–Sat. $$ (set lunch) $$$ (à la carte)
Run by an Italian-husband and Singaporean-wife team, the menu reflects this Italian-Asian marriage. Signatures include the tofu and vegetable tower, spaghetti with spicy crabmeat and prawns, and horlicks ice cream. There are just seven tables and the restaurant is perennially full. Diners call in advance – sometimes a month ahead – for dinner.

Da Paolo e Judie
81 Neil Rd. Tel: 6225 8306. Open: L and D Mon–Sat. $$$ (set lunch) $$$$ (à la carte)
www.dapaolo.com.sg
There are four Da Paolo eateries in Singapore, and seafood takes precedence at this sexy Italian place in a pre-war shophouse. If hankering after some seriously good pasta, you can always count on chef-owner Paola Scarpa. Try his linguine tossed with squid ink sauce – you get a black napkin to go with this. The bar is stunning – arrive early for pre-dinner drinks.

Pasta Brava
11 Craig Rd. Tel: 6227 7550. Open: L and D Mon–Sat. $$ (set lunch) $$$ (à la carte)
A real taste of Italy in a converted old Singapore shophouse. If you don't find the sauce you want for your pasta on the menu, chatty chef-owner Rolando Luceri will prepare anything that his available ingredients will allow. Check out his southern Italian signatures including the grilled vegetable-based antipasti and ravioli filled with pumpkin.

Senso
21 Club St. Tel: 6224 3534. Open: L Mon–Fri, D daily. $$ (set lunch) $$$$ (à la carte)
Drinks at the sleek bar should precede dinner at Club Street's most handsome restaurant. And if the weather permits, dine at the lovely al fresco courtyard. Chef-partner Diego Chiarini cites Alain Ducasse, whom he worked with in Monte Carlo, as one of his leading influences. The result – fine Italian fare, such as the carpaccio with winter black truffle puree, is the order of the day.

Spizza for Friends
29 Club St. Tel: 6224 2525. Open: L and D daily. $$
Spizza's winning formula: Italy-imported ingredients, a thin and crispy crust and a wood-fired oven. Try the Quinta Pizza – tomato, mozzarella and black truffles

topped with a cracked egg and the very special Isabella – mozzarella, parma ham and rucola salad. End with a sweet pizza – Zara comes dressed in melted chocolate, bananas and almond flakes.

Japanese

Ikukan
23 Mohd. Ali Lane. Tel: 6325 3362. Open: L Mon–Sat, D daily. $$ (set lunch) $$$ (à la carte)
Chef Hisaki Deguchi gives his charcoal grill specialties a delightful twist. Contemporary Japanese cuisine means you can savour pan-fried duck liver in teriyaki sauce with French wine in a sleek, minimalist decor. Traditional Japanese favourites aren't spared the stylish, modern touch either – your *sashimi* arrives in a carved ice bowl.

Local

Chinatown Complex Food Centre
Smith St. Open: B till late daily. $
American writer Patricia Schultz says Singapore's hawker centres, particularly Chinatown's, are among the 1,000 places to see before you die. The 233-stall complex is great for porridge (stall 103), Chinese desserts (stall 104) and steamed fish head (stall 119), among others. Also, the best local food are found along Smith Street in the

evening when the road closes to traffic.

Lau Pa Sat
Festival Market
18 Raffles Quay.
Open: 24 hours. $
www.kopitiam.biz

The cast-iron structure in the heart of the financial district has been here since 1894. Gazetted a national monument, the restored food centre now boasts 60 stalls and a side street peddling *satay* in the evening. What's hot: mutton soup (stall 30, street 3), Indian bread or *prata* (stall 26, street 3) and Indian vegetarian food (stall 84, street 7).

Maxwell Food Centre
Maxwell Rd, next to URA Ctr. Open: B till late daily. $

Join any of the long queues at one of Singapore's oldest food centres. Try the chicken rice (stall 10), herbal soups (stall 12), fried dough fritters (stall 28), fried sweet potato dumplings (stall 76), and claypot chicken rice (stall 53). Tip: Avoid lunch hours – executives arrive in droves from the nearby CBD offices.

Middle Eastern
Dharma's
40 Boat Quay. Tel: 6534 5100. Open: L Mon–Fri, D Mon–Tue till midnight, Wed–Fri till 3am; Sat 8pm–4am. $ (à la carte)

Blink and you may miss this hole-in-the-wall kebab shop. Chef Dharma Nand is finicky about quality. Your *naan* bread is always fresh from the tandoor, the meat juicy and tender, and the sauces are excellent. Everything is recommended especially the chicken *tikka* and onion *bahji* burger.

Modern European
Ember
Hotel 1929, 500 Keong Saik Rd. Tel: 6347 1928. Open: L Mon–Fri, D Mon–Sat. $$$ (set lunch) $$$$ (à la carte).
www.hotel1929.com

Chef-owner Sebastien Ng is one of Singapore's most talented young chefs. His Modern European cuisine is delightfully robust yet refined, and sometimes comes with wonderful Asian accents. Everything is good really, and you should definitely have the Maine lobster linguine in clam *jus* and slow-roasted lamb loin.

Salt
94 Amoy St. Tel: 6223 1266. Open: L Mon–Fri, D Tues–Sat. $$ (set lunch), $$$ (à la carte) Jimmy Chok, one of Singapore's most respected fusion chefs, whips out East-West dishes with aplomb at his friendly, homey restaurant. Chok does a braised lamb shank with oyster sauce and Chinese wine, and the seared salmon fillet comes with a ginger soy dressing. The six-course tasting menu of the restaurant's best dishes for dinner is good value for money.

Spanish
Streeters Restaurante Tapas Bar
35 Keong Saik Rd. Tel: 6221 1997. Open: L Mon–Fri, D Mon–Sat. $ (set lunch) $$$ (à la carte)

All the ingredients of a good Spanish-Mediterranean restaurant in the heart of Chinatown's red light district. Check the chalkboard for daily specials. What's recommended? The over 35 varieties of tapas, five types of paella, seafood stew, Spanish fish soup and lamb shoulder.

Thai
Basil Thai
28 Tanjong Pagar Rd. Tel: 6224 2262. Open: L and D Tues–Sun. $ (buffet lunch) $$ (à la carte)

Understandably, the Thai chefs here serve up a smattering of basil-inspired dishes along with the other classic northeastern Thai dishes. Must tries include the deep-fried basil leaf with cuttlefish, tom yam seafood soup with Thai herbs and pomelo-tossed rice.

Thanying
2/F, Amara Hotel, 165 Tanjong Pagar Rd. Tel: 6222 4688. Open: L and D daily. $$$ (à la carte) Thanying means "Thai noble lady". Indeed, this madam has cultivated a loyal following with her refined Thai cuisine. Whether it's the green curry or crispy boneless garoupa, every dish in the elegant teak-panelled dining room is beautifully presented. The extensive menu is complemented by a Thai dessert buffet.

Vegetarian
Lingzhi
01-01 Far East Sq, 7-13 Amoy St. Tel: 6538 2992. Open: L and D daily. $ (buffet lunch) $$
www.tunglok.com

This is how great vegetarian cuisine can be, thanks to executive chef Han Shujin who is well honed in the "imperial" style of Chinese vegetarian cuisine. The goodness of soy, mushrooms, nuts and vegetables are creatively employed and the beautifully presented dishes complement the restaurant's understated elegance.

WHATEVER...The Bookstore & Café
20 Keong Saik Rd. Tel: 6224 0300. Open: daily, 8am–10pm. $$.
www.whatever.com.sg

Yogis, swamis and mortals alike come to this tiny but lovely café for the soul-cleansing green tea soba noodle salad, organic pastas, wheat-free cakes and cookies and herbal teas. New Age books litter the shelves.

PRICE CATEGORIES

Prices for a three-course dinner per person without drinks and taxes:

$ = under S$20
$$ = S$20–$30
$$$ = S$30–$45
$$$$ = more than S$45

FENG SHUI PRINCIPLES

Is it science, art or just plain superstition? Feng shui is widely practised in Singapore, even by Westerners not easily swayed by unseen forces

ABOVE: auspicious Water Gate at Far East Square *(see page 111)*.

The Chinese believe that success or failure in a career or business, the state of a person's health, wealth and even relationships are all governed by *feng shui*. *Feng* (wind) *shui* (water) is a means of creating harmony between man and his surroundings to achieve balance and well being. It refers to the art of placing a building in relation to other structures in the area to create a balance. But it's not just orientation that counts; how a person's home or office is designed internally and how the furniture is arranged within also has an effect on the occupants' well-being.

This coincides with the Chinese concept of *yin* (negative/feminine) and *yang* (positive/masculine). Each cannot exist without the other. In life, if the *yin* and the *yang* is in balance, there will be harmony. The Chinese believe that *qi* – an invisible energy – flows through the universe and also the human body. The key to *feng shui* is effectively harnessing the flow of this *qi*.

ABOVE: the curve of Boat Quay in the Central Business District represents the belly of the carp. This auspicious shape drew many Chinese businessmen here in the early days and is probably the reason why the CBD grew around this part of the city. The fact that the river swells into a large body of water at this strategic point is another reason why many banks flourished here.

LEFT: the *luo pan* is an instrument used by *feng shui* masters to determine a person's most auspicious orientation. If for instance your best orientation is south according to your time and date of birth, then good fortune and success will follow if your office or home faces this particular direction.

ABOVE: the waters of the Fountain of Wealth *(see page 84)* in Suntec City supposedly bring good fortune to the person who touches it. In fact the entire Suntec City development – based on the human hand – was inspired by *feng shui* principles: its four 45-storey towers are the fingers while a shorter 18-storey building is the thumb. The fountain is held in the palm of the hand and since since water symbolises wealth, the significance is clear. Interestingly, the massive bronze fountain, which covers 1,683 sq metres (18,177 sq ft), is listed in Guinness World Records as the world's largest.

ABOVE: the Grand Hyatt Singapore *(see page 127)* was said to have fared poorly when it had conventionally angled doors. When the hotel was renovated in the mid 1990s, a *feng shui* master was consulted. He advised that the new doors be re-angled so that money would not "flow out into the streets" and voila, the hotel's fortunes have turned for the better.

THE TOOLS OF FENG SHUI

Bad *feng shui* can be countered by simple solutions such as hanging a mirror to deflect bad *qi* (pronounced "chi") or energy, or by re-orienting a door so that good *qi* will flow in. *Feng shui* tools abound to assist the masters in giving advice. Apart from the *luo pan* or compass *(see opposite)* which calculates a person's most favourable direction, the *pa kua*, or eight-sided Chinese trigam with a mirror in the middle, is another tool that is said to deflect bad *qi*. If the *pa kua* has a *yin* and *yang* symbol in the middle, it is used like a *luo pan* – as a means to identify problem areas and to rectify them.

Other principles which bring about harmonius *feng shui* include the use of the right colour, round shapes or symbolic "good luck" symbols such as a water fountain or pond. Crystals and wind chimes placed at certain strategic locations within the house or office are also used to enhance the flow of *qi*.

Others may prefer to turn to prayers at altars which pay homage to the the Fu Luo Shou, the Gods of Wealth, Health and Longevity *(see above)*. These gods are honoured with offerings like oranges (round in shape and bright in colour) laid out in "good luck" numbers such as five or eight.

LEFT: not many visitors are aware that *feng shui* principles are applied in Singapore's architecture. This old shophouse for instance was built with sharp corners to counter bad *qi* from the surrounding environment. The smooth cylindrical tower of Swissôtel The Stamford *(see page 86)* is deemed a good building as it allows *qi* to flow around it without obstruction. For more insights on this fascinating subject, book the "In Harmony with Feng Shui" tour with SH Tours (tel: 6734 9923; www.asiatours.com.sg)

ORCHARD ROAD AND SURROUNDS

International retailers jostle with homegrown stores
along the ultra-modern malls of Orchard Road.
And, when the shopping palls, the lush
Botanic Gardens offer a leafy retreat

Orchard Road is to Singapore what Fifth Avenue is to New York and the Champs-Élysées is to Paris – one interminable line of shops, shopping centres and hotels stretching from the top of the road where Plaza Singapura stands to the other end where Tanglin Road begins. But there is more to Orchard Road than just shops. It has a couple of leafy parks, a presidential palace, sidewalk cafés, and a charming enclave filled with some of Singapore's finest examples of Chinese Baroque shop- and terrace-houses.

Orchard Road derives its name from the sprawling orchards of nutmeg and pepper that once dominated the area in the 1840s. Plagued by frequent floods because of its location in a valley, a mysterious disease at the turn of the 20th century wiped out the plantations almost overnight. Stamford Canal – part of which runs below the pathway fronting Wisma Atria – was widened in 1965 to alleviate the flooding and from then Orchard Road took off. Today, the area is one of Singapore's most coveted business and residential addresses, full of swanky shopping complexes and multi-million dollar condominiums. The only vestiges of the past are found in the street names – inspired by planation owners like Scotts, Cairnhill and Cuppage.

Around Dhoby Ghaut

Orchard Road starts at the junction of Bras Basah and Handy roads. **Dhoby Ghaut MRT Station** marks the beginning of the road, once an area of grassy fields covered with linen left to dry in the sun by Indian-owned *dhoby* (laundries) that used to operate along the banks of the former Bras Basah Canal.

Facing the MRT station is the ageing redbrick **MacDonald House ❶**, built in 1949 for the Hong Kong and Shanghai Bank and one of the first

Map on pages 122–23

LEFT: perennial bustle outside Peranakan Place.
BELOW: Orchard Road street sign.

Sentry on duty at the Istana, the official residence of the President of Singapore. Watch the "changing of the guards" ceremony that takes place on the first Sunday of each month at 5.30pm. Forget about getting a glimpse of the palace building from the gates though: the grounds are so huge, all you can see is a never-ending expanse of greenery. Unknown to many people is the fact that Singapore's current president, S.R. Nathan, prefers to live in his own more humble abode in the east of Singapore, using the Istana only for receiving foreign dignitaries and for hosting state functions.

high-rise office buildings in the area. Most of the Victorian buildings that once lined this street have been bulldozed to make way for shopping malls. Still, history endures along the short stretch of buildings to the right of MacDonald House.

In stark contrast next door is the shimmering **Atrium @ Orchard**. This new glass and chrome S$268 million commercial complex is connected to Dhoby Ghaut MRT Station and consists of a shopping and office tower blocks linked by sky bridges.

Further along is **Plaza Singapura** while across the street at Penang Road is **Park Mall**, the first of the big shopping centres that have given Orchard Road its fame. Plaza Singapura is home to sprawling hypermart Carrefour, and five levels of restaurants and shops, as well as the Golden Village Cineplex. Park Mall is the haunt of new home owners and interior designers as its shops specialise in furniture and hip home decor.

The Istana

Just beyond Plaza Singapura is the **Istana ❷**, the official residence of Singapore's president. The palace and its sprawling gardens are strictly off-limits to the public, except on National Day and certain public holidays when the gates are thrown open to curious sightseers. The Istana was built in 1869 by the colonial architect J.F.A. McNair and it served as the residence of the British governor until the island became self-governing in 1959.

Facing the Istana squarely is **Istana Park ❸**, dominated by an imposing steel sculpture flanked by garden courtyards of heliconia and lotus-filled ponds, a pleasant place to stop for a drink at the park's café.

House of Tan Yeok Nee

Behind the park, at the corner of Clemenceau Avenue and Penang Road, is an old Chinese-style house that bears a discreet plaque hinting

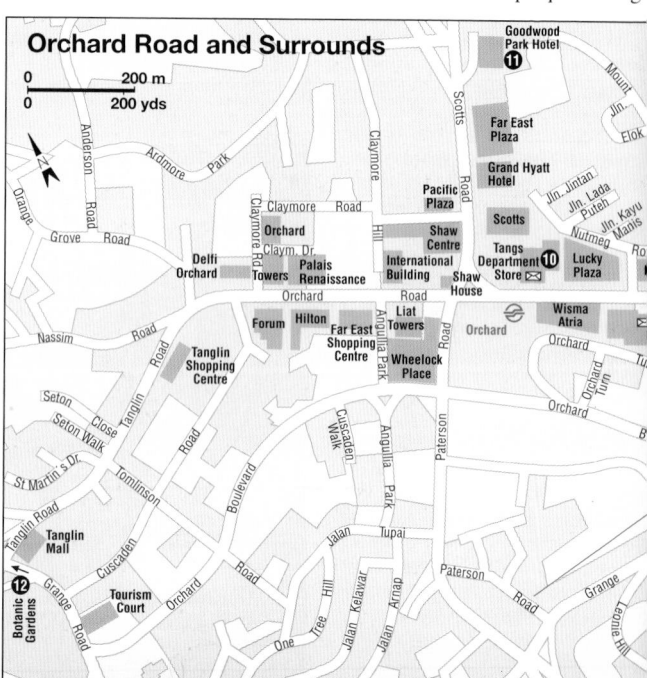

Orchard Road and Surrounds

0 — 200 m
0 — 200 yds

Goodwood Park Hotel ⓫

Far East Plaza

Grand Hyatt Hotel

Pacific Plaza

Shaw Centre

Scotts

Claymore Road

Orchard

Delfi Orchard

Claym. Dr.

Palais Renaissance

International Building

Tangs Department Store ⓾

Lucky Plaza

Orchard Road

Shaw House

Wisma Atria

Forum

Hilton

Far East Shopping Centre

Liat Towers

Orchard

Tanglin Shopping Centre

Wheelock Place

Orchard

Orchard Turn

Tanglin Mall

Tourism Court

Botanic Gardens ⓬

of its fascinating history. Rather unceremoniously called the **Chicago Graduate School of Business ❹**, this was the former **House of Tan Yeok Nee** – a name more befitting of its origins. Teochew cloth peddler turned wealthy gambier and pepper merchant, Tan Yeok Nee built his elegant Chinese-style house in 1885. Over the years, the mansion has variously served as the residence of a station master and a bishop, as a boarding school for girls, accommodation for officers of the Japanese Army during World War II and as the headquarters of the Salvation Army.

The house is a rare example of a typical Chinese southern-style courtyard house, with a grand entrance and sloping roofs with spiral ornamentation. The national monument, after undergoing extensive restoration work, was taken over by the school in 2000. It is not open to visitors but you could pretend to be an interested student and wander in!

Church of Sacred Heart

Further up Clemenceau Avenue on the right is **Tank Road** where three institutions stand in testimony of Singapore's polyglot character. First is the **Church of the Sacred Heart ❺**, one of the oldest Roman Catholic churches in Singapore (daily 7am–7pm; tel: 6737 9285). Founded in 1910 by a French Priest, the whitewashed building, beautifully lit at night, is built in the French Baroque style. Just next door is the four-storey **Teochew Building**, which has a green-tiled Chinese roof and a design that is likened to the *gong dian*, or imperial courts, of China. It is the headquarters for the Teochew-speaking Chinese clan in Singapore.

Chettiar Temple

Further down the road is the **Sri Thandayuthapani Temple ❻**, better known locally to most Hindus as the Chettiar Temple (6am–noon, 5–9pm; tel: 6737 9393). The temple,

The "gopuram" (or tower) that leads into the Sri Thandayuthapani Temple at Tank Road.

Map on pages 122–23

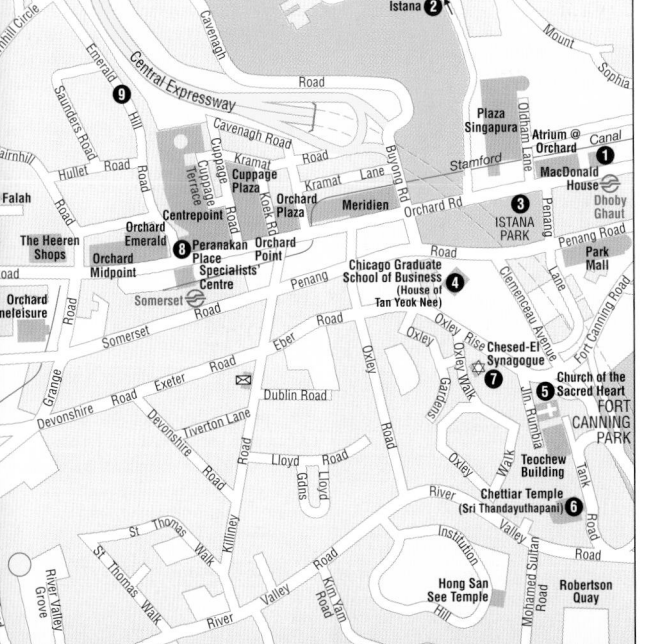

TIP

All of Singapore (and the region) comes out to shop during the Great Singapore Sale from end May to early July. It even has its own dedicated website: www.greatsingaporesale.com.sg

BELOW:
Emerald Hill's ornamental Chinese Baroque houses.

built in 1859, by the Chettiars, an Indian caste of moneylenders, is one of the Hindu community's most important monuments. Take a good look at the 48 glass panels on the roof, designed to capture the rays of the rising and setting of the sun. It is also here, during the annual Thaipusam festival, that hundreds of pilgrims, their bodies pierced by hooks, spears and spiked steel structures called *kavadi*, end their walk from the Sri Srinivasa Perumal Temple *(see page 140)* on Serangoon Road.

Chesed-El Synagogue

Just off Tank Road on Oxley Rise is the grandiose looking **Chesed-El Synagogue** ❼, the second synagogue to be built in Singapore *(see page 146)*. It dates back to 1905 and was funded by Manasseh Meyer, a prominent Jewish businessman (open only Monday service 7.30am; tel: 6732 8862). The Jewish population in Singapore today only numbers a few hundred, having shrunk from a high of 2,500 in the 1930s. At one time, it is said they owned half of the rental property on the island.

Le Meridien to Centrepoint

Back on Orchard Road, a block from the Istana is Le Meridien Hotel, with the **Le Meridien Shopping Centre** on its lower levels. The **Good Treat Foodcourt**, an air-conditioned food centre with mainly Thai food stalls, is worth stopping for a bite.

Past the nondescript **Orchard Plaza**, filled with equally tired looking shops, is **Orchard Point** with department store **OG** as the anchor tenant. Of more interest is the **Hemispheres** store on level three, which showcases the work of rising local fashion designers. Just next door is a pedestrian walkway called **H2O Zone** with restaurants and outdoor dining. Flanking it are **Cuppage Terrace**, with restored shophouses turned into bars and restaurants, and **Cuppage Plaza**.

Further along is **Centrepoint**, home to **Robinson's**, a large department store with history dating back to the 1850s. When its owners tried to sell the store in 2003, infuriated shoppers petitioned against its sale – such is the loyalty the store engenders among shoppers. The sale fell through in the end, much to the relief of older Singaporeans. Robinson's has some of the nicest sales staff in Singapore, and its eagerly awaited biannual sales are a big attraction.

Peranakan Place

Next door is charming **Peranakan Place** ❽ a complex of ornate Peranakan-style shophouses that have been transformed into a commercial hub. At its terrace café, patrons can sip iced lemon tea beneath swaying palm trees. More bar and café options abound in the adjoining shophouses. This area was once settled by the Peranakan people, or Straits-born Chinese, a unique culture that evolved through intermarriage between Chinese migrants and local Malay women in the 17th century *(see page 37)*.

Emerald Hill

Take time to explore the lovely old restored terrace houses further up the slope on **Emerald Hill** ❾. Once belonging to wealthy Peranakan families, the 30 or so homes on the slightly curved road were built between 1901 and 1925 in the so-called Chinese Baroque style *(see pages 148–49)*, typified by ornamental mouldings, shuttered wooden windows, pastel colours and colourful ceramic tiles. These houses were also the first to be given conservation status in 1981, which meant the owners could not alter their facades.

Look out for the four terrace houses numbering 39 to 45 with forecourts and gates topped with an ornate Chinese roof. No. 45, designed by M.T. Moh in 1903, is particularly outstanding – it features a Chinese grand entrance that was carefully restored by Chinese craftsmen. Keep an eye out, too, for the richly carved door of No. 127.

Megamalls galore

Across from Peranakan Place is **Specialists' Shopping Centre**, so

called because it is the hub of medical specialists. Its **John Little** department store is the budget-priced offshoot of Robinson's. After Peranakan Place are tiny malls almost back to back like **Orchard Emerald** and **Midpoint Orchard**.

Cross Cairnhill Road to **The Heeren Shops**, where the crowd is noticeably younger. Not surprisingly, Singapore's largest music store **HMV** has found a loyal following here and **The Annex**, on levels four and five, is a haven of funky street fashion – if you can tolerate the pounding techno. The outdoor **Spinelli's** cafe is perpetually filled with teenagers nursing their iced lattes.

On the opposite side, at the corner of Orchard and Grange roads, is **Orchard Cineleisure**, a complex of cinema halls, entertainment arcades and eateries, just behind the Meritus Mandarin Hotel.

Further along the same side of the road is the massive brown granite facade of **Ngee Ann City** with its twin towers. One of Southeast Asia's largest shopping malls, it has the Japanese **Takashimaya** department

Map on pages 122–23

Stores along Orchard Road try and out do one another with innovative window displays.

LEFT: Orchard Road poseurs.
BELOW: outside Ngee Ann City.

Detail from the Orchard Road MRT station's mosaic wall mural.

store and boutiques selling designer labels. The Louis Vuitton and Tiffany flagship stores are here as well as a Harrods store from London and half a dozen excellent restaurants on its upper floors. Singapore's largest bookstore, **Kinokuniya**, with 12,000 sq m (40,000 sq ft) of space, is found on the 3rd floor.

Beside it and linked to it by an underground tunnel is **Wisma Atria**, which houses the Japanese department store **Isetan**, as well as dozens of boutiques selling designer clothes and jewellery, restaurants, fast-food outlets and a terrace café.

Opposite Ngee Ann City is **The Paragon**, a swanky mall noted for hip designer boutiques like Miu Miu, Gucci, Escada and Bruno Magli, and its basement gourmet supermarket, the **Paragon Market Place**. There are also expensive furniture shops and the homegrown department store **Metro**.

In contast across Mt Elizabeth Road is the dowdy **Lucky Plaza**, a complex of shops offering cameras, watches, luggage and cheap hair accessories. One of the earliest shopping centres, Lucky Plaza has lost much of its former glitter. It is also the favourite Sunday hangout for hundreds of Filipino domestic workers on their day off from work.

Tangs

Adjacent to it is **Tangs Department Store** ❿, below the high-rise pagoda-roofed Marriott Hotel, at the corner of Scotts and Orchard roads. The store was founded by C.K. Tang, a Chinese Teochew who made his fortune in the early 1900s by cycling from house to house selling China-made lace to English families. Tang built his first store in 1932 at nearby River Valley Road, offering Oriental treasures and household goods. In 1958, Tang bought the land on which his store now sits for a song. The presence of a Chinese cemetery opposite his store didn't faze him even though his friends warned him about the bad *feng shui*.

His gamble paid off. Business outgrew the old building and the new store, which kept the ornate roof styled after the Beijing's Imperial Palace, is a well-loved Orchard Road icon. The five-storey store sells clothes, swimwear, shoes, jewellery, watches and electronics. It is particularly noted for its collection of cult skincare labels on level one and useful kitchen gadgets in the basement.

Scotts Road

On the other side of the street, at the corner with Scotts Road, is **Shaw House** – home to a branch of the Japanese-run **Isetan** department store. There are plenty of places to eat in this massive shopping complex, which also houses the **Lido Cineplex**. Next door is **Pacific Plaza**, with stores that cater largely to teens, including a huge Adidas shop and a stylish That CD store, the local equivalent of HMV.

Past the Royal Plaza Hotel is the striking red building called **DFS**

Galleria. This four-level temple to consumerism stocks an amazing variety of goods, from high-end clothing and shoes to a gourmet shop selling fine wines. Even if such things don't appeal, have a look at its ground level anyway – the kitschy interior combines elements of Chinese, Indian and Malay decor.

On the other side of the street is **Scotts Shopping Centre** with its numerous designer outlets, and next door to it the marble and glass **Grand Hyatt** hotel. The entrance to the hotel is set at an angle that is supposed to usher in good luck and prosperity, according to *feng shui*, or Chinese geomancy, experts *(see pages 118–19)*. The grand staircase in the lobby has 32 steps – a number when spoken in Cantonese sounds like the phrase for "life is easy". Pop into the hotel to soak in its luxurious surroundings, or have a cocktail at its stylish **Mezza9** restaurant.

Next door is **Far East Plaza**, a bit tatty around the edges but still popular. Its basement level shops, complete with artificial graffiti-painted walls, are filled with teen-friendly stores while upstairs are a handful of tattoo and body piercing shops.

Perched at the top of a gentle rise is the castle-like **Goodwood Park Hotel** ⑪, built in 1900 as the Teutonia Club for German residents in Singapore. Designed by R.A.J. Bidwell, the hotel has had a long and interesting history: during World War II, the Japanese used the building as a military headquarters, and, in 1945, the British turned its premises into a war crime court. Now a luxury hotel, high tea at its **Café L'Espresso** is a delightful affair.

The lower end of Orchard

Back at Orchard Road proper, across from Shaw House is a stunning glass pyramid – **Wheelock Place**, a complex of offices and restaurants designed by Japanese architect Kisho Kurokawa. **Marks and Spencer** is located in the basement and the American bookstore chain **Borders** fills the entire ground floor.

Next door is **Liat Towers**, mostly noted for its Hermes and Spanish-label Zara stores. Starbucks on the ground level is always abuzz with

Map on pages 122–23

TIP

Art lovers should check out The Art Gallery at The Paragon, which has 11 art galleries and a large display hall featuring regular art exhibitions.

BELOW: Wheelock Place – a glittering shopping palace.

Map
on pages
122–23

TIP

Explore the Botanic Gardens in the cool early morning air and watch out for its bird and animal life. Then join in the daily *tai chi* class (7am–8am), followed by breakfast amid tropical greenery at the Café Les Amis.

BELOW:
Botanic Gardens is a leafy retreat near Orchard Road.

people. Give tired Far East Shopping Centre a miss and head for the **Hilton Hotel** next door where its shopping gallery is another designer label haven for clothing and jewellery.

Across the road is the pretentious sounding **Palais Renaissance**, where local *tai tai* (bored rich housewives with money to burn) shop for designers' labels like Vera Wang, Prada, Versace and DKNY. Just next door is **Orchard Towers** with shops selling jewellery, silk and antiques followed by **Delfi Orchard**, with mainly beauty salons and bridal boutiques. Opposite is **Forum The Shopping Mall**, with an outlet of the international toy store Toys R Us as well as other children-friendly-stores.

Tanglin Road

Tanglin Road marks the end of Orchard Road, but the dividing line has blurred somewhat and Tanglin is often treated as an extension of Orchard Road. Just past Orchard Parade Hotel is **Tanglin Shopping Centre**, a great place to rummage for antiques and arts and crafts at stores like Renee Hoy Fine Arts and

Antiques of the Orient. At the end of Tanglin Road is **Tanglin Mall**, which has an excellent supermarket, sports music and clothing shops, as well as a food court and several restaurants.

Botanic Gardens

Slowly wind down at the **Botanic Gardens** ⑫ (daily 5am–midnight; free; www.sbg.org.sg), a short distance from Tanglin Mall, past the Gleneagles Hospital. Singapore's oldest national park was set up in 1859 and is known worldwide today as a living museum of tropical plants, with over 2,000 species of trees and shrub, and a centre for botanical research. Spacious and beautifully landscaped, with walkways winding around the expansive greenery, the gardens cover a sprawling 53 hectares (130 acres). It is the second patch of primary forest left in Singapore – Bukit Timah Nature Reserve *(see page 191)* is the other. It was at Botanic Gardens that Henry Ridley, its first director (1888–1912), developed the method of tapping the rubber tree.

The gardens can be explored in three sections. The main **Tanglin Core** features lush rainforest, Swan Lake, an 1860s bandstand and bronze sculptures by the British sculptor Sydney Harpley. The **Central Core** has the **National Orchid Garden** (daily 8.30am–7pm; admission charge) – where over 700 species of orchids are displayed *(see pages 132–33)* – and also **Palm Valley**, where there are regular open-air musical concerts and performances. The **Bukit Timah Core** features the Ecolake and gardens of herbs, spices and medicinal plants. The bird life of the gardens is surprisingly wide-ranging for an area of its size while squirrels and the green crested lizard may be spotted. There is also a **Visitor's Centre** (tel: 6471 7361) and souvenir shop, in addition to open-air **Café Les Amis**, and two restaurants. ❑

RESTAURANTS

Restaurants

American

Blu
24/F, Shangri-La Hotel, 22 Orange Grove Rd. Tel: 6730 2598. Open: D daily. $$$$ (set dinner) $$$$ (à la carte)
www.shangri-la.com
Why Blu still draws regulars all these years: fine Californian cuisine by chef Peter Schintler (who hails from Manhattan's Le Cirque and UK's Le Manoir Aux Quat Saisons), stunning city views, live jazz, snazzy touches such as the Philippe Starck lamps, Danny Lane's glass art, and definitely the cheongsam-clad all-female bartenders.

California Pizza Kitchen
01-42 Forum The Shopping Mall, 583 Orchard Rd. Tel: 6836 0110. Open: daily, 11.30am– 11pm. $$$
Trust this Beverly Hills import to come up with innovative salads, pasta and pizzas. Peking duck and Thai chicken are turned into toppings for the flavourful pizza crusts. The East-West dishes work well, especially Kung Pao spaghetti and Thai linguine.

DKNY Café
01-03 Palais Renaissance, 390 Orchard Rd. Tel: 6733 4226. Open: Mon–Sat 10.30am–7pm, Sun 11am–5.30pm. $$
Located within DKNY boutique, the fashionable New York-style deli is the place to see and be seen, park tired Blahnik-clad feet, rest shopping bags and bite into DKNY Club or hot pastrami sandwiches, smoked salmon bagels, Rocky Road fudge and a marbled orange blondie.

Hard Rock Café
02-01 HPL House, 50 Cuscaden Rd. Tel: 6235 5232. Open: Tues–Thur 11–2am, Fri– Sun 11–3am. $ (set lunch) $$$ (à la carte)
www.hardrock.com.sg
It's the same hard rocking formula that's amazingly still relevant today: American-sized portions, fun staff and a live band that brings the house down daily. The incredible set lunch deal is recession-proof but if you're feeling carnivorous, the oversized fajitas and burgers are always good bets. Don't forget the sinful brownie.

Tony Roma's
01-04/05 Orchard Hotel Shopping Arcade, 442 Orchard Rd. Tel: 6738 8600. Open: daily, 11.30am–11pm. $$$
www.tonyromas-mms.com
Pardon them when they unabashedly proclaim they serve the world's best ribs. You can't beat this American rib chain for tender fall-off-the-bone baby back ribs. Vegetarians do not despair; the Onion Loaf, Thai Peanut Salad and Sante Fe Salad are all excellent options.

Chinese

Crystal Jade Palace
04-19 Ngee Ann City, 391 Orchard Rd. Tel: 6735 2388. Open: L and D daily. $$ (set lunch) $$$ (à la carte)
Crisp, contemporary decor – apart from the kitschy etched glass windows. Excellent roast meat and "live" seafood such as the delicious baked prawns. Also runs **Hu Cui** (tel: 6238 1011), **Crystal Jade La Mian Xiao Long Bao** (tel: 6238 1661) and **Crystal Jade Kitchen** (tel: 6238 1411) in the same building.

Din Tai Fung
B1-03/06 Paragon, 290 Orchard Rd. Tel: 6836 8336. Open: Mon–Fri 11am–10pm, Sat–Sun 10am–10pm. $$
You notice the flurry of activity at the open concept kitchen before you realise diners are watching the chefs in action *and* lining up for their *xiao long bao*, or steamed pork dumpling that has exactly 18 pleats. Fans sing praises of the chicken soup and humble fried rice, too. No wonder *New York Times* ranked it one of the world's top 10 restaurants.

House of Mao Hunan Hot Pot
01-09/10 Orchard Hotel Shopping Arcade, 442 Orchard Rd. Tel: 6733 7667. Open: L and D daily. $$ (buffet only)
www.tunglok.com
A Mao-themed restaurant may be politically incorrect but diners lap up the Hunan-style hot pot, premium meat cuts, vegetables and accompanying piquant sauces. Select from the three types of soup – chicken, spicy Hunan or the restaurant's soup of the day. Unlimited helpings of *dim sum* are included in the feast.

French

Au Jardin
EJH Corner House, Singapore Botanic Gardens, 1 Cluny Rd. Tel: 6466 8812. Open: D daily, Br Sun. $$$$ (set dinner) $$$$ (à la carte)
www.lesamis.com.sg
"Au Jardin", meaning "in the garden" in French is appropriately set in a restored 1920s bungalow in the Botanic Gardens. At this highly acclaimed

PRICE CATEGORIES

Prices for a three-course dinner per person without drinks and taxes:
$ = under S$20
$$= S$20–$30
$$$ = S$30–$45
$$$$ = more than S$45

(and very expensive) restaurant, contemporary French flavours are as peerless as they should be. Choose from the lavish six-course *Menu Dégustation*, eight-course *Menu Gastronomique* and if you're adventurous, the 12-course *Menu de Renaissance*.

Les Amis
02-16 Shaw Centre, 1 Scotts Rd. Tel: 6733 2225. Open: L and D Mon–Sat. $$$$ (set lunch) $$$$ (à la carte)
www.lesamis.com.sg
Boasting one of the world's best wine lists, this chi chi restaurant understandably draws well-heeled regulars who appreciate French cuisine that's both delicate and flavourful. Resident chef Gunther Hubrechsen, ex-sous chef of the 3 Michelin-star L'Arpege in Paris helms the kitchen and woos with his carpaccio of scallops with fresh black truffles and braised veal cheeks.

Top of the M
39/F, Meritus Mandarin, 333 Orchard Rd. Tel: 6831 6258. Open: L Mon–Fri, D daily. $$$ (semi-buffet lunch) $$$$ (à la carte)
www.mandarin-singapore.com
At 173 metres above bustling Orchard Road, the city's first and tallest revolving restaurant is an old stalwart in the dining scene. The highlight is of course the ever-changing skyline. But accolades should go to the impeccable

service, exquisite French cuisine with an Italian twist, and fine wines.

Indonesian
Rendezvous
02-02/03 Hotel Rendezvous, 9 Bras Basah Rd. Tel: 6339 7508. Open: daily 11.30am–9.30pm. $$
Its history stretches six decades and the old steamy coffee shop is now a comfortable air-conditioned restaurant in Hotel Rendezvous. Still enduring are its fiery *nasi padang* favourites including their spicy thick curries and *sambal* seafood dishes. This would probably be your most expensive *nasi padang* meal in the Lion City but it's worth every single cent.

The Rice Table
02-09 International Bldg, 360 Orchard Rd. Tel: 6835 3783. Open L and D daily. Also at 43/45 Cuppage Rd. Tel: 6735 9117. $ (only buffet available)
For one price, you order as much Indonesian dishes your stomach can tolerate. Try the *tahu telor*, a tower of beancurd with shredded cucumber and sweet sauce, the tender spicy beef *rendang* and grilled chicken. Don't be shy to raise your hands for seconds.

Italian
Gusto Ristoranti Italiano
02-02/03 Wisma Atria, 435 Orchard Rd. Tel: 6341 9912. Open: daily,

noon–10pm. $ (set lunch) $$$ (à la carte)
Who would have thought quality Italian cuisine in a swish-looking space in the heart of Orchard Road could sport such down-to-earth prices? The best thing is, *everything* is delightful. The calamari is addictive, the lobster spaghetti is a treat that won't break the bank and chef Nino Gandolfi crafts one of the best gnocchis in town.

International
Baker's Inn
02-09 Paragon, 290 Orchard Rd. Tel: 6333 6647. Open: daily 10am–11pm. Also at: 01-17 The Atrium @ Orchard, 60B Orchard Rd. Tel: 6336 6006. $$$
www.bakersinn.com.sg
Singapore's most famous dessert place sports Laura Ashley-esque pink floral fabric on the wall and a dessert showcase unit that's designed like a jewellery box – dainty little cakes sit in there, waiting to be picked. Their soufflés are divine.

Blood Café
02-03 Paragon, 290 Orchard Rd. Tel: 6735 6765. Open: daily, 10.30am–9.30pm. $$
Tucked behind project-shopBLOODbros boutique, this trendy and perennially busy gay-friendly café has inspired East-West dishes, comfort food from all over the world and glorious desserts. You can't go

wrong with the daily specials on the chalkboard – try the blood caesar, cold tofu salad, and banana and mango crumble. Bugbear? – no reservations taken.

Crossroads Café
Marriott Hotel, 320 Orchard Rd. Tel: 6831 4605. Open: Sun–Wed 7–1am, Thur–Sat 7–3am. $$$
www.singaporemarriott.com
Whether nursing a juice or tucking into the platter of Thai-style spring rolls, *samosas* and chicken *satay*, this ever-bustling sidewalk café is the best place to watch Orchard Road pass by.

Halia
Ginger Garden, Singapore Botanic Gardens, 1 Cluny Rd. Tel: 6476 6711. Open: L and D daily, B Sat–Sun. $$ (set lunch) $$$ (à la carte)
To get to Halia (ginger in Malay) you navigate past a ginger garden to find the restaurant nestled amid lush tropical foliage. It's so tranquil you forget the city is just metres away. Lunch is a lighter menu of sandwiches and local favourites. Come dusk, a sublime Continental menu sees some ginger-inspired dishes.

Indochine Wisma Atria
1/F, 435 Orchard Rd. Tel: 6333 5003. Open: daily, 11–4am. $–$$$ (set lunch), $$–$$$$ (à la carte)
www.indochine.com.sg
A five-in-one dining-and-clubbing complex.

There's **PhoChine** for Indochinese cuisine, **The Sanctuary** for cold beer and **Oysta Bar** for champagne and oysters (what else?). The centre of attraction is the 18-metre long aquarium next to **Aquadisiac Club** and the chic East-West restaurant **Nude**.

mezza9

Grand Hyatt, 10-12 Scotts Rd. Tel: 6730 7189. Open: Mon–Sat noon–11pm, Sun 11.30am–11pm. $$ (set lunch) $$$$ (à la carte) The oh-so-chic Takashi Sugimoto-designed restaurant features show kitchens for *sushi*, *yakitori*, seafood, Western and Chinese dishes as well as deli and dessert counters, walk-in wine cellar and a martini bar. It's so cleverly designed you can sit anywhere, order from the various show kitchens, and still watch the chefs in action.

TeaSpa

05-43 Paragon, 290 Orchard Rd. Tel: 6333 8646. Open: Sun–Thur noon–9pm, Fri–Sat noon–10pm. $$ (set lunch) $$$ (à la carte) www.teaspa.com.sg This low-key place has over 80 varieties of tea blends for every ailment – migraine, stress and even PMS – and there are teas to heal, detox and boost your immunity. In addition, the small but thoughtful East-West menu and restful ambience make Tea-Spa a fine place to soothe frazzled nerves.

Japanese

Akashi

B1-9/10/11 Tanglin Shopping Centre, 19 Tanglin Rd. Tel: 6732 4438. Open: L and D daily. Also at: B1-01/02 Paragon, 290 Orchard Rd. Tel: 6735 8887. $$$ They say eat where the locals eat. It's a good sign that Akashi is well patronised by the expat Japanese community. The constant buzz, efficient and no-nonsense waitresses, the food, especially the reverse California roll, *ebi miso yaki* (grilled *miso* prawns) and smooth *tara inaniwa udon* noodles all keep its regulars returning for more.

Sushi Tei

05-01/04 Paragon, 290 Orchard Rd. Tel: 6235 1771. Open: daily 11.30am–10pm. Also at: 02-13 Ngee Ann City, 391 Orchard Rd. Tel: 6737 8878 and 01-21 Far East Plaza, 14 Scotts Rd. Tel: 6733 0111. $$ www.sushitei.com The Sushi Tei chain has perfected the art of serving fresh *sushi* and *sashimi* on a conveyor belt. Their hot food items such as salmon belly soup are always delicious, and there's fresh-from-the-tank lobster *sashimi* if you're feeling indulgent. *Sushi* fans will love the innovative creations such as the Dragon Roll, a King prawn and avocado *sushi* shaped like a dragon.

Local

Newton Circus

Bukit Timah Rd. (near Newton MRT) Open: L till late daily. $$ Best visited at night. Ignore the touts, make sure prices are posted prominently and you've one of Singapore's best local food experiences. Good bets include seafood (stalls 8 and 52), Hainanese chicken rice (stall 17), grilled chicken wings (stall 43), fishball noodles (stall 64), fried carrot cake (stall 13) and local spring rolls (stall 68).

Prima Taste

01-63/64 Centrepoint, 176 Orchard Rd. Tel: 6887 3786. Open: daily 11am–10pm. $ www.pfs.com.sg When a restaurant calls itself a "True Singapore restaurant", it usually spells tourist trap. Luckily Prima Taste isn't one of those. The tiny air-conditioned café is a hot lunch spot and sees locals happily tucking into Hainanese chicken rice and prawn noodles.

Scotts Picnic Foodcourt

Basement, Scotts Shopping Centre, 6 Scotts Rd. Open: daily 10.30am–10pm. $ Singapore's first air-conditioned foodcourt is still among the best. Korean delicacies, Indian *naan* breads, Hainanese beef noodles and Italian pastas are among the 17 stalls selling affordably-priced international cuisine.

Takashimaya Food Village

Basement Two, Takashimaya, 391A Orchard Rd. Open: daily 10am–9.30pm. $ Food lovers are spoiled for choice. Nibble your way through 50 stalls peddling Indonesian cakes, Thai fried rice, Vietnamese spring rolls, English fish and chips, Japanese *ramen* and cream puffs – it's truly a United Nations of cuisines. It's impossible to find a seat at meal-times, so arrive very early or late for a table.

Peranakan

House of Peranakan Cuisine

Meritus Negara, 10 Claymore Rd. Tel: 6733 4411. Open: L and D daily. $$ *Asian Wall Street Journal* has hailed its fish head curry as the best dish in Singapore. That's because one of Singapore's best Peranakan restaurants has recipes that are three generations old. Must-tries: Nonya flowercrab, braised duck, stewed pork and *ayam buah keluak* (stewed chicken with Indonesian black nuts).

PRICE CATEGORIES

Prices for a three-course dinner per person without drinks and taxes:
$ = under S$20
$$= S$20–$30
$$$ = S$30–$45
$$$$ = more than S$45

ORCHIDS IN A GARDEN CITY

Singapore helped the orchid industry bloom and commercial producers in Southeast Asia now export millions of dollars' worth of flowers each year

Singapore owes its success in orchid growing to a tropical climate and the pioneering orchid hybridisation work of the Botanic Gardens *(see page 128)*. The seeds of Singapore's orchid industry were sown in 1893 when Agnes Joaquim showed Henry Ridley, the gardens' first director, a mauve orchid bloom in her garden. It was a new natural orchid hybrid – a cross of *Vanda hookeriana* and *Vanda teres*. The Botanic Gardens began producing the hybrid, the *Vanda* Miss Joaquim *(above)* and distributed it to growers in Singapore and Malaya.

It was under Eric Holttum, the garden's director (1925–49), that the orchid industry bloomed. The popularity of *Vanda* Miss Joaquim convinced him that orchids of similar quality could be produced by hybridising. In 1928, he set up a laboratory and experimented with the asymbiotic method of culture, which involved germinating orchid seedlings from a single pod. The first *Spagthoglottis* hybrids flowered in 1931, and soon, other orchid hybrids were produced, starting a thriving cut-flower industry.

Today, the Botanic Gardens has a sprawling National Orchid Garden with over 1,000 species of orchids and 2,000 hybrids bred over the last 70 years. It frequently produces orchid hybrids named after VIPs on state visits; in the garden's Burkill Hall visitors can gaze at *Dendrobium* Margaret Thatcher or *Dendrobium* Benazir Bhutto.

RIGHT: attempts to promote a national dress using the orchid as a motif have failed to catch the public's imagination. Various design contests have been held in previous years, resulting in outfits that combine ethnic Chinese, Malay and Indian dress with orchid motifs. The results have been a *couture* nightmare in most cases. These days, the only people who wear clothing with orchid motifs are politicians keen on promoting a national identity, and tour guides – like the one pictured here.

LEFT: a wax figure of Agnes Joaquim, an Armenian resident in Singapore who discovered the orchid hybrid named after her. Agnes' life story is recounted at Sentosa's Images of Singapore exhibit *(see page 155)*. Agnes was a keen gardener who particularly excelled at cultivating orchids. Her hybrid the *Vanda* Miss Joaquim won the 1899 Flower Show in Singapore, but, sadly, she died three months later of cancer. In 1981, the hybrid was recognised as Singapore's national flower.

ABOVE: *dendrobium* hybrids are the most common type of orchids, with well over 1,000 species. It produces pretty flowers that are diverse in colour and form. *Vandaceous* hybrids are the second most common hybrids, mainly used for breeding: they are showy plants and are frequently used in landscaping and in the cut-flower trade. Most of the hybridisation work that the National Orchid Garden undertakes involve these two main groups of orchids. Pictured here is the vandaceous hybrid *Aranda* Noorah Alsagoff.

ABOVE: many newly created hybrids are named after special state visitors, like this one called *Dendrobium* Benazir Bhutto. The first VIP orchid was named *Aranthera* Anne Black in 1956, after Lady Black, wife of the former governor of Singapore, Sir Robert Black. Other VIP orchids include *Dendrobium* Margaret Thatcher, *Dendrobium* Memoria Princess Diana and *Vandaenopsis* Nelson Mandela.

TEST TUBE ORCHIDS

The National Orchid Garden's well-regarded hybridisation programme takes place in the temperature-controlled Tissue Culture Laboratory. The key to successful hybridisation is in creating sterile conditions for the seedlings to grow. A single pod placed in a flask germinates more effectively than what nature can achieve, resulting in several healthy seedlings. A pod yields about 20 orchid plantlets in each flask. When the tiny plants are over 3 cm (1¼ inches) in height and have developed roots, they are ready to be transferred from the flask to the pot. Amateur horticulturists can buy these flasks and bring them home to grow their very own orchids. Detailed instructions are given with each purchase.

Another major centre for orchid cultivation in Singapore is the Mandai Orchid Gardens *(see page 194)* in the north of Singapore. An amazing variety of blooms are grown here, both for the local market as well as for export. Visitors frequently buy a box of orchid sprays to bring home; with proper care, the blooms will last for several weeks.

LEFT: the National Orchid Gardens, located in the Central Core of the Botanic Gardens, offer orchid seedlings for sale to budding gardeners. These tiny plants are nurtured in convenient ready-to-take-home flasks like this. Obviously you need to make sure that the climate back home is conducive for the cultivation of orchids – there is no sense in taking them home to a cold winter!

LITTLE INDIA AND KAMPUNG GLAM

To experience the sensory impact of the subcontinent,
take a stroll along Little India's Serangoon Road,
then step south into a slightly different world,
that of the Malay enclave of Kampung Glam

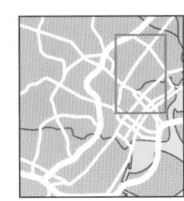

Most Asian cities grew in ramshackle fashion, but Singapore was planned from the very start. Raffles, on his second visit to the island in 1822, sketched a masterplan for his trading entrepot that divided urban Singapore into various ethnic districts.

Little India was a later addition, a suburb that grew up around a camp for Indian convict workers. It was never intended to be an enclave for Indian migrants who had Kampung Chulia (an area now marked by Chulia and Market streets in the CBD) designated to them by Raffles. But the abundant grass and water that had made the Serangoon area an attractive place for cattle-breeding attracted both Indian proprietors and labourers in the 1840s. Some of the cattle owners even brought labourers from their hometowns in India to work for them. One of them was I.R. Belilios, a Venetian Jew from Calcutta who brought nearly all his Bengali staff with him.

Cattle trading soon took off. The animals were also used for driving machines and for transportation, which in turn spawned a spectrum of economic activities such as wheat grinding, and pulled in even more Indians to the area. Retail and commercial activities developed to cater to the burgeoning population's needs, and by the turn of the 20th century, the area began to take on the character of an Indian neighbourhood.

Little India today

Step into **Serangoon Road** – the main road that runs into the heart of Little India – today and the same ambience still persists. Indeed, the visitor is plunged into the subcontinent, with undulating music punctuated by car horns and bicycle bells, women in vivid saris and the pungent nose-tickling aroma of spices.

Map
on page
136

LEFT: Little India fabric vendor.
BELOW: religious posters for sale along Serangoon Road.

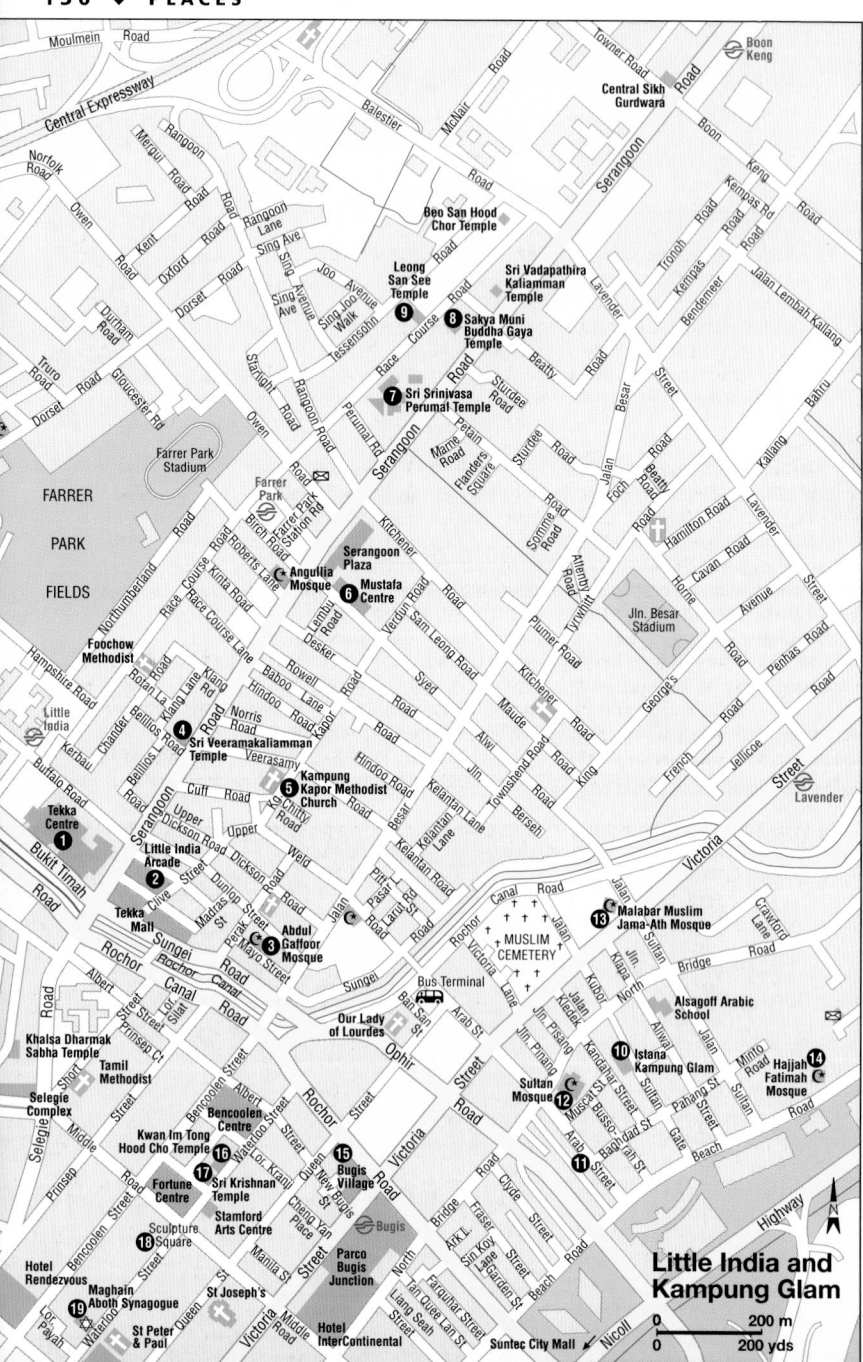

Little India and Kampung Glam

0 ———————— 200 m
0 ———————— 200 yds

The sights, sounds and smells of India are unmistakable. At street corner stalls, jasmine flowers perfume the air as they are deftly strung into garlands for use in Hindu temples in the neighbourhood. In restaurants, people eat curried rice off banana leaves with their fingers, and you may chance upon the *roti prata* man, twirling lumps of dough into the air in ever increasing circles and then pan frying them on a hot griddle. Dunked in curry, it makes for a delicious breakfast.

Tekka Centre

Just at the corner of Serangoon Road and Bukit Timah Road lies **Tekka Centre ❶**. Tekka means "bamboo shoot" in Teochew, and the name was adopted as a profusion of bamboo once grew here in the past. Stalls selling Malay, Chinese and Indian food draw sizeable crowds for breakfast. Tekka also has a "wet market" with an amazing array of fresh produce, offering herbs such as fresh dill and sweet basil, and vegetables seldom found elsewhere. Upstairs are clothing, brassware and antiques shops.

The market once occupied a sprawling site on Serangoon Road and was known as Kandang Kerbau ("cattle pen" in Malay) Market, after the cattle station that marked the site. In fact Tekka Centre is sometimes referred to by this old name.

Modernisation today encroaches on this largely low-rise ethnic quarter with new (and often ugly) structures like the six-storey shopping complex, **Tekka Mall** opposite Tekka Centre. Opened in 2003, it houses a hypermarket, food court, fast food outlets and shops.

Little India Arcade

Opposite is **Little India Arcade ❷** flanked by Hasting Road and Campbell Lane. Located in a restored art deco-style shophouse built in 1913, the arcade houses a food court with stalls offering South and North Indian dishes. Souvenir stalls abound in an open courtyard selling incense sticks, ayurvedic herbal oils and handicrafts from India. Savoury snacks such as fried lentils and *muruku* savouries are also sold at counters at the arcade's Serangoon Road entrance.

For S$3, you can have your fortune told by a green parakeet – with the help of its able-bodied human assistant of course.

LEFT: twirling *roti prata* – a delicious breakfast treat.
BELOW: fragrant flowers to adorn the hair.

Little India is a vegetarian's fantasy come true – there are heaps of shops doling out "thosai", a rice-flour based pancake eaten with a selection of vegetable curries. Komala Vilas and Ananda Bhavan, at No. 76 and No. 58 Serangoon Road, respectively, are particular favourites.

BELOW: a henna tatooist at work.

Around Serangoon Road

Serangoon Road and the side streets that lead off it, like Campbell Lane, Dunlop Street, Clive Street and Upper Dickson Road, are lined with brightly lit shops spilling over with spices, fabrics, brassware and glittering jewellery. Here you can buy homemade yoghurt wrapped in a plastic bag for a dollar on the "five-foot way" (the mandatory five-foot wide corridor that fronts all shop-houses – as decreed by Raffles), maybe see an old man wrapping areca nut, gambier, tobacco and lime in *seray* (betel nut leaf) to be chewed for a narcotic-like effect or a green parakeet choosing tarot cards based on Hindu mythology for S$3 (just outside Komala Vilas Restaurant at 76 Serangoon Road).

In the handful of jewellery shops run by Indian goldsmiths (most are now owned by Chinese), take a closer look at the cabinets in which silver amulets depicting parts of the body such as arms, legs or feet are displayed. Depending on which limb or organ of the body has been inflicted, the Hindus will buy the amulet representing it and present it as an offering in the temple in the hope that the gods will get the message and relieve their pain.

Streets such as Dickson, Dunlop and Clive once led to the private residences of Europeans who settled near the Race Course when it was completed in the 1840s while those like Belilios and Desker reflect the names of its former cattle owners.

Be sure to explore **Campbell Lane**, which bursts into colour at the first light of day with stalls offering floral garlands and jasmine flower bunches which Indian women use as hair adornments. **Jothi Music Corner** (tel: 6292 7173) on this street is popular with local Indians for its selection of VCDs from Bollywood and Bhangra music CDs.

Further on the right, **Dunlop Street** teems with tireless hawkers peddling fruits and vegetables all day. **Royal Saree Palace** at 132 Dunlop Street (tel: 6336 7885) is a good place to shop for exquisite silk saris as is the massive fabric emporium **Haniffa Textiles** at 60 Serangoon Road (tel: 6299 3709).

Indian Beauty Secrets

Thanks to Hollywood celebrities, Indian beauty practices never looked so hip. Whether you're looking for a henna tattoo or Ayurvedic massage, Little India is your one-stop beauty spot – the Indian way, of course. Call at Vanessa Beauty Salon & Henna Artwork Creations for henna body art and henna hair colouring (22 Buffalo Road, tel: 6291 0977). Susiee House of Beauty swears by its secret herbal formula that halts hair loss after a few treatments (32-A Buffalo Road, tel: 6292 6720). Threading is an art and if your therapist does it right, removing facial hair with a thread is painless. Try Rupini's Beauty (24/26 Buffalo Road, tel: 6291 6789).

Abdul Gaffoor Mosque

Little India is famous for not just Hindu temples, but shrines representing the spectrum of faiths practised in Singapore. Tucked away at 41 Dunlop Street is the lovely old **Abdul Gaffoor Mosque ❸** (daily 5.30am–9pm; tel: 6295 4209). Originally built in 1859 and named after a South Indian lawyer's clerk, the Arabian- and Renaissance-style mosque is an oasis of calm.

The prayer hall, decorated with Moorish arches, has a tableau tracing the origins of Islam. Outside prayer times, the mosque is occupied by devotees who drop by to spend time to read the Koran or to chat.

Veeramakaliamman Temple

Return to Serangoon Road, where at No. 141 is **Sri Veeramakaliamman Temple ❹**, dedicated to the multi-armed Goddess Kali, the manifestation of anger in the face of evil (daily 5.30am–12.15pm, 4–9.15pm; tel: 6295 4538). In one of her images, she is shown ripping a hapless victim apart. As consort to Shiva, the goddess is also known as Parvati in her benign form; therefore she is both loved and feared. Dating back to 1881 and built by indentured Bengali labourers, the temple's main shrine has a striking statue of Kali, with her sons – Ganesh, the Elephant God, and Murugan, the Child God – depicted on either side.

Tuesdays and Fridays are considered sacred days and are especially busy with devotees streaming in to pray and ask for blessings.

Kampung Kapor Church

On the opposite side of Serangoon Road, a walk down Veerasamy Road leads to the corner where it connects with Kampung Kapor Road. Here stands a gem of a little church – the **Kampung Kapor Methodist Church ❺** with Dutch-style gabled roofs (call ahead to view; tel: 6293

7997; www.kkmc.org.sg). Formerly known as the Straits Chinese Methodist Church, it was built in 1930 to cater to a largely Peranakan congregation from Melaka. Its history dates back to 1890 when Methodist missionary Sophia Blackmore started the first Malay-language church service in Singapore.

Mustafa Centre

Back on Serangoon Road, a 15-minute stroll past the Moorish-style **Angullia Mosque** on the left takes you to a decidedly secular temple to consumerism. Located on the left along Syed Alwi Road, the sprawling **Mustafa Centre ❻** is a three-storey shopping complex that is hugely popular with bargain hunters (daily 24 hours, tel: 6419 0500). It's also the only department store in Singapore that offers retail therapy round the clock, thanks its far-sighted Indian owner who is dubbed Singapore's Retail Raja.

Tourists and "foreign workers" from India often come here to shop for goods to take home to the sub-continent. There is a mind-boggling

> Map on page 136

BELOW: Goddess Kali image at the Sri Veeramakaliamman Temple.

Little India comes alive in October or November each year (depending on the lunar calendar) for the annual Deepavali light-up. This is one of the best times to visit this area.

BELOW:
blowing his trumpet at the Srinivasa Perumal Temple.

range of goods – from household appliances and luggage to computers, cameras and food items. In fact the store has done so well for itself that it has spawned a café and a small hotel, plus an extension of the mall across Verdun Street.

Srinivasa Perumal Temple

Further along Serangoon Road, the great *gopuram* (tower) of the **Sri Srinivasa Perumal Temple ⑦**, built in 1855, is visible, showing the different incarnations of Vishnu (daily 6.30am–noon, 6–9pm; tel: 6298 5771; www.heb.gov.sg).

The *gopuram* graces the entrance of Hindu temples and consists of an odd number of tiers, the actual configuration depending on the money contributed to build it. Perumal Temple's five-tier *gopuram* was a donation from P. Govindasamy Pillai, one of the earliest Indian migrants who made good. He ultimately set up a chain of popular general goods stores in Little India and was known for his philanthropic works, a legacy continued by his sons today.

Perumal Temple is at the centre of

the Hindu trinity made up of Brahma the Creator, Vishnu the Preserver and Shiva the Destroyer. The temple is dedicated to Krishna, one of the incarnations of Vishnu. Perumal is another name for Krishna and statues of him – coloured blue to signify blue-blood – are everywhere in the temple. There are also statues of his two wives, Lakshmi and Andal, the goddesses of Beauty and Wealth respectively, and of his mount, the mythical Garuda bird. The temple ceiling is dominated by a colourful circular pattern depicting the nine planets of the universe.

The annual Thaipusam procession sets off from here. Devotees, their tongues and cheeks pierced by metal skewers and carrying *kavadi* (cage-like constructions decorated with wire and peacock feathers), make their way to the Sri Thandayuthapani Temple in Tank Road *(see page 123)*.

Petain Road houses

A little further from Perumal Temple, on the opposite side of Serangoon Road, is **Petain Road** which, like many of the nearby roads that were built after World War I, was named after men who had distinguished themselves in World War I battles. Petain Road was named after the Marshal of France, Henri Philippe Petain (1856–1951).

The street was once a swampland filled with vegetable gardens. In 1916, the swamps were drained, the farmers forced out, and the area was converted into a residential neighbourhood. It is here that architecture typical of 1920s can be seen at its best. Called Chinese Baroque or Singapore Eclectic *(see pages 148–49)*, it is a blend of European, Malay, Indian and Chinese influences.

The row of 19 ornate terrace houses share the same characteristics – carved wooden eaves found in Malay houses, Indian-style stucco pillars, classical-inspired columns and pilasters, facades made up largely of colourful Spanish floral tiles and Chinese symbols in the bas-relief plaster work depicting animals and flowers. Look out for the beautifully tiled covered "five-foot" walkway linking the houses.

Sakya Muni Buddha Gaya

Race Course Road may have lost its glamour of a racing track and its horses, but there is a pair of very different Chinese temples worth visiting. At 366 Race Course Road is the the stunning **Sakya Muni Buddha Gaya Temple ❽**. Also known as the Temple of 1,000 Lights, a 15-metre-high (49-ft) Buddha image sits amidst a halo of lightbulbs, on top of a base depicting scenes from the life of Prince Siddharta Gautama (daily 8am–4.45pm; tel: 6294 0714). Worshippers may illuminate the lights around the statue for a small donation or have their fortune told by spinning a wheel on the left of the prayer hall.

The temple began as a wooden shelter in 1927 by Thai monk Vutthisasara. Its immense popularity

saw a grander building being built in the 1930s, with funds from Aw Boon Haw and Aw Boon Par, the brothers behind the Haw Par Villa in Pasir Panjang Road *(see page 164)*. Guarding the entrance of the temple are a pair of ferocious-looking tigers.

Leong San See Temple

The richly carved and ornately decorated **Leong San See Temple ❾** (Dragon Mountain Temple) at 371 Race Course Road just across the street is dedicated to Kuan Yin, the Chinese Goddess of Mercy (daily 6am–6pm; tel: 6298 9371).

The temple, dating back to the late 1800s, bears the image of Confucius at its altar and is popular with many parents who bring their children here to pray for success at examinations and filial piety. Established by Reverend Chuan Wu, what was once a lodge for the sick in 1926 is now an elaborate temple built on funds donated by prominent merchant and philanthropist Tan Boon Liat. Note especially the dragon sculptures on top of its roofs. At the back is a courtyard with old ancestral tablets.

Map on page 136

At Leong San See Temple in Race Course Road, joss sticks are burnt as supplication to the ancestral gods.

BELOW: giant Buddha statue at Sayka Muni Buddha Gaya Temple.

TIP

When in Arab Street, do what Arabs do – try smoking fruit-flavoured tobacco through water, better known as *shisha*. This Middle Eastern tradition can be experienced at Café Le Caire (39 Arab Street, tel: 6292 0979) and the lovely Arabian-themed Samar Café (19 Baghdad Street, tel: 6398 0530).

BELOW:
Arab Street shop spilling over with all manner of baskets.

Kampung Glam

Raffles allocated this area, a neighbouring district of Little India, to Sultan Hussein, the Malay ruler of Singapore who signed two treaties in 1819 and 1824, ceding the island to the British. Here the sultan built a palace for his family and homes for his royal retainers who had followed him from Riau.

Today, the sleepy neighbourhood is landlocked, but in former times it ran along the shore (hence the name Beach Road) with many of the houses built on stilts above the tidal mud flats. Much of Kampung Glam was mangrove swamp when it was drained in the 1820s. The name means "Village of the Glam Tree" in Malay. The bark of these trees (*melaleuca leucadendron*) had medicinal value and was used by the Malays to caulk their ships, although it would be difficult to find a glam tree in the area today.

Istana Kampung Glam

At the very heart of the district, at 73 Sultan Gate, is **Istana Kampung Glam ❿**, the old royal palace, built in the early 1840s by Sultan Ali Iskandar Shah on the site of the original wooden palace constructed by his father, Sultan Hussein. Erected on stilts, the original building was styled after a Malay palace with a verandah on the upper floor. Istana Kampung Glam was said to have been designed by George Coleman, who combined traditional Malay motifs with the Palladian style, though there is no concrete proof that he was its architect.

Freshly restored in 2004, the palace has been converted into a **Malay Heritage Centre** (daily 9am–6pm; museum closed Mon 9am–2pm; free except for museum and cultural shows; tel: 6332 7980; www.malayheritage.org.sg). On the grounds are a museum housing eight galleries of Malay history and culture, an archaeological excavation site where original artefacts were found – 17th-century tin coins bearing evidence of trade between Malays and the Dutch, and umbilical cords of newborns dating back to early 19th century among others – a spice garden and carts selling Malay snacks and crafts. Its adjacent canary yellow two-storey **Gedung Kuning** (Yellow Mansion), built for Tengku Mahmoud, grandson of Sultan Hussein, is now the **Tepak Sireh Restaurant** (*see page 147*).

Arab Street

Arab traders, together with Bugis, Javanese, Boyanese, Banjarese, Sumatrans, Malays and people from the Riau Islands, eventually settled in the area, transforming Kampung Glam into a commercial hub, especially along **Arab Street ⓫**, four blocks away, which still draws those looking for bargains in textiles, lace, basketware and haberdashery.

In Arab Street, you can shop for batik cloth, either in sarong lengths, or fashioned into clothes, table linen and paintings. Baskets of every

shape, size and colour are piled on the pavement. There's leatherware and ethnic jewellery, too, as well as gold and silver, embroidered *songket* fabric and alcohol-free perfumes. Try **Rishi Handicrafts** at 58 Arab Street (tel: 6298 2408) for rattan and bamboo products) or **Royal Fabrics** across the street at No. 87 (tel: 6396 5820) and **Silk Junction** at No.115 (tel: 6293 6083) for every manner of sequined and embroidered textiles.

Sultan Mosque

Dominating the *kampung* (village) skyline is the great golden dome of **Sultan Mosque** ⑫, completed in 1928 (daily 9am–1pm, 2–4pm, Fri 2.30–4pm; tel: 6293 4405). Swan and Maclaren, the architectural firm responsible for the mosque, adopted the design of the Taj Mahal and combined it with Persian, Moorish, Turkish and classical themes. It is the largest mosque in Singapore, where the muezzin calls the faithful to prayer five times a day; the women to their enclave upstairs, and the men to the main prayer hall. With its striking golden domes and soaring minaret, this is one of the loveliest and most important places of Muslim worship in Singapore.

Bussorah Street

The most enchanting view of the mosque is from the corner of Bussorah Street and Baghdad Street. Part of **Bussorah Street**, whch is lined with charming 19th-century restored shophouses, has been closed to traffic. Bussorah Street is a treasure trove of shops selling Asian and Muslim-inspired crafts, like the **Malay Art Gallery** at No. 31 (tel: 6294 8051); look out for its selection of *kris*, or traditional Malay daggers.

The street was once part of the "Pilgrims Village" in early days when steam ships plied the sea. Bussorah and other nearby streets used to house *haj* pilgrims travelling enroute to Mecca from East Asia. Today, however, the colourful if a little sleepy streets have been transformed into a delightful shopping area, peppered with Arabic-style cafés and restaurants serving Middle-Eastern cuisine, a magnet for young urban Malays in the evenings.

Map on page 136

Bussorah Street door detail showing Arabic influences. Stroll along Bussorah Street during the Muslim Ramadan month when it is filled with stalls selling Malay food for the ritual sundown breaking of fast.

BELOW:
Sultan Mosque.

Religious Tensions

Singapore's enviable record of religious and ethnic harmony is not one that was won lightly. The country has twice been wracked by communal riots, once in 1950 when the British still ruled Singapore and again in 1964 during the brief period when Singapore was part of an ill-fated union with Malaysia. These sobering experiences convinced the government that inter-religious peace in a multi-ethnic society like Singapore was fragile and needed to be cultivated through even-handed state policies.

Government policies aside, a live-and-let-live attitude of religious tolerance and the belief that each religion has its merits helps Singaporeans cope with each other's religious practices in close proximity. This, however, does not imply the complete absence of religious tension – in fact the potential for religious friction is ever present. In the early 1980s for example, a Christian charismatic offshoot in Singapore actively converted huge numbers of Chinese from the Buddhist and Taoist faiths. These new converts in turn began to engage in aggressive proselytisation, and by the late 1980s, started to target the Malays, causing considerable reli-

gious and ethnic tension. Because Islam is central to their identity, the Malays perceived these efforts as an attack on their community as well as their religion. The stress this caused was considered sufficiently serious for the state to intervene and pass a Maintenance of Religious Harmony Bill in 1990, which empowers the state to place a restraining order on individuals who engage in aggressive evangelism.

More recently, tensions simmered in February 2002 when four Muslim girls were suspended from school for wearing their *tudung* (headscarf). The schools maintained the need for uniformity in their institutions – in line with official policy – causing an uproar among certain Muslim religious groups here, as well as in neighbouring Malaysia.

The geopolitics of religion, too, influences the state's perceptions of certain ethnic groups, in this case the Malay community. Singapore has always perceived itself and been viewed by others as a "Chinese state" because of its Chinese majority, yet geopolitically it is situated in a Malay- and Muslim-dominant region. This has given Singapore's Malays a political significance in excess of their size, both as the indigenous minority and in the larger context of the region they live in.

Yet at the same time, the prevailing perception has been that the Malays' loyalty to religion is at times greater than their loyalty to the nation. When the Allied forces attacked Iraq in 1991 following its invasion of Kuwait, a local newspaper poll indicated that six out of 10 Malays disapproved of the attack, compared to three out of 10 Singaporeans. The 9/11 terrorist attacks in New York and Washington DC and the subsequent arrest of 15 Al-Qaeda-linked terrorists in Singapore in January 2002 raised similar concerns.

Such damaging perceptions have had repercussions for the Malays. Because their loyalty is perceived to be divided, they have in the past been consciously disadvantaged in national service and employment in the armed forces. Although the government maintains that the situation has improved, the Malay perception that they are institutionally discriminated against continues to prevail.❑

LEFT: worshippers at Sultan Mosque.

Malabar Jama-Ath Mosque

Kampung Glam has several other beautiful mosques. At the corner of Jalan Sultan and Victoria Street is the humble **Malabar Muslim Jama-Ath Mosque ⑬** in blue-coloured mosaic, a quiet place of worship with a bygone ambience that harkens back to the era when the *kampung* was founded (daily 5.30am–9pm; tel: 6294 3862). The mosaic tiles were only added after the mosque opened in 1963. The islands's oldest Muslim cemetery lies beneath fragrant frangipani trees a little further along Victoria Street opposite Jalan Kledek.

Hajjah Fatimah Mosque

Behind Jalan Sultan and off Beach Road is the lovely **Hajjah Fatimah Mosque ⑭** built by a British architect in 1846 (daily 9am–9pm; tel: 6297 2774). The structure is named after a faithful Muslim woman who, after her husband's death, ran his shipping business so well that the proceeds enabled her to build the mosque on the site of their home, which had been demolished after it was ravaged by a fire. Its Gothic-style spire which tilts at six degrees has earned the mosque the nickname Leaning Tower of Singapore.

Bugis Village

Leaving Kampung Glam behind, head down Beach Road towards the corner of Rochor Road and Victoria Street to reach **Bugis Village ⑮**. The name is inspired by the former **Bugis Street**, arguably Singapore's most infamous attraction and known for its street food, raucous entertainment and uninhibited transvestites in days gone by – until it was demolished years ago to make way for an MRT station. Some of the old Bugis Street attractions are back in its new guise as Bugis Village but it is a pale imitation of its former self. The old shophouses have been restored and some of the original hawkers have returned. Rows of tightly packed stalls peddling clothes, bags and watches lend a bazaar-like atmosphere but this sterile impostor cannot match the buzz of the original Bugis Street.

Across Bugis Village is **Parco Bugis Junction**, a mall that features

Colourful pajamas for sale at Bugis Village's streetside vendors.

BELOW: Arab Street shoppers in Islamic dress and head scarf *(tudung)*.

Map on page 136

Map
on page
136

Temple detail from the Sri Krishnan Temple at Waterloo Street – this one depicts Hanoman, the Monkey God.

BELOW: Kwan Im Tong Hood Cho Temple with Sri Krishnan Temple behind it.

a glass-covered air-conditioned "street" with boutiques and cafés. Forming part of the complex is the **Hotel InterContinental**, using shophouse architecture as its theme.

Kwan Im Tong Hood Temple

At nearby **Waterloo Street**, a show of ethnic amicability is demonstrated at the Buddhist **Kwan Im Tong Hood Cho Temple** ⑯ (daily 6.15am–6.15pm; tel: 6337 9227). Both Chinese and Hindus are equally comfortable saying their prayers at this temple or at Sri Krishnan Temple *(see below)*, both of which sit side by side along this pedestrianised street. The temple was rebuilt in 1895 and again in 1982 to cater to the increasing number of devotees who come here to pay their respect to the deities. Chief among them is Kuan Yin, or the Goddess of Mercy, sitting in a heavily gilded altar.

Sri Krishnan Temple

Standing just next door, Chinese can be seen offering incense sticks to Lord Krishna (the Hindu equivalent of Kuan Yin) and other Hindu deities

at **Sri Krishnan Temple** ⑰ (daily 6am–noon, 5.30–9pm; tel: 6337 7957). Although it wasn't till the 1980s that the present elaborately carved tower entrance was added, the temple has sat on the same site since the 1870s. What began as a modest shrine at the foot of a tree is now an important place of worship with an adjacent building dedicated to cultural and spiritual classes.

Sculpture Square

Across Sri Krishnan Temple is a designated arts strip near the Singapore Art Museum *(see page 88)*. The area is home to local arts groups like Action Theatre, the Young Musicians' Society, the Singapore Calligraphy Centre and Stamford Arts Centre, where artists work on disciplines ranging from Indian music to Chinese dance and Italian opera. The arts hub is also home to the Nanyang Academy of Fine Arts, and by the end of 2006, the LaSalle-SIA College of the Arts.

The lovely **Sculpture Square** ⑱ at the junction of Waterloo Street and Middle Road was constructed in 1870 as a church and a girl's school (Mon–Fri 11am–6pm, Sat–Sun noon–6pm; tel: 6333 1055; www.sculpturesq.com.sg). The chapel, with its 19th-century arc windows and circular vents, is one of the few Gothic-style buildings still standing in Singapore today. Restored and opened in 1999 as the Sculpture Square, it's the only space in Singapore dedicated to 3-dimensional art.

Maghain Aboth Synagogue

At 26 Waterloo Street stands yet another institution that is testimony to Singapore's multi-racial society: the Victorian-style **Maghain Aboth Synagogue** ⑲. Erected in 1878, this was the first synagogue to be built for the Jewish community in Singapore (viewing strictly by appointment only; tel: 6337 2189). ❏

RESTAURANTS

Restaurants

Indian

Ananda Bhavan
01-10, Blk 663 Buffalo Rd. Tel: 6294 0684. Open: daily 7.30am–10pm. Also at: 58 Serangoon Rd. Tel: 6297 9522. $
www.anandabhavan.com
You order, take a queue number and wait for your number to be called before collecting your scrumptious South Indian meal. While waiting, read all about the virtues of vegetarianism posted on the wall. One of the vignette reads "the strength of an elephant is sustained on a vegetarian diet".

Banana Leaf Apolo
54/56/58 Race Course Rd. Tel: 6293 8682. Open: daily 10.30am–10.30pm. $$
www.bananaleafapolo.com
Never mind the unimaginative, fluorescent-lit space. The perennially busy restaurant fills up quickly. Its *the* place for spicy South Indian food served on banana leaves. Everything looks good and the busy but efficient waiters are ever-ready to help if you need recommendations. Must tries: *masala* prawns and chicken.

Delhi
60 Race Course Rd. Tel: 6296 4585. Open: daily 11.30am–11.30pm. $$

Small, cosy and very popular Northern Indian restaurant. The menu here is extensive but staff will help. Start with the sizzling mixed grill. The Delhi prawns, Delhi butter chicken and *naan* breads are all excellent.

Komala Vilas
76-78 Serangoon Rd. Tel: 6293 6980. Open: daily 7am–10.30pm. Also at: 82 Serangoon Rd. Tel: 6294 3294; and 12-14 Buffalo Rd. Tel: 6293 3664. $
www.komala-vilas.com
This boisterous, charming Little India institution is the place for saffron rice accompanied by an array of vegetable curries, *vadai* (savoury fritter) and Indian breads such as wholewheat *bhattura* and *chapati*, and rice flour-based *thosai*. Sauces and dips are replenished as desired and you should definitely eat with your fingers.

Roshni Fine Indian Dining & Lounge
48 Serangoon Rd. Tel: 6292 4808. Open: daily 11.30am–11pm. $ (buffet) $$ (à la carte)
The decor is far from "fine dining" but it's still a pleasant to wind down from the bustle of Little India. The menu features the usual North and South Indian suspects and the buffet is good value for money. A Hindi band performs every night.

Muthu's Curry
78 Race Course Rd. Tel: 6293 2389. Open: daily 10am–10pm. $$
The locals are passionate about their fish head curry and Muthu's Curry inevitably comes up as one of the top places to sample this dish. It has been serving their award-winning fish head curry since 1969. That's not all. The chicken, mutton and prawn dishes are always good bets – and they're all served on a banana leaf, of course.

Singapore Zam Zam Restaurant
697-699 North Bridge Rd. Tel: 6298 6320. Open: daily 8am–11pm. $
A rough and ready place serving Indian-Muslim specialities. The fragrant mutton or chicken *briyani* (saffron rice) is robustly spicy as are the flaky bread, called *murtabak* when stuffed with minced mutton or chicken, and *prata* when eaten plain and dipped in curry.

Malay

Tepak Sireh Restoran
73 Sultan Gate. Tel: 6396 4373. Open: L and D daily. $ (buffet lunch and dinner) $$ (à la carte)
www.tepaksireh.com.sg
This resplendent mustard-coloured building adjacent to the Istana Kampung Glam was originally built for Malay royalty. Its recipes,

reportedly handed down from generations, lives up to expectations. Order the spicy and tender beef *rendang*, chicken curry and pandan tea.

Hajjah Maimunah Restaurant
11 Jalan Pisang. Tel: 6291 3132. Open Mon–Sat 11am–9pm. $
Self-service Malay restaurant that's always packed to the gills: just point to the dish and it will be served with fluffy rice. The tender and spicy beef *rendang* and *sotong bakar* (grilled squid) are heavenly.

Middle Eastern

Samar Café
19 Baghdad St. Tel: 6398 0530. Open: daily noon–3am. $ (set lunch) $$$ (à la carte)
The Middle Eastern menu is small (try the hummus with freshly baked bread) and it's a lovely spot to chill out after exploring Arab Street. In fact, you may want to lie on the cushions upstairs and smoke away the day's stress on their *shisha* pipes.

PRICE CATEGORIES

Prices for a three-course dinner per person without drinks and taxes:
$ = under S$20
$$= S$20–$30
$$$ = S$30–$45
$$$$ = more than S$45

SINGAPORE SHOPHOUSES

Of all the architectural styles in Singapore, none is as unique as the lavishly decorated shophouses found in the city's older neighbourhoods

ABOVE AND LEFT: the Late Shophouse Style – built between 1910 and the late 1930s – is the most florid of all the shophouse styles, with lavishly decorated facades and the most ornate details. The house above can be found at the corner of Lorong 19 and Lorong Bachok in Geylang. The detailed plasterwork framing the windows on the left is from a shophouse in Syed Alwi Road.

Known as Chinese Baroque or Singapore Eclectic architecture, these shophouses sport a rich mix of Malay, Chinese and European architectural details, all giving a distinctive look to Singapore's urban landscape. The shophouse was so called because the lower floor was used for business while the upper level as living quarters. The design, initiated by Raffles, had detailed specifications to achieve conformity. They were arranged in a linear form and built of masonry with tile roofs. Linking the shophouses was a covered path called the "five-foot way" because the width between the building and the street had to be exactly five feet. The style later evolved to two-storey residential terrace houses that housed occupants on both floors. Over the years, five distinct shophouse styles developed: Early, First Transitional, Late, Second Transitional and Art Deco – many of which have been restored to their original splendour.

ABOVE: Boat Quay *(see page 113)* was where *coolies* (labourers) once lugged sacks of rice, spices and other goods on their backs from "bumboats" along the Singapore River to the shophouses on the shore. Today, its restored shophouses have been turned into a thriving nightlife hub.

LEFT: Detail of a bas-relief Sikh guard with rifle and bayonet – taken from the Late Shophouse at Lorong Bachok *(see top)*.

BELOW: the Art Deco Shophouse Style is the most recent of styles, mainly built between 1940 and 1960. It is probably the least common of the styles and the most European in character. This particular stretch of houses is found along Bukit Pasoh Road near Chinatown. The private forecourt area with a gate and a balcony on the upper floor is another one of its traits.

BELOW: the Early Shophouse Style, as the name implies, was the first of the shophouses that was erected in the 1840s. Kampung Glam and Little India have the best examples of such houses. With their squat upper levels and simple lines unadorned of detail, they resemble dolls' houses. The shophouse is not unique to Singapore: it can be found in Melaka and Penang in neighbouring Malaysia, which together with Singapore, was known as the Straits Settlements during colonial times.

BELOW: the First Transitional Shophouse Style which dates back to the early 1900s took on an extra floor in order to maximise on space. Once dilapidated and shunned, many old shophouses are much sought after properties these days because of their unique facades and historical value. Strict guidelines govern the restoration of shophouses, many of which have been turned into chic restaurants, bars and boutique hotels as well as offices for advertising and publishing firms.

BELOW: the Second Transitional Shophouse Style of the late 1930s onwards was a little less florid than its predecessor, the Late Style. Still, it combined both Asian and European architectural influences, including Malay-style wooden eaves, Corinthian columns and pilasters, Palladian-style arches, French windows with timber louvres and semi-circular fanlights as well as European glazed ceramic tiles and bas reliefs depicting motifs from Chinese mythical tales, and flowers and animals.

SENTOSA AND THE SOUTHERN ISLANDS

It's easy to escape from the frenzied city to Sentosa island, a playground of attractions and lovely beaches. The other southern islands, in contrast, are tiny specks of sand visited by few people

Sometimes it's easy to forget that Singapore is in the tropics, so take the opportunity to get offshore and enjoy a little island hopping. The most popular of the outlying islands is **Sentosa**, which has become a major resort and recreation area over the last decade after its previous life as a military base. Several other islands can be easily reached from the mainland, ranging from tiny specks like the Sisters' Islands to larger ones like St John's.

Sentosa's origins

Sentosa was once called Pulau Blakang Mati, which means "island at the back of which lies death" in Malay, so-called because the frequent outbreaks of disease there had claimed the lives of many of its islanders. It was also a refuge for pirates in the 19th century before it was turned into a military fortress by the British – who positioned guns towards the sea thinking this would best protect their colony of Singapore. But history proved them wrong and during World War II, Singapore succumbed to the Japanese who came not by sea but overland through the peninsula of Malaya (now Malaysia).

When the British withdrew their military presence in Singapore in 1968, the government decided to transform the former garrison island of 395 hectares (976 acres) into a leisure resort for both tourists and locals. But first, a more appealing name had to be found. A contest was held and the winning name, Sentosa ("Isle of Peace and Tranquillity" in Malay) was picked, and in 1972, Sentosa welcomed its first visitors in its new role as a tropical island retreat.

A whole day should be set aside for Sentosa; in fact, there is probably enough to keep visitors busy for a few days. Touted as a major attrac-

Map on page 152

LEFT: lush grounds of the Shangri-La Rasa Sentosa Resort. **BELOW:** the good life on Siloso Beach.

tion in most guidebooks, Sentosa suffers from having too many attractions – although some are outstanding, others have fizzled out despite a great start. Choosing the right attractions to visit can make the difference between a great day out on Sentosa and a disappointing one.

A number of sights on Sentosa recently closed or are languishing due to a lack of visitors. To reinvigorate the island, the Sentosa Development Corporation is spending a whopping S$7 billion dollars – spread over a 10-year period – on villa-style resorts, waterfront homes and entertainment outlets, possibly even a theme park. Already plans are afoot to replace the ageing monorail system that serves the island with the new Sentosa Express, a light rail system that links up direct to the HarbourFront MRT Station.

Sentosa Cove, an extension of the eastern end of the island next to Tanjong Beach, is being developed into

an upmarket residential project with marina facilities. Also under construction is a luxury hotel designed by Norman Faster. Called The Knolls, it will be ready in 2007. There are also talks of linking Sentosa to the Southern Islands and developing a mega resort similar to the ocean-themed Atlantis in the Bahamas.

Getting to Sentosa

The island can be reached by cable car or land. The more scenic option is by cable car, shuttling 65 metres (213 ft) above the water from stations at Mount Faber (see page 161) and the HarbourFront Centre to Sentosa. The lofty ride offers a bird's-eye view of the city and the busiest container port in the world (cable cars run daily 8.30am–9pm; tel: 6270 8855; www.cablecar.com.sg – packages, including admission fees and a guided tour of Sentosa are available).

From HarbourFront Centre, you can take a taxi, bus or walk across

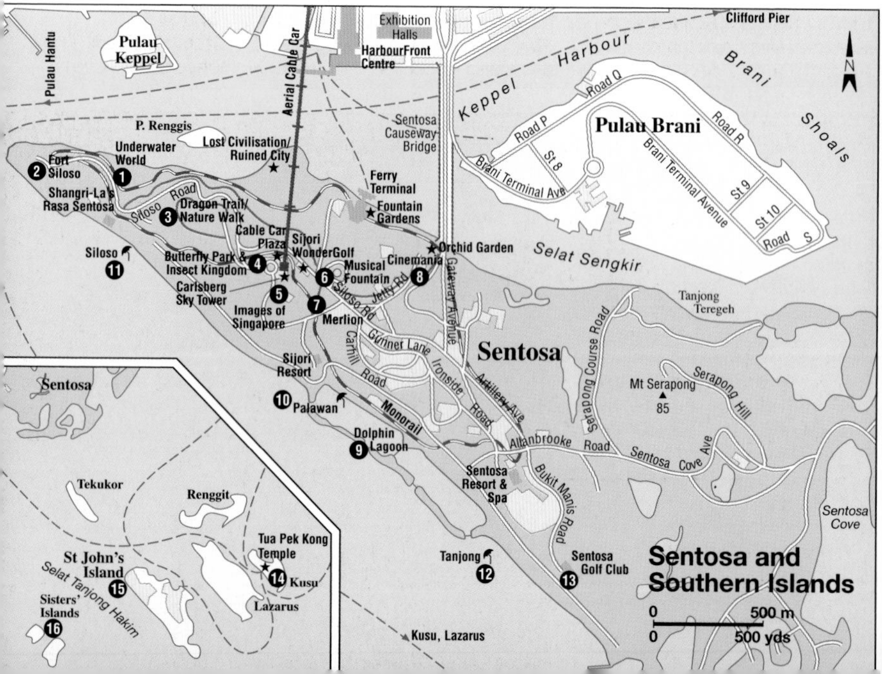

Once on Sentosa, use the free monorail service to get around the island.

the 700-metre (2,297 ft) causeway that links Sentosa to mainland Singapore. Most visitors take the train to the HarbourFront MRT station and walk to the nearby HarbourFront Centre Bus Terminal to catch the Sentosa Bus to the island (Sun–Thur 7am–11pm and Fri–Sat and holidays 7am–12.30am; S$1). Once on the island, free buses and the monorail make getting around easy.

A basic admission fee of S$2 includes access to all the park areas and beaches, plus unlimited monorail rides on Sentosa. All the major attractions on the island, however, have separate admission charges, which can all add up. The best deals are package tickets which include transportation and entry to multiple attractions on Sentosa (tel: 1800 736 8672 or visit www.sentosa.com.sg for more information).

Underwater World

A short ride on the monorail to the station M2, past the gimicky **Lost Civilisation** and **Ruined City** – a not-too-convincing attempt to recreate the remains of some ancient civilisation through carved stones and elaborate gateways – is the **Underwater World ❶**. This is one of Asia's best aquariums and a must-see while at Sentosa (daily 9am–9pm; admission charge; tel: 6275 0030; www.underwaterworld.com.sg).

One of the highlights at this attraction is the transparent acrylic tunnel with a moving walkway that leads under huge tanks containing some 2.8 million litres of water and over 2,500 tropical sea creatures – from bright, luminous reef-dwellers to sinister stingrays and sharks. Nasty stone fish, sea urchins and moray eels lurk behind the rocks and amid colourful corals. At 11.45am, 2.30pm and 4.45pm daily, you can watch these denizens of the deep being hand-fed by divers.

The more adventurous can opt for a "Dive with the Sharks" and swim amongst these fearsome sea creatures while intrepid scuba-certified divers can sign up for the "Extreme Bull Shark Encounter". There's also a "Dive with the Dugong" option for the shark-shy. Extra charges apply for these special encounters and

Map on page 152

TIP

Cycling is a great way to explore Sentosa – rent a bicycle from rental kiosks at the Ferry Terminal or along the beach, pick up a Cycle Track Route Map (available at the kiosks) and just pedal away.

BELOW:
face-to-fish at the Underwater World.

advance reservations are essential.

Another rivetting exhibit is the **Singapore Wetlands** display at the Changing Exhibit Hall, where visitors enjoy close encounters with the usually hard-to-spot freshwater and estuarine creatures, including mudskippers and monitor lizards.

Also worth seeing is the **Dugong Cove**, where a dugong that was rescued from the seas off Pulau Ubin in 1998 and rehabilitated at Underwater World currently resides. The gentle sea creature, with its curiously shaped body and tail – long thought to have inspired sailors' tales of the mermaid – is named Gracie.

If there in the evening, be sure to join the **Night Ocean Discovery** programme (daily 6.45–9pm). Visitors are given a torch to help navigate their way through a darkened oceanarium, where nocturnal marine creatures dart to life. Look out for a spectacular exhibit of underwater fireflies and a chance to witness the restless sharks hunting for prey.

Note: your ticket to Underwater World includes admission to the Dolphin Lagoon (*see page 156*).

To get your money's worth, choose a bright haze-free day to ride up the 110-metre (360-ft) Carlsberg Sky Tower.

BELOW: Singapore's war history comes alive at Fort Siloso.

Fort Siloso

Located at the western tip of the island and walking distance from the Underwater World is **Fort Siloso ❷**, Singapore's only preserved coastal fort (daily 9am–7pm; entrance fee). The fort's numerous guns and tunnels were built for the defence of Singapore by the British – albeit facing the wrong direction – during World War II. This historical landmark, enhanced by lush greenery and landscaping, is another one of Sentosa's must-see sights.

Used as a prisoner-of-war camp during the Japanese Occupation (1942–45), the fort offers a one-stop overview of World War II history. A tram takes visitors from the foot of the hill through a series of films and exhibits detailing the fort's history, including its role during the war. Bunkers, tunnels and a six-inch gun that can "load and fire" add a fillip to this real-life vignette of Singapore's wartime past.

The displays at the adjoining **Surrender Chamber** takes you through the years of World War II with photographs, films, wartime mementoes and wax figures depicting surrender by the British in 1942, and then by the Japanese in 1945.

Dragon Trail/Nature Walk

If there is time to kill and you have small children with you, take them to the nearby **Dragon Trail/Nature Walk ❸**, a trail through 1.5 km (1 mile) of secondary forest with the opportunity to observe tropical flora and fauna as well as small animals like long-tailed macaques, squirrels, geckos and spotted doves.

You also take a detour up to the summit of **Mount Imbiah**, a former gun battery, and be rewarded with views of the Western Anchorage and nearby Indonesian islands.

Around the Cable Car Plaza

Clustered around the Cable Car Plaza area are a number of fairly interesting sights. First off is the **Butterfly Park & Insect Kingdom ❹** – a real treat for nature lovers (daily 9am–6.30pm; admission charge). The first has some 2,500 live butterflies from more than 50 species that flit and flutter between lush tropical plants in a large enclosed garden while the adjacent attraction has more than 3,000 mounted bugs, including some of the world's largest and rarest creepy crawlies.

It's near impossible to miss the island's latest attraction – the 110-metre (360-ft) tall **Carlsberg Sky Tower** (daily 9am–9pm; admission charge). The disc-shaped air-conditioned cabin slowly spins up a central column and, on a clear day, offers a panoramic view of Sentosa, Singapore and its surrounding islands.

Images of Singapore

South of the Cable Car Plaza is the **Images of Singapore ❺**, which was closed for major upgrading at time of press. When re-opened in June 2005, the revamped exhibit will comprise three experiences –

Warehouse of the Four Winds, Singapore Adventure and Singapore Celebrates. The exhibit promises to take visitors through Singapore's history and give them a sneak preview of the country's rich cultural diversity through multimedia shows and walk-through settings.

Around the Musical Fountain

Continue on the monorail or bus back to the Ferry Terminal where there are restaurants, the outdoor **Sentosa Food Centre** and souvenir shops, as well as a bicycle hire kiosk. Behind the food centre is the **Sentosa Orchid Garden** with its collection of orchids from all over the world. Flanking the Fountain Gardens is the **Enchanted Grove of Tembusu** comprising 2 hectares (5 acres) of majestic Tembusu trees and MacArthur Palms creating a cool shady canopy for strolls.

A short walk from either the Ferry Terminal or Cable Car Plaza is the fun **Musical Fountain ❻** which comes to life each evening with a spectacular show called *Magical Sentosa*, combining the use

Map on page 152

An exotic bug – one of 3,000 – on display at Sentosa's Insect Kingdom Museum.

BELOW:
Sentosa's Musical Fountain display.

Orchid lovers will find all manner of these delicate blooms at the Sentosa Orchid Garden.

BELOW: beach volleyball action at Palawan Beach.

of laser lights, dancing jets of water and fire (two shows at 7.40pm and 8.40pm daily; free). The S$4-million spectacle also features a live actor and computer animation.

Then go for a stroll in the lovely **Fountain Gardens** or take the lift up to the top of the gigantic 37-metre (120-ft) high **Merlion ❼** – the half-lion and half-fish creature that has become the tourist symbol of Singapore – for views of the harbour and surrounding Southern Islands, and on a clear day, even the Riau islands of Indonesia.

The **Herb and Spice Garden** along Merlion Walk (behind the statue) has a collection of over 250 species of traditional herbs and spices – the whiff of lemon grass, basil and kaffir lime can be intoxicating – and is worth a stroll if you have time.

Other attractions

Cinemania ❽ (daily 11am– 8pm; admission charge) is probably not worth your time unless you have small children with you. Visitors are strapped into computer synchronised seats that claim to simulate every

bump and hair-raising moment of roller coaster rides and speed races – but it's not quite the real thing. Another attraction, the kitschy **VolcanoLand**, is in imminent danger of being closed due to falling visitor numbers (daily 1–6.30pm; admission charge). Its attempt to recreate the Mayan civilisation with rather plasticky props and a lame roller coaster ride holds little appeal.

Dolphin Lagoon

Your ticket to the Underwater World includes admission to the **Dolphin Lagoon ❾**, along Palawan Beach (daily 10.30am–6pm). The performing stars are the endangered Indo-Pacific Humpbacked, or pink dolphins, which endear themselves to the crowd with their tail-flapping antics (which incidentally has drawn flak from animal welfare groups worldwide). "Meet the Dolphin" shows take place daily at 11am, 1.30pm, 3.30pm and 5.30pm. In addition, up to eight people can sign up to swim with the dolphins at 10am daily. Advance reservations are required (tel: 6275 0030).

Beaches and bars

Sentosa's other great appeal is recreation, especially watersports and golf. White sands stretch some 3 km (2 miles) along the southern shore, interspersed by scenic saltwater lagoons and coconut groves. Each of the three beaches, Siloso, Palawan and Tanjong, has its own character, and they are probably Singapore's most pleasant stretches of sand – if you disregard the views of scores of container ships in the distance.

Watersports enthusiasts should head for either **Palawan Beach ⑩** or **Siloso Beach ⑪**, where windsurfers, canoes and pedal boats can be hired. In addition, a new sea sports centre called **Azura**, offering powerboat charters and wakeboarding facilities, opened at Siloso Beach recently. Beach volleyball has also gained popularity in recent years, attracting a lively crowd of bikini-clad girls and bare-chested young turks to the beaches, especially on the weekends. Not surprisingly, many come to just watch the fun. Throughout the year, events like sand-sculpting competitions, jazz evenings, bazaars and beach soccer tournaments keep Sentosa's beaches a hotbed of activity. If you prefer peace and quiet, head for **Tanjong Beach ⑫** at the eastern end of the island. Getting from one beach to another is easy: a beach train plies all three beaches daily from 9am–7pm.

After the sun goes down, the action on Siloso Beach revs up on Friday and Saturday nights when a mix of fun-loving locals and expatriates descend on beach pubs like **Sunset Bay** (daily 10am–10pm, Fri till midnight, Sat till 2am). The action gets even hotter when the occasional foam party – where people dance, as opposed to bathe, in giant plastic pools covered in suds – are held at Palawan Beach's **Bora Bora Beach Bar** (Mon–Fri 11am–9pm, Fri–Sat 11am–11pm).

Golf

The **Sentosa Golf Club ⑬** near Tanjong Beach sees avid golfers playing on its two 18-hole par 72-championship courses. Offering a golfing experience of a different kind is the **Sijori WonderGolf** near the Cable Car Plaza with 54 putting greens set in three fun courses (daily 9am–7pm; admission charge). Players have to go up and down landscaped slopes and negotiate their way through caves, waterfalls, ravines, streams, ponds and geysers.

Island accommodation

Those who want an extended beach holiday can check into any of three hotels on the island. There are two five-star properties, the beachfront **Shangri-La's Rasa Sentosa Resort** on Siloso Beach, and the stylish **The Sentosa Resort**, within walking distance from Tanjong Beach. A mid-priced option is the **Sijori Resort Sentosa**, housed in a row of old prewar buildings *(see Travel Tips page 217)*. Budget accommodation at hostels, campsites and chalets is also available on the island.

TIP

For those with derring-do, the Flying Trapeze! at Shangri-La's Rasa Sentosa Resort on Siloso Beach has professional trapeze artistes on hand to teach juggling and acrobatic stunts (Mon–Fri 9am–6pm, Fri–Sat 9am–7pm).

Map on page 152

BELOW: poolside at The Sentosa Resort.

Even if you decide not to spend the night on Sentosa, consider having a lesiurely rub-down at the **Spa Botanica**, (daily 10am–10pm; tel: 6371 1318; www.spabotanica.com) set in lush landscaped gardens adjacent to The Sentosa Resort. The outdoor spa garden has float pools, therapeutic mud pools and garden labyrinths as well as a yoga and pilates studio. A scrub followed by a blissful massage at the outdoor pavilion is a wonderful treat.

Southern Islands

Beyond Sentosa is an archipelago of tiny islands that lie within Singapore's territorial waters, ranging from uninhabited coral outcrops to popular weekend retreats like Kusu and St John's. Because thousands of ships ply the Straits of Malacca and Singapore harbour each year, the government has been especially vigilant in preventing water pollution and protecting the natural beauty of these islands.

Many islands are still enveloped in coral reefs, and Singapore's Nature Society has successfully completed a coral conservation project to transplant reefs that are threatened by land reclamation and industry. Two entire reefs have been moved thus far from the endangered waters around Pulau Ayer Chawan and Buran Darat to new homes off the south coast of Sentosa.

Meanwhile, the government is drawing up plans to establish marine conservation areas to protect the reefs near Sudong, Hantu, Semakau and St John's Island. Two of the offshore islands can be reached by regular ferry service from mainland Singapore; to reach the others, join a tour or hire a boat from Clifford Pier *(see text box below)*.

Kusu island

Kusu Island is a place of both rest and worship. Also called Turtle Island, legend has it that two shipwrecked sailors – one Chinese, one Malay – were saved when a giant turtle transformed itself into an island. Each man gave thanks according to his own beliefs, and so today the Taoist temple of **Tua Pek Kong** with its turtle pool and the

BELOW: temple pavilion at Kusu Island.

temple pavilion at Kusu Island.

Getting to the Islands

Ferries to **Kusu Island** and **St John's Island** leave from the Sentosa Ferry Terminal (Mon–Sat 10am and 1.30pm; Sun 9am, 11pm, 1pm, 3pm and 5pm). The round-trip fare for the 30-minute ferry ride includes admission. The ferry stops at Kusu first on the way to St John's. Call 1800 736 8672. **Lazarus**, **Sisters'** and **Hantu** islands are not served by regular ferries, so you have to hire the slow "bumboats" at Clifford Pier. An alternative way to see the harbour and islands is on the *Cheng Ho*, a replica Chinese junk which cruises the southern islands with a brief stopover at Kusu (tel: 65339811; www.watertours.com.sg).

Muslim *keramat* (shrine) on the hill are popular places of pilgrimage.

In the ninth month of the lunar calendar, usually straddling October and November, both Malays and Chinese people from Singapore flock to the island in droves. The Chinese arrive with candles, joss sticks and other offerings, and then make straight for the temple where they pray for prosperity, good luck and fertility. Offerings of flowers, fruit, eggs and chickens are left before the gods in the shrine. The Malay pilgrims on the other hand climb the 122 steps to their shrine to offer their prayers to Allah.

Other islands

Plans to develop the neighbouring **Lazarus Island** into a tropical beach resort are underway. **St John's Island** ⓖ, which is reputedly haunted by spirits according to local rumour, was where Raffles anchored before meeting the Temenggong, or Malay chief, on the Singapore River in 1819. The island served as a quarantine centre for immigrants until the 1950s when it was used as a holding centre for political detainees. In 1975, St John's was turned into a holiday haven with lagoons, shady paths and picnic spots, making it a popular weekend venue. These days, however, the island is losing its allure somewhat as one-third of the island has been turned into a Tropical Marine Science Institute, and another third into a detention centre for illegal immigrants.

The two **Sisters' Islands** ⓰, made up of Pulau Subar Darat and Pulau Subar Laut, are also favourite spots for relaxation and diving, although the waters can sometimes be murky. Likewise, **Pulau Hantu** or Ghost Island, to the northwest of Sentosa – said to be haunted by a Malay warrior – attracts mainly divers and fishermen to its waters.

There are other more obscure islands in this area, like Pulau Sekang, but they are more difficult to get to and not worth the effort.

If you're planning to explore the southern islands, be sure to bring your own picnic basket as the islands do not offer food or drinks, or facilities of any sort. ❑

Each year, pilgrims to Kusu Island release baby terrapins at its Tortoise Sanctuary. The act is supposed to bring one good luck.

Restaurants

Italian

Trapizza
10 Siloso Beach Walk. Tel: 6376 2662. Open: Tue–Thur and Sun 11am–9pm, Fri–Sat 11am–10pm. $$$
The Italian-style family restaurant sits on Siloso Beach next to a trapeze. On a hot day, nothing beats a scoop of mango sorbet and a mug of cold beer. Wait for the sun to set and wind down with their hearty salads, delicious pastas and excellent pizzas from the wood-fired oven. Don't forget to order Italian wine or a glass of grappa to go with your meal.

Seafood

Sharkey's
Shangri-La Rasa Sentosa, 101 Siloso Rd. Tel: 6275 0100. Open: D daily. $$$
The waterfront Sharkey's is the best place on the island – and one of Singapore's best places – for local seafood. Forget cutlery. Use your fingers for the massive seafood platter and the Sri Lankan crabs – which can be done any way you desire – fried with pepper, simmering in Thai curry, wok-fried with chilli sauce or steamed with Chinese herbs.

The Cliff
The Sentosa Resort & Spa, 2 Bukit Manis Rd. Tel: 6275 0331. Open: D daily. $$$$
www.thesentosa.com
One of Singapore's most beautiful and dramatic restaurants sits at the edge of a cliff and offers a view of lovely lush surrounds and the South China Sea. In fact, the artful and sensuous Yasuhiro Koichi-designed restaurant and chef de cuisine Shawn Armstrong's elegant contemporary seafood-inspired dishes seem a perfect marriage. Oysters are served six ways and the lobster sausage is out of this world.

PRICE CATEGORIES

Prices for a three-course dinner per person without drinks and taxes:
$ = under S$20
$$ = S$20–$30
$$$ = S$30–$45
$$$$ = more than S$45

SOUTHERN AND WESTERN SINGAPORE

The south has some tranquil green oases worthy of a ramble. To the west is Jurong, where a number of family-friendly attractions are found amid the city's most hardworking industrial zone

The west coast of Singapore has a split personality. On one end, it comprises industrial areas with docks, factories and refineries; on the other, it is a major recreation zone that embraces some of Singapore's top green spaces and theme parks. The Ayer Rajah Expressway (AYE) leads into the heart of the west, linking downtown Singapore with a bustling industrial suburb called Jurong. But a more pleasant way to explore the coast is by way of Telok Blangah and Pasir Panjang roads, which hug the coast.

Start exploring the west coast from the south – from the top of **Mount Faber ❶** to be precise, which offers panoramic views of the city and the massive port area. Alternatively, ride the cable car (daily 8.30am–9pm; admission charge; tel: 6270 8855; www.cablecar. com.sg) to Sentosa for a bird's-eye view of the harbour.

Mount Faber is a misnomer as it's only 105 metres (345 ft) high. Formerly called Telok Blangah Hill, it was renamed in 1845 after Captain C.E. Faber of the Madras Engineers constructed the narrow serpentine road leading to the summit in order to install a new signal station to replace the one on Pulau Blakang Mati (Sentosa today).

The sprawling rainforest-covered park which surrounds Mount Faber is one of the oldest in Singapore; be sure to stop at the various look-out points on the way up. At the summit, the Marina Deck, built like the deck of a ship, has good views of the city and port. In the evenings, **Altivo Bar** (tel: 6377 9618) here offer opportunities to linger with a drink.

Bustling port

The Port of Singapore is the world's busiest in terms of shipping tonnage, and also Asia's main trans-shipment hub. The major port terminals lie in

Map on page 162

LEFT: dragon slayer at the Haw Par Villa. **BELOW:** Singapore's port is the busiest in the world.

the south and southwest of the island stretching from Tanjong Pagar just outside the CBD to Jurong in the west.

The port's main terminal has 200 shipping lines with connections to 600 ports all over the world. Its four container terminals – Tanjong Pagar, Keppel, Brani and Pasir Panjang – with a total of 37 berths – operate as one integrated facility. If you peer down from Mount Faber, you will see the massive Keppel and Brani container terminals at its foot.

HarbourFront Centre

Also at the base of Mount Faber is the **HarbourFront Centre** ❷, which houses a shopping mall. The northeast line, the world's first fully automated and driverless metro system, runs past here. The adjacent Cable Car Tower is where the cable cars from Mount Faber stop to pick up passengers for the ride to Sentosa. Adjoining the HarbourFront Centre is the **Singapore Cruise Centre**, where passenger ships from all over the world dock.

Mosques and mansions

The next landmark is the **Masjid Temenggong Daeng Ibrahim** ❸ on Telok Blangah Road, near the HarbourFront Centre and opposite the causeway to Sentosa (daily 5.30am–9pm, tel: 6273 6043). Daeng Ibrahim was the son of Abdul Rahman, who was the Temenggong (chief) of Singapore when Raffles landed in Singapore in 1819. The Temenggong and his followers at that time lived around the south bank of the Singapore River, which Raffles had intended to develop. They were persuaded by Raffles to move to Telok Blangah. Soon others followed, including Arabs and Indonesian immigrants, turning the area into a Malay enclave. Adjacent to the mosque is the *makam* (tomb) of Temenggong Abdul Rahman.

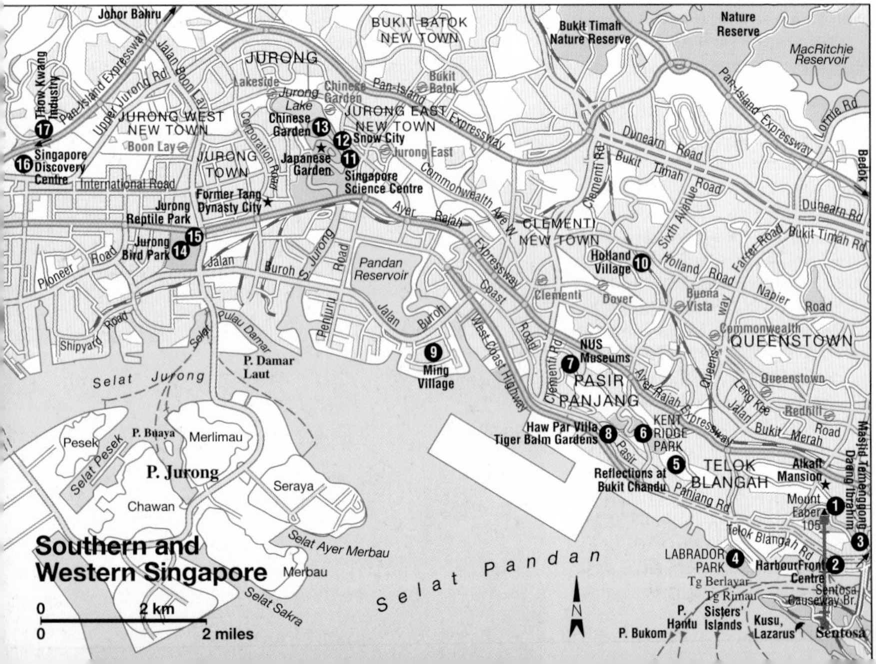

Further up is **Telok Blangah Green**, which sits in the middle of tropical gardens with walkways, picnic areas and an exercise course. The opulent house near the crest of the green, named Telok Blangah Hill Park, is **Alkaff Mansion** which has been restored to its 1920s splendour and transformed into a romantic bar and restaurant. Built by the wealthy Alkaff Arab trading family who lived and entertained here in its heyday, the mansion is currently closed for a major refurbishment.

Labrador Park

The western end of Keppel Harbour is marked by a small cape called **Tanjong Berlayar**. The British Army engineers built a powerful bastion here in 1892. They installed six-inch guns and christened their citadel the Labrador Battery, believing that it would forever protect imperial shipping. The builders never would have guessed that within a century, their sturdy ramparts would become a park.

Labrador Park ❹ houses the World War II gun batteries, bunkers and other relics that have been restored and trace a chapter of Singapore's war history (daily 7am–7pm). An aerial staircase built into the edge of the secondary forest offers a panoramic view of the sea. The staircase also descends to the jetty and the shore where the **Tanjong Berlayar Plaza** is located. This waterfront promenade offers a romantic stroll in the evenings when the harbour lights come on. There are also a number of forest trails that make for pleasant walking *(see text box below)*. To get to the park, turn into Labrador Villa Road off Pasir Panjang Road, across PSA Building.

Bukit Chandu

Further west at 31K Pepys Road (off Pasir Panjang Road) is a World War II monument called the **Reflections at Bukit Chandu ❺** (Tue–Sun 9am–5pm; admission charge; tel: 6375 2510; www.S1942.org.sg). It is dedicated to the heroes of the 1st and 2nd Battalions of the Malay Regiment, who along with the British, Australian and Kiwi forces, fought 13,000 Japanese soldiers at

Map on page 162

BELOW: bronze sculptures at Bukit Chandu.

Labrador's History Trail

Labrador Battery, where Labrador Park now sits, was part of the gun system that defended Singapore in WW II. Today, the park's History Walk traces the paths around the old defensive structures. Story boards posted in the 17-hectare (42-acre) park explain the development of the battery and its fortification. The Bunker Path winds around underground chambers, gun emplacements, an 1892 ammunition storeroom, a six-pounder quick-fire gun and remains of an old fort wall, among others. At the foot of the park is an opening in the Straits of Singapore – once known as Keppel Passageway and used by sailors and traders to sail into Singapore.

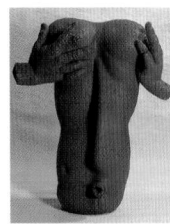

Singapore sculptor Ng Eng Teng's work entitled "I See". His works can be seen at the NUS Museums in Kent Ridge.

BELOW: Haw Par Villa was built by the founders of the Tiger balm ointment.

the Battle of Pasir Panjang in 1942.

The five galleries, showcasing artefacts and multimedia interactives, provide rich insight into the war, while the *Sounds of Battle* video in the theatre practically transports you onto the battlefield with realistic sound effects of machine gun fire and human cries.

Kent Ridge area

Heading along Pasir Panjang Road, a right turn to South Buona Vista Road leads to the lush **Kent Ridge Park ❻** (daily 7am–7pm). From the bluff you can see dozens of ships anchored in the western harbour and the myriad southern islands of Singapore. The workout course here is popular with joggers from the nearby university and science park.

Along nearby Kent Ridge Crescent is the **National University of Singapore** (NUS), which houses the first-rate **NUS Museums ❼** (Mon–Sat 9am–5pm, Thur 9am–9pm; free; tel: 6874 4616; www.nus.edu.sg/museums). Its three galleries are well curated and worth a detour.

The impressive **Lee Kong Chian Art Museum**, named after the first Chancellor of the former University of Singapore, is noted for its collection of Chinese art spanning some 7,000 years of civilisation and culture. There are close to 4,000 pieces of artwork, which include paintings and calligraphic works as well as ceramics, bronzes and sculptures.

The **South and Southeast Asian Gallery** mirrors classical traditions as well as modern trends and comprises ceramics, textiles, sculpture and paintings. Be sure to stop at the **Ng Eng Teng Gallery**, which houses the works of the late Ng Eng Teng, Singapore's foremost sculptor and known for his whimsical renditions of the human form.

Haw Par Villa

In vivid contrast to the museum exhibits are the somewhat bizarre displays at **Haw Par Villa ❽**, also known as Tiger Balm Gardens, at 262 Pasir Panjang Road (daily 9am–7pm; free except for Jade House; tel: 6872 2003). This collection of rather grotesque statues illustrates various Chinese mythological themes, and notorious crimes and vices from Singapore's history. These gaudy exhibits are the only remaining collection of this genre in Asia, and for this reason a must-see.

Haw Par Villa (Villa of the Tiger and the Leopard) was built by Aw Boon Haw (Gentle Tiger) for his brother Aw Boon Par (Gentle Leopard) in 1937. The Aw brothers were philanthropists who made their fortune with Tiger Balm, the cure-all that has now become world famous. In 1990, the gardens were transformed into Haw Par Villa Dragon World, billed as the world's first high-tech Chinese mythological theme park. However, the appeal of animated attractions and roller-coaster type rides did not last and Haw Par Villa reverted to its original self – a collection of bizarre tableaux depicting Chinese legends and folktales. The 1,000 statues and 150 tableaux may be too gory for some, but they were meant to be a lesson in morality, reflecting the brothers' beliefs in the values of filial piety. Be sure to walk through the **Ten Courts of Hell**; visitors cringe at the kinds of torture meted out to wrongdoers, such as disembowelment or immersion in a wok of boiling oil.

Among the statues are brief glimpses of the brothers' lives. There are photographs of the old villa and their quirky collection of cars – one was even painted with tiger stripes and a tiger head fashioned out of metal mounted on the bonnet. The original villa was torn down by Boon Haw when Boon Par died in 1945. Boon Haw turned Haw Par Villa into public property as a way to preserve Chinese culture and to impart the values of the past to modern Chinese.

Restoration works are underway to breathe new life into the attraction. A replica of the Tiger car, remodelled from a 1925 Buick, now stands at the original site of the Aw garage outside the Ten Courts of Hell. The private jade collection of the Aw family is displayed at the **Jade House** (the Aw family's original 1930s Jade House in Nassim Road was torn down in 1990). In December 2004, the new **Hua Song Museum** opened, connecting the Chinese diaspora with photographs and artefacts donated by overseas Chinese.

Ming Village

A detour off Pasir Panjang Road to the West Coast Highway leads to the **Ming Village** ❾ at 32 Pandan Road (daily 9am–5.30pm; free; tel: 6265 7711). Here you can watch potters and painters painstakingly recreate beautiful Ming blue and white porcelain by hand. On the same premises is the **Royal Selangor Pewter Museum**, which has fine pewterware – made from 97 percent tin and 3 percent alloy – on display and for sale (daily 9am–5pm; free). You can see a collection of vases, photo frames, tea sets and goblets, including reproductions of oil lamps and wine decanters, from London's Victoria & Albert Museum.

Map on page 162

Giant mask at the Haw Par Villa.

BELOW:
Ming Village pottery artist.

TIP

Holland Village is a good place to pick up ethnic items and handicrafts. Lim's Arts & Living at Holland Road Shopping Centre (02-01, tel: 6467 1300) has one of the widest selections.

BELOW: kids will love the interactive Science Centre.

Holland Village

Holland Village ⑩, once hailed by Prime Minister Goh Chok Tong as being "bohemian", is actually far from radical. It is really a charming village-like enclave well-loved by expats, locals and students from surrounding tertiary institutions.

The village is a wedge bounded by Lorong Liput, Lorong Mambong and parts of Holland Road and Holland Avenue. No one knows exactly how the area got its name, but it's common speculation that it was perhaps the favourite place of residence for the Dutch in colonial times. When the British troops were still in Singapore, Holland Village and nearby **Chip Bee Gardens** across Holland Avenue were their preferred place of abode; long after they left (in 1968), the semi-detached bungalows and terraced houses in which they used to live are still much sought after among new expat arrivals to Singapore. As if to relive its Dutch roots, **Holland V Shopping Mall** at the junction of Lorong Liput and Lorong Mambong sports a windmill atop its roof.

Holland Village has always had a reputation as a fashionable place to wine and dine. Chic restaurants and lively sidewalk cafés abound in the village and at Chip Bee Gardens, now home to gourmet grocers, trendy restaurants and art galleries. A gamut of cuisines is offered, from Mexican and South Seas-inspired to Indian and Italian. The area is particularly vibrant at night.

Like the rest of Singapore, however, Holland Village will inevitably favour the new over the old, the polished over the dilapidated. Already the old rattan and porcelain shops have been taken over by newer but more humdrum stores, the old market currently sticks out like a sore thumb and may just be "refurbished" to be in line with clean and tidy Singapore. Even the artistic community that has burgeoned at Chip Bee Gardens is a coordinated effort by the powers that be.

Singapore Science Centre

Anchoring the west coast is **Jurong**, an industrial area where about 300,000 or 10 percent of Singaporeans are employed. There are more than 2,600 factories in this part of the island. Nevertheless, it's not all work and no play, for Jurong has a number of parks, gardens and wildlife collections.

Some 15 km (9 miles) to the west of the HarbourFront Centre, about a 20-minute drive along the Ayer Rajah Expressway (AYE), is the family-friendly **Singapore Science Centre ⑪** at 15 Science Centre Road (Tues–Sun 10am–6pm, closed Mon; admission charge; tel: 6425 2500; www.science.edu.sg). The principles of flight, the animal kingdom and the complex world of electronics and the human body are just some of the subjects embraced by the 1,000 exhibits in its 12 galleries.

These innovative and hands-on displays have never failed to enthrall adults and children since the centre

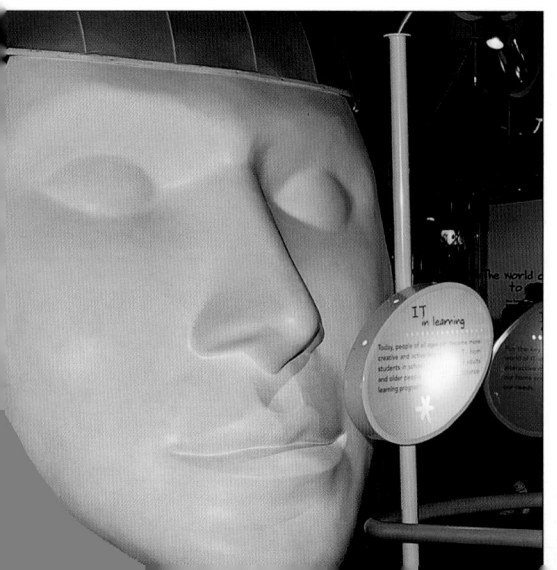

opened in 1977. One highlight is the interactive **Mind's Eye** gallery where visitors experience optical illusions – watch how the body can miraculously "disappear". Another highlight is the **Infocomm Xperience** hall, an exhibition featuring IT in education, at work, at play, in the home and on the move. A S$38-million revamp in 2000 saw new facilities being added, including the **Kinetic Garden** – an interactive garden with 35 sculptures, exhibits and water features – as well as an Annex Building featuring technology-based changing exhibitions.

The adjacent **Omni-Theatre** presents several wide-screen omnimax movies each day (starting at 10am with the last screening at 8pm; admission charge) with images on a 5-storey high hemispheric screen and sound from 72 amplifiers.

Snow City

Right next to the Omni-Theatre is **Snow City** ⑫, possibly the coolest attraction in town – in terms of degrees Celsius (Tues–Sun 10.30am–6.30pm; public holidays

Map on page 162

9am–8pm; admission charge; tel: 6337 1511; www.snowcity.com.sg).

The arctic playground contains a 1,200-sq metre (13,000-sq ft) **Snow Chamber** which allows tropical-bred locals a chance to snowboard, ski and snow tube down a three-storey high incline and doll up in full winter gear. Warning: you may not want to bother with this place if you've experienced the real thing.

Chinese/Japanese gardens

A short drive around Jurong Lake at Yuan Ching Road is the **Chinese Garden** ⑬ and right next door to it the **Japanese Garden** (both open daily 6am–11pm; free except for Bonsai Garden; tel: 6261 3632).

These two distinctly different gardens next to each other are joined by the **Bridge of Double Beauty**. The Chinese Garden (Yu Hwa Yuen) is a collection of theme gardens in the style of the Summer Palace in Beijing. The landscaping, inspired by the Sung Dynasty, is a harmonious blend of natural elements. The lovely pagoda affords a nice view of the garden in its lake-side setting.

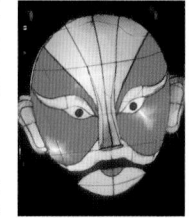

In September or October each year, depending on the lunar calendar, the Chinese Garden is illuminated with thousands of lanterns.

BELOW:
Chinese Garden pavilions at sunset.

Housing the Masses

Singapore has the second-highest population density in the world after Hong Kong, with 5,771 people per sq km. Even with ongoing reclamation, the land area cannot be increased much more, so there is a pressing need to optimise its use.

Once out of the city centre, the predominant image is of high-rise, high-density public housing, for 86 percent of Singaporeans live in apartment blocks designed by the Housing and Development Board (HDB). Incredibly, more than 90 percent of these households own the apartments they live in, subsidised in part by the government.

Singapore's public housing programme began in 1960. Building homes was a priority and by 1999, the HDB had designed and constructed over 800,000 units, most of which are located in self-contained New Towns. Singapore adopted the New Town typology, probably because of its close association with British planning practice in the 1950s and 1960s.

Each of the 21 New Towns is planned for about 250,000 to 300,000 residents, with essential facilities provided. These include commercial facilities such as cinemas, shopping malls and supermarkets; institutional facilities like libraries, schools and community centres; and recreational facilities such as sports complexes and swimming pools. Each town is divided into neighbourhoods of about 24,000 residents and each neighbourhood is further divided into precincts of between 2,000 and 3,000 residents. The larger facilities are sited at the town centre, which is also the transportation hub for bus and MRT stations. In the town centres are a range of eating places, malls and shops.

The earliest designs of apartment blocks were kept simple to facilitate speedy construction but, today, Singapore's younger generation are more demanding. The basic housing provision that satisfied their grandparents and even their parents is no longer sufficient. This has presented a challenge to the HDB who since 1992 have responded with better designs for new flats and a programme of upgrading existing public housing, starting with 30-year-old blocks of flats. Various means have been explored to achieve character: buildings of different height, articulated roof forms and special architectural features. Natural elements like gardens and fountains are also incorporated to enhance the character of each new town.

Public housing has also become increasingly integrated with the private sector. The most recent development is the concept of a waterfront town in the north of the island. Called Punggol 21, it has a planned mix of public and private housing.

Public housing in other parts of the world has generally received bad press but in Singapore it has worked remarkably well; in 1991 the "quality-of-life" in Tampines New Town (in the east of Singapore) was recognised with a United Nations World Habitat Award. To quote Rem Koolhaas: "The Singapore model stands out as a highly efficient alternative in a landscape of near universal pessimism... a pertinent can-do world of clearly defined ambitions."

To many Westerners it looks monotonous, but public housing in Singapore is studied with curiosity by planners around the world who are astounded by its success. ❑

LEFT: typical public housing.

Another attraction here is the Yun Xiu Yuan or Garden of Beauty, which is a Suzhou-style *penjing* (bonsai) garden with more than 1,000 bonsai. This is one of the largest *penjing* collections outside China and includes many valuable plants such as a pair of 200-year-old *Podocarpus* trees shaped like lions. In September/October each year, the Chinese Garden becomes ablaze with pretty lighted lanterns during the annual Mid-Autumn Festival celebrations *(see pages 48 and 51)*.

The adjacent Japanese Garden (Seiwaen), with its accent on simplicity, exudes a sense of peace and tranquillity with its Zen rock gardens, stone lanterns, ponds and shrubs.

Jurong Bird Park

Just off the Ayer Rajah Expressway is **Jurong Bird Park** ⓮ (daily 8am–6pm; admission charge; tel: 6265 0022; www.birdpark.com.sg). Colourful macaws welcome visitors at the entrance of this 20-hectare (49-acre) park – home to 8,000 birds of 600 different species from all over the world. Acknowledged as the leading bird park in the region and known for its commitment to avian conservation, the park attracts well over a million visitors every year.

There is much to see and do to occupy your time. Exhibits like the **Penguin Parade** recreate an Antarctic habitat for penguins, puffins as well as four species of flying seabirds. Outside, brightly coloured parrots enjoy the sunshine and delicate pink flamingoes wander in and out of the **Flamingo Lake**. More than 100 species of Southeast Asian birds fly almost free in the enormous walk-in **Waterfall Aviary** which reproduces the atmosphere of a rainforest.

The **Lory Loft**, launched in June 2004, is the park's fourth walk-in free flight aviary and the world's largest of its kind. Built to simulate Australia's vast rural landscape, visitors on boardwalks and bridges suspended in mid-air at a height of 12 metres (39 ft) mingle with 1,000 free-flying Lory birds at treetop level.

Another highlight is the **Hornbill and Toucan Exhibit**, which has one of the world's largest collections of Asian hornbills and South American toucans. Also unique is the **World of Darkness**, a nocturnal bird house which uses a reversed lighting system so that during the day when there are visitors, it is night inside. Six aviaries feature night birds from different habitats around the world. They range from the snowy owl from the tundra to the buffy fish owl from the mangrove forest.

A relaxing way to explore the park is by the Panorail (daily 9am–5pm; admission charge) so named because of the panoramic vistas it affords.

Included in your ticket is admission to the highly entertaining bird shows. These are held throughout the day but the most popular are the **All Star Birdshow** with cockatoos, pelicans and hornbills at 11am and 3pm daily, and the **Birds of Prey** at

Resident macaw at the Jurong Bird Park.

BELOW: birds of a feather at the Jurong Bird Park.

Map on page 162

Map on page 162

Pottery being dried inside the "dragon" kiln at Thow Kwang Industry in Jurong.

BELOW: snap-happy crocodiles at the Jurong Reptile Park.

10am and 4pm daily. Check the information board at the entrance for the day's schedule of shows.

Jurong Reptile Park

Opposite the Jurong Bird Park at 241 Jalan Ahmad Ibrahim is **Jurong Reptile Park** , where creatures that have changed little since prehistoric times roam (daily 9am–6pm; admission charge; tel: 6261 8866; www.reptilepark.com.sg). Iguanas, Giant Aldabra Tortoises from the Indian Ocean, anacondas from the Amazon, araipamas, a type of freshwater fish that can grow up to 7 metres (22 ft) and 5-metre (16½-ft) long crocodiles are on display.

You can watch the fascinating hand feeding of crocodiles (they leap and snatch at their food) at 10.30am and 5pm daily, or see them perform in the Reptile Show, also featuring cobras, at 11.45am and 2pm each day (extra 4pm show on Sat–Sun). Daily guided tours at 11am, after crocodile-feeding sessions, also feature the feeding of iguanas and other reptiles. Animal lovers are advised to skip this attraction.

Discovery Centre

Just off the Pan Island Expressway (PIE) at 510 Upper Jurong Road is **Singapore Discovery Centre** (Tues–Sun 9am–7pm; closed Mon except public holidays; admission charge; tel: 6792 6188; www.sdc.com. sg). The centre is a one-stop complex for children that tells the defence history of Singapore through images, shows and high-tech displays.

Many of the displays are interactive and hands-on – the kids will be able to talk to a robot, go on a motion simulator ride, shoot a couple of rounds at the computer-simulated firing range with real M-16 rifles, or watch a 3-D movie at the iWERKS, a five-storey high theatre.

Thow Kwang Industry

Tucked at the end of Jurong, near the Nanyang Technological University, is **Thow Kwang Industry** , a sprawling 3,000-sq metre (32,300-sq ft) porcelain- and earthernware-filled space in the middle of a forest (daily 9am–5pm; tel: 6265 5808; www.tkpotteryjungle.com).

To get there, take a taxi from the Boon Lay MRT station to 85 Lorong Tawas, where the "dragon kiln" carries on the ancient 2,000-year tradition of firing pottery. Called a dragon kiln because of its 40-metre (132-ft) length, it is filled with as many as 2,000 to 4,000 pieces of ceramics before being fired twice a year (in June and November). The dragon kiln has its origins in Shantou, China, and the one in Lorong Trawas was started by a migrant family from there.

Now run by the third generation Tan family, it is the only surviving dragon kiln in Singapore. Visitors can also see local potters honing their craft. A large variety of pottery pieces from all over Asia are on sale, including figurines, vases, jars and table lamps. Purchases can be shipped home, if required. ❑

RESTAURANTS

Restaurants

Brazilian

Brazil Churrascarla
14-16 Sixth Ave. Tel:
6463 1923. Open: D
daily. $$$ (buffet only)
A lively restaurant
favoured by carnivores,
thanks to *pasedors* who
come to your table to art-
fully shear slices of skew-
ered meats onto your
plate. Technically, you
should be a meat lover –
there are 15 cuts to
choose from – though a
salad buffet is available.

French

Au Petit Salut
01-54 Chip Bee Gardens,
Blk 44 Jalan Merah
Saga. Tel: 6475 1976.
Open: L and D daily
(closed Sat L). $$ (set
lunch) $$$$ (à la carte)
www.aupetitsalut.com
Petite this French restaurant may be, but it is big
on flavours. Chef de cui-
sine Philippe Nouzillat
brings diners traditional
Southern French cuisine
with contemporary
touches. Signatures
include the red wine
braised beef cheeks,
stewed white beans with
duck leg confit, and warm
Manjari chocolate cake.

Italian

Da Paolo La Terazza
01-56 Chip Bee Gardens,
Blk 44 Jalan Merah
Saga. Tel: 6476 1332.
Open: L and D daily
(closed Tues). $$ (set
lunch) $$$$ (à la carte)
www.dapaolo.com.sg
One of Singapore's best
Italian restaurant chains
is as stylish as ever
despite expansion in
recent years. This branch
manages to ooze sophis-
tication yet remain laid-
back. Owner-chef Paolo
Scarpa's pastas are
always excellent – in
fact, you won't go wrong
with any of the pasta
dishes on the menu.

Michelangelo's
01-60 Chip Bee Gardens,
Blk 44 Jalan Merah
Saga. Tel: 6475 9069.
Open: L and D daily
(closed Sat L) $$ (set
lunch) $$$ (à la carte)
www.michelangelos.com.sg
Chef-owner Angelo
Sanelli is like your big
Italian mama – fastidi-
ous, funny and an
accomplished chef. And
if you're permanently
glued to your cellphone,
he'll admonish you, too.
After all, when you're
dining at this romantic
Italian-Australian restau-
rant, what could be more
important than his food?

Sistina Ristorante
01-58 Jalan Merah Saga,
Blk 44 Chip Bee
Gardens. Tel: 6476
7782. Open: L and D
daily. $$$
www.sistina.com.sg
The humble pizza is
transformed to a high-cui-
sine treat under the skill-
ful hands of owner-chef
Simon McLoughlin. There
are over 50 types of top-
pings including scallops
and oysters. Whether
regular or thin crust,
topped with goat cheese
or rosemary-infused
lamb, there's an exten-
sive collection of New
World wines to comple-
ment your gourmet pizza.

Japanese

Shiro
24 Greenwood Ave. Tel:
6462 2774. Open: L and
D Mon–Sat. $$$ (set
lunch) $$$$ (à la carte)
Walk-ins are not enter-
tained at this reserva-
tions-only 30-seater in a
sleepy neighbourhood.
Persist, and you'll find
yourself sampling exquis-
ite haute Japanese cui-
sine in minimalist but
intimate surrounds. The
nine-course *Kaiseki* meal
is a sublime experience.

Mediterranean

Original Sin
01-62 Jalan Merah Saga,
Blk 43 Chip Bee Gar-
dens. Tel: 6475 5605.
Open: L and D daily
(closed Mon L). $$ (set
lunch) $$$ (à la carte)
www.originalsin.com.sg
Whether you're on an
ovo-lacto diet, a vegan or
just plain health-con-
scious, chef-owner
Marisa Bertocchi ensures
there's something imagi-
native for everyone. Her
mezze platter, *moussaka*,
Four Seasons pizza and
tiramisu would convert
even the most hardened
meat lover.

Mexican

Cha Cha Cha
32 Lorong Mambong,
Holland Village. Tel:
6462 1650. Open: Sun–
Thur 11.30am–11pm,
Fri–Sat 11.30am–mid-
night. $$$
It's a subdued little spot
where you will find good
south-of-the-border food
– *chimichangas*, *fajitas*,
burritos – along with a
relaxed atmosphere and
great margaritas.

Local

SoulFood by Makansutra
01-01 Matrix Block, 30
Biopolis St. Tel: 6478
9570. Open: daily
8am–10pm. $
www.makansutra.com
SoulFood is a fantasy
turned dream for K.F.
Seetoh, one of Singa-
pore's most famous food
personalities. The air-conditioned space houses
11 of the Who's Who of
the local food scene.
Learn about hawker food
from the vignettes posted
outside every stall.

PRICE CATEGORIES

Prices for a three-course
dinner per person without
drinks and taxes:
$ = under S$20
$$ = S$20–$30
$$$ = S$30–$45
$$$$ = more than S$45

THE EAST COAST

The palm-fringed East Coast offers visitors a taste of Malay culture in Geylang Serai, watersports at East Coast Park's beach, history in Changi, and the chance to unwind on rural Ubin island

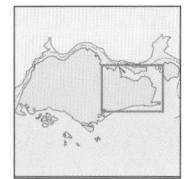

The East Coast is one of Singapore's most eclectic neighbourhoods and has a good mix of ethnic groups. Numerous churches, several mosques, and Chinese and Indian temples bear witness to this. The east is also a popular food hub, with many good restaurants and hawker fare – lots of it. Until the 1970s, when a huge chunk of the east coast shoreline was reclaimed, the sea was right at the doorstep of many of the bungalows that lined Tanjong Rhu, Fort Road and Meyer Road.

Today, instead of the sea lapping the shores of these houses, it's the expressway called the East Coast Parkway (ECP) stretching all the way from Tanjong Rhu to Changi Airport. Part of the reclaimed land has been transformed into a park which has become a pleasant waterfront playground for the residents of the east coast. Courting couples and families often come here to stroll in the evenings and enjoy the sea breezes. In the place of rambling seaside bungalows, there are now towering high-rise apartment blocks with sweeping views of the sea.

Kallang

Kallang – the part of the east coast closest to downtown – is a massive sports and entertainment hub. Major sporting events are held at the **National Stadium**, while the wedge-shaped **Singapore Indoor Stadium**, designed by Kenzo Tange, plays host to both sports and concerts.

On the fringes of the Indoor Stadium along the edge of the Kallang River is **Stadium Waterfront** with riverfront bars and restaurants – a particularly lovely spot in the evening. Just next to the Indoor Stadium is another restaurant cluster known as **Oasis Complex**. Mock horror theatre-restaurant **Igor's** is located here *(see page 184)* and is a fun night out.

Map on page 212

LEFT: yachting at the East Coast.
BELOW: Igor's at the Stadium Waterfront makes for a ghoulish night out.

Dancer wearing elaborate headgear at the Malay Village in Geylang.

Geylang

Colourful **Geylang** is further east, a short walk from the Paya Lebar MRT station. It is an area is full of contradictions: Buddhist temples coexist with brothels. Many visitors are surprised to learn that prostitution is legal in Singapore. "Working" women are licensed and brothels operate in designated red-light areas. On some streets in Geylang, women may draw unnecessary attention to themselves if they are unaccompanied.

Ironically, some of Geylang's best restaurants, **Geylang Famous Beef Kway Teow** *(see page 185)* at Lorong 9 for instance, are located around these streets. Food-mad Singaporeans seem more concerned with finding a table to care about the area's seedy repute. Geylang is a well-known hotspot for good hawker-style food and it really comes alive after midnight. This is also the place for durians, the pungent fruit that elicits a love-it-or-hate-it response. A string of street-side durian stalls are found along **Sims Avenue**, across Lorong 15.

Geylang Serai

Travelling further east, **Geylang Serai** lies at the end of **Geylang Road**. Although Geylang Serai is not one of the original districts established by Raffles, it has a strong ethnic flavour. More than Kampung Glam *(see page 142)*, this is the heart of Malay society and culture in Singapore, and home to many of the island's best Malay restaurants. The Malays had been living in a village built on stilts at the mouth of the Singapore River when Raffles arrived in 1819. When the Malays were asked to move in 1840, they chose Geylang as their new home.

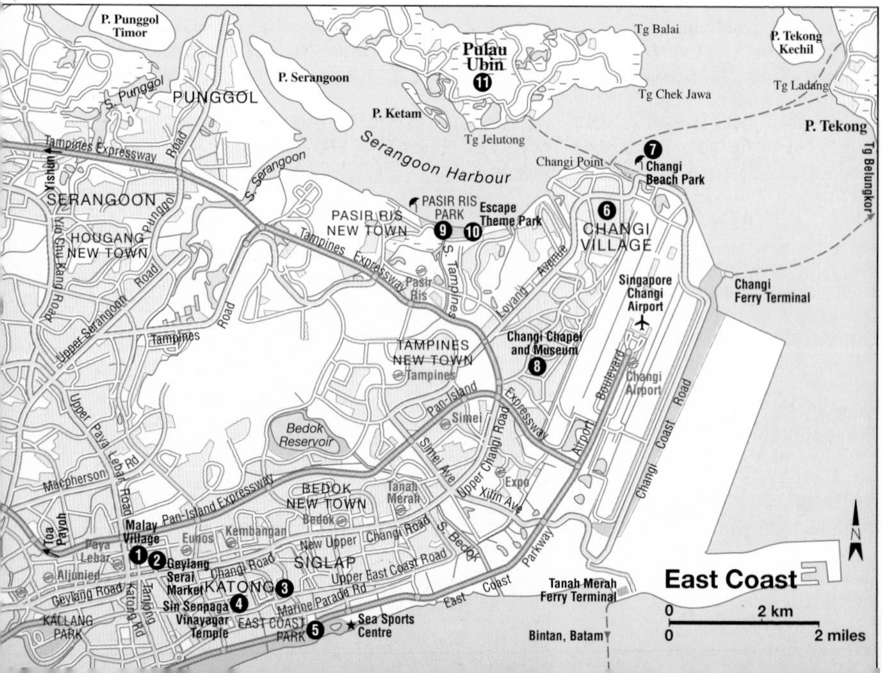

Originally covered by coconut and rubber plantations and *serai* (lemon grass) fields, by the early 20th century Geylang had become urbanised with rows of two- and three-storey shophouses and terrace houses similar to those found in Chinatown and Kampung Glam. Indeed, some of the Chinese Baroque shophouses *(see pages 148–49)* here rank among the best preserved in Singapore. They are more flamboyant in the use of details such as tiles, motifs and bas-relief mouldings. The shophouses are tucked along the numerous *lorong* (lanes) between Geylang Road and Sims Avenue; perhaps the best examples can be seen in Lorong 35, Lorong 24A, Lorong 24, Lorong Bachok and Lorong 19.

Today, the heart of Geylang Serai is the section of Geylang Road between Jalan Eunos and Aljunied Road, lined with numerous restaurants and shops that are often open until late at night. **Jalan Eunos**, a public housing estate nearby, is another Malay-dominated enclave.

Malay Village

Dominating the area is the **Malay Village ❶** opposite Paya Lebar MRT station (daily 10am–10pm; free except museums; tel: 6748 4700). The village, or *kampung*, draws together various aspects of Malay art, music, history and food in a setting comprising traditional *bumbung panjang* (long roof) or *rumah Melayu* (Malay house) architecture – wooden and thatched-roof buildings with high-pitched roofs and steep, slightly flared sides.

The village houses a rather banal **Cultural Museum** with a display of traditional *keris* (daggers), musical instruments and typical Malay household items and an elaborate bridal chamber. The other equally ho hum attraction, **Kampung Days**, is a recreation of a typical Malay village) in the 1950s and 60s.

There are two dining options: the **Floating Seafood Restaurant** sits on stilts above a fish pond and serves Chinese-style seafood dishes (tel: 6740 8647). **Attie Food Court** has Malay dishes such as *satay* and Indonesian fried rice from 6–11pm. There are also some shops selling batik, spices and handicrafts. Sadly, despite its attempts to promote Malay culture and renewed efforts to re-package it, the Malay Village never quite got off the ground.

Map on page 174

TIP

Geylang is one of the best places to see how different cultures can coexist harmoniously. Along Geylang East Avenue 2, the ornate Sri Sivan Temple sits next to the Tang dynasty-style Foo Hai Ch'an Monastery.

LEFT AND BELOW: ceremonial umbrella and Javanese doll display at the Malay Museum.

Geylang Serai Market

A block's walk from the Malay Village leads to the flats of Geylang Serai where wooden houses on stilts once stood. Behind the flats is the **Geylang Serai Market ❷**, a fascinating "wet market" of stalls under a zinc roof and manned by genial owners. You will find a wide range of produce, especially hard-to-find vegetables favoured by the Malays. Prices here are considered to be among the lowest in Singapore. If there's one place that doesn't look like squeaky clean Singapore, this is it. The pungent smell of freshly slaughtered poultry mingles with fragrant hot-off-the-wok banana fritters, and its narrow alleys are congested and wet. It's a fast disappearing sight – the market and food centre will be torn down in 2006 and rebuilt in a style reminiscent of Malay architecture.

Joo Chiat and Koon Seng

Opposite the Malay Village is **Joo Chiat Complex** and the Joo Chiat area, which together with Katong (*see page 177*) is a stronghold of the Peranakan community – descendants of early Chinese immigrant men who married local Malay women (*see page 37*). Joo Chiat Complex houses low-cost government-built flats on the upper floors and shops on the lower levels. It replaced the former Joo Chiat Market where in the old days trishaws used to wait to ferry the sarong-clad Peranakan *bibik* (elderly ladies) and their laden baskets back to their homes after shopping. Today, Joo Chiat Complex is noted for its plethora of textile shops.

The Peranakan *bibik* have all but dispersed from Joo Chiat, but the area still has traces of its rich Straits Chinese heritage. **Kway Guan Huat** still produces by hand wafer-thin *poh piah* "skins" on griddles (95 Joo Chiat Road; tel: 6344 2875). The skins are used to wrap the myriad ingredients which make up *poh piah* or spring rolls, a delicious Peranakan dish that requires tedious preparation. The process of making the skins from dough can be seen from 9am to noon.

Perhaps the finest examples of Peranakan heritage are the beautifully restored Chinese Baroque

Katong Antique House at 208 East Coast Road is a treasure trove of Peranakan artefacts.

BELOW: fish-happy Geylang Serai Market vendor.

shophouses *(see pages 148–49)* along **Joo Chiat Road** and **Koon Seng Road**, built in the 1930s. The richly decorated facades testify to the wealth of the original homeowners.

Katong

Joo Chiat Road connects with East Coast Road and an old suburb called **Katong ❸**. This area has long enjoyed a reputation for good food. Gentrified in appearance these days, the neighbourhood, with traces of its Eurasian and Peranakan past, is on the brink of losing its old-world charm. As with the now-sanitised Chinatown, the newly refurbished prewar shophouses are no longer affordable to old-timers who once plied their trade in the area. Recently, businesses in Katong have joined forces to keep the Peranakan culture alive and restore the area to its glorious old days.

Key among them is **Katong Antique House**, at 208 East Coast Road, where a collection of age-old Peranakan artefacts are displayed by its Peranakan owner, Peter Wee (viewing by appointment only; admission charge to gallery; tel: 6345 8544). This century-old shophouse has been home to five generations of Straits Chinese families. The gallery on level two showcases Wee's private collection of porcelain, beaded shoes, *kebaya* (traditional embroidered blouses) and silver items among others. Typical spices used by the Peranakan in their cooking such as *belacan* (prawn paste) and curry powder are also on sale.

More traces of Peranakan culture can be seen further down the road. **Glory** (tel: 6341 1749) at 139 East Coast Road is best known for its pineapple tarts and traditional Peranakan confectionery, while **Kim Choo Kueh Chang** at No. 109/111 (tel: 6741 2125) sells delicious rice dumplings wrapped in fragrant pandan leaves. Nonya dumpling wrap-

ping demonstrations are offered daily – call for appointment.

Two doors away at No. 113 is **Rumah Bebe** (tel: 6247 8781), a treasure trove of Peranakan artefacts in a 1928 Peranakan-style shophouse. A tour around its premises allows a peek into a traditional Peranakan house setting – check out the lovely bridal chamber on level two. Look out also for intricate *kasut manik manik*, dainty slippers made of fine beadwork. The owner Bebe Seet is regarded as an expert in the art of beading, a craft that is fast disappearing in urban Singapore. She can customise beaded shoes (beadwork classes are also available) and *kebaya* outfits for visitors.

Peranakan culinary classes are offered at Rumah Bebe and a few doors away, at **True Blue** restaurant, at No. 117 *(see page 185)*. Peranakan fare is in fact Singapore's very own fusion cuisine, blending Chinese and Malay cooking styles and ingredients with flair. A number of restaurants in the area offer authentic Peranakan fare – like **Casa Bom Vento** and **Guan Hoe Soon** *(see page 185)*.

Map on page 174

TIP

One of Katong's stalwarts must surely be the Chin Mee Chin Confectionery, where two generations of Katongites have snacked on their famous toasted bread with *kaya* (coconut jam) and cakes (204 East Coast Road; tel: 6345 0419).

BELOW: handmade beaded Peranakan slippers.

BELOW:
roof detail from the Sri Senpaga Vinayagar Temple.

Senpaga Vinayagar Temple

The ornate **Sri Senpaga Vinayagar Temple ❹** sits at 19 Ceylon Road, just off East Coast Road (daily 5.30am–12.30pm, 5.30–9pm; tel: 6345 8176). The present building, rebuilt bteween 2001 and 2003, features a 5-tier, 72-ft *rajagopuram* (royal entrance tower) sculptured according to Indian Chola traditions. Unique features abound at this Hindu temple: the granite footstone at the temple's entrance is a feature found in ancient Chola temples; *dwarapalakas* (gatekeepers) at the base tier of the tower entrance are apparently not found anywhere else in Asia; and its *vimanam* (temple dome) is covered in gold.

The temple's history dates back to the 1850s when Ceylonese Tamil Ethirnayagam Pillai built a thatch-roof temple under a *senpaga* tree on the banks of a pond where a statue of Lord Vinayagar was believed to be found. It moved to its present site in the early 1900s. A bomb damaged the temple during World War II though the main shrine remained intact. Today, the temple remains an important place of worship for the Hindu community in the east coast.

Siglap

Further up is Upper East Coast Road and another suburb, **Siglap**, made up of a number of private housing estates of bungalows and terrace houses like Frankel (built by a Jewish developer) and Opera Estate (with street names like Tosca Terrace and Aida Avenue), and stylish condos. Rows of newly built terraces with shops, alfresco wine bars, smart cafés and restaurants on the ground floor and apartments on the upper floor have proliferated here. Weekends often see the most crowds and parking is sometimes a problem.

East Coast Park

The visitor's first encounter with Singapore starts with the lush east coast while travelling into town from Changi Airport. The area could be aptly described as Singapore's "riviera" with coconut groves and sandy beaches on one side of the coastal highway, and expensive condos on the other. The east coast is packed at weekends as Singaporeans escape for a day at the beach, but during the week the beaches and picnic areas are blissfully quiet.

East Coast Park ❺ stretches for more than 10 km (6 miles) along the coast between Changi Airport and Marina Bay. Fringed with casuarinas and coconut palms, the park affords superb views of ships anchored in the Straits of Singapore. The sea breeze blows gently and it's often peaceful enough for birds to flock to special tall-grass sanctuaries found along the coastline.

The park is the playground for residents living in the eastern part of the island. *Tai chi* practitioners can be seen exercising in the park as early as 6am, together with joggers and cyclists. Picnic tables and barbecue pits are set up under the trees, and on weekends campers pitch their colourful tents. As always in Singapore, there are plenty of eating places, from burgers and pizzas to mouthwatering local seafood.

The beach gets very crowded on the weekends especially around car park C3 where Marine Cove and McDonald's are, but there's always plenty of space for a picnic in the coconut groves and wooded areas behind the shore. Swimming is pleasant here (don't expect crystal clear waters) but at least the water and beaches are clean. Basic accommodation is available at the beachfront **Costa Sands Resort** if you want to spend a few days here (tel: 6442 7955; www.costasands.com.sg).

Like Sentosa, there is plenty here to keep you occupied. The **Sea Sports Centre** (1212 East Coast Parkway; tel: 6449 5118) offers surfboards and sail boats for hire. Bicycles and roller blades can be hired from several kiosks in the park for use along the 12-km (7-mile) bike path along the coast.

Other recreational diversions include tennis courts, a golf driving range, an indoor mini golf adventure, a water park, fitness courses and a 10-pin bowling alley.

East Coast dining

Many people come to the East Coast just to eat, especially at the popular **East Coast Seafood Centre**, housing several restaurants near the swimming lagoon. The specialties here range from steamed *garoupa* fish in ginger and soya sauce, to chilli or pepper crabs and grilled butter prawns. A stone's throw away is the popular **East Coast Lagoon Food Village** where some stalls are so popular that it is not uncommon to find queues 10 people deep.

A few kilometres further (towards the city) is **Marine Cove**, another restaurant and recreation hub. A number of good restaurants are found here (Tung Lok Seafood Gallery, The Mango Tree, among others), and there are also pubs where you can sit out in the open air to enjoy the fresh sea breezes. **Bernie's BFD** (ask them what the acronym stands for) is noted for its huge margaritas *(see page 184)*.

The East Coast is a popular spot for windsurfers and sailors alike.

BELOW:
roller bladers at
the East Coast Park.

Changi Village

Before Changi Airport was opened in the early 1980s, the rustic and laidback **Changi Village ❻** was the only reason to venture to the far eastern shore of Singapore. This sleepy corner of the island is a charming slice of old Singapore and is home to a splendid variety of old trees (the magnificent Shorea Gibbosa tree with a cauliflower-like crown at the junction of Netheravon Road and Turnhouse Road is believed to be one of the last two left standing in Singapore). The stretch of sea here is a favourite rowing area for kayakers. The horizon is often dotted with the sails of dinghies and keelboats manned by weekend sailors from the nearby sailing clubs.

Once considered the boondocks, the seafood restaurants and pubs flanking Netheravon Road in Changi Village have revived the bustling atmosphere the place enjoyed when the British troops were stationed here. **Le Meridien Changi Village Hotel** (tel: 6379 7111) offers the only hotel accommodation in the area.

Take time to wander along the village's sleepy streets. Old black-and-white photographs of the village can be seen at **George Photo** (01-2000, Block 1; tel: 6545 1509). Down the same street, **Salvation Army Thrift Shop** has interesting stuff (01-2078, Block 4, tel: 6545 5722).

Changi Village Food Centre behind offers some of the island's best local fare – and not surprisingly gets very crowded at weekends.

A short walk away is the **Changi Point Jetty**, which offers a ferry service to Pulau Ubin *(see pages 182–83)* and to Tanjong Pengelih, the jump-off point for mountain biking trips to **Penggarang**, at the southeastern tip of Johor in Malaysia.

Changi Beach Park

The footbridge nearby leads to **Changi Beach Park ❼**, a short but pleasant stretch of sand with views across the water to Malaysia and Pulau Tekong island, which is a Singapore military training area. It isn't as popular as the East Coast Park and therefore far less crowded.

Look out for the **Changi Beach Massacre Site** nearby, marked by a storyboard, where 66 male Chinese civilians were killed by a Japanese firing squad on 20 February 1942. The same spot is a campsite and popular picnic spot.

Changi Chapel/Museum

The Japanese Imperial Army turned barracks built by the British into a POW camp at Changi after they captured Singapore in early 1942. This camp became a notorious hell hole where both military and civilian prisoners were interned by the thousands. Many of the POWs were sent to work at the Thailand-Burma railroad, including the infamous Bridge of the River Kwai, but those who remained at Changi weren't much better off. They had to endure appalling conditions, described in a number of poignant books, includ-

East Coast Lagoon Food Village (see page 184) has more than half-dozen satay stalls; one of the best is Haron's at No. 55.

BELOW:
seafood restaurants are abundant on the East Coast.

ing *King Rat* by James Clavell – who was a POW at Changi himself.

Changi Prison still exists today, but it's now a place for criminals. The historic **Changi Chapel and Museum ⑤**, formerly located next door to Changi Prison, moved to its new site in nearby Upper Changi Road North in 2001 (daily 9.30am–4.30pm; free; tel: 6214 2451; www.changimuseum.com).

The museum focuses on the memories and lives of both POWs and civilian internees who survived the horrific Japanese Occupation (1942–45) with a collection of wartime memorabilia, including drawings by W.R.M. Haxworth and photographs by George Aspinall (taken and developed in great danger when he was interned by the Japanese). Life as a POW is depicted in searing clarity here.

Particularly compelling are the **Changi Murals**. Painted by British POW Stanley Warren, the five murals, each depicting the life of Christ, are replicas of the restored originals at Changi Camp. The Changi Chapel, a symbolic replica

of the one at Changi Prison, is housed in the open-air courtyard (visitors are welcome to join the Sunday service, which takes place from 9.30am to 11.30am). There are also video screenings and rare books depicting life during the war years.

Johore Battery

Further up off Upper Changi Road North, along Cosford Road, lies the **Johore Battery** (daily 8am–5pm; free; tel: 6546 9897), a former gun emplacement with a labyrinth of underground tunnels built by the British in 1939. The battery displays a replica of the 15-inch "monster guns" – the largest to be installed outside Britain during World War II and capable of firing at battleships over 20 miles (32 km away).

Pasir Ris Park

Pasir Ris at the northeast coast of Singapore and the end of the eastern MRT line is home to the idyllic **Pasir Ris Park ⑦**, another pleasant stretch of beach that overlooks Pulau Ubin just across the waters. Part of the park, near car park C (entry via Pasir

Map on page 174

TIP

One of the best ways to get close to the sea without getting wet is via the boardwalks built along the rugged coastline of Changi. The 1.2-km (¾-mile) boardwalk stretches from Changi Sailing Club to Changi Beach Club.

BELOW: poignant notes left behind in rememberance of war heroes at the Changi Chapel.

Ris Green road), encloses a reserve which protects an area of mangrove swamp, where many migrating shore birds feed and build their nests.

A wooden boardwalk leads across the mud flats and brackish ponds, with signboards that provide descriptions of the flora and fauna. Note: the boardwalks are currently closed for repair and will reopen in the middle of 2005. However, nature lovers can still derive much pleasure from **Sungei Api Api** nearby. ("Sungei" is "river" in Malay and "Api Api" is a mangrove variety). A bridge spanning the river connects car parks C and D. This river is one of the few remaining natural rivers in Singapore and about 26 species of mangrove have been documented at this mangrove swamp. If flora and fauna does not interest you, spend a lazy afternoon relaxing or swimming at this undulating stretch of sand.

Fisherman's Village near car park D offers fishing opportunities at a pond. A string of beach pubs, cafés and restaurants are also located along this side of the beach.

Twin theme parks

The **Escape Theme Park** ❿ at 1 Pasir Ris Close is an ideal playground for families with restless children (Sat–Sun and public and school holidays 10am–10pm; admission charge; tel: 6581 9112; www.escape themepark.com.sg). The gravity-defying rides and speed races will appeal to thrill seekers and speed demons. The adjacent **Wild Wild Wet** water theme park promises more thrills and spills of the watery kind with rides like the Tsunami and snake-like Ulah-lah (Sat–Sun and public and school holidays 10am–7pm, Mon and Wed–Fri 1–7pm; admission charge; www.wildwildwet.com).

Both parks are part of a larger development called **Downtown East**, a leisure, food and shopping hub that also provides comfortable chalet-style accommodation at reasonable rates (tel: 6582 3322; www.ntucclub.com.sg).

Pulau Ubin

Just off the northeastern tip of Singapore is the island of **Pulau Ubin** ⓫, which basks in the Johor Straits, a stone's throw from the Malaysian coast. A 15-minute boat ride from **Changi Point Jetty** *(see page 180)* is all it takes to reach Ubin, measuring just 8 km (5 miles) across and 1.5 km (1 mile) wide. Left behind by developments on the main island, Ubin was for a long time the last stronghold of old Singapore. Despite scars caused by quarrying, its pastoral charm remains intact, a tapestry of sandy roads, prawn farms, abandoned rubber plantations and coconut groves. An information kiosk run by the National Parks (daily 8.30am–5pm; tel: 6542 4108) has a map and leaflets detailing the flora and fauna of Ubin and things to do on the island.

Ubin's main "town centre" is no longer a sleepy hollow. The handful of grocery stores have taken on a lucrative sideline renting mountain

BELOW: get an adrenalin high at Escape Theme Park.

bikes, and the coffee shops of old have turned themselves into seafood restaurants. These services cater to the ever-increasing crowds from the mainland, especially during weekends and holidays. Most visitors walk around Ubin although mountain biking is also popular. Taxis can also be hired near the ferry pier, but agree on the fare first before hopping in.

A naturalist's paradise

Pulau Ubin is one of Singapore's last great nature areas, with vast tracts of secondary jungle and mangrove swamp that sustain a wide variety of animals such as the flying fox, long-tailed macaque and monitor lizard, and birds like the ruby-cheeked sunbird, kingfishers, brahminy kite, white-bellied fish eagle, buffy fish owls and various types of egrets and herons.

Fish and prawn farming are a source of income for the island's inhabitants. The island has a population of about 100 people, most of whom live in wooden houses surrounded by fruit orchards. Apart from bird watching, visitors to Ubin can go fishing or crabbing in the mangrove swamps. The best angling spots are near the Ketam Channel (between Ubin and its sister island, Pulau Ketam), and along waterways near the coast during high tide.

A walk in the swamps or forest may reveal unexpected surprises such as sightings of an oriental whip snake curled up on a tree or fruit bats rustling in the trees in the evenings. There are wild orchids and flowers to be found and if one is lucky, carnivorous pitcher plants with insects trapped in their huge pitcher cups.

Accommodation is available at the **Marina Country Club Resort** which offers cottage-style rooms with a focus on outdoor activities like canoeing, rock climbing, mountain biking and treks (tel: 6542 9590; www.marinacountryclub.com.sg).

There are two beaches on the island – **Noordin** and **Mamam** – where visitors can pitch tents. In recent years, plans to develop Ubin have been shelved after the public voiced its concerns, preferring to leave the island as the last bastion of rural Singapore. ❑

Map on page 174

A brahminy kite swoops in for the kill over the waters off Pulau Ubin.

BELOW: trail riding at Pulau Ubin.

Chek Jawa

Call it nature's outdoor classroom if you wish. Thanks to passionate nature lovers, Chek Jawa at Pulau Ubin's southeast coast has been saved from reclamation. The vast expanse of sand and mud flats is so fertile it has created an astonishing marine biological diversity and a coastal ecosystem found nowhere else in Singapore. The wetland with several habitats – seagrass bed, rocky shore, sand bar, mud flats and mangrove forest – teems with endangered flora and fauna. The two-hour guided tour takes place during low tide and must be booked in advance. Schedules are posted on www.nparks.gov.sg (tel: 6542 4108) and tours get booked up quickly.

RESTAURANTS

American

Bernie's BFD

East Coast Recreation Ctr, 1000 East Coast Parkway. Tel: 6244 4434. Open: Mon–Thur 4pm–2am, Fri 4pm–3am, Sat noon–3am, Sun noon–2am. $$$
With an energetic band, tanned women in tight outfits, oversized burgers and steaks, intoxicating margaritas and beach-front location, no wonder Bernie's is such a hit.

Indian

The Mango Tree

1000 East Coast Parkway, B23. Tel: 6442 8655. Open: L and D Mon–Fri, Sat–Sun 11.30am–11pm. $$$
www.themangotree.com.sg
Named after the tree standing outside, this seafront restaurant is so lovely you want to linger over your meal, watching the cyclists whizzing past or just staring at the deep blue – with an endless supply of mango *lassi*, of course. The hospitable staff, in all-white

Punjabi outfits, the decor, modern with Indian accents, and the menu, featuring the best of India's coastal regions, all lend a sophisticated but relaxed air.

Vansh

01-04 Singapore Indoor Stadium, 2 Stadium Walk. Tel: 6345 4466. Open: L and D daily. $$ (set lunch) $$$$
Have you stumbled upon a setting for an Austin Powers film? The setting is so bold, yet so sexy baby, you may just want to sip the Kamasutra cocktail horizontally – on the low lounge chairs around the open tandoor kitchen. Modern Indian cuisine means everything is individually plated and creatively presented.

Italian

Al Forno

400 East Coast Rd. Tel: 6348 8781. Open: L and D daily. $$$
Al Forno means "The Oven" and Italian owner-manager Alessandro Di Prisco has certainly won many hearts (and stomachs) with his lip-smacking pizzas and calzones. That's because they are lovingly crafted by Italian chefs before they go into a large wood-fired oven. So is the seafood spaghetti – wrapped in foil so that it is juicy yet oh-so *al dente*.

Porta Porta

971 Upper Changi North Rd. Tel: 6545 3108. Open: L and D Tues–Sun. $$ (set lunch) $$$$ (à la carte)
Run by a husband-and-wife team, Italian Nino Laino and Singaporean Rozianah Baharudin, who make you feel so at home you'd think you've been invited to a home-style Italian dinner. The irrepressible Nino loves to talk and he can whip up anything you desire, if ingredients permit. The great value house menu offers a sampling of Laino's specialties.

International

Igor's – The Main Event

01-02A Oasis Complex, 50 Stadium Blvd. Tel: 6440 2725. Open: D Thurs–Sat and eve of public holidays. $$$$ (set dinner with show)
www.igors.com.sg
Camp it up at this horror-themed restaurant, where skeleton chandeliers loom overhead and sculpted bats peer from doorways. Cocktails are dispensed at the Devil's Distillery Bar by ghoulish waitstaff. Don't get spooked by the hefty admission fee – it includes a tour through the monster-infested Demon Dungeons, dinner in the Grand Haunted Dining Hall and rowdy live stage shows.

Shore Restaurant

National Service Sea Sports Ctr, 11 Changi Coast Walk. Tel: 6546 7703. Open: L and D daily. $$$
Changi's best-kept secret is where you tuck into beef curry, lamb chops and black pepper crabs with your feet in the sand, metres away from the sea. Service is good, prices are amazingly down to earth and the seafood barbecue on Friday and Saturday evenings are great fun.

Local

Changi Village Food Centre

Blk 2, Changi Village Rd. Open: B till late daily. $
It's most famous for *nasi lemak*, a coconut-based rice dish. Just S$2 gets you rice with fried chicken, ikan bilis (fried whitebait) and egg. Many Malay stalls offer this dish but the longest queues are at stall 57. Also check out Charlie's Snack Bar at stall 8 for fish and chips and over 50 varieties of beer.

East Coast Lagoon Food Village

East Coast Parkway, next to car park E2. Open: B till late daily. $
Where else can you have some of the best local food in a lovely Indonesian-style structure and just a stone's throw away from the sea?

Make a beeline for the curry puffs (stall 28), barbecued pork noodles (stall 45) and vermicelli with *satay* sauce (stall 17). There are at least a dozen *satay* stalls but No. 55 (Haron's) is the best. Best visited at night when all the stalls are open.

Singa Fiesta

Pasir Ris Park, near car park D. Open: D daily. $–$$$

It's the only hawker centre in Singapore that sits right on the sand beach. You can even park your bums on the sand and disregard the wooden benches if you desire. Seafood is the mainstay though stalls offer *satay*, Thai pineapple fried rice and pasta. What's beach dining without a cold, cold beer? Alcohol and fruit juices are sold under a thatched roof.

Geylang Famous Beef Kway Teow

237 Geylang, Lorong 9. Open: Mon 5pm–3am, Tues–Sun 11–3am. $

It's indeed famous. Just look at the number of cars risking parking fines just for a plate of beef noodles. Industrious chef-owner Leong Wan Hui serves up to 700 plates of it on a Saturday night. It's the super-tender beef slices and thick gravy of black beans and chilli that make this dish stand above others. Also try her other stir-fry dishes such as ostrich with spring onions, and sweet and sour pork.

Marine Parade Laksa

Nan Sin Food Ctr, 57/59 East Coast Rd. Open: daily 10am–6pm, closed alternate Tues. $

Laksa is noodles with a curry-like, coconut-based soup. This particular stall is said to have pioneered Katong *laksa*, the now-famous variety that has even warranted a story in *The New York Times*. You can ask for clams (or without) and you eat the short noodles with your spoon – no chopsticks required.

Peranakan

Casa Bom Vento

467 Joo Chiat Rd. Tel: 6348 7786. Open: L and D Tues–Sun. $$

Never mind the non-existent decor, the home-style Eurasian and Peranakan dishes are so delicious word of mouth alone has kept this modest establishment going. Owner-chef Gladys Chee's traditional oxtail stew requires a day's advance order. But if you just turn up, her Devil's curry and stingray with peppercorn and curry leaves are superb.

Guan Hoe Soon

214 Joo Chiat Rd. Tel: 6344 2761. Open: L and D daily, closed Tues. $$
www.guanhoesoon.com

Singapore's oldest Peranakan restaurant was a mere coffeeshop when it was founded in 1953 by an enterprising Hainanese man. Despite some attempts at modernisation in the 1980s, its old world ambience is

still palpable. You can't go wrong with traditional Straits Chinese dishes such as *satay babi* (pork satay curry), *ngo hiang* sausage and *ayam tempra* (chicken stew).

True Blue

117 East Coast Rd. Tel: 6440 0449. Open: L and D Tues–Sun. $$

You may miss the entrance to this lovely restaurant if you aren't vigilant. Up a staircase, past owner Benjamin Seck's personal collection of Straits Chinese antiques, you settle in a tastefully adorned space. Seck's mom, Daisy Seah, has a formidable reputation in the Peranakan circle. Her *ayam buah keluak* (chicken with Indonesian black nuts) is divine.

Seafood

East Coast Seafood Centre

1110 East Coast Parkway, car park E1. $$$

A collection of informal, family-type seafood restaurants that fill up on weekends. A good seaside place to gorge on seafood prepared Singapore-style. Prices are reasonable unless you order Sri Lankan crabs. Good bets include **Red House** (tel: 6442 3112); **Jumbo** (tel: 6442 3435); **Long Beach** (tel: 6448 3636) and **Lucky View** (tel: 6242 1011).

Hua Yu Wee

462 Upper East Coast Rd. Tel: 6442 9313. Open: D daily. $$$

Housed in a slightly battered Chinese mansion, families flock in droves to this nondescript restaurant for its Singapore-style seafood dishes that always satisfy. Their chilli and pepper crabs, butter prawns and seafood rolls are highly recommended.

Palm Beach Seafood Restaurant

Kallang Leisure Park, 5 Stadium Walk. Tel: 6344 3088. Open: L and D daily. $$$

Whether there's a concert at the nearby Indoor Stadium or not, this is a firm favourite with locals who come for the chilli and black pepper crabs, black sauce prawns, deep-fried baby squid and crisp *yu char kway* rolls. Ask for fried *mantou* (Chinese buns) to mop up the sauce from the chilli crabs.

Tung Lok Seafood Gallery

2/F, Building B, East Coast Recreation Ctr, 1000 East Coast Parkway. Tel: 6246 0555. Open: L and D daily. $$$$
www.tunglok.com

Who says you can't negotiate crab claws and business deals simultaneously? The mod dining room, vigilant waitstaff, beautifully presented dishes and creative menu (like barramundi steamed with gooseliver sauce and prawns with *wasabi* mayo) are all geared towards impressing your VIP guests.

CENTRAL AND NORTHERN SINGAPORE

A verdant oasis of green marks the centre of the island
where Singapore's remaining natural habitats are
found. But it's not all flora and fauna as the area
also hosts some age-old Chinese temples

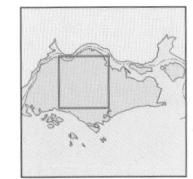

Central and Northern Singapore are a paradox. The two areas house some of the island's most heavily populated districts yet contain, at the same time, most of its pockets of nature. In fact, these parts of the island offer such large tracts of tropical forest, mangrove and swamp that getting close to nature here is as much a part of Singapore life as eating and shopping.

Lian Shan Shuang Lin

Some 5 km (3 miles) north of Orchard Road is **Lian Shan Shuang Lin Monastery ❶** (daily 8am–5pm; tel: 6259 6924). Better known as Siong Lim Temple, it is located in Toa Payoh, one of Singapore's oldest Housing and Development Board (HDB) estates.

Its full name, Lian Shan Shuang Lin Shi, means "Twin Grove of the Lotus Mountain Temple". Completed in 1912, the temple was modelled after Xi Chan Si, a well-known *cong lin* temple in Fuzhou. *Cong lin* means "layers of forest" and Xi Chan Si is a monastery that was built according to an established layout which allows monks to move around to a set pattern to perform rituals. This enables them to find their way about in any *cong lin* temple they might be in, whatever its size.

Siong Lim Temple was the result

of one man's dream, Low Kim Pong (1838–1908), a Buddhist who was a successful trader, land owner and a leader of the local Fujian community.

The story goes that one day in 1898, Low had a dream in which he saw a golden light shining from the west. He found out, the next day, that his son had the same dream. Taking it as an omen, father and son went to the harbour and waited. At sunset, a boat sailed in from the west, carrying a family of 12 Buddhist monks and nuns who were on their way

Map
on page
188

LEFT:
weekend warriors
at Bukit Timah
Nature Reserve.
BELOW:
Lian Shan Shuang
Lin Monastery.

Bundles of "hell money", which the Chinese burn as offerings to the deceased.

back to China after six years of pilgrimage in India, Sri Lanka and Burma. It was Low's dream come true. Inspired, he persuaded the group to stay and promised to build a Buddhist monastery for their use.

It was a massive exercise that took over 10 years to finish. The work was done in stages and with substantial funds donated by Low. Though he did not live to see the completion, his name has always been associated with it. In fact, it was often referred to as Low Kim Pong's temple.

Over the years, the Siong Lim Temple deteriorated and in 1991, it

underwent major restorations. Four of its structures were restored – the impressive **Entrance Hall** topped by a granite wall panel depicting scenes of Chinese culture and history, the **Drum Tower** and **Bell Tower** flanking the main courtyard, and the **Main Hall** housing the key altar.

The Main Hall is the hub of the monastery and is noted for the beauty of its decorative panels, wood carvings and sculptures of deities. Other secondary buildings of no architectural value that were added over the years were replaced with new ones built in traditional

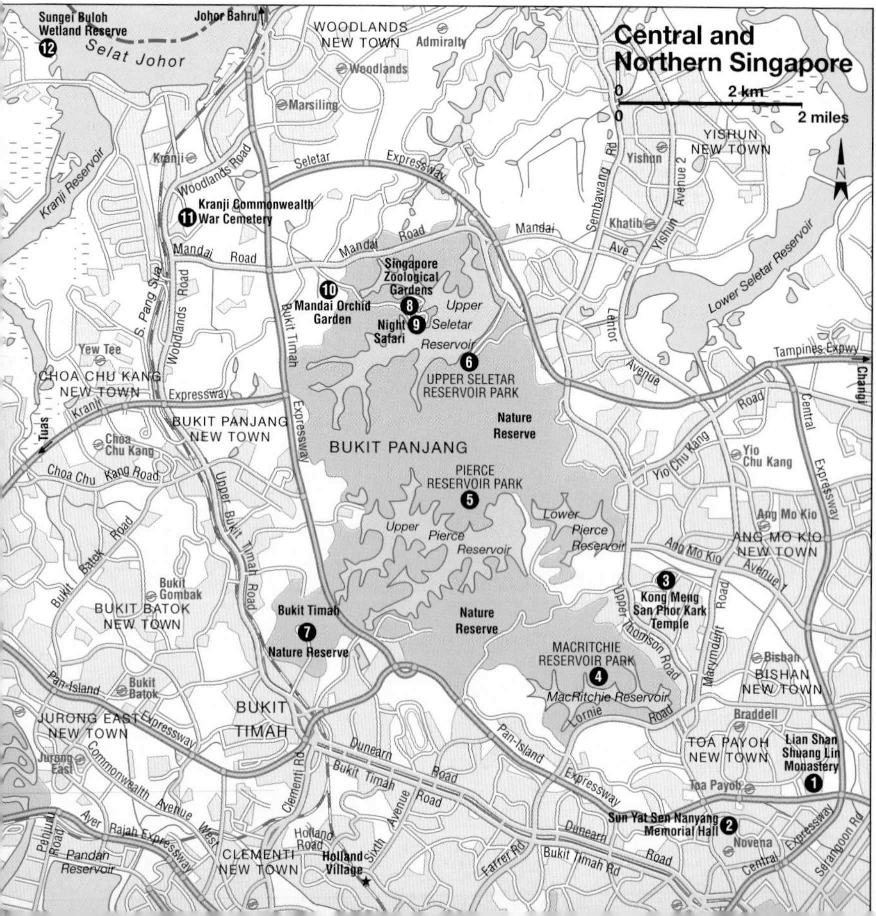

Central and Northern Singapore

0 — 2 km
0 — 2 miles

N

Sunget Buloh Wetland Reserve ⑫
Selat Johor
Johor Bahru
WOODLANDS NEW TOWN
Admiralty
Woodlands
Marsiling
Kranji
Seletar
Yishun
YISHUN NEW TOWN
Khatib
Kranji Reservoir
Woodlands Road
Kranji Commonwealth War Cemetery ⑪
Mandai Road
Mandai
Sembawang Rd
Yishun Avenue 2
Lower Seletar Reservoir
Yew Tee
Singapore Zoological Gardens ⑧
Mandai Orchid Garden ⑩
Night Safari ⑨
Upper Seletar Reservoir
Lentor
Tampines Expwy
CHOA CHU KANG NEW TOWN
Expressway
BUKIT PANJANG NEW TOWN
UPPER SELETAR RESERVOIR PARK ⑥
Nature Reserve
Avenue
Yio Chu Kang
Choa Chu Kang
Choa Chu Kang Road
Upper Bukit Timah Expressway
BUKIT PANJANG
PIERCE RESERVOIR PARK ⑤
Lower Pierce Reservoir
Yio Chu Kang
ANG MO KIO NEW TOWN
Ang Mo Kio Avenue 1
Bukit Gombak
Bukit Batok
Upper Pierce Reservoir
Ang Mo Kio
BUKIT BATOK NEW TOWN
Bukit Timah
Nature Reserve ⑦
Nature Reserve
Kong Meng San Phor Kark Temple ③
Bishan
BISHAN NEW TOWN
Pan-Island Expressway
Bukit Batok
BUKIT TIMAH
MACRITCHIE RESERVOIR PARK ④
MacRitchie Reservoir
Braddell
JURONG EAST NEW TOWN
Jurong East
Commonwealth Avenue
Dunearn Road
Bukit Timah Road
Pan-Island Expressway
TOA PAYOH NEW TOWN
Lian Shan Shuang Lin Monastery ①
Toa Payoh
Clementi Rd
Sixth Avenue
Holland Road
Holland Village
Farrer Rd
Bukit Timah Rd
Dunearn Road
Sun Yat Sen Nanyang Memorial Hall ②
Novena
Central Expressway
Serangoon Rd
Ayer Rajah Expressway
Pandan Reservoir
CLEMENTI NEW TOWN

style. Then in June 2002, the new seven-storey granite **Dragon Light Pagoda** – topped with a golden spire – was completed by craftsmen from China, culminating a 11-year restoration programme that had cost over S$40 million.

Although the farms and villages that used to surround Siong Lim Temple have been replaced with high-rise apartment blocks and the Pan-Island Expressway, the traditions of the temple continue to endure.

Sun Yat Sen Memorial Hall

On the other side of the Pan-Island Expressway is national monument **Sun Yat Sen Nanyang Memorial Hall ②**, a lovely two-storey Victorian-style bungalow at 12 Tai Gin Road (Tues–Sun 10am–5pm, Sat 10am–10pm; admission charge; tel: 6256 7377). Dating back to the 1880s, look out for the seated statue of Sun Yat Sen, the leader of China's nationalist movement, just in front of the building in the garden.

In 1906, when Dr Sun Yat Sen arrived in Singapore to drum up support for his nationalist cause

among the *Nanyang* (overseas Chinese), he was given the villa for his use. It was here that he plotted the overthrow of the Qing Dynasty in China. It was also at the villa that the Tong Meng Hui Nanyang Branch was founded and the villa was made its Southeast Asian quarters. Soon after, the bungalow became known as the Sun Yat Sen Villa.

After the successful revolution in China in 1911, the villa fell into disrepair. It was sold to an Indian merchant who left it unoccupied. Then, in 1938, a group of philanthropists, who were members of the Tong Meng Hui society, bought the building with the purpose of preserving it.

In 1942, during World War II, the Japanese used the villa as a communications centre, and in 1945, it became the headquarters of the Singapore Branch of the Kuomintang. In 1951, the villa was handed over to the Singapore Chinese Chamber of Commerce and Industry to manage. It was restored in 1965 and turned into a library and museum. In 1966, on the centenary of Dr Sun's birthday, the villa opened to the public.

Map on page 188

Sun Yat Sen travelled to many parts of the world, including Singapore, to drum up overseas Chinese support to overthrow China's Qing dynasty.

BELOW:
Sun Yat Sen Nanyang Memorial Hall.

Don't be tempted to feed the animals at the reservoir parks. The monkeys have been known to behave viciously.

BELOW: a nun in repose at Kong Meng San Phor Kark Temple.

In 1997, the villa was closed for major refurbishments and re-opened four years later on the 135th anniversary of the famed revolutionary's birth. Five exhibition halls are now spread over two storeys. Among them is a set of life-sized wax figures showing Dr Sun holding a secret meeting at the villa. The Father of Modern China's revolutionary activities in Southeast Asia are also told through some 400 photographs.

Kong Meng San Temple

Five kilometres (3 miles) north of the villa is the **Kong Meng San Phor Kark See Temple** ❸, located at Bright Hill Drive (daily 6am–9:30pm; tel: 6458 4454; www.kmspks.org). Built in 1989, it is Singapore's largest Buddhist temple and one of the largest temple complexes found in Southeast Asia.

Spread over 12 hectares (29 acres) of land, its gilded roofs are visible from afar. It's easy to get lost among the many halls of prayer and meditation. The **Hall of Great Compassion** houses a 9-metre (30-ft) high Goddess of Mercy, Kuan Yin, carved

in marble. This Bodhisattva image is crafted in the Indian tradition and has 1,000 arms and eyes. Look out also for one of Southeast Asia's largest images of the Medicine Buddha, which sits beneath a golden stupa in the **Pagoda of 10,000 Buddhas**.

Also on the grounds is a Bodhi Tree (the Buddha gained enlightenment under such a tree), a home for the aged, a crematorium and a columbarium. There is also a pond housing turtles and an enclosure where doves are released every year as a merit-making gesture on Vesak Day, which celebrates Buddha's birth, death and attainment of *nirvana*.

In May, Vesak Day celebrations are held here on a grand scale, sometimes stretching over three weeks, and visitors are welcome.

Central Catchment Reserve

West of the temple is a lush green expanse known as **MacRitchie Reservoir Park** ❹ which, together with the **Pierce Reservoir Park** ❺ further north (comprising the Upper Pierce and Lower Pierce parks) and **Upper Seletar Reservoir Park** ❻, form what is collectively known as the **Central Catchment Nature Reserve**, one of four gazetted nature reserves in Singapore (all open daily 6.30am–7.30pm; free; www.nparks.gov.sg). The other protected green areas on the island are Bukit Timah Nature Reserve, Sungei Buloh Wetland Reserve and Labrador Nature Reserve. Together, they comprise some 3,347 hectares (8,271 acres) – which is no mean feat in land-scarce Singapore.

The Central Catchment Nature Reserve consists of a rich mixture of secondary and primary forests, and contain a surprising array of species, including the lesser mousedeer, pangolin and flying lemur. The reservoirs – MacRitchie, Upper and Lower Pierce and Upper Seletar – trap rain water caught and filtered

by the natural vegetation. The Central Catchment Nature Reserve also contains the only patch of freshwater swamp remaining in Singapore.

The reservoirs are surrounded by landscaped parks that are popular with joggers and mountain bikers. **MacRitchie Reservoir** particularly, with its boardwalks bordering the water's edge and well-posted signboards, make for scenic tramps (*see text box below*). Picnickers are a common sight on weekends.

MacRitchie can be accessed via Lornie Road, Upper and Lower Pierce Reservoirs via Upper Thomson Road and Seletar Reservoir via Mandai Road. A map of the Central Catchment Nature Reserve can be obtained from Bukit Timah Nature Reserve Visitor Centre, or downloaded from www.nparks.gov.sg.

Bukit Timah Nature Reserve

To the west of MacRitchie is **Bukit Timah Nature Reserve ❼** (daily 6.30am–7.30pm; free; www.nparks. gov.sg). This reserve is found in the geographic centre of Singapore, 12 km (7 miles) from the city, and most easily reached by taxi. After the taxi turns into Hindhede Drive from busy Upper Bukit Timah Road, the reserve's moist and dark green quietness, overlaid by the uninterrupted buzzing of cicadas, will seem almost unreal, an isolated patch of land showing how the region would look if man had not intervened.

The reserve's car park is surrounded by new private housing estates. At the **Visitor Centre** (daily 8.30am–6pm; tel: 1800 468 5736) is an exhibition of Bukit Timah's history, including its role in the war years and Singapore's flora and fauna. A collection of old photographs includes one of the last tiger that was shot in Singapore in 1924.

The reserve includes Singapore's highest hill, **Bukit Timah**, at a mere 164 metres (532ft), and protects 163 hectares (403 acres) of the nation's only virgin lowland rainforest.

Much of Singapore's forest was intensively logged right till the middle of the 19th century. In 1884, in response to research on climatic changes arising from deforestation, Bukit Timah was declared a nature

Map on page 188

TIP

Fit and feeling adventurous? Head to Bukit Timah Nature Reserve. Past the three caves along Cave Path, up Tuip Tuip Path through Dairy Farm Loop, you'll cross a stream, scramble up a steep slope then walk some distance before coming to Seraya Hut – it offers a view of picturesque Singapore Quarry.

BELOW: MacRitchie Reservoir Park.

Into the Woods

MacRitchie's easiest trails are the six boardwalks along the forest fringes. The trails – from 450 metres (¼ mile) to 2.2 km (1½ miles) are named after native trees. Four of these, Prunus, Petai, Chemperai and Jering, skirt the edge of the reservoir and are accessible from MacRitchie's only car park at Lornie Road. Five other tramps, from one to five hours, bring you deeper into the bush. The seven-storey Jelutong Tower offers a view of the forest canopy. The fastest way to get there is a 5.5-km (3½-mile) tramp through Lornie Trail and Golf Link. For the truly indefatigable, a 9.5-km (6-mile) trail from MacRitchie leads to the foot of Bukit Timah Hill – plan for half a day.

For a walk on the wild side, have breakfast (9am) or afternoon tea (4pm) with unusual company like otters and pythons. After that, have your picture taken with orangutans. Call the zoo at tel: 6269 3411 for information.

BELOW:
common treeshrew
at Bukit Timah
Nature Reserve.

reserve. Over the past 100 years, boundary changes have reduced the size of the reserve, and poaching of timber and animals have reduced its ecological diversity. Today, most large mammals, including tiger, leopard and deer, are extinct in Singapore as are ecologically sensitive birds such as hornbills, trogons and broadbills.

To explore the reserve, follow the asphalted road from the car park to the hilltop. Many trees along this road are labelled in English and with scientific names, and give the newcomer to the tropics a feeling for the enormous diversity of plant species in Southeast Asia. In fact, noted conservationist Dr David Bellamy has pointed out that the number of plant species in the reserve exceeds that found in the whole of North America. Although few mammal species have survived, the frequently-heard hissing identifies slender squirrels and plantain squirrels. Another squirrel-like mammal with a long pointed nose is the unrelated common treeshrew.

Bukit Timah Hill is a popular training spot for mountaineers.

Understandably, it gets crowded on weekends – if you're planning a trek, weekdays are your best bets. There are five trails, all clearly marked and with varying levels of difficulty, taking from 45 minutes to two hours to complete. There is a also a challenging 6-km (4-mile) long mountain bike trail for enthusiasts. Free brochures and trail maps are available from the Visitor Centre.

Though the view from the hilltop is unspectacular, it is a good place to wait for white-bellied sea-eagles or brahminy kites, and the besotted birdwatcher can meet the challenge of identifying at least nine species of swifts and swallows. The view over the protected forest of several water reservoirs makes visitors forget that they are in one of the world's most densely populated cities.

Zoological Gardens

About 15 km (9 miles) northeast of the reserve at Mandai Lake Road is **Singapore Zoological Gardens** ⓑ, (daily 8.30am–6pm; admission charge; tel: 6269 3411; www.zoo.com.sg). Occupying 28 hectares (69 acres) of greenery just beside the Upper Seletar Reservoir, the zoo stands out in nearly every category by which animal collections are judged: variety of wildlife (more than 4,000 animals from 410 species), open-air enclosures that present animals in their natural environment, captive breeding of endangered species, and attractive landscaping. But where the zoo really excels is melding education and entertainment into a delightful combination that reaches out to both adults and children.

It would be hard to find a zoo elsewhere in the world with a more creative approach to wildlife display. Modern glass enclosures offer visitors an underwater view of crocodiles and pygmy hippos in their riverine environment, while polar

bears swim in deep blue waters. Gibbons leap through the trees, as rhinos share space with antelopes in a stunning recreation of the African plains. The home for the **Elephants of Asia** – one of its newest exhibits – is reminiscent of the logging areas in the hill tracts of Arakan in Burma. The zoo also has the world's largest captive orangutan colony.

A popular attraction is the **Fragile Forest** – an ecological wonder highlighting the interplay between animals and plants living in the rainforest, and man. The first zoo exhibit to display invertebrates and vertebrates under one roof, the Fragile Forest features a walk-through flight area and four centres showing various ecosystems. Venture into the flight enclosure and look out for tamarins, marmosets, lemurs, sloth, parakeets and butterflies.

Animal shows are performed several times each day at the zoo's open-air amphitheatre. One features reptiles and primates (orangutans, chimps and gibbons) while others feature elephants and sea lions. Feeding times of the various animals are posted near the park entrance; the most spectacular feasts are at the polar bear and lion habitats.

The little ones will be enthralled with **Children's World**, which provides close encounters of the animal kind. They can stroke animals, see baby chicks hatch from their eggs, watch an Aussie sheep dog at work, or take a ride on a miniature train.

Night Safari

The world's first night wildlife park, the **Night Safari 9** is next door with 1,200 nocturnal animals in 47 recreated habitats including a Nepalese river valley, Malaysian rainforest, Himalayan foothills and African plains (daily 7.30pm– midnight; admission charge; tel: 6269 3411; www.nightsafari.com.sg).

The Night Safari features after-hours hunters such as tigers and lions, as well as lesser known creatures like the Himalayan tahr mountain goat, babirusa pig, one-horned rhino and barasingha swamp deer. It may not be a real safari but it's probably the closest you can get to feeling you're in the wilderness. With

Map on page 188

TIP

Visiting Singapore Zoo and the Night Safari on the same day? Save money by buying a combined Zoo and Night Safari entrance package. Call 6269 3411 for information.

LEFT AND BELOW: albino python and a pair of hippos at the Zoological Gardens.

Orchids from Mandai Orchid Gardens can be packed for the flight back home.

clever unobstrusive lighting and realistic habitat recreations, visitors do feel they are in the middle of a thick tropical jungle on a moonlit night. Free-ranging deer and other small animals wander to the tram, which makes a 45-minute journey around the park. Even tigers and lions appear to be roaming freely in their natural enclosures, oblivious to observers just a stone's throw away. Walking trails are clearly marked and there are rangers to guide you along the way – there is no danger of stepping on a lion's tail! Just remember that flash photography is prohibited.

Not to be missed is the interactive **Creatures of the Night** show (daily 8 and 9pm) featuring 19 species of night animals including the puma, leopard cat and spotted hyena.

Mandai Orchid Garden

West of the zoo along 200 Mandai Lake Road is the **Mandai Orchid Garden ⑩**, on a hillside covered with a riot of glorious colour (daily 8am–5.30pm; admission charge; tel: 6269 1036). This lush garden has one of the world's finest displays of orchids in all shapes, shades and sizes. Growing in a mixture of charcoal and brick chips, orchids clamber up poles in vivid profusion, while others hang in delicate sprays from suspended pots.

The brilliant orchids are exported all over the world from here. Visitors can make their selections to take away, boxed for the flight. In cool climes, the blooms can last several weeks if the stems are regularly trimmed and the water changed.

Kranji War Cemetery

Farther west along along Woodlands Road is **Kranji Commonwealth War Cemetery ⑪** (open daily during daylight hours; free; tel: 6269 6158). Allied soldiers who were killed in Singapore in World War II and two of Singapore's past presidents lie buried in this state cemetery. In the middle of the cemetery is the **War Memorial**. The names of 24,346 men who died in various battles in the Asia-Pacific are engraved on it. The design of the memorial is symbolic, representing the three arms of the service – army, air force and navy.

Sungei Buloh Reserve

On the extreme northwest coast of Singapore is the **Sungei Buloh Wetland Reserve** ⑫, about 15 km (9 miles) west of the Kranji War Memorial (Mon–Fri 7.30am–7pm; Sat–Sun, public holidays 7am–7pm; admission charge; www.sbwr.org.sg). Located at Neo Tiew Crescent, this reserve is remarkable for the abundance and diversity of its birdlife. It has been estimated that over 212 species of birds can be seen here. This reserve is also one of the few spots in Singapore where endangered heron species nest and breed.

A boardwalk guides visitors through part of the park, with hides at regular intervals from which birds can be observed and platforms that jut out at vantage points to offer better views. There are four trails, ranging from 30 minutes to five hours, including one through a mangrove. The Visitor Centre (tel: 6794 1401) has more details on these and also screens an informative 10-minute audio-visual show at its theatrette.

The old freshwater fish ponds still remain, green with algae and surrounded by mangroves. Some of the fish still thrive, and with the farmers long gone, birds have a heyday. Collared as well as white-throated kingfishers sit on the low stakes by the bunds, waiting to swoop while cinnamon and yellow bitterns stalk the reedy edges.

But it is the migrating waders, of which more than 20 species have been sighted feeding on exposed mud-beds, that are the stars of the reserve. From as early as September to April, large flocks of plovers, sandpipers, stints, curlews, godwits and egrets gather to feed on the mud exposed by the ebbing tide.

With the rapid reclamation of coastal areas in other parts of Singapore, the sanctuary now stands out as its last significantly sizeable feeding ground for migrating wading birds. The ornithological importance of the site is underlined by the fact that Singapore is the last stopover in the migration path down the Malaysian peninsula before the thrust to regions further south. ❏

Map on page 188

A crimson sunbird – one of several migratory birds sometimes spotted at Sungei Buloh Wetland Reserve.

Restaurants

French

Vis-A-Vis
12 Chun Tin Rd. Tel: 6468 7433. Open: L and D daily. $$ (set lunch) $$$$ (à la carte)
www.vis-a-vis.com.sg
Reward yourself with a lobster thermidor after a rigorous trek at nearby Bukit Timah Nature Reserve. This charming French restaurant has a seasonal menu offering snails, quail, foie gras and all things French, along with a reasonably good wine list.

International
Restaurants In the Wild
Singapore Zoological Gardens, 80 Mandai Lake Rd. Tel: 6269 3411. Open: daily 9am–5pm. $
Located within the zoo grounds, this jungle-themed and family-friendly restaurant has something to please everyone. The three sections – Jungle Flavours, Jungle Tandoor and Forest Fare – offer fish and chips, pasta and local dishes such as chicken rice, tandoori chicken and curry dishes.

Local
The Roti Prata House
246M Upper Thomson Rd. Tel: 6459 5260. Open: daily 7–1am. $
Enjoy your *roti prata* bread crispy or paper thin, with cheese or filled with chicken, mutton, sardine or vegetables. Then work off the calories at MacRitchie Reservoir Park – just 15 minutes' walk from here.

Peranakan
Ivins
207 Upper Thomson Rd. Tel: 6254 1877. Open: L and D daily; closed Thur.

$ (set lunch); $$ (à la carte)
Droves of people come here for delicious Peranakan fare at down-to-earth prices. A lavish meal of chilli prawns, spring rolls, honey pork and stewed chicken with Indonesian black nuts can be had for a song.

PRICE CATEGORIES

Prices for a three-course dinner per person without drinks and taxes:
$ = under S$20
$$ = S$20–$30
$$$ = S$30–$45
$$$$ = more than S$45

EXCURSIONS

Pristine beaches ringed by coral reefs offshore and luxury
resorts on land are a short ferry ride away. If history
beckons instead, then the ancient trading empire
of Melaka is the perfect getaway

A short trip north across the causeway from Singapore brings the traveller to Johor Bahru in Peninsular Malaysia. There is not much of interest at this border town but further afield are two spots worth visiting. One is the idyllic island of Pulau Tioman and the other is the historic trading port of Melaka (or Malacca), founded by Sultan Parameswara in the 15th century.

Lying within sight of Singapore's southern shore is the Riau archipelago of Sumatra in Indonesia. While largely a tropical backwater, change has come swiftly to the sleepy island of Pulau Bintan in recent years. Part of it is industrial but the northern coast, where the sandy beaches of Pasir Panjang are found, has been developed into a major beach resort, with a string of luxury hotels.

PULAU TIOMAN

Over 60 volcanic isles in the South China Sea make up the Johor group, six of which have tourist facilities. These islands are protected as marine parks and have prolific and diverse marine life, much of it endemic to the area. The largest of these islands, **Pulau Tioman**, is believed to be named after the *burung tiong* (mynah bird), said at one time to proliferate on the isle. Tioman was mentioned before AD 1000 in what was perhaps the first guide to the peninsula. Arab traders then noted in their "sailing directions" that Tioman offered good anchorage and freshwater springs. Centuries later, the island's southern twin peaks, called Ass's Ears, at Mukut in the south, also guided Chinese traders between the 12th and 17th century, as evidenced by Ming and other pottery shards found in caves and on the beaches.

Today, Tioman's beaches continue to attract tropical island fans, including divers and snorkellers, who come

PRECEDING PAGES:
Malay boys in their
traditional finery.
LEFT: picture
perfect beach at
Pulau Tioman.
BELOW: reef fish
and diver at
Pulau Tioman.

The blue parrot fish makes an audible crunching sound when it feeds on coral polyps.

to explore the marine park's underwater life. The main beaches fringe the west coast, and all are mainly lined with small chalet-type accommodation run by local Malay families. Somehow, luxury resorts have not found their way to Tioman. The island's only comfortable large hotel is the **Berjaya Tioman Beach Resort** at Tekek beach (tel: 609-419 1000; www.berjayaresorts.com).

The tiny town centre is at **Tekek**, where the jetty, airstrip and shops are. The long beach, shaded by casuarina and coconut trees, is fronted with chalets and restaurants. The island's only road goes from here south to the the Berjaya Resort, which has its own golf course. North of Tekek are the smaller beaches of **Air Batang** (better known as ABC after the original chalet operation there) and **Salang**, which have nice mangrove areas. These three beaches have the closest access to the coral reefs.

South of Tekek are **Nipah**, a quiet stretch with chalet accommodation, and **Mukut** down south at the base of the Twin Peaks, whose view of the blue ocean is obscured by nei-

ther islands nor passing ships. Two other stretches on the west coast are not so pretty: **Genting**, which sits on rocks, and **Paya**, which has no beach to speak of, although both have plenty of accommodation. **Juara** is the sole beach on the east coast, a long white stretch with less tree cover but no coral reefs.

Snorkelling and diving

Tioman has large coral reefs on the west coast, most of which are close to shore. A feature of its marine life is its giant seafans, particularly at the top dive spot of **Pulau Tulai** (Coral Island), whose shallow waters are popular with snorkellers. **Cebeh** reef provides some nice swim-throughs, and there are pretty submerged coral gardens at **Golden Reef**. **Rengis** is an accessible site with an occasional slight drift as is **Jahat**, just south of Mukut.

The 55 km (35 miles) to Tioman can be covered in 30 minutes by scheduled ferry from **Mersing** (try to get there in the morning) on the Malaysian mainland. A high-speed ferry also services Singapore, although much quicker is the Berjaya Air plane from Singapore, which has the bonus of spectacular views.

MELAKA

Along the western coast, the North-South Highway from Johor leads to the state of **Melaka**, or Malacca as most people know it. Melaka is a town with a glorious past. In the 1400s, it was a small settlement of sea gypsies. Then Parameswara arrived, a Malay prince fleeing from his own invaded domain of Temasek (Singapore). While out hunting he encountered a tiny *kancil* (mouse deer) which managed to intimidate his dogs; he took this as a sign that this should be the site of his new capital. By the end of the 15th century, Melaka had become the centre of a great trading empire and held an

undisputed claim over the southern Malay peninsula.

Geography was responsible for Melaka's multi-cultural history. Located at the mouth of the Melaka River, astride the maritime route linking the Indian Ocean with the South China Sea, it was at Melaka that the monsoon winds met. Junks from China were driven up the Straits of Melaka by the northeast monsoon, as were the ships of the traders from the Indonesian archipelago. The goods were then traded at Melaka's port. When the winds changed, the southwest monsoon assisted the same vessels to return home.

The small colony of Chinese merchants who stayed behind married local Malay women and these unions founded the Peranakan community, one of the most colourful Chinese fraternities in the region today.

Melaka's golden age came to an end when it fell in 1511 to the Portuguese. The port was theirs for more than 100 years before they were ousted by the Dutch. After 150 years of occupation, the Dutch in turn ceded the land to the British.

Stadthuys

Melaka's past is contained within its 1-km (½-mile) historic centre, easily covered on foot, or on a leisurely trishaw ride through the narrow streets past old temples and mosques, ruins and epitaphs. Trishaw drivers make fine guides, as they know the sights and speak English. As usual, bargain before you get on.

The best place to begin your tour is in the centre, near the bridge built on the site where the Portuguese made their final successful assault on the town. Located here is the **Melaka Tourist Information Centre** (daily 9am–4.30pm), where you can get maps, brochures and also book the 45-minute river cruise up **Sungai Melaka**.

The maroon-coloured building facing what is sometimes known as the Red Square, is **Stadthuys**, which houses the **History, Ethnography and Literature Museum**. (Tues–Sun 9am–6pm; admission charge). The Stadthuys was erected in 1650 and is the oldest known Dutch building still standing in Asia. The handsome General Post Office next to it is also of Dutch origin, and is now the **Youth Museum**.

Perpendicular to the Stadthuys is the fabled **Christ Church**, with its bright red exterior. The church is full of old, engraved tombstones, many telling a grim tale of the hardships the early European settlers faced.

St Paul's Hill

The only remnants of Portuguese architecture are on the slopes of **St Paul's Hill**, behind the square. When the Portuguese conquered Melaka, they were determined to make it one of the mightiest strongholds in the Orient. Hundreds of slaves and captives hauled stones from demolished mosques and elaborate tombs to build the **A Famosa** fortress, of which only the remains

BELOW:
Christ Church was built with bricks shipped all the way from Holland.

of the entrance called the **Porta de Santiago** is left standing today.

Erected in 1511 by the Portuguese, it once enclosed a castle, two palaces and five churches. The fortress withstood attacks for 150 years before succumbing to the Dutch in 1641 after an eight-month seige. It was repaired by the Dutch only to be blown to pieces by the British at the beginning of the 19th century.

At the top of St Paul's Hill are more ruins. In 1521, a chapel, later renamed **St Paul's Church**, was built by a Portuguese *fidalgo* to fulfil a vow he made on escaping death in the South China Sea. It was later taken over by the Jesuits (St Francis Xavier was temporarily enshrined here in 1552) and the Dutch later used the church as burial grounds.

Antiques and curios

Walk towards the bridge near the Red Square, and cross over to the west bank. **Jalan Tun Tan Cheng Lock** – called **Heeren Street** by the Dutch – is named after a leading Peranakan politician and architect. At No. 48–50 is the fascinating

Antique Peranakan silver belt. Look out for items like these at antiques shops along Melaka's Jonkers Street.

BELOW: Porta de Santiago – what is left of the old fort.

Baba Nonya Heritage Museum, where you can explore the interior of a typical Peranakan house (daily 10am–12.30pm and 2–4.30pm; admission charge). Opt for the guided tour to learn more about this house's fascinating history.

Parallel to this road is **Jalan Hang Jebat**, better known as **Jonkers Street**, Melaka's main tourist drag. The street contains every imaginable trade: hairdressing salons, wooden clogs shops, coffin makers, apothecaries with Chinese herbs on display, sign printers, an acupuncture clinic, furniture makers, souvenir shops, antiques shops, restaurants and more.

Places of worship

On parallel Jalan Tokong are three of the oldest places of worship in Malaysia. The **Cheng Hoon Teng Temple** (Temple of Bright Clouds), founded in 1645, is dedicated to three deities: Kuan Yin, the Goddess of Mercy, Kwan Ti, the God of War who "triples" as the patron saint of wealth and tradesmen, and Ma Choe Poh, the Queen of Heaven. There's a stone inscription commemorating

Admiral Cheng Ho's visit to Melaka in 1406. An illustrious envoy of the Ming emperor and famous adventurer, Cheng Ho was also the city's earliest Chinese pioneer.

Along Jalan Tukang Emas road is **Masjid Kampung Kling** (Kampung Kling Mosque), the town's oldest mosque, built in 1748 in typical Sumatran style. The cemetery encloses the tomb of Sultan Hussein of Johor, who ceded Singapore to Raffles in 1819. Also on the same street is the **Sri Poyyatha Vinayagar Moorthi Temple**. Built in the 1780s, it is the country's oldest Hindu temple and dedicated to Vinayagar or Ganesh, the Elephant God.

Bukit Cina

Away from Melaka's centre is another historical hill, housing some 12,000 graves. While most names and dates on the tombstones at **Bukit Cina** (China Hill) have been eroded, what remains is the legacy of Ming Princess Hang Li Poh who was married to Sultan Mansur Shah of Melaka in the mid-15th century. The princess's followers built a well at the foot of the hill, whose waters soon became as legendary. After Admiral Cheng Ho supposedly drank from the well, its water attained an extraordinary purity and never dried up, even during the most severe drought.

Portuguese traces

Head northwest from the well to Jalan Bendahara and **St Peter's Church**, where the country's most elaborate Good Friday services are held. The church was built in 1710 by the descendants of Portuguese soldiers who were given amnesty by the Dutch when the Portuguese garrison was forced into submission.

The legacy of the Portuguese is far greater than their ruins. In 1604, 200 mixed marriages had taken place. After 400 years, many Portuguese Eurasians in Melaka continue to speak Cristao, a medieval dialect of southeastern Portugal that is spoken nowhere else today.

At the **Portuguese Settlement**, 3 km (2 miles) from the centre, the dwellings resemble Malay *kampung* houses with wooden walls in soft hues of blue and green and capped by zinc roofs. There is little for tourists here, except some Portuguese restaurants that organise cultural performances on Saturdays. The best places to meet locals are the open-air cafés around **Portuguese Square**, which serve spicy seafood dishes and beer.

PULAU BINTAN

Nearly three times the size of Singapore **Pulau Bintan** (1,030 sq km/398 sq miles) is the largest of all the Riau islands. Other than its northern shore, it remains a largely undisturbed expanse of jungle, swamp and mountains – the highest point is Gunung Bintan at 335 metres (1,100 ft) – with isolated *kampung* that betray little modern influence.

The island's major port and "capital" is **Tanjung Pinang**, on the southwest coast, about two hours

Almost four centuries ago, a Portuguese historian said "Whosoever holds Melaka has Venice by the throat", in reference to the former's strategic trade position along the Straits of Melaka.

BELOW: roof detail from the Cheng Hoon Teng Temple.

from Singapore's Tanah Merah Ferry Terminal by high-speed ferry. Tanjung Pinang is the ancient capital of the Riau province and is a bustling town with traces of Malay, Chinese and Dutch influences. **Jalan Merdeka** is the main street running east–west through the city.

Senggarang, a *kampung* (village) on the far side of the Riau River from Tanjung Pinang, is noted for its **Heaven, Sea and Earth Temples** which are at least 280 years old. The miracle of the three temples surviving a blaze that razed the rest of Senggarang a few decades ago was not lost on devotees for whom worship at these temples has always been central to their lives.

Penyengat Island

More than any other place in the Riau archipelago, the island of **Pulau Penyengat** near Tanjung Pinang is considered the cradle of Malay civilisation. During the 18th and 19th centuries, this tiny island was the home base of the sultans of Riau, with a lavish court and royal city. The book, *Bustanul Katibin*,

Grounds of the Royal Graveyard at Pulau Penyengat.

BELOW:
poolside at the Angsana Resort.

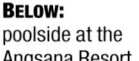

the first on Malay grammar, was published here in 1857, laying the foundation for Bahasa Indonesia, the *lingua franca* of the Indonesian archipelago. The Riau sultanate prospered until 1910 when the Dutch ended its autonomy.

More than 2,000 people live on the island today, spread among five *kampung*. Most people stay in simple wooden houses and nearly every home has a tidy garden. Penyengat is a fascinating insight into what life must have been like in Singapore before modernisation took over.

The island's **Sultan's Mosque** (Masjid Raya Sultan Riau), built in 1818, remains the most important place of Muslim worship in the Riau islands. Directly east of the mosque is a the **Royal Graveyard** (*komplex makam*) where many of the sultans are buried. The most important is that of the **Tomb of Engku Puteri**, also known as Raja Hamidah (1760–1812), the wife of the Sultan of Johor, who received the Riau islands as part of her wedding dowry. Hamidah is considered a Muslim saint and her tomb is a place of pilgrimage for people from all over Riau.

On a hill overlooking the town is restored **Bukit Kursi Fort**, one of three forts built in the 19th century as a defence against the Dutch.

Bintan's beaches

Trikora Beach in eastern Bintan is an unspoilt coconut palm-fringed strip of white sand beach with turquoise waters. There are a few thatched-roof restaurants, and several hotels and guest houses for those who want to spend the night.

From Trikora, a road leads all the way to the northern tip of the island to **Pasir Panjang Beach** where the massive waterfront development called **Bintan Resorts** is found. Most visitors from Singapore arrive at the nearby **Bandar Bentan Telani Ferry Terminal** direct from

Singapore, a 45-minute ferry ride away. The beach resort project, spreading along 103 km (64 miles) of prime shoreline on the north coast, comprises a number of luxury hotels, golf courses, seasports and other recreational facilities.

The chalet-style **Mayang Sari Beach Resort** (tel: 6323 6636; www.nirwanagardens.com) occupying one of the loveliest stretches of white sand beach, offers a laid-back atmosphere amid swaying palms. Next door is the **Mana Mana Beach Club** (tel: 6339 8878; www.manamana.com) with a watersports centre and 50 cabana rooms amid a coconut grove. Heading east is the 245-room **Nirwana Gardens** (same contact details as Mayang Sari above). Right on its sandy beach too is a watersports centre and the **Kelong Seafood Restaurant**, set on stilts over the sea.

Past the headland is the **Angsana Resort & Spa** (tel: 6489 5788; www.angsana.com) on its own beach and offering 135 rooms in tranquil surroundings. Hugging one end of this beach and built into the cliffside are the 70 luxury Balinese-style hill-top villas (some with private swimming pool) that make up the **Banyan Tree Bintan** (tel: 6849 5800; www.banyantree.com). Also to be found here is an 18-hole Greg Norman-designed golf course.

After a brief respite is the **Club Med Ria Bintan** (tel: 6830 0830; www.clubmed.com), which has waterfront villas, and seasports and recreational facilities, including a circus trapeze school for children and a 27-hole golf course designed by Gary Player. This is followed by **Bintan Lagoon Resort** (tel: 6223 3223; www.bintanlagoon.com), with rooms, villas and a golf club with two 18-hole golf courses designed by Greg Norman and Ian Baker-Finch.

Most Bintan visitors tend to be Singapore holiday makers seeking a beach escape from the city. Unfortunately, the luxury hotels in this area and its infrastructure feels like an extension of Singapore, without its frenetic city pace. Visitors who want to experience Indonesia are advised to get out of the hotels and explore Bintan's more remote areas. ❏

LEFT: dreamy Bintan sunset.

Getting There from Singapore

Pulau Tioman
Berjaya Air flies (40 minutes) to Tioman from Singapore once daily (tel: 6481 6302; www.berjaya-air.com). Cheaper is the fast ferry (4½ hours) operated by Penguin Ferry Services (tel: 6542 7105) from Tanah Merah Ferry Terminal to Tioman's Berjaya Beach Resort once daily except during the Oct–Mar monsoon season.

Malacca
The most cheapest option is the air-conditioned Malacca-Singapore Express bus (tel: 6293 5915). Coaches depart from Lavender bus station hourly from 8am to 7pm daily and take 4½ hours. Alternatively book a package tour with hotel and sightseeing included. A day trip is tiring so plan on an overnight. Contact Gunung Raya (tel: 6294 7711; www.gunungraya.com) or Grassland Express (tel: 6293 1166).

Pulau Bintan
Bintan Resort Ferries (tel: 6542 4369) has regular ferry services (45 mins, up to 7 times daily) from Tanah Merah Ferry Terminal to Bandar Bentan Telani Ferry Terminal. Penguin Ferry Services (tel: 6542 7105) has ferries (2 hours) serving Tanjung Pinang up to 5 times daily.

TRANSPORT

GETTING THERE AND GETTING AROUND

GETTING THERE

By Air

There are some 70 scheduled airlines operating over 3,000 flights a week to **Changi Airport** with its two terminals, **Terminal 1** (T1) and **Terminal 2** (T2). The terminals – which can handle over 5,000 passengers per hour during peak periods – are linked to each other by the Sky Train. With such high passenger traffic, the airport has been conceived for maximum comfort and convenience – in other words, it's a great airport to wait out a delayed flight!

Singapore's airport is a multi-award winner: readers of Britain's *Business Traveller* magazine, for instance, have voted it the world's best for an extraordinary 16 years (since 1991). When the S$1.5 billion Terminal 3 opens in 2006, Changi Airport will expand its handling capacity from 25 to 60 million passengers a year.

Airport Facilities

The range of services available at the airport are superb: a post office, foreign exchange outlets, courtesy phones for local calls, free and paid broadband Internet access, a transit hotel, spa,

swimming pool, gym, TV lounges and cinema, games arcade, supermarkets, clinics and left-luggage services, among others, many of which operate 24 hours.

Disabled travellers are well catered for with specially designed telephones, toilets, ramps and elevators.

This being Singapore, food and shopping options are plentiful. There are over 100 shops selling everything from cosmetics to candies, tobacco to toys, liquors to lingerie – all at prices

that are no higher that what you get downtown. For the hungry traveller, cuisines that cater to different palates are dished up in 25 cafés and restaurants.

Transit passengers who have a minimum of 5 hours' layover time before catching their connecting flight can book a 2-hour Free Singapore Tour. The counter opens for registration from 8.30am to 4.30pm daily; tours are available from 10am to 5pm on a first-come first-served basis.

Free maps and guides of the

KEY AIRLINE OFFICES

Air New Zealand
24-08 Ocean Building
10 Collyer Quay
Tel: 6535 8266
www.airnewzealand.com.sg

British Airways
06-05 Cairnhill Place
15 Cairnhill Road
Tel: 6589 7000
www.britishairways.com

Lufthansa
05-01 Palais Renaissance
390 Orchard Road
Tel: 6835 5933
www.lufthansa.com.sg

Northwest
08-06 Odeon Towers
331 North Bridge Road
Tel: 6336 3371
www.nwa.com.sg

Qantas Airways
06-05 Cairnhill Place
15 Cairnhill Road
Tel: 6589 7000
www.qantas.com

SilkAir
08-01 Temasek Tower
8 Shenton Way
Tel: 6223 8888
www.silkair.com

Singapore Airlines
02-38/39 The Paragon
290 Orchard Road
Tel: 6223 8888
www.singaporeair.com

United Airlines
01-03 Hong Leong Building
16 Raffles Quay
Tel: 6873 3533
www.unitedairlines.com.sg

city are available, including copies of the airport magazine, *Changi*, which details all the airport services. If you need help, look out for the Information and Customer Service counters scattered in both terminals or the 24-hour help phones. These phones will link you to the appropriate customer service officers.

For more information on airport services contact **Changi Airport Customer Service** (tel: 6541 2267; www.changiairport. com.sg). For information on flight arrival and departure times, contact tel: 1800 542 4422.

Flying from UK and US

The national carrier Singapore Airlines (SIA) is based at Changi Airport and flies to some 60 cities in 38 countries. Its sister carrier SilkAir serves over 20 Asian cities.

There are regular daily flights out of London and major European cities direct to Singapore. Flying time is between 12 to 13 hours. Many UK and Europe travellers heading to Australia and New Zealand often use Singapore as a transit point to break the long journey. From Singapore it is another 4½ hours to Perth, 7½ hours to Sydney and Melbourne, and 10 hours to Auckland.

Flying from US takes longer; a flight from Los Angeles or San Francisco which crosses the Pacific Ocean takes about 16 to 18 hours with a stop in Seoul, Taipei or Tokyo along the way. From New York, flight time is about 22 hours including transit time.

The good news for long-haul travellers from the US was the start of Singapore Airlines' non-stop flights from Los Angeles to Singapore in early 2004; in June it began operating the first non-stop flight from New York to Singapore. These flights typically shave 2 to 4 hours off flying time.

Singapore is also an excellent base for travel to Southeast Asian destinations like Bali, Phuket, Koh Samui, Langkawi, Penang and Siem Reap (Angkor Wat) among others, many of which are served by SilkAir.

Regional budget carriers – a recent phenomena in Southeast Asia – like Air Asia and Valuair – recently started flying out of Singapore, with others (like Tiger Airways, a start-up by Singapore Airlines) in the offing. All this competition is of course good news for travellers to this region.

As a major hub in Southeast Asia, Singapore is an excellent place to puchase air tickets to the region and beyond.

By Sea

Arriving slowly by sea is a pleasant experience. You get to savour the journey as you sail in past myriad other vessels lying at anchor, watching the skyline clarify into looming skyscrapers. Singapore, incidentally, is the world's busiest port in terms of tonnage.

Most visitors arrive at the **Singapore Cruise Centre** (tel: 6321 2803; www.singaporecruise. com) located at the HarbourFront Centre. The facility is also used by several regional cruise operators such as Star Cruises and by many large cruise liners stopping over on their long voyages from around the world.

Tanah Merah Ferry Terminal (tel: 6540 8087), located near Changi Airport, handles boat traffic to the resorts on the north shore of Indonesia's Bintan island as well as Tanjung Pinang, its capital, and to Nongsa, on neighbouring Batam island. Ferries to Malaysia's Tioman island and Sebana Cove also depart from here.

Changi Ferry Terminal (tel: 6545 3600), also near Changi Airport, handles regular ferry services to Tanjung Belungkor, on Malaysia's east coast.

By Train

Coming by train through Malaysia and then across the Causeway at Woodlands in the north of Singapore is a leisurely way to arrive. Malaysia's **Keretapi Tanah**

REGIONAL TRAVEL

Singapore is a perfect place from which to explore the region. When looking for good deals, it's best to check out the travel agents' section of the classified advertisements in *The Straits Times*. Destinations in Peninsular Malaysia can be easily accessed by road, rail, sea and by air, while the islands of Batam and Bintan in Indonesia are connected by ferries. Other destinations of interest in the region are a short flight away.

Another interesting option is cruises to ports of interest in Indonesia, Malaysia and Thailand. Contact **Star Cruises** (www.starcruises.com; tel: 6226 1168/6223 0002).

Melayu (KTM) has two lines: one links Singapore to Kuala Lumpur, Butterworth, Alor Setar and north across the Thai border into Bangkok, and the other branching off at Gemas and connects to Tumpat, near Kota Bahru along Malaysia's east coast.

Both Malaysian and Singapore immigration facilities are located at Woodlands. For more information, call the Singapore office of the **Malayan Railway Station** (tel: 6222 5165; www.ktmb.com.my) at Keppel Road.

If money is no object, plump for the **E&O Express** (tel: 6392 3500, www.orient-express.com), the ultimate recreation of a bygone age of romantic Asian rail travel. Decked out in the E&O livery of cream and racing green, it carries a maximum of 132 passengers on the 2-night trip from Bangkok through southern Thailand, Butterworth to Kuala Lumpur and Singapore.

This luxury does not come cheap; the one-way 2-night Singapore–Bangkok trip which takes 42 hours over a 1,943-km (1,205-mile) route starts from S$2,720 per person (twin-share) inclusive of meals.

By Bus/Coach

There are good roads down the west and east coasts of Peninsular Malaysia crossing either the Causeway at Woodlands or the Second Link in Tuas into Singapore. The Second Link is far less prone to the frequent congestion that the Woodlands checkpoint experiences.

Private air-conditioned buses run from Hatyai in Thailand and many towns in Malaysia to Singapore. The ride from Hatyai takes about 15 hours with stops for refreshments and arrives in Singapore at Golden Mile Complex along Beach Road. Call **Gunung Raya** (tel: 6294 7711, www.gunung raya.com) for bus tickets to Hatyai.

Hasry (tel: 6294 9306; www.hasryexpress.com) as well as Gunung Raya above have buses which connect Singapore to key Malaysian cities like Kuala Lumpur, Penang and Malacca. Buses arrive and leave from its Lavender Street office.

Plusliner (tel: 6256 5755; www.plusliner.com) has a fleet of Plusliner buses and more luxurious NiCE "executive" 26-seater coaches which link Kuala Lumpur and other major Malaysian cities to Singapore. Especially popular is its NiCE Singapore-Kuala Lumpur coach, which departs from Copthorne Orchid Hotel at Dunearn Road and arrives at Kuala Lumpur's KTM Station about 5 hours later.

GETTING AROUND

From the Airport

The airport authority's aim is for arriving passengers to be on their way to their hotels within 30 minutes of landing. As a result, the formalities are brief and luggage arrives in no time.

Changi Airport is linked to the city centre by the East Coast Parkway (ECP) and to the other parts of Singapore by the Pan-Island (PIE) and Tampines (TPE) expressways. There are five types of transport from the airport – taxi, car, bus, airport shuttle and MRT.

By Taxi

At both Terminals 1 and 2, the taxi stand is situated on the same level as the Arrival Hall. A surcharge of S$3 (or S$5 from 5pm–midnight Fri–Sun) applies in addition to the fare shown on the taxi meter. There are two other surcharges which are added to the fare where applicable: for rides between midnight to 6am and ERP (Electronic Road Pricing) tolls (see page 210). Taxi fare to the city centre will cost around S$15, excluding the surcharges. Travel time to the city centre is about 20 to 30 minutes, depending on traffic conditions.

By Private/Rented Car

If you are being picked up by a private car in Terminal 1, inclined travelators in the Arrival Hall descend to ground level, which leads to the Passenger Crescent where a private car pick-up point is located. In Terminal 2, the car pick-up point is on the same level as the Arrival Hall. If you're renting a car, the car rental counters are located at Terminal 2.

By Public Bus

In the basement of both terminals are public bus depots. Buses depart between 6am and midnight daily, and information on bus routes is available at the bus stands. Service No. 36 gets you direct into the city. You'll need to have the exact fare as no change is given on board.

By Airport Shuttle

The comfortable airport shuttle called **Maxicab** operates between the airport and major hotels in the city, with flexible alighting points within the Central Business District (CBD). Tickets at S$7 for adults and S$5 for children are available at the shuttle counters located at both terminals.

By Mass Rapid Transit

The MRT link to Changi Airport is situated underground in Terminal 2. Trains leave every 12 minutes and a ride to the city centre – City Hall MRT station – takes about 27 minutes and costs S$1.40. Note: some trains do not go direct to the city so you have to switch lines at Tanah Merah MRT station.

Orientation

Singapore lies 137km (85 miles) north of the equator and is separated from Peninsular Malaysia in the north by the Straits of Johor. To its east, west and south, it is surrounded by the sprawling Indonesian archipelago.

Singapore consists of the main island, 682 sq km (263 sq miles) in area, and some 60 other small islands, making up a total land area of 714 sq km (275 sq miles). North to south it stretches for about 23 km (14 miles); east to west, the distance is roughly 42 km (26 miles). This land mass is constantly growing, however, as a result of ongoing land reclamation projects.

Singapore is an easy city to get around. The hardy walker can cover most areas of interest such as the Singapore River area, Chinatown, Civic District, Arab Street, Little India and the Orchard Road area on foot. These and all the outlying places of attractions can be reached easily using the city's excellent public transport (MRT and buses) or by taxi.

What is more, there are no great distances to cover. From the Central Business District (CBD) it takes you no more than 20 to 30 minutes to Changi Airport, about 30 minutes to the western tip (Jurong) and a little more than 35 minutes all the way to the Woodlands Causeway.

The east coast area has some of Singapore's older and more traditional neighbourhoods (Katong and Geylang, for example) and two major beach parks (East Coast and Pasir Ris) with cycle paths, exercise stations,

TRANSPORT

and picnic and camping grounds. The central and northern areas of the island still have some forest reserves while the west, although largely industrialised, has a few key tourist attractions.

Public Transport

Singapore's public transport system is comprehensive, efficient and cheap. If you prefer to take a guided tour, see the **Sightseeing Tours** section *(pages 229–30).*

Mass Rapid Transit (MRT)

The MRT system *(see map on back flap)* started in 1988 and has now grown to 131 air-conditioned trains serving 63 stations along the **East-West Line**, the **North-South Line** and, most recently, the **North-East Line**. The last line started operations in July 2003 as the world's first driverless mass rapid transit system. Together they cover a total route length of 100 km (62 miles). A fourth line, the **Circle Line**, is under construction and due for completion in 2010.

In addition, a Light Rapid Transit (LRT) system services the towns of Bukit Panjang and Sengkang and soon, Punggol.

During any one day this modern people-mover transports over a million passengers in comfort and with clockwork precision. The six-car trains, each of which can accommodate 1,800 persons, travel at 45 kmh (30 mph) and arrive at each of the 63 stations every few minutes. About one third of the stations are underground. Depending on the station, the first train rolls out at about 5.15am; last trains run until around 12.49am.

The system is easy to use: there are six MRT interchanges, City Hall, Raffles Place, Dhoby Ghaut, Tanah Merah, Outram Park and Jurong East, where you can switch from one line to another. Fares are easy to figure out and collection is automatic: magnetically-coded cards cost between 80 cents and S$1.80 for single trips, plus a S$1 deposit. You can purchase tickets at any MRT station from the General Ticket Machines. Flash your ticket at the electronic card reader on the entry turnstile and walk through when the green indicator comes on. When you arrive at your destination, flash your ticket at the reader on the exit turnstile to pass through. At the end of the trip, make sure you insert your card into the General Ticket Machine to get back your S$1 deposit.

For added convenience buy a stored-value **TransitLink ez-link Card**. These cards *(see text box below)* give users the advantage of a small discount when connecting from buses to MRT and vice versa.

Buses

Around 11,000 buses operated by **Singapore Bus Service** (SBS) and **SMRT Buses** (formerly called Trans-Island Bus Services) ply 256 routes covering practically every corner of the island. Buses (single and double-deckers with or without air-conditioning) run from around 6am to 11.40pm, with an extension of about half-an-hour for both starting and ending times on weekends and public holidays.

Fares are cheap (minimum 70 cents on non-airconditioned buses; maximum S$1.70 on air-conditioned buses) depending on the number of sectors. Have loose change ready; bus drivers are generally helpful and will tell you the exact fare on boarding. Tickets are issued by automatic dispensers on board.

For convenience, buy a stored-value ez-link Card, which can be used on both buses, and MRT and LRT trains *(see text box below).*

Taxis

More than 18,000 taxis ply the roads and are a popular mode of transport; but be warned that

ACCOMMODATION ACTIVITIES A – Z

HOW TO USE THE EZ-LINK CARD

If you're in Singapore for a few days and plan to move around a lot by public transport, it makes sense to buy the **TransitLink ez-link Card**, which is a stored-value card for use on the MRT, LRT and buses. The ez-link Card can be purchased at ticket offices at all MRT stations and bus interchanges for a minimum of S$15. This card is worth for rides up to S$7, and can be topped up at ticket offices when the value runs low. When the card is returned at the end of your trip, S$3 is refunded. Although the remaining S$5 is a non-refundable administration charge, this far outweighs the convenience of having this card.

Both the MRT and buses use the so-called contactless "smartcard" system – aimed at speeding up queue lines.

To use the ez-link Card, flash or tap it on electronic readers mounted at bus entrances and entry turnstiles of MRT stations, which automatically deducts the maximum fare. When you arrive at your destination, flash the card at the exit reader so that the unused portion of the fare is credited back into the card.

A helpful source for information on using the MRT system and buses is the **TransitLink Guide** (S$1.50 per copy), available at all TransitLink ticket offices. It gives complete details of MRT and bus routes, and contains a section on services to major tourist spots. Or contact:
• **TransitLink:** tel: 1800-767 4333; www.transitlink.com.sg;
• **SMRT Corporation:** tel: 1800-336 8900; www.smrtcorp.com.sg;
• **SBS Transit:** tel: 1800-287 2727; www.sbstransit.com.sg;
• **SMRT Buses:** tel: 6482 3888; www.smrtbuses.com.sg.

during morning and evening rush hours, and when it rains, it is almost impossible to get one if you haven't booked ahead.

Singapore's taxis are clean and generally in good condition. Most drivers speak or understand some English. Still, make sure the driver knows exactly where you want to go before starting out. Tipping is not necessary.

In 2004, the existing three taxi companies – CityCab, Comfort and TIBS – were joined by three new competitors, Premier Taxi, Smart and Trans-Cab. All taxis, regardless of company, have either SH or SHA on their licence plates. Each taxi may carry a maximum of four adult passengers. All taxis are metered with a flagfall of S$2.40 for the first kilometre and 10 cents for every 200 to 225 metres thereafter, or 30 seconds of waiting time.

Most taxi stands are found just outside shopping centres, hotels and other public buildings. You may join the queue at these places or flag one along the road. However, thanks to a very efficient computerised booking system, it has become increasingly difficult to flag down cruising taxis during peak hours.

A long list of extra charges in addition to the fare shown on the meter are applicable:
• S$3 (or S$5 from 5pm–midnight Fri–Sun) for trips originating

TAXI NUMBERS

Booking taxis in advance is recommended; try one of the following companies:
• **CityCab:** 6552 2222;
www.citycab.com.sg
• **Comfort:** 6552 1111;
www.comfort-transportation.com.sg
• **Comfort Limousine Cab**:
6552 2828;
• **SMRT Taxi:** 6555 8888;
www.smrttaxis.com.sg
• **Premier Taxi:** 6363 6888
• **Smart:** 6485 7700
• **Trans-Cab:** 6287 6666

from Changi and Seletar airports;
• midnight surcharge of 50 percent for trips between 11.30pm and 6am;
• S$1 peak period charge for trips between 7.30 to 9.30am and 5 to 8pm from Monday to Saturday;
• S$1 for trips leaving the CBD (Central Business District) between 5 and 8pm from Monday to Thursday and 5pm to 12 midnight from Friday to Saturday;
• S$1 public holiday surcharge from 6pm on the eve of a public holiday to midnight the next day;
• A 10 percent charge for credit card payment; and
• Booking fee of S$3.20 for current bookings and S$5.20 when booking at least half-an-hour in advance. Fancier Limousine Cabs cost S$8 to 10 for current bookings and S$12 to 20 when booked at least half-an-hour in advance.
• Finally, under the ERP (Electronic Road Pricing) system, additional charges (between 30 cents and S$2) apply when the taxi passes ERP gantry points along the ECP (East Coast Parkway), CTE (Central Expressway), PIE (Pan Island Expressway) and Nicoll Highway during morning peak hours, and from 7.30am to 7pm in the CBD area where ERP gantry points are located.

Trishaws

The quaint trishaw, a bicycle with a sidecar, has virtually disappeared from Singapore's streets. Today, it exists only for tourists who want to experience something of the old days.

For more information on trishaw tours, ask your hotel concierge or tour desk. Otherwise, just turn up at the trishaw station behind Bugis Village next to Fu Lu Shou Complex and find a driver, usually between 5 and 11pm. The other place to book trishaws is the **Chinatown Trishaw Tour** office at Kreta Ayer Square, opposite Sago Street (tel: 6339 6833).

A tour around town including Chinatown, Arab Street and Little

India for around 30 to 45 minutes should cost about S$25. For safety, it's best to wait until heavy traffic has dispersed after 8pm.

A word of caution: be sure you agree upon a fare before getting on. Licensed riders are distinguished by their coloured badges.

Driving

Thanks to an efficient public transportation system, it is highly unlikely that the average visitor is going to drive. But if you do, Singapore has great roads and driving is relatively painless – compared to the rest of Asia. Keep a lookout though for drivers who routinely don't switch on indicator lights to signal their intention, and annoying tailgaters and lane drifters on expressways.

Rental companies will provide the wheels as long as you have a valid international driver's licence. Self-drive cars are not cheap and cost from S$175 for a 1.3-litre car to S$295 for a 2-litre car per day including mileage but not insurance. These rates are only applicable for driving in Singapore; taking the car to Malaysia will cost you extra.

Before you head out, stock up on parking coupons and make sure you have a complete understanding of the Electronic Road Pricing system *(see page 90)*.

A valid driver's licence from your country of residence or an international driver's licence is required for driving in Singapore. Driving is on the left and wearing of seat-belts and the use of special child-seats is compulsory. Speed limits are 50 kmh (30 mph) in residential areas and 80 to 90 kmh (50 to 56 mph) on expressways.

Contact any of the following car rental companies:
Avis, tel: 6737 1668;
www.avis.com.sg
Hertz, tel: 1800-734 4646;
www.hertz.com.sg

Smaller companies, however, listed in the Yellow Pages under "Car Rental" offer lower rates and are more open to negotiation.

ACCOMMODATION

WHAT'S AVAILABLE, WHERE TO LOOK, AND WHAT YOU'LL HAVE TO PAY

Choosing a Hotel

In terms of accommodation, amenities and service standards, Singapore's top-end hotels easily compare with the best in the world. Deluxe, first-class and business-orientated hotels all have conference and business facilities, in-room computer ports, cable TV and IDD phones.

There are price categories to suit all pockets. No doubt, accommodation in Singapore is more pricey than in some Southeast Asian cities, but keep an eye out for promotional rates offered by top hotels – these can go as low as 50 percent off the published rates. It's also worth surfing the web for online reservation deals. If you intend to stay longer, you might want to consider checking into a serviced apartment. Singapore's serviced apartments generally offer all the amenities of 4- to 5-star hotels, but come with the added facilities of a fully-equipped kitchen and dining area, for significantly lower rates than a hotel room. Although many are available on a short-term basis, the savings really add up when you take a long-term lease.

The number of backpacker hostels here have decreased with the recent demolition of old buildings on Bencoolen Street,

the once traditional backpacker haunt. What's left is rather dismal, and for the price you pay in some, you're probably better off in a good budget hotel – it costs only marginally more, but in return you get much cleaner beds and greater security.

Hotel Areas

Most visitors stay in the city centre, especially around the Civic District and Orchard Road areas. The former is where you'll find attractions like the Singapore Art Museum and Esplanade – Theatres on the Bay as well as a thriving nightlife scene, while the latter is the city's shopping hub.

For those who want to avoid the crowds (which can get quite chaotic on weekends) and stiff prices, head for the atmospheric charm of Chinatown or Little India. Here you will find budget accommodation in small hotels occupying old-style shophouses. The East Coast area is also worth considering for its laid-back appeal, range of local food options, proximity to the beach, and generally lower rates. Even closer to sun, sand and sea is Sentosa. Hotels on this holiday island are mainly luxury resorts so be prepared for their higher-than-mainland rates. Singapore's efficient transportation system,

however, makes getting around a breeze, so even if you're staying in the suburbs, the city is still within easy reach.

Prices & Bookings

When making reservations directly with the hotel – even from the airport – ask for discounts or special rates. Hotels in this section are listed according to price ranges. Rates are subject to 10 percent service charge, 5 percent GST (Goods and Service Tax) and 1 percent cess (tax), shown as the $-rate+++.

If you arrive without prior hotel reservations, the **Singapore Hotel Association** (SHA) counters at Singapore Changi Airport's Terminals 1 and 2 arrival halls can help you with bookings. At Terminal 1, the East counter opens 10am to 11.30pm daily while its West counter is open 24 hours. At Terminal 2, the North counter opens daily 7am to 11pm, and the South counter opens 24 hours. Alternatively, you may book online at the SHA's website: www.stayinsingapore.com.sg. Peak seasons include the local school holidays in June and December when occupancy levels rise. But unless there is a big convention in town or a regional crisis, you should have no problem being accommodated at the last minute.

THE CIVIC DISTRICT

HOTELS

Luxury

The Fullerton
1 Fullerton Square
Tel: 6733 8388
Fax: 6735 8388
www.fullertonhotel.com
The city's former
General Post Office, this
restored historical land-
mark sits in the heart of
the Civic District, along
the Singapore River and
is only a 5-minute walk
to the Raffles Place MRT
station. Business trav-
ellers will appreciate its
proximity to the financial
district and its contem-
porary Art Deco interior
filled with Philippe
Starck fittings. Café, a
fine-dining Chinese
restaurant and trendy
bar on site. One Fuller-
ton across the road
entices with more water-
front wining and dining
options. (400 rooms)

Raffles Hotel
1 Beach Road
Tel: 6337 1886
Fax: 6339 7650
www.rafffleshotel.com
The city's most famous
(and most expensive)
luxury hotel, beautifully
restored to its former
grandeur. A total of 14
restaurants and bars,
offering everything from
fine-dining continental
and American-style deli
to innovative fusion and
refined Chinese. Expect
old-world atmosphere
and charm, although
part of the hotel is now

an upmarket shopping
annexe. Across the road
is the City Hall MRT
station. (103 suites)

**The Ritz-Carlton
Millenia**
7 Raffles Avenue
Tel: 6337 8888
Fax: 6337 5190
www.ritzcarlton.com
Striking modern hotel,
with an impressive con-
temporary art collection
and Singapore's largest
guest rooms (and stun-
ning bathrooms with
views to match).
Located beside the
Suntec conference
centre and 10 minutes'
walk away from the City
Hall MRT station.
Restaurants serving
Western and fine
Cantonese cuisines,
plus a poolside seafood
restaurant. The bar with
a riveting glass sculp-
ture as its talking point
is perfect for after-din-
ner drinks. (610 rooms)

Expensive

**Conrad Centennial
Singapore**
2 Temasek Boulevard
Tel: 6334 8888
Fax: 6333 9166
www.conradhotels.com
Stylishly modern busi-
ness hotel adjacent to
the Suntec convention
centre and mall, Marina
Square and Millenia
Walk, making it a great
location for both busi-
ness and shopping.
Facilities include a health
club and spa, and out-
door swimming pool with
bar. Excellent Chinese

restaurant and popular
24-hour café. Only a 10-
minute walk from City
Hall MRT. (509 rooms)

The Oriental
5 Raffles Avenue
Tel: 6338 0066
Fax: 6339 9537
www.mandarinoriental.com
Thoroughly modern
despite its name, with
an elegant interior of
mainly black marble.
The rooms on the high
floors offer excellent
views of the surrounding
Marina bay. Located
opposite Suntec City
and next to Marina
Square shopping mall
and 10 minutes' walk to
City Hall MRT station.
Restaurants comprise
an all-day café, an Amer-
ican-style steakhouse, a
Chinese restaurant, an
open-air Italian eatery
and trendy Japanese
bistro. (527 rooms)

Pan Pacific
7 Raffles Boulevard
Tel: 6336 8111
Fax: 6339 1861
www.singapore.panpac.com
John Portman-designed
5-star hotel with a lofty
35-storey atrium and
comfortable good-sized
rooms. Well located
beside Suntec City and
the international con-
vention centre, and 10
minutes' walk from the
City Hall MRT station.
Cantonese restaurant
with grand views (from
37th floor), traditional-
style Japanese restau-
rant with garden; Italian
and North Indian
restaurants, bakery and
lounge bar. (784 rooms)

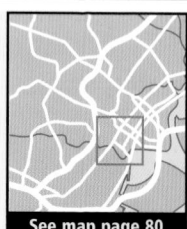

See map page 80

Swissôtel The Stamford
2 Stamford Road
Tel: 6338 8585
Fax: 6338 2862
www.swissotel-thestamford.com
Formerly the Westin
Stamford (the world's
tallest hotel until it was
supplanted in mid-
1999), this newly-
refurbished hotel sits
above the City Hall MRT
station and is located
beside the CBD and
colonial Civic District,
and is practically part of
a large shopping com-
plex. Business centre,
convention centre and a
huge number of restau-
rants and bars (includ-
ing the excellent rooftop
Equinox complex), plus
a luxurious spa and well
equipped fitness
centre. (1,200 rooms)

Moderate

Allson
101 Victoria Street
Tel: 6336 0811
Fax: 6339 7019
www.allsonhotels.com
Close to the museum
district and City Hall
MRT station and good
value for money. Its
recent major refurbish-
ment means spanking
new rooms and lobby

area. The guest rooms have been spruced up and furnished in rosewood and leather furniture. Facilities include outdoor swimming pool and health centre. Restaurants serving local, continental, Chinese and Japanese food. (450 rooms)

Carlton
76 Bras Basah Road
Tel: 6338 8333
Fax: 6339 6866
www.carlton.com.sg
Right in the heart of the museum district, and near the Chjimes entertainment area, this business-class hotel has a great location. The Premier rooms in the new Annex Wing offer luxuries such as marble bathrooms and flat-screen TVs. The hotel also has an award-winning Cantonese restaurant and 24-hour café. A

5-minute walk to City Hall MRT station. (630 rooms)

Grand Plaza Parkroyal
10 Coleman Street
Tel: 6336 3456
Fax: 6339 9311
www.parkroyalhotels.com
This business hotel near City Hall MRT is a combination of both traditional and modern architecture. Located just across popular sights like the Armenian Church, Asian Civilisations Museum and Fort Canning Park. Dining options include a Chinese restaurant, brasserie, and al fresco grill. Also known for its marine-themed spa. (326 rooms)

Hotel Rendezvous
9 Bras Basah Road
Tel: 6336 0220
Fax: 6337 3773
www.rendezvoushotels.com
Right next door to the Singapore Art Museum and close to the Civic

District. Its Rendezvous Restaurant is known for its famous spicy Nasi Padang (Indonesian-style rice and curries) The Palong Lobby Bar is the ideal spot to relax after sightseeing or a long business day. A 5-minute walk to Dhoby Ghaut MRT station. (300 rooms)

Budget

Hangout@Mt.Emily
10A Upper Wilkie Road
Tel: 6438 5588
Fax: 6339 6008
www.hangouthotels.com
Brand new and funky budget-class hotel conveniently located near the Civic District and its tourist attractions. Clean and comfortable but expect no frills. You sleep in Zonk Out rooms, meet fellow travellers in the Veg Out lounge, surf

the web at the Log Out room, eat at the Pig Out café, do your laundry at the Wash Out room and exercise at what else but the Work Out room. A 10-minute walk to Dhoby Ghaut MRT station. (61 rooms with ensuites and 25 dorm-style beds with shared facilities)

Strand
25 Bencoolen Street
Tel: 6338 1866
Fax: 6338 1330
www.strandhotel.com.sg
Clean and comfortable and one of the better budget hotels around. Close to the museum district and Chijmes, and within walking distance to the top end of Orchard Road and a 10-minute walk from Dhoby Ghaut MRT station. Its Blabbers Café on the ground level is great for coffee and sandwiches. (130 rooms)

CHINATOWN AND CENTRAL BUSINESS DISTRICT

HOTELS

Expensive

Grand Copthorne Waterfront
392 Havelock Road
Tel: 6733 0880
Fax: 6737 0880
www.millenniumhotels.com.sg
A modern business hotel only a short distance from the CBD and

PRICE CATEGORIES

Price categories are for a double room without breakfast and taxes:
Luxury = over S$300
Expensive = S$200–300
Moderate = S$100–200
Budget = under S$100

Orchard Road. Sitting by the Singapore River, it has four executive club floors, a large conference centre with business facilities, a piano bar with al fresco dining options, and a good Italian restaurant. Guest rooms are all equipped with broadband Internet access. (538 rooms)

M Hotel Singapore
81 Anson Road
Tel: 6224 1133
Fax: 6222 0749
www.mhotel.com.sg
Excellent location in the financial district for business travellers and only 5-minutes' walk from the Tanjong Pagar MRT station. After a recent S$30-million refurbishment, it now

offers wireless Internet access throughout the hotel and top-notch business facilities including fully-furnished and serviced offices. All rooms have harbour or city views; Japanese restaurant, café and a jazz bar. (412 rooms)

Moderate

Amara
165 Tanjong Pagar Road
Tel: 6879 2555
Fax: 6224 3910
www.amarahotels.com
Newly upgraded hotel with chic modern décor located within the Central Business District. Has a spa, fitness centre, swimming pool and tennis courts. Dining

See map page 102

options include award-winning Thai restaurant, Thanying, as well as a Chinese restaurant and coffeeshop. Short walk to Tanjong Pagar MRT station. (380 rooms)

Berjaya Hotel
83 Duxton Road
Tel: 6227 7678
Fax: 6227 1232
www.berjayaresorts.com
A boutique hotel occupying a row of beautifully

restored shophouses in the heart of China-town's conservation area. Houses fine French restaurant L'Aigle d'Or and a bar. Rooms are smallish, but the Garden suites have a little courtyard. Note: there is no pool or fitness centre. Ten-minute walk to Tanjong Pagar MRT station. (48 rooms)

Furama
60 Eu Tong Sen Street
Tel: 6533 3888
Fax: 6534 1489
www.furama.com
After a recent S$22-million renovation to woo business travellers, its rooms are now comfortable and cosy. Good location for shopping and nightlife as it's near Boat Quay, Clarke Quay and Chinatown. Restaurants serve local, Western and Chinese food, plus a bar. Ten-minute walk to Chinatown MRT station. (354 rooms)

Hotel 1929
50 Keong Saik Road
Tel: 6347 1929
Fax: 6327 1929
www.hotel1929.com
Ultra hip boutique hotel in the heart of China-town that has made the headlines in various design magazines (it won the Architectural Heritage Award in 2003). Highlights here include a rooftop jacuzzi, a well-known contemporary European restaurant, and retro vintage furniture in the rooms. (32 rooms)

Novotel Apollo
405 Havelock Road
Tel: 6733 2081
Fax: 6733 1588
www.novotelapollo.com
Situated between China-town and Orchard Road and within walking distance to Clarke Quay. The new Tropical Wing caters to business travellers and has the requisite facilities. Restaurants

serve local, Indonesian and Chinese food. Outram Park MRT station is a good 15–20-minute walk. (480 rooms)

Budget

Chinatown
12–16 Teck Lim Road
Tel: 6225 5166
Fax: 6225 3912
www.chinatownhotel.com
No-frills budget business hotel with friendly and efficient service in the heart of Chinatown. Rooms are tiny but modern, clean and comfortable. Five minutes' walk to Outram Park MRT station. (42 rooms)

Damenlou
12 Ann Siang Road
Tel: 6221 1900
Fax: 6225 8500
www.damenlou.com
Quaint small hotel with a good Chinese restaurant. Within walking distance to Chinatown, Tanjong Pagar MRT

station, dining hub Club Street and CBD. Rooftop garden has views of Chinatown. (12 rooms)

The Inn
36 Temple Street
Tel: 6221 5333
Fax: 6225 5391
www.theinn.com.sg
Five restored Chinatown shophouses reflecting the Peranakan heritage make up The Inn. Has a business centre, café and bar. Three-minute walk to Chinatown MRT station. (42 rooms)

Royal Peacock
55 Keong Saik Road
Tel: 6223 3522
Fax: 6221 1770
www.royalpeacockhotel.com
Boutique hotel inspired by a Baroque theme and jewel-toned colours. Rooms have plush purple carpeting, red walls and wooden sleigh beds. Café and bar on site. Only a 10-minute walk to Outram Park MRT. (79 rooms)

ORCHARD ROAD

HOTELS

Luxury

Four Seasons
190 Orchard Boulevard
Tel: 6734 1110
Fax: 6733 0682
www.fourseasons.com/singapore
A statement in under-stated elegance, this hotel is located just behind the Orchard Road shopping area. Luxurious interiors, large plush rooms of at least 48 sq metres (515 sq ft) and expensive artworks belie its rather plain facade. Restaurants serving

contemporary fare and refined Cantonese cuisine, plus a cosy al fresco bar with views of Orchard Road. Pool, fitness centre/spa and air-conditioned tennis courts – a dream in humid sticky Singapore. Five-minute walk to Orchard MRT station. (254 rooms)

Grand Hyatt
10 Scotts Road
Tel: 6738 1234
Fax: 6732 1696
www.singapore.grand.hyatt.com
A stone's throw from Orchard Road and its MRT station. Minimalist, almost stark decor, comfortable rooms and excellent service are its

defining hallmarks. Italian restaurant, stylish mezza9 restaurant with elegant martini bar, and a cafe.The Hyatt's free-form pool with lush gardens is a haven in this busy neck of the woods. (693 rooms)

Shangri-La
22 Orange Grove Road
Tel: 6737 3644
Fax: 6737 3527
www.shangri-la.com
A lush green haven just outside the city area. Very popular with its discerning business clientele. Three towers set in luxuriant gardens; extensive renovation of guest rooms, public areas and pool area in

See map pages 122–23

1999. Its luxurious Valley Wing, refurbished in 2004, is where visiting heads of state and other VIPs stay. Superb Cantonese and classy Californian eateries, excellent Japanese restaurant and a 24-hour coffee shop. Only drawback is that it's not very convenient for public transportation and is a good 15-minute walk to the Orchard MRT station. (760 rooms)

Expensive

Goodwood Park
22 Scotts Road
Tel: 6737 7411
Fax: 6732 8558
www.goodwoodparkhotel.com.sg
Charming historical building dating back to 1900. Situated near the heart of Orchard Road and Orchard MRT station. This landmark used to serve as a social club for the German community. Today, it's a luxury hotel with suites that open out to the swimming pool. Five eateries including a grill, Chinese restaurant and coffee lounge for local high tea. (235 rooms)

Hilton International
581 Orchard Road
Tel: 6737 2233
Fax: 6732 2917
www.singapore.hilton.com
The city's longest operating 5-star hotel with a shopping arcade housing international fashion boutiques. Also conveniently located near shopping malls and 10 minutes' walk from Orchard MRT station. Fine-dining Western restaurant, as well as a bakery and café. (423 rooms)

Marriott
320 Orchard Road
Tel: 6735 5800
Fax: 6735 9800
www.marriott.com
The pagoda-roofed hotel at the corner of Scotts and Orchard roads is a well known landmark and just opposite the Orchard MRT station. Its location is perfect for shopping and nightlife.

Popular café with outdoor seating, Chinese restaurant serving *dim sum* and a poolside cafe. The famous Tangs department store is just next door. (382 rooms)

Meritus Mandarin Singapore
333 Orchard Road
Tel: 6737 4411
Fax: 6732 2361
www.mandarin-singapore.com
Serious shoppers would do well to stay here as all the major malls and boutiques (and two MRT stations) are within walking distance. Continental cuisine served in Singapore's highest revolving restaurant plus an excellent Chinese restaurant; its 24-hour Chatterbox coffee house is noted for its local specialty of Hainanese chicken rice. (1,200 rooms)

The Regent
1 Cuscaden Road
Tel: 6733 8888
Fax: 6732 8838
www.regenthotels.com
Another chic hotel, in keeping with the Regent brand name. Expect well appointed rooms and excellent service. Café with both Western and Asian dishes and Cantonese gourmet restaurant serving *dim sum*. Orchard MRT station is a good 10–12-minute walk away. (439 rooms)

Sheraton Towers
39 Scotts Road
Tel: 6737 6888
Fax: 6737 1072
www.starwood.com/sheraton
Swanky and well-run hotel close to Newton MRT station, and a short walk to the start of Orchard Road. Executive tower rooms come with butler service. Speciality restaurants serving Chinese and

Italian fare, and a café with local and Western food (which also serves an excellent brunch on Sunday). (413 rooms)

Moderate

Hotel Asia
37 Scotts Road
Tel: 6737 8388
Fax: 6733 3563
www.hotelasia.com.sg
Ageing but still good value-for-money 3-star hotel close to Newton MRT station and the popular Newton food centre. The café serves local and Western fare, including delicious Indonesian-style *nasi padang*. Cantonese restaurant has good *dim sum* for lunch. (146 rooms)

Crown Prince
270 Orchard Road
Tel: 6732 1111
Fax: 6732 7018
www.crownprince.com.sg
Recently renovated and smack in the middle of Orchard Road and surrounded by an array of shopping malls. Has both Japanese and Sichuan restaurants plus the 24-hour Swensen's café which serves American-style fare and ice-creams. Conveniently located between Somerset and Orchard MRT stations. (332 rooms)

Orchard
442 Orchard Road
Tel: 6734 7766
Fax: 6733 5482
www.orchardhotel.com.sg
Good Orchard Road location opposite the Hard Rock Café. Deluxe rooms in the Claymore Wing have recently been refurbished. The lobby coffee shop serves both buffet and à la carte meals; the Cantonese restaurant is

one of the best in town and is popular for *dim sum*. (672 rooms)

Phoenix
277 Orchard Road
Tel: 6737 8666
Fax: 6732 2024
www.hotelphoenixsingapore.com
Excellent value for its fantastic location on Orchard Road. At its doorstep is the Somerset MRT station. Most rooms have computers with e-mail and Internet access, and personal massage couches. Its popular café serves a value-for-money buffet. (392 rooms)

Royal Plaza On Scotts
25 Scotts Road
Tel: 6737 7966
Fax: 6737 6646
www.royalplaza.com.sg
Owned by the Sultan of Brunei, this business hotel has an excellent location for shopping. Perks include complimentary mini-bar in all rooms, and special discounts at the adjacent DFS Galleria mall. The poolside café serves Italian fare, while the restaurant is popular for its high-tea buffet. (500 rooms)

York
21 Mount Elizabeth
Tel: 6737 0511
Fax: 6732 1217
www.yorkhotel.com.sg
A small hotel with a quiet location behind Scotts Road, but close to Orchard Road shopping, nightlife and MRT

PRICE CATEGORIES

Price categories are for a double room without breakfast and taxes:
Luxury = over S$300
Expensive = S$200–300
Moderate = S$100–200
Budget = under S$100

TRANSPORT

ACCOMMODATION

ACTIVITIES

A – Z

station. The rooms have been recently spruced up and are now more contemporary in decor. Good café serving Western and local cuisines, and a bar. (403 rooms)

Budget

The SHA Villa
64 Lloyd Road
Tel: 6734 7117
Fax: 6736 1651
www.sha.org.sg
Formerly known as Regalis Court Hotel, this small, restored bungalow has a unique character and a Peranakan-inspired decor. The laid-back, homey environment will make you feel like you're staying in a guesthouse. Only a 10-minute walk to Somerset MRT station. (40 rooms)

RELC International House
30 Orange Grove Road
Tel: 6885 7888
Fax: 6733 9976
e-mail: relcih@singnet.com.sg
Humble neighbour to the upscale Shangri-La Hotel but manages to impress nevertheless with its much, much lower rates. Rooms are spacious with balconies, and business travellers will appreciate its well-equipped conference rooms. Good Chinese restaurant. Orchard MRT station however is a 15-minute walk away. (128 rooms)

YMCA International House
1 Orchard Road
Tel: 6336 6000
Fax: 6337 3140
www.ymca.org.sg
Situated at the top end of Orchard Road, bordering the colonial Civic District and a stone's throw to Dhoby Ghaut MRT station. It has conference facilities, café, rooftop swimming pool, fitness centre, squash and badminton courts, and a McDonald's in the lobby. Choose from guest rooms with attached bathrooms or four-person dormitories. (111 rooms)

Apartments

The Ascott
6 Scotts Road
Tel: 6735 6868
Fax: 6733 7561
www.the-ascott.com
Located within walking distance to the Orchard MRT station and popular shopping centres (in fact it sits over one). Has 153 self-contained luxury studios, one- and two-bedroom and penthouse units with fully equipped kitchens. Other facilities include fitness centre, business centre, swimming pool and a laundry room. Ideal for long stays. Minimum 1-week lease.

Orchard Parksuites
11 Orchard Turn
Tel: 6839 1233
Fax: 6737 5463
www.fareastsvcapts.com.sg
Luxurious apartments in the heart of Orchard Road just next to the Orchard MRT station. In the opulent lobby sits a baby grand piano, and the swimming pool has piped-in underwater music. Floor plans vary from one-bedroom lofts to the four-bedroom penthouse suite; minimum 1-week lease.

LITTLE INDIA

HOTELS

Expensive

Inter-Continental
80 Middle Road
Tel: 6338 7600
Fax: 6338 7366
www.singapore.
intercontinental.com
Stylish hotel with some rooms built in the shophouse style. Located between Little India and the Civic District; near

museums and beside Bugis Junction shopping complex and Bugis MRT station. Casual Mediterranean-style restaurant, elegant Chinese restaurant serving *dim sum* and creative Cantonese dishes, Japanese restaurant and jazz bar. The Asian artworks scattered throughout the hotel is a nice touch. (406 rooms)

Moderate

Albert Court
180 Albert Street
Tel: 6339 3939
Fax: 6339 3252
www.albertcourt.com.sg
Boutique hotel just adjacent to the Little India district. The interior decor is nostalgically charming, with carved

Peranakan teak furnishings and old brass electrical switches, but the comforts are thoroughly modern. Continental café and bar. No pool. Five minutes' walk from Little India MRT station. (136 rooms)

New Park
181 Kitchener Road
Tel: 6291 5533
Fax: 6297 2827
www.parkroyalhotels.com
Located near the bottom end of Serangoon Road close to the 24-hour Mustafa Centre (great for shopping) and next to Farrer Park MRT station. Rooms are spacious and feature the usual comforts. Café serving Asian and Western cuisines, and a Cantonese restaurant. Conference facilities,

See map page 136

executive floors, fitness centre and swimming pool. (531 rooms)

Budget

Broadway Hotel
195 Serangoon Road
Tel: 6292 4661
Fax: 6291 6414
www.geocities.com/broadwayhotel
Basic but comfortable no-frills hotel in the heart of Little India and close to the famous "banana leaf" restau-

rants of Race Course Road. Rooms are decent enough for the price and all were renovated in 1999. Only a short walk to Little India MRT station. (63 rooms)

Perak Lodge
12 Perak Road
Tel: 6299 7733
Fax: 6392 0919

www.peraklodge.net
With a charming location in Little India, Perak Lodge occupies a restored shophouse. Lovely atmosphere with friendly staff. Only five minutes' walk from Little India MRT station. It has a lovely courtyard with fish pond. All rooms

come with electronic room safes and breakfast. (34 rooms)

aRoundCactus Hotel
407 Jalan Besar
Tel: 6391 3913
Fax: 6391 3238
www.cactushotelsg.com
This newly revamped hotel on the outskirts of Little India has a nice

vibe, and clean double, twin or four-person dormitory-style rooms. All rooms are air-conditioned and come with attached bathrooms and TV. About 5-minutes' walk from Lavender MRT station and near a large 24-hour hawker centre. (30 rooms)

SENTOSA

ACCOMMODATION

HOTELS

Luxury

The Sentosa
2 Bukit Manis Road
Tel: 6275 0331
Fax: 6275 0228
www.thesentosa.com
Stunning resort-style hotel located on a forested hill on Sentosa island. Features both hotel-style rooms and suites as well as villas with private pools.

Linked by a path directly to the beach. You may just want to park yourself at this idyllic retreat and not venture into the city. Terrace café and the superb Cliff restaurant, which serves seafood and Continental cuisine in a picturesque location. The sea-facing bar is perfect for sunset cocktails. Be sure to book a massage at its adjacent Spa Botanica, set in lush gardens. (214 rooms and villas)

Expensive

Shangri-La's Rasa Sentosa Resort
101 Siloso Road
Tel: 6275 0100
Fax: 6275 0355
www.shangri-la.com
This is Singapore's only true beachfront hotel, located along Siloso Beach on Sentosa Island. Restaurants serving seafood, international and Italian cuisines, plus café, lobby lounge and poolside bar. Not the most

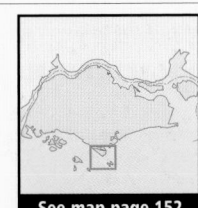

See map page 152

convenient place to stay for access to the city, but the resort offers extensive recreational activities, from sailing to cycling, so there is plenty to do. Ideal for families. (459 rooms)

EAST COAST

HOTELS

Moderate

Grand Mercure Roxy Hotel
50 East Coast Road
Tel: 6344 8000
Fax: 6344 8010
www.accorhotels-asia.com
Value-for-money 4-star hotel with Parkway Shopping Centre just opposite and a short walk to the East Coast beach. Chic modern design with spacious rooms, café and Thai restaurant. No MRT station nearby, but buses

across the street service the city. (482 rooms)

Le Meridien Changi Village
1 Netheravon Road
Tel: 6379 7111
Fax: 6545 0112
www.lemeridien.com
A S$45-million renovation has completely transformed this former transit hotel into a chic modern resort. Convenient location for Changi Airport and Singapore Expo. Free shuttle to both the airport and the city. Both Changi Beach and Changi Village nearby are great places to chill out. (380 rooms)

Budget

Betel Box Hostel
200 Joo Jiat Road
Tel: 6247 7340
www.betelbox.com
One of the best backpacker hostels in this neck of the woods. Owned by seasoned backpackers who know what the budget traveller wants. Clean, air-conditioned dormitory-style rooms in a quaint shophouse setting with Asian furniture. Paya Lebar MRT station is a 15-minute walk away.

Malacca Hotel
97–99 Still Road
Tel: 6345 7411

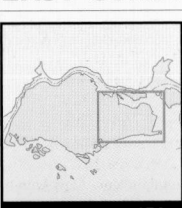

See map page 174

Fax: 6440 5121
www.malacca.com.sg
Budget hotel with few facilities – there's no pool or restaurant. But its location is convenient for exploring the heritage-rich Katong area and East Coast Park. Ten-minute walk from Eunos MRT station. (29 rooms)

TRANSPORT

ACCOMMODATION

ACTIVITIES

A – Z

A CTIVITIES

THE ARTS, NIGHTLIFE, SHOPPING, SPORTS, SIGHTSEEING TOURS, CHILDREN'S ACTIVITIES

THE ARTS

Singapore is trying to make a name for itself as Asia's centre of the arts and entertainment by staging regular theatre, dance, music and opera events and also by encouraging home-grown productions. The Singapore Arts Festival (www.singaporeartsfest.com) around June is an annual 3-week long celebration of the arts, with international acts from all over the world showcasing their talents.

Performing Arts Venues

DBS Arts Centre
20 Merbau Road
Tel: 6733 8166
Performing venue of the Singapore Repertory Theatre.
Esplanade – Theatres on the Bay
1 Esplanade Drive
Tel: 6828 8222
www.esplanade.com
Sprawling 6-hectare (15-acre) performing arts centre with world-class concert hall and theatres.
Jubilee Hall
Raffles Hotel
1 Beach Road
Tel: 6412 1319
A theatre playhouse designed in late Victorian style featuring plays, musicals and concerts.

Kallang Theatre
1 Stadium Walk
Tel: 6345 8488
Home of mainly big-name stage productions.
Nanyang Academy of Fine Arts
151 Bencoolen Street
Tel: 6331 0386
www.nafa.edu.sg
The academy's Performing Arts Building has regular concerts.
The Arts House
1 Old Parliament Lane
Tel: 6332 6900
www.theartshouse.com.sg
The latest arts centre, housed in the Old Parliament House.
The Black Box
Fort Canning Centre
Tel: 6338 4077
Residence for local arts group Theatreworks.
The Substation
45 Armenian Street
Tel: 6337 7535
www.substation.org
Multi-media arts centre and venue for cutting-edge works.
Victoria Concert Hall
11 Empress Place
Tel: 6338 4401
www.vch.org.sg
Singapore Symphony Orchestra holds occasional concerts here.
Victoria Theatre
9 Empress Place
Tel: 6338 8283
Venue for international and local theatre and musicals.

Singapore Indoor Stadium
2 Stadium Walk
Tel: 6344 2660
www.singaporeindoorstadium.com
Asian and international concerts are held in this large sports and entertainment centre.

Music and Dance

Singapore Dance Theatre
Fort Canning Centre
Tel: 6338 0611
www.singaporedancetheatre.com
Critically acclaimed dance company with an active calendar of performances.
Singapore Symphony Orchestra
11 Empress Place
Tel: 6338 1230
www.sso.org.sg
Singapore Symphony Orchestra gives regular concerts at the Esplanade – Theatres on the Bay, often with eminent guest conductors and famous soloists from all over the world.

Theatre

For a complete listing on local theatre companies and updates on arts performances, check www.singaporetheatre.com.
Action Theatre
42 Waterloo Street
Tel: 6837 0842
www.action.org.sg
Notable theatre group that

stages mainly contemporary plays on topical issues, and big musicals.

The Necessary Stage
278 Marine Parade Road
Tel: 6440 8115
www.necessary.org
A major theatre company in Singapore with a strong youth theatre emphasis.

Theatreworks
The Black Box
Fort Canning Centre
Tel: 6338 4077
www.theatreworks.org.sg
A leading local avant-garde theatre company; stages works at the Black Box.

Singapore Repertory Theatre
DBS Arts Centre
20 Merbau Road
Tel: 6733 8166

BUYING TICKETS

Tickets for events can either be obtained directly at the ticket offices of performance venues or at the outlets of SISTIC and Ticketcharge.

SISTIC outlets: Alliance Francaise, Bishan Junction 8, Chinese Opera Teahouse, Cold Storage Jelita, DBS Arts Centre, Downtown East, Esplanade – Theatres on the Bay, Millenia Walk, Parco Bugis Junction, Parkway Parade, Raffles City Shopping Centre, Scotts Shopping Centre, Singapore Conference Hall, Singapore Indoor Stadium, Specialists' Shopping Centre, Suntec City Mall, Tampines Mall, Victoria Concert Hall, Wisma Atria. Hotline: 6348 5555, fax: 6440 6784; www.sistic.com.sg.

Ticketcharge outlets: Centrepoint, Century Square, Chijmes, Forum – The Shopping Mall, Great World City, Jurong Point, Marina Square, Singapore Visitor Centre@Orchard, Substation, Tanglin Mall, West Mall. Hotline: 6296 2929, fax: 6296 9897; www.ticketcharge.com.sg.

www.srt.com.sg
Leading theatre group that focuses on performances with a strong Asian theme.

Chinese Opera

Outdoor performances are staged in suburban neighbourhoods during the seventh month of the Chinese lunar year (August/September). During this time, Taoists believe that the gates of hell are thrown open allowing the spirits of the deceased to wander the earth. To appease them, Chinese operas and pop concerts (*getai*) are staged along with offerings and sumptuous banquets. For year-long performances, contact **Chinese Opera Teahouse** at Smith Street in Chinatown. Performances every Friday and Saturday at 7pm, tel: 6323 4862; www.ctcopera.com.sg).

Cinema

There are more than 50 cinemas on the island, showing everything from Hollywood blockbusters to art movies and Chinese and Indian dramas. Details are published daily in the *Life!* section of *The Straits Times*. Censorship – while recently relaxed – keeps out films dealing with themes which are too sexually explicit or on subjects deemed undesirable. R21 films are for those over 21 years old, M18 or Mature 18 is for 18 years and above, NC-16 stands for No Children Under the Age of 16, G is for general viewing and PG indicates that parental guidance is advisable.

Cineplexes offer a choice of several movies in smaller theatres. The main ones are at Bugis Junction, Great World City, Orchard CineLeisure (has 24-hour screenings on Fri, Sat and eve of public holidays), Plaza Singapura, Shaw Centre and Suntec City.

The annual **Singapore Film Festival** offers a chance to view critically acclaimed films which normally are subjected to a lim-

ited distribution. The well-received cinefest usually takes place in April – check website www.filmfest.org.sg for updates. In addition, the **Singapore Film Society**, an active organisation of dedicated movie buffs, holds weekly screenings of non-mainstream films for its members (tel: 9017 0160, www.sfs.org.sg).

Art Galleries

The many art galleries here offer a whole gamut of choices – from rare European masterpieces to modern abstracts by young local artists. Most galleries offer a worldwide delivery service.

Art-2 Gallery
01-03 MITA Building
140 Hill Street
Tel: 6338 8713
www.art2.com.sg
Collection includes sculptures, ceramics, paintings, and prints from around the region.

Art Forum
82 Cairnhill Road
Tel: 6737 3448
www.artforum.com.sg
Well-established gallery in an old-style shophouse, with a focus on contemporary Asian art.

Artfolio
02-25 Raffles Hotel Shopping Arcade, 328 North Bridge Road
Tel: 6334 4677
www.artfolio.com.sg
Contemporary Asian art, including works by prominent Malaysian-born artist Eng Tay.

Art Seasons Gallery
5 Gemmill Lane
Tel: 6221 1800
www.artseasons.com.sg
International contemporary art pieces are housed in this three-storey gallery above a wine bar.

Plum Blossoms
01-02 MITA Building
140 Hill Street
Tel: 6339 9768, and
02-37 Raffles Hotel Shopping Arcade, 328 North Bridge Road
Tel: 6334 1198
Collection includes museum-quality Asian art, Chinese porcelain and textiles and Vietnamese art.

TRANSPORT

ACCOMMODATION

ACTIVITIES

A – Z

Singapore Tyler Print Institute
41 Robertson Quay
Tel: 6336 3663
www.stpi.com.sg
Gallery and teaching facility for
artists housed in a restored 19th
century warehouse – its
inaugural exhibition featured
renowned contemporary artist
Frank Stella.

Soobin
01-10 MITA Building
140 Hill Street
Tel: 6837 2777
Specialising in Southeast Asian
and Chinese Art.

The Substation Art Gallery
45 Armenian Street
Tel: 6337 7535
www.substation.org
Exhibits experimental, original
and traditional art forms.

NIGHTLIFE

General

The island's days as a risqué
port may be over – the opium
dens and the Bugis Street transvestites are long gone – but the
city's nightlife scene is alive and
booming, with stylish new bars
and clubs opening all the time.
Recent laws have allowed
dancers to get on top of bars and
do their thing, and some
nightspots, away from residential
areas, can remain open throughout the night.

Whether you plan to rip it up
on the dance floor, unwind with a
glass of premium vino, down a
frothy pint or join a snaking
queue of trendy young things at
the newest, hottest nightspot,
there are enough choices to
satisfy party animals of all
inclinations (and budgets).

The best time to enjoy your
favourite bar is during "Happy
Hours", usually between 5–8 or
9pm, when prices are more
affordable. At clubs, a cover
charge of between S$15–30 will
give you admission on Friday and
Saturday nights and a drink.

Boat Quay/Circular Road

Boat Quay's stretch of pubs and
restaurants, occupying old shophouses beside the Singapore
River, has lost some of its initial
gloss, but it still makes for a
lively night out. Here you will find
pubs and eateries offering a
blend of wining and dining under
antique street lamps and stars.

Either take the MRT to Raffles
Place or ask the taxi driver to drop
you at UOB Plaza, from where you
can walk to the waterfront.

Bar Opiume
1 Empress Place
Asian Civilisations Museum
Tel: 6339 2876
www.indochine.com.sg
Not quite Boat Quay but across
the river, this place attracts a
chi chi crowd with its stunning
view of the Singapore River, ultra-
cool decor and a vodka bar.

BQ Bar
39 Boat Quay
Tel: 6536 9722
A mixed crowd of locals and
expats come here for its laid
back house and jazz tunes and
reasonably priced drinks. Complimentary bar snacks like olives,
carrot and celery sticks and
bruschetta with your drinks.

Harry's Bar
28 Boat Quay
Tel: 6538 3029
An institution with the pin-striped
investment crowd who gather to
cut business deals and to take in
the moody jazz and blues sessions performed nightly.

Jazz at South Bridge
82B Boat Quay
Tel: 6327 4672
Set up by an ex-architect and jazz
enthusiast. Performances by jazz
musicians and jam sessions are
held regularly at this venue – with
sections catering to the "serious
listener", "borderline listener"
and "boozers".

Mag's Wine Bar-Bistro
86 Circular Road
Tel: 6438 3836
A nice little place with a good
wine list, cigars and a congenial
atmosphere. Owner Mag cooks
up a storm in the kitchen too.

Molly Malone's Irish Pub & Grill
42 Circular Road
Tel: 6536 2029
One of the best Irish pubs anywhere in Asia. This very traditional bar oozes quaint cosy
charm, and is always busy with
those inclined towards Irish-style
dark beers and roast beef with
Yorkshire pudding.

The Penny Black
26/27 Boat Quay
Tel: 6538 2300
Popular with the financial district
crowd, this upmarket "public
house" serves great pub lunches
of sandwiches and steaks, meat
pies, and fish and chips – all
washed down by English ales like
Ruddles and Old Speckled Hen.

Clarke Quay and Riverside Point

Further up the river is **Riverside
Point**, with **Clarke Quay** across
the river. The nearest MRT station
is Clarke Quay.

Attica
01-13/13/14 Clarke Quay
3A River Valley Road
Tel: 6333 9973
www.attica.com.sg
An open courtyard setting with
lush greenery and a fountain is
the perfect setting to unwind to
Latin, jazz and funk. Upstairs is
the highly regarded Coriander
Leaf restaurant (see page 96).

LOCAL LISTINGS

Visitors can obtain information
on the arts, nightlife, shopping
and eating out through several
publications available free at
hotels, shopping centre information counters and STB
visitor centres. Singapore This
Week, The Singapore Visitor,
and WHERE Singapore maga-
zines are full of useful information as are I-S and Juice
magazines, especially for listings of hot bars and clubs.

The Straits Times' What's
On section and 8 Days magazine provide useful information
as well but they are not free.

Brewerkz
01-05/06 Riverside Point
30 Merchant Road
Tel: 6438 7438
www.brewerkz.com
Micro-brewery, pub and restaurant rolled into one. To taste all six types of beer, try a six-beer sampler then go for a 12-, 16- or 24-ounce glass of your favourite; the India Pale Ale is a local favourite.

Café Iguana
01-03 Riverside Point
30 Merchant Road
Tel: 6236 1275
Sample over a 100 different tequilas – just not all at once. Their margaritas are recommended and wine is available too, along with a Tex-Mex menu.

China Bar
01-01 Central Mall
7 Magazine Road
Tel: 6536 2047
Uninhibited dance joint, where the live rock band and bar-top dancing are big hits on Friday and Saturday nights.

Coco Carib
Blk 3C Clarke Quay
River Valley Road
Tel: 6332 6028
Chill out to the sounds of reggae and resist the urge to *rrrrhumba* as you dine al fresco on Caribbean cuisine.

Crazy Elephant
01-06/07 Clarke Quay
3E River Valley Road
Tel: 6337 1990
This small, smoky den is always full of people jamming to the great house band playing passionate jazz and heartfelt blues. The outdoor tables are usually busy, but they're the nicest places to sample the pizzas, pastas and sandwiches.

1 Nite Stand Bar & Comedy Club
01-15/20 Clarke Quay
3A River Valley Road
Tel: 6334 1954
www.the1nitestand.com
A place to down a beer while laughing your head off at some of the best international comedians that fly in to entertain every last Wednesday–Saturday nights of the month.

Civic District
The watering holes in this area are strewn over quite a large area, from **One Fullerton** near Merlion Park at the waterfront to the **Raffles City** and **Suntec City** areas to historic **Chijmes** – a convent school that had its church (gasp!) turned into a performance hall and the classrooms into shops, bars and restaurants. Some of the Civic District's most spectacular hotels also boast great bars to chill out at.

Balaclava
01-01B Suntec City Convention Centre, 1 Raffles Boulevard
Tel: 6339 1600
The ultra-chic decor – featuring red armchairs, lamps, screen dividers, and interesting textures – is a perfect backdrop to the great live music and stylish crowd. There is ample space for intimate parties.

Carnegie's
01-01 Far East Square
44–45 Pekin Street
Tel: 6534 0850
Popular with expatriates, this bar was one of the first to introduce bar-top dancing. Hearty Western-style meals and good drink deals are available throughout the week; Ladies' Night on Wednesdays is especially well-received.

Chihuly Lounge
7 Raffles Avenue
Ritz-Carlton Millenia
Tel: 6337 8888
Soak in the fabulously modern, architectural drama of this hotel and enjoy a quiet drink amid the glow from Dale Chihuly's spectacular glass sculptures.

China Jump Bar and Grill
B1-07/08 Fountain Court
Chijmes, 30 Victoria Street
Tel: 6338 9388
Trendy cocktails and enormous servings of typical American diner-fare. Live band Jive Talkin' keeps the dance floor crowded.

Equinox
2 Stamford Road
Swissôtel The Stamford
Tel: 6431 5669
www.equinoxcomplex.com
This exclusive dining complex on the 68th–72nd floors houses five restaurants and bars offering a huge selection of cocktails and wines and *the* best views of the city skyline. Dancing takes place at its 71st-floor **New Asia Bar** after 10pm on Fridays and Saturdays, while **City Space** on the 70th floor is a classy bar with the best seats in the house to see the eye-popping skyline.

Father Flanagan's Irish Pub
B1-06 Chijmes, 30 Victoria Street
Tel: 6333 1418
Barrels, brewing implements and wall murals were sourced from Ireland while music by the Chieftains, U2 and Van Morrison enhance the atmosphere. Extensive menu, with dishes like smoked bacon soup, Irish stew, and beef and Guinness pie.

Long Bar
1 Beach Road, Raffles Hotel
Tel: 6412 1229
The languorously colonial Raffles Hotel's bar still serves the famous Singapore Sling. No one cares about Singapore's anti-litter laws here: patrons are expected to toss empty shells of peanuts onto the floor!

Ocho
01-12/13/14 Chijmes
30 Victoria Street
Tel: 6883 1508
A Spanish-themed tapas bar with a lovely al fresco area makes a cosy spot to down a hearty jug (or two) of sangria.

Paulaner Bräuhaus
02-01 Millenia Walk
9 Raffles Boulevard
Tel: 6883 2572
German pub/brewery which serves up a large selection of light and dark brews, along with a menu of German dishes.

Post Bar
The Fullerton Hotel
1 Fullerton Square
Tel: 6733 8388
This art-deco inspired bar at a former post-office-turned-luxury-hotel is where the city's hip come to be seen. The high prices don't seem to put people off. The seafood and oyster bar is a highlight here.

Club Street

Club Street reinvented itself in the late 1990s and is now a lively entertainment strip populated with trendy restaurants and bars.

Bar Sa Vanh
49 Club Street
Tel: 6323 0145
This ethnic-inspired bar somehow manages to exude tranquillity with its waterfall, fish pond and opium beds. Upstairs is an equally stylish restaurant serving Indochinese cuisine.

Barrio Chino
60 Club Street
Tel: 6324 3245
A Latin-American-influenced joint; try its potent signature Mucho Macho cocktail.

Beaujolais
1 Ann Siang Hill
Tel: 6224 2227
One of Singapore's first wine bars remains one of the most romantic places for a candle-lit rendezvous.

The Club by Aphrodisiac
47B Club Street
Tel: 6325 8616
Offers aphrodisiac-inspired cocktails and a dance floor.

Mohamed Sultan Road

Since the late 1990s, Mohamed Sultan Road has etched itself on Singapore's clubbing map. Today, the stretch – which also includes Robertson Walk and Robertson Quay – is home to more than 30 watering holes. Many bars have opened and closed over the past few years, but there's always another eager entrepreneur ready to take over a vacant spot in the island's nightlife mecca.

BAR
01-23 Robertson Walk
11 Unity Street
Tel: 6738 1318
The spacious drinking hole serves up premium champagnes, cocktails and wine, and attracts showy types.

CU Bar
15 Mohamed Sultan Road
Tel: 6738 9050
The place to shake your booty on the bar tops, or to ogle the sexy lasses strutting their stuff.

Dbl-O
01-24 Robertson Walk
11 Unity Street
Tel: 6735 2008
Pronounced "Double-O", this club is high on the glamour quotient and an excellent place to people-watch. Plays a mix of house, disco, garage and retro.

Madam Wong's
28/29 Mohamed Sultan Road
Tel: 6834 0108
Tried-and-tested pub, and probably the first nightspot to draw the clubbing crowds to this area.

Next Page
17 Mohamed Sultan Road
Tel: 6235 6967
Popular with the 30-something crowd, the pub has a distinct Oriental decor with Chairman Mao memorabilia and wooden booths.

Siam SupperClub
01-53 UE Square
207 River Valley Road
Tel: 6732 0937
Acid jazz grooves dominate along with plush booth seats in this cosy drinking den.

The Liquid Room
03-05 The Gallery Hotel
76 Robertson Quay
Tel: 6333 8117
www.theliquidroom.com.sg
The ground floor is Soundbar@ Liquid Room, where you can listen to down-tempo beats. Upstairs is where the dance action is. Plays mainly trance and progressive house, and has hosted several well-known DJs.

Zouk
17/19/21 Jiak Kim Street
Tel: 6738 2988
www.zoukclub.com.sg
Not quite Mohammed Sultan Road but close to it, Singapore's hippest club in a converted warehouse is a must-go for serious clubbers – all the international magazines have raved about this place. The bustling **Wine Bar** plays acid jazz as a prelude to the cutting-edge dance music that rules on the main dance floor. The smaller **Phuture** caters to a hip-hop crowd while **Velvet Underground** is where an older and more beautiful crowd converges.

Orchard Road

You can bar-hop all night long on Orchard Road. The Peranakan Place area has a concentration of cosy pubs favoured by expatriates, and most of the major hotels along Orchard Road have decent in-house bars.

Alley Bar
2 Emerald Hill
Tel: 6738 8818
Scores high on ambience with its cosy Peranakan-inspired interior and black marble bartop. *Dim sum* bar snacks provide an unusual twist.

Anywhere
04-08/09 Tanglin Shopping Centre
19 Tanglin Road
Tel: 6734 8233
This place has been around for over two decades, but still rocks with local band Tania. Lead singer Alban is a consumate entertainer.

Bar None
Marriott Hotel, 320 Orchard Road
Tel: 6222 8117
Packs in the crowds loyal to resident live rock band 9Lives. This place is long-time fixture on the nightlife circuit.

Brix
Grand Hyatt, 10-12 Scotts Road
Tel: 6416 7107
Offers a sophisticated environment for after-work gatherings; the bar is divided into the quiet Whisky Bar, the relaxing Wine Bar and the livelier Music Bar.

Hard Rock Café
50 Cuscaden Road
Tel: 6235 5232
If you really need another Hard Rock T-shirt, head to the American import famous for its diner food and rock 'n' roll memorabilia.

Ice-Cold Beer
9 Emerald Hill
Tel: 6735 9929
The name says it all – this is the place to chug down, literally, ice-cold beer. The jumbo-sized hot dogs are perfect with beer.

Muddy Murphy's Irish Pub
B1-04 Orchard Hotel Shopping Arcade, 442 Orchard Road
Tel: 6735 0400
A thriving Dublin-styled pub where taps flow with Guinness and

Kilkenny. It's standing room only on most Friday nights.

Que Pasa
7 Emerald Hill
Tel: 6235 6626
It's smoky, lined with crates and barrels of wine, and is always full. Premium wines are served upstairs amid the atmosphere of a cigar club. Excellent tapas menu.

Sentosa Island

The party continues on further away, on Sentosa. Come on a sunny afternoon and you may think you're in Venice Beach, as buff bodies parade around the timber decking and palm trees. It's a great spot to watch the sunset – try to ignore the oil tankers – and in between drinks you can join the ongoing volleyball games.

Sunset Bay
40 Siloso Beach Walk
Tel: 6275 0668

Bora Bora Beach Bar
Palawan Beach
Tel: 9005 4238

Gay and Lesbian Venues

Singapore's unofficial gay hangout is Tanjong Pagar, where most of the gay bars are located. Straight clubs like Centro at One Fullerton also hosts gay nights on Sundays, while Velvet Underground at Zouk attracts a mixed straight and gay crowd.

Backstage Bar
13A Trengganu Street
Tel: 6227 1712
Cosy place with a Broadway theme. Discreet rainbow flag outside proclaims its inclination.

Taboo
65-67 Neil Road
Tel: 6225 6256
A perennial favourite among local and foreign gay men, Taboo's new location boasts three levels of partying. Expect long queues on Friday and Saturday nights.

Water Bar
38/39 Craig Road
Tel: 6221 5739
Affliated to Taboo, this club plays pop tunes to the happy (and obviously gay) dance crowd.

Cabaret

Boom Boom Room
01-01 Far East Square
130 Amoy Street,
Tel: 6435 0030
www.boomboomroom.com.sg
Head here for one of the most outlandish evenings that Singapore has to offer. Risqué cabaret-styled entertainment reigns in this small club with riotously funny song-and-dance acts every night. Singapore's most celebrated tranny, Kumar, who gained notoriety with his outrageous drag performances, rules the stage here on most weekends. Some of the obviously local references will go over most visitors' heads but there is enough to make visitors double up in laughter.

The Neptune
Level 7 Overseas Union House
50 Collyer Quay
Tel: 6224 3922
This huge theatre-restaurant is a big draw for Chinese business-men entertaining clients, and is famous for its twice-nightly (8pm and 9.30pm) topless showgirl revues. A bizarre leftover from former decades, it seems. You can go just for the show or dine on its noteworthy Cantonese dishes.

An Evening of Horror

Igor's – The Main Event
01-02A Oasis Complex
50 Stadium Boulevard
tel: 6440 2725
www.igors.com.sg
This fun place is a ghoulish mix of food, theatre and music entertainment. Before you can sit down to dinner in the Grand Haunted Dining Hall, you'll have to pass through the Demon's Dungeon, a horror maze that's really more cheesy than scary. Dinner is a high-energy affair accompanied by a suspense-thriller stage performance starring Igor himself. This theatre-dining experience comes on every Friday and Saturday, 7pm to 1am.

SHOPPING

General

All large stores operate on a fixed price system but in smaller shops, prices are sometimes negotiable and bargaining can be a fun experience. Traditionally, the first customer is said to bring luck, so an early start can save you some money. Find out the seller's "best price", ask for a little below that, then plead and joke, perhaps even begin to move towards the exit of the shop.

No vendor sells below cost as he claims, so don't worry and just enjoy the fun. Comparing prices at different places for the same item is definitely worth your while, especially for high-end goods such as watches, cameras and computers.

There are unspoken rules, though, in the bargaining game. Let the vendor know if you intend to pay by credit card (to allow for the surcharge) and if you have bargained for a while and agreed on a price, you are under a moral obligation to buy.

Keep a lookout for shops bearing the **CaseTrust** logo – an indication of both reliability and competitive pricing, as they are recognised by the **Consumers Association of Singapore** (CASE). The **Singapore Tourism Board** (STB) also encourages shops to work on their reputation and treat their clientele courteously. By the same token, it blacklists errant retailers, all in the spirit of protecting the visitor's interest. You can view the list of errant retailers at www.visitsingapore.com.

See also chapters on Shopping (page 66) and Orchard Road (page 121).

Complaints

Be on your guard against touts offering free shopping tours, special discounts and pirated goods. Complaints about unethical practices or excessively rude service

TRANSPORT

ACCOMMODATION

ACTIVITIES

A – Z

should be made to: **CASE** (tel: 6463 1811). You can also lodge a complaint with the **STB** (tel: 1800 736 2000).

Visitors may also take unscrupulous vendors to court. The **Small Claims Tribunal** (tel: 6435 5937) has a fast-track system for tourists. Cases will be heard within 2 or 3 days. A S$10 fee is payable and no legal representation is necessary. Or go online to the **e@dr Centre** of the Singapore Subordinate Courts (www.e-adr.org.sg), where disputes can be mediated via e-mail.

GST REFUND

There is a 5 percent Goods and Services Tax (GST) imposed on most goods and services. To qualify for a refund, a visitor must spend at least S$300 at a single retailer, or shops which are part of the same retail chain, or pool receipts of S$100 or more from stores which participate in the **Global Refund Tax Free Shopping** scheme. Note: refunds are only given for visitors who depart Singapore by air. Designated stores will display a Tax Free Shopping sticker. The goods purchased must be for export only. The refund may be made either by cash, cheque or through your credit card.

Claim forms and the correct procedure on how to make a claim can be obtained at all participating retailers.

Accumulated shopping cheques can be cashed at Changi Airport's **Global Refund Counter** (tel: 6225 6238; www.globalrefund.com). Please note that the purchased goods have to be presented so head for the Refund Counter *before* checking in bulky purchases. Hand-carried items can be verified at the Refund Counters located after the immigration checkpoint.

What to Buy

Cameras

Singapore is one of the best places in Southeast Asia for the duty-free purchase of cameras, lenses and photographic equipment. Prices are good, and the selection enormous, from idiot-proof automatics to the latest digital models.

With all purchases either get an international guarantee, or opt for directly-imported goods intended for the local market, and save on the price. If you don't see what you want in the shop, ask, because it will be brought to you in no time.

Centrepoint, Sim Lim Square and Raffles City Shopping Centre have several specialist camera stores. Peninsula Plaza and the Peninsula Hotel's shopping arcade, both on Coleman Street, are also excellent places for cameras and camera equipment. **Albert Photo**, 01-06 Orchard Towers, tel: 6235 2815.

Cathay Photo Store, 01-07/08 Peninsula Plaza, tel: 6338 0451; 02-219 Marina Square, tel: 6339 6188.

The Camera Workshop, 01-31, 3 Coleman Street, tel: 6336 1956. Also trades in used cameras and has a repairs service.

Computers/Electronics

Being such a wired country, computer buffs have a wide choice of PCs, Macs, laptops, palmtops, PDAs and a complete range of software, peripherals and accessories. Don't forget to check if the voltage of the equipment is compatible with that of your home country.

The law comes down hard on bootleg software and frequent raids are carried out at shopping malls specialising in computers – so buy the genuine stuff and ask for a guarantee.

The range of hi-fi equipment, video recorders and CD and DVD players is also vast.

The best selection is found at

Funan The IT Mall on North Bridge Road and **Sim Lim Square** on Rochor Canal Road. Other places to buy are:

Best Denki, 03-400 Marina Square, tel: 6337 3323; 05-01/05 Ngee Ann City, tel: 6835 2855; 04-09/12 Plaza Singapura, tel: 6333 0110. This large chain of stores can be found in many major shopping centres (the above locations are located in the city centre).

Harvey Norman, 03-08 Centre-point, tel: 6732 8686; 03-22 Raffles City Shopping Centre, tel: 6339 6777; 02-001 Suntec City Mall, tel: 6332 3463. Another reliable chain store for electricals and electronic goods.

Watches

Watches are sold tax-free – from a lifetime's investment in a Rolex to a plastic Swatch. There are, of course, fakes or "copy-watches" – buy these at your own risk.

The Hour Glass, 01-36A Lucky Plaza, tel: 6733 1262; 01-02 Ngee Ann City, tel: 6734 2420; 01-01 Peninsula Plaza, tel: 6337 8309; 01-09/11 Scotts Shopping Centre, tel: 6235 7198.

Rolex, 01-01 Tong Building, 302 Orchard Road, tel: 6737 9033.

Sincere Fine Watches, 01-18/22 Lucky Plaza, tel: 6737 4593; 01-12 Ngee Ann City Tower B, tel: 6733 0618; 01-013 Suntec City Mall, tel: 6337 5150.

Swatch, 01-41 Raffles City Shopping Centre, tel: 6334 5951; 02-098 Suntec City Mall, tel: 6821 3016; 01-08 The Heeren Shops, tel: 6737 1917.

Watches of Switzerland, 01-09 Scotts Shopping Centre, tel: 6737 3708.

Traditional Jewellery

Many of the traditional gold jewellery shops sell mainly pure 22–24K yellow Chinese gold, which is also an investment as it can be traded in for cash at the current gold price. Dealers are centred in South Bridge Road, Chinatown, Little India and Arab Street. At these shops nothing is price-tagged because gold is sold according to the day's gold rate. However, you can haggle over the charge for workmanship.

Little India Goldsmiths, 01-05/06, Blk 664 Buffalo Road, tel: 6294 5000.

Poh Heng, 01-17 People's Park Complex, tel: 6535 0960.

Modern Jewellery

For more innovative designs, look out for the **Risis** brand (www.risis.com.sg) which has found a way of preserving orchid blooms by dipping them in pure 22K gold to preserve their beauty forever. They are worn as rings, earrings, pendants or bracelets. Leaves and ferns, too, are similarly treated to make delicate, unique pieces of jewellery.

Contemporary designer jewellery shops are mainly found along Orchard Road. Most of the stuff is set in 18K white or yellow gold and encrusted with diamonds, rubies, emeralds, pearls, and other semi-precious stones.

Bvlgari, 01-08 Hilton Hotel Shopping Gallery, tel: 6737 1652.

Je Taime, 02-12C/D Ngee Ann City Tower B, tel: 6734 8211.

Larry Jewellery, 01-38 Raffles City Shopping Centre, tel: 6336 9648; 02-12A Ngee Ann City, tel: 6235 5848.

Lee Hwa, B1-30 Wisma Atria, tel: 6736 0266; 01-05 Plaza Singapura, tel: 6341 9341.

Soo Kee, 01-11 Wisma Atria, tel: 6733 0433; 02-21 Parco Bugis Junction, tel: 6337 2933.

TianPo Jewellery, 01-43/46 Centrepoint, tel: 6235 1889.

Tiffany, 01-05 Raffles Hotel, tel: 6334 0168; 01-05/02-05 Ngee Ann City Tower B, tel: 6735 8823.

Fashion

Whether it's foreign or local designer labels, batik, silk or chiffon, off-the-rack or made-to-measure, Singapore offers it all. Donna Karan, Chanel, Giorgio Armani, Helmut Lang, Issey Miyake, Gucci, Paul Smith, Ralph Lauren, Versace and dozens of

other top international designers have boutiques here. Most are found along Orchard Road within the multi-storey shopping centres. For teenage fashion and streetwear, head to The Heeren Shops and Fast East Plaza.

Local designers like Benny Ong, Celia Loe, Thomas Wee and Song and Kelly offer a fusion of Eastern fabrics and Western chic. Local boutiques offer their own modern designs, which are well suited to the local climate and style as well as representing good value. Try the following:

Hemispheres Designers' Gallery, 03-00 Orchard Point, tel: 6238 2135.

M)Phosis, 01-12 Raffles City Shopping Centre, tel: 6336 6739; B1-10 Ngee Ann City, tel: 6737 2190; B1-28 City Link Mall, tel: 6884 4481.

projectshopBLOODbros, 02-33 Paragon, tel: 6735 0071; B1-02A, Ngee Ann City, tel: 6887 4942; 01-16 Wisma Atria, tel: 6737 8058.

Song+Kelly21, Level 3 Isetan Orchard, Wisma Atria, tel: 6732 2057; 01-24 Forum The Shopping Mall, tel: 6735 3387.

The Island Shop, 02-17 Tanglin Mall, tel: 6836 1322.

Woods & Woods, 02-23 Raffles City Shopping Centre, tel: 6338 6775.

Many tailors can run up suits in 24 hours, copy clothes or work from patterns. It's best to allow more time, be as specific as possible and to insist on more than one fitting. Tailor shops are usually located in shopping centres along the Orchard Road belt.

If interested in Asian textiles and ethnic wear, seek out the ethnic districts. Generally, good places to shop for textiles include Arab Street for batiks and chiffons, Little India for sari silks and Chinatown for Chinese silk.

Books and Music

CDs are often cheaper here than elsewhere, and with many well-stocked bookstores, you won't be short of reading material either.

Borders, 01-00 Wheelock Place,

tel: 6235 7146. One of the largest selection of books plus a CD section and a café/bistro.

Kinokuniya, 03-09 Ngee Ann City, tel: 6737 5021. The largest bookstore in Singapore. Also has smaller outlets at 03-09/12 Bugis Junction (tel: 6339 1790) and 03-50 Liang Court (tel: 6337 1300).

MPH Bookstore, B1-26A CityLink Mall, tel: 6835 7637; 01-01/02, 63 Robinson Road, tel: 6222 6423; 02-24/25 Raffles City Shopping Centre, tel: 6336 4232; B1-155/157 Parkway Parade, tel: 6348 1483.

Times – The Bookshop, 04-09 Centrepoint, tel: 6734 9022; 04-01 Plaza Singapura, tel: 6837 0552; 02-054 Suntec City Mall, tel: 6336 9391; 03-01 OUB Centre, tel: 6557 2923.

Select Books, 03-15 Tanglin Shopping Centre, tel: 6732 1515 Specialises in books on Southeast Asia.

HMV, 01-11 The Heeren Shops, tel: 6733 1822. Huge three-level music shop with specialist jazz and classical CD sections.

That CD, 01-01 Pacific Plaza, tel: 6734 2276. Stylish two-level music store with very helpful staff.

Antiques

Exotic treasures from all over the region can be found in Singapore. Antique desks, chairs, tables, vases, statues, mirrors and opium beds from all over Asia are just some of the items available. Many of these pieces have been restored to their original beauty and reputable dealers can usually provide certificates of authenticity. Check shops in Raffles Hotel Shopping Arcade and Tanglin Shopping Centre, in particular, which is well known for its antiques dealers. Reproduction furniture also makes an attractive buy: look around Dempsey Road and Holland Village.

Akemi Gallery, 02-07 Tanglin Shopping Centre, tel: 6735 6315.

Antiques of the Orient, 02-40 Tanglin Shopping Centre, tel: 6734 9351.

Kwok Gallery, 03-01 Far East Shopping Centre, tel: 6235 2516.
Lim's Arts and Living, 02-01 Holland Village Shopping Centre, tel: 6467 1300.
Lopburi, 01-04 Tanglin Place, tel: 6738 3834.
Pagoda House Gallery, 02-34 Raffles Hotel Shopping Arcade, tel: 6883 0501; 143/145 Tanglin Road, Tudor Court, tel: 6732 2177.
Renee Hoy Fine Arts, 01-44 Tanglin Shopping Centre, tel: 6235 1596.

Oriental Carpets

Oriental carpets range from tribal rugs to exquisite silk carpets, and they come from China, India, Pakistan, Iran or Turkey, each with its own distinctive style. Buying at one of the regularly held auctions in a hotel is an exhilarating experience and great bargains can be had if you know your merchandise. Uncertain buyers, however, are advised to take their time in shops.
Amir & Sons, 03-01/07 Lucky Plaza, tel: 6734 9112.
Eastern Carpets, 03-27 Raffles City Shopping Centre, tel: 6338 8135.
Jehan Gallery Pte Ltd, 01-01, 6 Dempsey Road, tel: 6475 0003
Mohammad Akhtar Carpets, 01-14 Tanglin Shopping Centre, tel: 6733 1130
The Orientalist Carpet Gallery, 02-00, 2 Tanglin Road, tel: 6235 3343.
Qureshi's Carpets, 05-12 Centrepoint, tel: 6235 1523.

Shopping Areas

Shopping in the main city area is mostly confined to contemporary goods, the likes of which you find in most large cities. For more colour and Asian flavour, head out to the ethnic neighborhoods.

Orchard Road

This is by far the most famous shopping precinct, an endless stretch of smart boutiques, malls and department stores. The shopping tends to be more upmarket, so don't expect bargains unless you're here during the sales periods. Following are some of Orchard Road's major shopping centres and department stores (see page 121):
Centrepoint, 176 Orchard Road, tel: 6235 6629.
DFS Galleria, 25 Scotts Road, tel: 6229 8100.
Far East Plaza, 14 Scotts Road, tel: 6734 2325.
Forum The Shopping Mall, 583 Orchard Road, tel: 6732 2469.
Isetan, Wisma Atria Shopping Centre, tel: 6733 7777; also at Shaw Centre, tel: 6733 1111.
John Little, Specialists' Shopping Centre, tel: 6737 2222.
Lucky Plaza, 304 Orchard Road, tel: 6235 3294.
Marks & Spencer, L1 & L2 Centrepoint, tel: 6734 1800; B1 & B2 Wheelock Place, tel: 6733 8122; 03-22 Paragon, tel: 6732 9732.
Metro, Paragon, 290 Orchard Road, tel: 6835 3322.
Ngee Ann City, 391 Orchard Road, tel: 6733 0337.
Orchard Point, 160 Orchard Road, tel: 6735 0500.
Orchard Towers, 400 Orchard Road, tel: 6734 2326.
Pacific Plaza, 9 Scotts Road, tel: 6733 5655.
Palais Renaissance, 390 Orchard Road, tel: 6738 2393.
Paragon, 290 Orchard Road, tel: 6738 5535.
Park Mall, 9 Penang Road, tel: 6339 4031.
Plaza Singapura, 68 Orchard Road, tel: 6332 9298.
Robinson's, 05-05 Centrepoint, tel: 6733 0888.
Scotts Shopping Centre, 6 Scotts Road, tel: 6734 7560.
Tanglin Mall, 163 Tanglin Road, tel: 6736 4922.
Tangs, 320 Orchard Road, tel: 6737 5500.
Tanglin Shopping Centre, 19 Tanglin Road, tel: 6737 0849.
The Heeren Shops, 260 Orchard Road, tel: 6733 4725.
Wisma Atria, 435 Orchard Road, tel: 6235 2103.

Civic District

Although the shopping in this area is scattered over a wider area, most of the shopping centres are connected to City Mall MRT station by a series of underground (air-conditioned) walkways.
CityLink Mall, 1 Raffles Link, tel: 6339 9913.
Marina Square, 6 Raffles Boulevard, tel: 6339 8787.
Marks & Spencer, Level 2 Raffles City Shopping Centre (inside Robinson's department store), tel: 6339 9013.
Millenia Walk, 9 Raffles Boulevard, tel: 6883 1122.
Raffles City Shopping Centre, 252 North Bridge Road, tel: 6338 7766.
Raffles Hotel Shopping Arcade, Raffles Hotel, Beach Road.
Robinson's, Raffles City Shopping Centre, tel: 6216 8388.
Suntec City Mall, 3 Temasek Boulevard, tel: 6821 3668.

Chinatown

Just launched in June 2004 is the **Chinatown Night Market**, which sees **Sago Street**, **Pagoda Street** and **Trengganu Street** closed to traffic in the evenings (Sun–Thurs 5–11pm and Fri–Sat 5pm–1am). The market has over 200 street stalls hawking all manner of goods, from contemporary jewellery and bags by young designers to more traditional Chinese goods, like calligraphy, lanterns, masks and embroidery. These complement the old shophouses that line these streets, occupied by retail stores and restaurants.

Be sure also to visit **People's Park Complex** and **People's Park Centre** along Eu Tong Sen Street for fabrics, gold jewellery, watches, cameras and clothes. **Yue Hwa Emporium** at the corner of Upper Cross and Eu Tong Sen streets, housed in an old Chinese-style building, offers everything imaginable from China. At the corner of Upper Cross Street and New Bridge Road is **Chinatown Point**, another haven for Chinese arts and crafts.

Arab Street

In **Arab Street**, off Beach Road, and its adjoining streets, a strong Muslim atmosphere lingers from the early years of Singapore when Malays, Bugis and Javanese settled here. Prayer mats, holy beads and lace skullcaps for those who have made the pilgrimage to Mecca are all sold here. It is also *the* place for cheap batik and textiles including everything a tailor needs: lace, sequins, beads, buttons and bows. Other good buys are baskets, leather bags, purses and shoes.

Within walking distance of Arab Street at the corner of Rochor Road and North Bridge Road is **Parco Bugis Junction**, with a unique glass-covered, air-conditioned "shopping street". It also houses the Seiyu department store, a cineplex and trendy boutiques and cafés.

Little India

Singapore's **Little India**, comprising Serangoon Road and the neighbouring side streets, is where everything from spices to Indian silk saris from the subcontinent are found. There are too many shops to list but it's unlikely that you'll leave this fascinating area empty handed.

Little India Arcade at the corner of Serangoon and Hastings roads is a charming cluster of shophouses with interesting Indian paraphernalia. Further up Serangoon Road at 145 Syed Alwi Road is the 24-hour **Mustafa Centre**, a sprawling department store that will meet most of your retail needs – from electronics and clothing to groceries.

Holland Village

Holland Shopping Centre, in Holland Village, just outside of the centre of town, is the expatriate haven. There is a large supermarket on the ground level and a host of shops selling bags, shoes, jewellery and clothes. Be sure to visit **Lim's Arts & Living** at 02-01 (tel: 6467 1300), a real oriental treasure trove spread over three

floors. Along **Lorong Mambong** are shops selling an eclectic mix of things, from Asian arts and crafts to home furnishings.

Suburbs

Venture further out of the city area to the heartlands where most locals live and you'll find better bargains and lower prices. The range of shops and services is surprisingly wide, with huge modern complexes that can rival those in town. Try larger estates such as **Tampines** or **Bishan** (both easily accessible by MRT).

SPORTS

Spectator Sports

Cricket

Singapore Cricket Club
Connaught Drive
Tel: 6338 9271
Holds regular weekend matches from March to October. Access to the club is restricted to members, but visitors can watch games at the Padang on most weekends from 10am for free.

Horse Racing

Singapore Turf Club
1 Turf Club Avenue, Kranji
Tel: 6879 1000
www.turfclub.com.sg
The four-level grandstand accommodates 30,000 race goers. The club incorporates all the best features from race courses the world over. Races are run 32 weekends each year during the racing season. Check the Turf Club website for exact dates.

The race track is easily accessible by MRT (Kranji station) public buses and taxis. Admission is S$3 (non-air-conditioned stands) and S$7 (for air-conditioned stands); S$20 gives you access to a special club area. Dress code applies: no shorts or slippers for public grandstands; no jeans, shorts or collarless shirts for members' areas.

Soccer

Football Association of Singapore
100 Tyrwhitt Road
Tel: 6348 3477
www.sleague.com
Singapore has its very own professional football club, the S-League. Check its website for details of matches and venues.

Rugby

SCC International Rugby Sevens
Connaught Drive
Tel: 6338 3121
www.sccrugbysevens.com
The annual International Rugby Sevens tournament is held at the Padang. Teams from around the world come to compete in this action-packed sporting event. Check website for exact dates.

Participant Sports

Bowling

There are several bowling alleys spread across the island, many of them in the suburbs and some, like Superbowl, are open 24 hours. Shoes are available for hire and charges are reasonable. Remember to book a lane before you go, especially on weekends. Expect to pay between S$2 and S$3.90 per game.
Kallang Bowl
5 Stadium Walk, Leisure Park
Tel: 6345 0545.
Superbowl
15 Marina Grove, Marina South
Tel: 6221 1010.

Golf

Singapore is said to have more golf courses per capita than any other place on earth. Many of these are designed by leading course architects.

Many of the clubs welcome non-members. Green fees range from as little as S$70 on weekdays to as much as S$240 on weekends when nearly every course in Singapore is crowded. Caddies cost S$15–30.
Keppel Club
Bukit Chermin Road
Tel: 6273 5522

TRANSPORT
ACCOMMODATION
ACTIVITIES
A – Z

A 18-hole, par 71 course. The front nine is over rolling hills, while the back nine cuts across wooded flatlands. Open to visitors both weekdays (S$110) and weekends (S$180).

Raffles Country Club
450 Jalan Ahmad Ibrahim
Tel: 6861 7655
Offers a choice of two 18-hole courses, the tree-shaded Palm Course or the picturesque Lake Course. Open to visitors week-days (S$126–S$178).

Sentosa Golf Club
27 Bukit Manis Road
Tel: 6275 0022
Two 18-hole courses near the The Sentosa resort. Visitors are welcome on both the Serapong and Tanjong courses on week-days (S$231).

Singapore Island Country Club
180 Island Club Road
Tel: 6459 2222
One of the world's most beautiful places to tee off, set amid park-land and jungle on the shores of MacRitchie Reservoir. Four 18-hole courses are open to mem-bers' guests; weekday play is S$100–S$120 and weekend play is S$200–S$240 depending on the course played.

Racquet Sports

Many hotels have tennis courts. Otherwise, the island offers a number courts for hire.

Kallang Tennis Centre
52 Stadium Boulevard Road
Tel: 6348 1291
Charges S$9.50 for weekend and primetime play (6–9pm) and S$3.50 at other times for tennis. Hourly fees for squash are S$5 and S$10 (for weekends and from 6pm onwards).

Singapore Tennis Centre
1020 East Coast Parkway
Tel: 6442 5966
Charges S$8.50 per hour on weekdays and S$12.50 on week-ends and between 6–9pm.

Tanglin Squash & Tennis Centre
5 Stevens Road
Tel: 6734 0707
Charges between S$2.50–3.60 for tennis or squash.

Watersports

Singapore is one of the few places where you can walk out of the airport terminal and be on a beach in less than 10 minutes. There is a plethora of water-sports available: windsurfing, sailing, canoeing, waterskiing and wakeboarding. **Sentosa Island** and **East Coast Park** are the most obvious choices for a day at the beach because of easy access and variety of activities.

Windsurfing and Sailing

Seasports Centre
1210 East Coast Parkway
Tel: 6449 5118
Located just behind the East Coast Lagoon Food Village, it offers both a one-day windsurfing crash course or a more relaxed 2-day course at the same price: Cost is S$90 (minimum four people) or $280 (individual). Windsurf boards can be rented for S$23 (for two hours).

Laser sailing lessons are also available: S$300 for 4 half-day lessons or 2 full days (minimum four people) or $600 (individual). A single laser boat is hired out for $25 an hour.

Waterskiing and Wakeboarding

Extreme Sports
Kallang Riverside Park
Tel: 6344 8813
www.extreme.com.sg
You can both ski or wakeboard at Kallang River; costs S$90 per hour on weekdays and S$120 on weekends, inclusive of equip-ment rental. Beginner lessons (4 sessions) cost S$150.

Punggol Marina
17th Avenue, 600 Punggol Road
Tel: 6386 3891
Offers waterskiing and wake-boarding; a boat with driver and gear costs S$80–90 an hour.

Trail Sports

Singapore is great for hikers, bik-ers and runners. The island is quite flat – perfect for beginners. At the same time, there is enough rugged topography for those who crave challenges. The island's longest jogging and bik-ing paths run through **East Coast Park**, a total length of 10 km (6 miles) between Fort Road and Sungei Bedok. The route winds along the sea's edge, through coconut palms and bird sanctuar-ies. Bikes and roller blades can be rented from several places in East Coast Park for around S$6–10 an hour.

The best areas for off-road running and bike riding – and also one of the best places for a walk in the jungle – is the **Central Catchment Nature Reserve**, which comprises the MacRitchie, Pierce and Upper Seletar reser-voir parks. The parks are espe-cially popular with mountain bikers and bird watchers.

Trails and unpaved roads lead through secondary rainforest, swampland and around the edge of scenic lakes. Monkeys frolic in the jungle and you can spot many different types of tropical birds.

An alternative off-road venue is **Pulau Ubin**, a maze of country roads winding through old rubber and fruit plantations.

Other popular walking and running spots include the **Botanic Gardens** with an entrance at the corner of Holland and Cluny roads, **Labrador Park** at the foot of Alex-andra Road, **Kent Ridge Park** near the National University of Singa-pore, **Bukit Batok Park**, near the town of the same name, and **Bukit Timah Nature Reserve** (see the respective Places chapters for more information on the above).

Reverse Bungy

G-Max Reverse Bungy
Clarke Quay
River Valley Road
Tel: 6338 1146
www.gmax.co.nz
For a thrilling adrenaline rush, try Singapore's first G-Max Reverse Bungy at Clarke Quay. You're seated in an open-air capsule and hurled into the air 60 metres from the ground at a speed of 200 km per hour. The 5-minute ride costs S$30 per person.

SIGHTSEEING TOURS

Special Interest Tours

If pressed for time, take the standard 3½-hour **City Tour** (S$29) offered by a number of tour agencies. This coach tour normally includes a drive along Orchard Road to the colonial heart of Singapore, with a stop along the Singapore River. Tours continue to the financial district, and then to Chinatown, Mount Faber with its panoramic views, Botanic Gardens and end at Little India.

More novel are the special-interest tours that the STB has devised with several tour agencies. The **Flavours of Singapore** (S$29) tour begins at the Spice Garden (Fort Canning Park) and continues on to sample local cuisines with visits to Little India, Geylang Serai, Katong and Chinatown. **Heartlands of Singapore** tour (S$29) is for those interested in the everyday life in Singapore's suburban housing estates. The **In Harmony with Feng Shui** (S$35) tour focuses on *feng shui* or geomancy, the ancient Chinese practice of harnessing the powers of nature to promote business, good fortune and general well-being. The tour visits a *feng shui* centre and shows examples of *feng shui* application in local architecture.

STB's visitor information centres (*see page 238*) and its website www.visitsingapore.com has full details of the tours available. Otherwise, contact any of the tour operators listed here or your hotel concierge.
Holiday Tours & Travel/Tour East, tel: 6738 2622, www.toureast.com.
RMG Tours, tel: 6220 1661, www.rmgtours.com.
Sentosa Discovery Tours, tel: 6270 8855; www.sdtours.com.sg.
SH Tours, tel: 6734 9923; www.asiatours.com.sg.
Singapore Explorer, tel: 6339 6833; www.singaporeexplorer.com.sg.

Singapore Trolley

Another sightseeing option is the **Singapore Trolley**. These are brown and maroon old-fashioned tram buses that ply a route through Orchard Road, Chinatown and Clarke Quay. You can purchase a ticket from the driver for S$14.90 (adult), S$9.90 (child) which allows unlimited rides for the day and includes a "bumboat" ride. You can hop on at any designated stop along the bus route, or at the Clarke Quay taxi stand. Contact **Singapore Explorer** at tel: 6339 6833; www.singaporeexplorer.com.sg.

SIA Hop-On

This tourist bus service plys the major landmarks and attractions around the city area, from Bugis through Chinatown and Orchard Road to the Botanic Gardens. As its name implies, you hop on (and off) as you wish along various designated stops. One-day tickets are S$3 for Singapore Airlines and SilkAir passengers visiting Singapore, free for SH Tours' customers and S$6 (adult), S$4 (child) for other passengers. SIA Hop-on is operated by **SH Tours** – for more information call 6734 9923; www.asiatours.com.sg.

DIY Walking Tours

Singapore's streets are safe, and although it's generally hot and humid, the covered walkways lining many streets can make walking pleasant and also protect you from the sun and the occasional downpour.

A permanent **Heritage Trail** has been set up at the **Civic District**, **Chinatown** and **Little India**. Strategic markers placed along the trail in these areas will guide you along a walking route and provide nuggets of information on the area's historical sights. You can also obtain Heritage Trail maps of the Civic District, Little India and Chinatown from STB's visitor centres.

Guided Walking Tours

Original Singapore Walks promises to "bring people into places most other tours don't". Hosted by personable and energetic guides who inject humour and insider knowledge into the walks, itineraries include the red-light district of Chinatown, the hidden charms of Little India, and even one to Singapore's (supposedly) haunted grounds in search of spirits. No pre-booking is necessary. All you need to do is show up at the designated meeting place (usually at an MRT station) at the tour time and pay on the spot. All tours cost S$15 each except for the By the Belly of the Carp tour which costs S$20. Contact **Journeys** at tel: 6325 1631; www.singaporewalks.com.

River and Harbour Cruises

A range of cruises are on offer, from modern catamarans to traditional *tongkang* (Chinese junks). You can even board the hardy "bumboat" which used to be the traditional way of travelling on the Singapore River in days gone by. Bumboat cruises, operated by **Singapore River Cruises** (tel: 6336 6111; www.rivercruise.com.sg), depart at 15-minute intervals from 9am–10.30pm daily from the following jetties: Merlion Park, Esplanade, Boat Quay, Liang Court (near Clarke Quay) and the Raffles Landing Site. The boats ply two routes: tickets for the 30-minute route cost S$12 while the 45-minute route costs S$15. You can choose to return to where you boarded the boat or get off at any of the designated stops along the way (just let the boat driver know beforehand).

Chinese junk cruises, lasting about 2 to 3 hours, depart from Clifford Pier. They all cover the same route with some stopping at Kusu, Lazarus or St John's Island. The *Fairwind* junk cruises twice daily (10.15am and 3pm) at S$20 for adults and S$10 for children. Dinner cruises

(6–8.30pm) cost S$36 for adults and S$18 for children. Call **Eastwind**, tel: 6533 3432.

The *Cheng Ho*, a replica 15th-century Chinese junk, has a similar cruise daily at 10.30am (S$23 for adults and S$12 for children). It also has high-tea at 3pm (S$29 for adults, S$14 for children) and dinner cruises at 6.30pm (S$49 for adults, S$25 for children). Contact **WaterTours** at tel: 6533 9811 for bookings.

Nature Tours

Subaraj Rajathurai (mobile: 9650 5183; e-mail: serin@swiftech.com.sg) is an enthusiastic and knowledgeable voice on conservation and eco-tourism. He takes visitors on educational and entertaining nature rambles through Singapore's wildlife reserves.

Brewery Tours

Tours can also be arranged for groups of 20–40 people at the **Tiger Brewery** (tel: 6860 3007; www.tigerbeer.com.sg), which brews Singapore's favourite beer.

DUCKTours & HiPPOtours

A half-boat, half-truck amphibious vehicle is your mode of transport in the zany **DUCKtours**. Your trip goes from land to river and covers several tourist sights. Tickets for the 60-minute tour (S$33 adults, S$17 children) can be bought at Suntec City Mall and at the Animal Farm @ Orchard, next to the STB Visitor Centre at the corner of Orchard and Cairnhill roads. Tours operate from 9.30am to 7pm daily (tel: 6338 6877; www.ducktours.com.sg).

Also available are open-top double decker buses called **HiPPOtours**. You can hop on or off at designated stops during the way. The daytime tour operates from 10am–6pm but can be uncomfortably hot in Singapore's weather. Much better is the evening tour from 6.30–10.30pm (S$33 adults, S$17 children).

Customised Tours

A personal guide can come up with an excursion to suit your specific needs and interests and provide you with snippets of gossip and inside information. Call **Tourist Guides Association**, tel: 6339 2114. For half-a-day, English-speaking guides charge about S$50; foreign language guides S$85.

Taxi Tourist Guides

It's often been said that Singapore taxi drivers are an opinionated lot, so it only makes sense to turn them into tourist guides. The **Taxi Tourist Guide** organised

COOKING CLASSES

at-sunrice
Fort Canning Centre
Tel: 6336 3307
www.at-sunrice.com
Offers guided tours of the nearby Spice Gardens followed by a variety of cooking classes, from half-day to two weeks. Strong emphasis on the cuisines of Southeast Asia. Hands-on classes are taught by chefs from the region.
Coriander Leaf
02-12 Clarke Quay
Tel: 6732 3354
www.corianderleaf.com
Chef-owner Samia Ahad of acclaimed Coriander Leaf restaurant conducts classes at her cooking studio for small groups of 10. The 4-hour classes (Italian, Mediterranean, Indian and Middle Eastern fare) are informal and chatty affairs, with plenty of useful advice thrown in.
Raffles Culinary Academy
Raffles Hotel
Tel: 6412 1256
www.raffleshotel.com
Offers a variety of cooking demonstration classes featuring both Asian and Western cuisines. Courses are hosted by the hotel's renowned chefs.

by the STB and the Singapore Taxi Academy allows visitors to explore Singapore at their own pace with a trained taxi driver who doubles up as a tourist guide. Call the STB (tel: 1800 736 2000) for more information.

CHILDREN'S ACTIVITIES

The **Singapore Zoological Gardens** is one of the best zoos in the world. Enjoy breakfast with wildlife, watch various animal shows or visit Children's World. The **Night Safari**, next door to the zoo, is not to be missed either. Walking trails and trams provide exciting adventures at this wildlife park.

Children will also be enthralled by the "All Star Birdshow" at the **Jurong Bird Park**, by hornbills perched on a keeper's arm or by falcons swooping down for food at the "Birds of Prey" show.

Sentosa Island is full of fun things to do. **Underwater World** offers a Touch Pool of marine creatures while its sprawling beaches make fine picnic spots.

Escape Theme Park at Pasir Ris offers go-karts and fun rides from choo choo trains to pirate ships and ferris wheels. Just next door is **Wild Wild Wet**, a water theme park with exciting rides and lagoons to laze in.

East Coast Park is a pleasant stretch of beach where bicycles, roller blades, windsurfers and barbecue pits are available for hire. Thickly-forested **Bukit Timah Nature Reserve** is great for jungle walks.

The **Singapore Science Centre** has hundreds of hands-on exhibits that will delight children. And don't forget the **Singapore Discovery Centre** which has a five-storey-high IWERKS Theatre screen, technological and military exhibits, and a computer-simulated shooting gallery. *(See the Places section for more details of the above sights.)*

A - Z

A HANDY SUMMARY OF PRACTICAL INFORMATION, ARRANGED ALPHABETICALLY

A ddresses

Singapore is one of the easiest Asian cities to navigate, with efficiently laid out streets and well-posted signs. The number preceding the road name in an address indicates the building or block number on that road, and in the case of high-rise buildings, the number of the floor precedes the shop's unit number. For example, 02-11 Centrepoint, 176 Orchard Road means the shop is unit number 11 on the 2nd floor of the Centrepoint building at 176 Orchard Road.

Animal Quarantine

The minimum quarantine period for animals from countries other

than Australia, New Zealand, Ireland and the UK is 30 days. Contact the **Agri-Food & Veterinary Authority of Singapore** (tel: 6227 0670; www.ava.gov.sg).

B udgeting your Trip

Accommodation can cost anywhere from S$10 for a bed in a dormitory with shared facilities to S$40 a room in a budget hotel to more than S$300 per night in a top-end luxury hotel.

Food is cheap – you can eat very well at a hawker centre for less than S$5 – and so is public transportation (S$0.70 to S$1.80 per trip on the bus or MRT). Taxi rides in Singapore are reasonably priced as well; short journeys around the city centre

will cost between S$5–8.

If you live frugally, it's possible to survive on a budget of S$50 a day. If, however, you intend to live it up by eating out at good restaurants and checking out the city's nightspots, be prepared to budget about S$30 for a 2–3 course meal (without drinks), and a similar amount for entry into the clubs (inclusive of one drink). Drinks at bars are cheaper than at clubs but the best deals are during "Happy Hours" from about 5–8pm.

Business Hours

Business hours are generally from 9am until 5pm. Government offices are open Monday to Friday and on Saturday mornings; hours vary between 8–9am and 5–6pm, and till 1pm on Saturdays.

Department stores and shops open from about 10–11am until about 9pm. Most are also open on Sundays including those in Little India and Chinatown.

Banks are open from 10am until 3pm on weekdays, and 9.30–11am on Saturdays.

Business Travellers

As a country aggressively promoting free trade and foreign investment, Singapore is a good place for businesspeople. International-class hotels have business centres with all the requisite services. Other support services, such as office rental, staff hiring and translation and interpretation services, are all easily available.

Singapore's modern and efficient airport, telecommunications and superb infrastructure have all helped to make it one of the leading convention cities in the world. There are several world-class venues for large conventions and exhibitions. For details on conventions, contact the **Singapore Tourism Board** *(see page 238)*. For information on starting a business in Singapore, contact the **Singapore Economic Development Board**, tel: 6832 6832; www.sedb.com.

Climate

Singapore has a tropical climate. Maximum daytime temperatures seldom exceed 33°C (91°F) and rarely drop much below 23°C (73°F) at night. Average maximum temperature is 32.4°C (90°F), the average minimum is 25.3°C (77.5°F). Most of the rain falls during the northeast monsoon (Nov–Jan) and to a lesser degree during the southwest monsoon (May–Sep). Thunderstorms, though, can occur throughout the year. Generally the weather is hot with high humidity levels, averaging 80.4 percent daily. The average rainfall is 1,119 mm (44 inches).

What to Wear

Light summer clothes that are easy to move around in, and preferably in porous cotton, are the right choice for a full day out in town. After work and on weekends, most Singaporeans favour very casual clothing.

Wear a white or light-coloured shirt and tie if you have business meetings. Jackets and ties are usually out of place except for very formal functions.

Most hotels and restaurants don't impose a strict dress code. While slippers and shorts are taboo at clubs, casually dressed – but not sloppy – diners are generally welcomed at most restaurants, and increasingly so as many upmarket dining hubs have al fresco seating. To be sure, call in advance to check on an establishment's dress code.

If visiting temples and mosques, avoid wearing brief shorts and scanty tops *(see also "Etiquette" page 233).*

Crime & Safety

Singapore is a safe country with a very low crime rate. "A low crime rate doesn't mean no crime", though, warns a police poster. So, it's prudent to watch out for pickpockets and snatch thieves. There is occasional youth gang activity but it seldom – if at all – involves visitors. For police assistance call 999.

Women Travellers

Women in Singapore enjoy equality and more freedom when compared to other countries in the region. Because of this, there is little or no sexual harassment – a fact foreign women will appreciate. Women travellers can also expect to walk safely in Singapore's streets even when alone and late at night. Although shorts and sleeveless t-shirts are acceptable, women travellers should still exercise common sense when it comes to dressing. Topless bathing is not permitted at the beaches.

Customs Regulations

There is no restriction on the export or import of the amount and type of currency. Duty-free allowance per adult is 1 litre of spirits, 1 litre of wine or port and 1 litre of beer, stout or ale. No duty-free cigarettes are allowed into Singapore although they may be purchased on the way out.

Duty-free purchases can be made both upon arrival and departure except when returning to Singapore within 48 hours. This is to prevent Singaporeans from making a day trip out of the country to stock up on duty-free goods. In addition, passengers arriving from Malaysia are not allowed duty-free concessions.

The list of prohibited items includes drugs (the penalty for even small amounts can be death); firecrackers; obscene or seditious publications, video tapes and software; reproduction of copyright publications, video tapes or discs, records or cassettes; seditious and treasonable materials; endangered wildlife or their by-products; chewing tobacco and imitation tobacco products; and chewing gum other than for personal use.

A complete list of prohibited, restricted and dutiable goods is available from the airport's **Customs Duty Officer**, tel: 6542 7058 (Terminal 1), tel: 6546 4656 (Terminal 2), or check the **Singapore Customs** website at: www.customs.gov.sg.

Disabled Travellers

There is a growing awareness of the special needs of disabled people. The **National Council for Social Services** (tel: 6210 2500; www.ncss.org.sg) has a booklet titled *Access Singapore*, which gives details of facilities for the disabled. The **Disabled People's Association of Singapore** (tel: 6899 1220; www.dpa.org.sg) is another good information source.

Some of the newer buildings are designed with the disabled in mind, but generally if one is confined to a wheelchair, getting around by public transport is a big problem. Only CityCab and SMRT *(see page 210)* have taxis that are large enough to accommodate wheelchairs.

Electricity

Electrical supply is 220–240 volt, 50 Hz. Most hotels will supply transformers for 110–120 volt, 60 Hz appliances.

Embassies & Consulates

Office hours of foreign missions vary and locations may change. Call to confirm before visiting. For a full listing, check the STB website at: www.visitsingapore.com.
Australia: 25 Napier Road, tel: 6836 4100; www.australia.org.sg.
Britain: 100 Tanglin Road, tel: 6424 4200; www.britain.org.sg.
Canada: 14-00 IBM Towers, 80 Anson Road, tel: 6325 3200; www.cic.gc.ca.
New Zealand: 15-06 Ngee Ann City Tower A, 391A Orchard Road, tel: 6235 9966; www.nzembassy.com.
USA: 27 Napier Road, tel: 6476 9100; http://singapore.usembassy.gov.

Emergency Telephone

Fire, Ambulance: 995
Police: 999
Police Hotline (non-emergency): 1800-255 0000
Ministry of Health Hotline: 1800-333 9999

Entry Requirements

Visas & Passports

Visitors need to satisfy the following requirements before they are allowed to enter:
• Passport valid for at least 6 months;
• Confirmed onward or return tickets;
• Sufficient funds to maintain themselves during their stay in Singapore;

• Visa, if applicable.
Citizens of British Commonwealth countries (except India and Pakistan), UK, European Union, Canada and the USA do not require visas. Such visitors will automatically be given a 30-day social visit pass when arriving at the airport, in the form of a stamp in their passports.
Check with your local Singapore embassy or consulate if you need a visa for entry, the rules of which are regularly subject to change, or look up the Singapore **Immigration and Checkpoint Authority** (ICA) website at: www.ica.gov.sg.
In addition, the visitor must hand in a completed disembarkation/embarkation card to the immigration officer. Upon immigration clearance, the disembarkation portion will be retained while the embarkation card returned to the visitor. When the visitor leaves Singapore, the embarkation portion must be handed to the immigration officer.

Visa Extensions

Your social visit pass can be extended by another 2–4 weeks by submitting the requisite form at the ICA's **Visitor Services Centre**, 4th Storey, ICA Building 10 Kallang Road, tel: 6391 6100. Forms may be downloaded directly from the ICA website at www.ica.gov.sg. Note: a local sponsor is required in order to apply for an extension of the social visit pass. The easier way to extend your stay is to leave the country, say to Johor Bahru across the border in Malaysia, for a day and have your passport re-stamped on entry into Singapore.

Etiquette

Some local customs and habits recall inherited traditions and a familiarity with local mores, but, generally, with everyday etiquette being relaxed and fairly cosmopolitan, visitors behaving courteously stand little chance of unintentionally giving offence.

For deeper insights on local traditions though, read JoAnn Meriwether Craig's *Culture Shock! Singapore (see page 239).*

In Public

What is more obvious however are law-enforced rules governing public behavior, some of which carry hefty fines. There are usually clear signs explaining what you can or cannot do. In general be mindful of the following:
Road Crossing – Pedestrians must use a designated crossing if one is available within 50 metres (165 ft), or else risk a fine of up to S$500 for jaywalking. Designated crossings are zebra crossings, overhead bridges, underpasses, and traffic light junctions fitted with red and green pedestrian signal lights.
Littering – Much pain has been taken by the government not only to keep Singapore's streets clean but also to inculcate civic-conscious habits in its citizens. Litter bins are found everywhere and make it inexcusable to litter. Offenders are subject to a fine of up to S$500 (be it a bus ticket, a cigarette butt or a sweet wrapper). Repeat offenders are also sentenced to participate in a corrective work order programme where they have to collect rubbish in a public place for a period of time.
Toilets – Failure to flush urinals and water closets after use in public toilets (hotels, shopping complexes, etc.) can result in a S$500 fine. It is interesting to note, however, that to date no one has ever been convicted of this "crime". Still, take no chances.
Smoking – Smoking is banned in public buses, MRT trains, taxis, lifts, theatres and cinemas, government offices, air-conditioned restaurants, shopping centres, supermarkets – in fact, all covered areas. The only exception to this rule are pubs, bars, discos, karaoke lounges and similar nightspots. If you have to smoke in a restaurant, choose one that

TRANSPORT

ACCOMMODATION

ACTIVITIES

N – A

has an outdoor dining terrace. There is a fine of up to S$500 for the first offence. Signboards that serve as reminders are on display in such places. Youths under 18 years are prohibited to buy cigarettes and smoke in public.

Chewing Gum – Contrary to belief, you won't go to jail for chewing gum. The ban – imposed in the late 1980s because the authorities got fed up with people sticking wads of used gum on train and cinema seats – covers only the sale and importation of chewing gum, not the actual act of gum chewing. Many Singaporeans are known to "smuggle" in a couple of sticks when they return from abroad for their own consumption. Remember to just chew them, not hawk them at street corners or stick them under seats when no one is looking.

Note: A new law passed in 2003 allows the sale of gum with therapeutic value, for instance, nicotine-laced gum to help smokers kick the habit. These can only be bought from the pharmacist, not off the shelves.

Public Transport – No eating, drinking and smoking aboard buses and MRT trains is allowed. And commuters are banned from carrying smelly durians on board MRT trains too!

Private Homes

If you are invited to the home of a local, it is customary to take a small gift along – whether some cakes or pastries, fruit, chocolates or flowers. Never bring alcohol, wine or beer to a home of a Muslim though.

Most Singaporeans remove their shoes at the door so as not to bring dirt into the house. No host would insist that visitors do the same, but it is only polite to follow this custom.

Asian meals are usually served family-style in large bowls or plates placed in the centre of the table, with diners helping themselves to a little from each bowl or plate. Piling up your plate with food is impolite.

Temples and Mosques

Removing one's shoes before entering a mosque or an Indian temple has been a tradition for centuries. Inside, devotees do not smoke, yet neither of these customs generally apply to Chinese temples where more informal styles prevail. Visitors are most welcome to look around at their leisure and stay for religious rituals except in some mosques. While people pray, it is understood that those not participating in the service will stand aside. A polite gesture would be to ask permission before taking photographs: the request is seldom, if ever, refused. Modest clothing is appropriate for a visit. Most temples and mosques have a donation box for funds to help maintain the building. It is customary for visitors to contribute a token amount before leaving.

G ay & Lesbian Travellers

Engaging in homosexual activity is an offence – which doesn't mean it is non-existent. In fact, several establishments now attract a gay crowd (see page 223 for gay and lesbian nightlife venues). In general, Singapore society is still fairly conservative when it comes to gay public displays of affection, and these actions are likely to draw stares. But that's as much reaction as you'll get as Singaporeans do not usually react aggressively to homosexuality (see also text box on page 56).

The local gay rights advocacy group **People Like Us** (www.plu-singapore.com) has not been allowed to register as a legitimate society and only operates as an online portal. Some useful websites on Singapore's gay scene are found at www.fridae.com and www.utopia-asia.com.

H ealth & Medical Care

Most of Singapore is as sparkling clean as billed. Safe drinking water and strict government control of all food outlets make dining out a great experience.

Singapore is malaria-free although dengue fever, spread by daytime mosquitoes, occurs occasionally in the older residential neighbourhoods. However, there is no cause for alarm as these are not areas usually frequented by tourists.

Yellow fever vaccinations are unnecessary unless arriving from infected areas.

If travelling to less developed countries in the region, the **Travellers' Health & Vaccination Clinic** (tel: 6357 2222) at Tan Tock Seng Hospital (Moulmein Road) is an excellent place for vaccinations and booster shots against tropical diseases.

Hospitals

Singapore has the best healthcare facilities in the region. Medical services in both government and private institutions are excellent. Government and private hospitals are found all over the island. They compare favourably with those in the West. The hospitals here are advanced and well-equipped to cope with the most complicated and difficult procedures. Most of their services are available to non-citizens but at substantially higher rates. For this reason, ensure that you have bought adequate travel insurance policy.

Singapore General Hospital
7 Outram Road
Tel: 6222 3322
www.sgh.com.sg
Excellent public hospital with the best facilities in the city.

Mount Elizabeth Hospital
3 Mount Elizabeth Road
Tel: 6737 2666
www.pgh.com.sg
Private hospital close to Orchard Road. Has both a walk-in clinic and emergency services.

KK Women & Children's Hospital
100 Bukit Timah Road
Tel: 6293 4044
www.kkh.com.sg
Specialises in obstetrics, gynaecology, children and infant

care. It has a 24-hour women's clinic and a children's emergency department.

Raffles Hospital
585 North Bridge Road
Tel: 6311 1111
www.raffleshospital.com
Has a 24-hour walk-in clinic; it also provides a 24-hour house, hotel and ship-call service.

Clinics

There is no shortage of private clinics in Singapore. All doctors speak English and at least one other language. They are professionally trained either here or abroad and an average cost per visit varies between S$25–35 for a practitioner and S$35–70 for a first consultation by a specialist. Ask your embassy or hotel reception to recommend a private practitioner or specialist.

Pharmacies

In Singapore, most clinics also dispense medication but there are also numerous registered pharmacies with a qualified pharmacist on duty. The largest ones include **Guardian Pharmacy** at Changi Airport, Ngee Ann City, Centrepoint, Plaza Singapura, Raffles City Shopping Centre, Tangs, Marina Square, Bugis Junction, Suntec City Mall; and **NTUC Healthcare Pharmacy** at Raffles City Shopping Centre, Tanglin Mall, Great World City and Tiong Bahru Plaza. Most pharmacies also stock personal care, baby products, hair care products, toiletries, cosmetics, vitamins, nutritional supplements and even unrelated items like gift cards and sweets.

I nternet

There are far fewer cyber-cafés in Singapore compared to Asian cities like Bangkok and Kuala Lumpur, partly because many Singaporeans have home computers and access to high-speed broadband services. The following cyber-cafés are centrally located in the city.

Chills Café
01-07, 39 Stamford Road
Tel: 6883 1016
Open daily 9am–12 midnight.
Cyberstar ComCentre
15 Beach Road
Tel: 6334 1232
Open 24 hours.
Hotels catering to a business clientele also offer such facilities, albeit at higher rates. Travellers with their own laptops and wireless cards can surf at any of the wireless surf zones in cafés, restaurants, libraries and hotels around Singapore. Contact service providers like **SingTel** (tel: 68486933; www.singtel.com) and **Starhub** (tel: 6825 5000; www.starhub.com) for details on how to hook up locally.

L eft Luggage

Counters that provide baggage storage services can be found at both Terminals 1 and 2 at the Changi Airport, and are open 24 hours daily (tel: 6542 2061).

Lost Property

The loss of your passport or valuables should be reported immediately to the local police. Call 1800-255 0000 or head to the police headquarters at 391 New Bridge Road, Police Cantonement Complex. For loss of items in taxis, buses and MRT trains, contact the respective transport service operator (see pages 209–10).

M aps

Excellent Singapore maps, with areas of interest to the visitor shown in detail, are freely available at Changi Airport's arrival hall and throughout the city.

Most bookshops also stock maps of Singapore and the region. Particularly good is the **Insight Fleximap Singapore**, laminated for durability and easy folding. For a comprehensive street atlas, get a copy of the **Mighty Minds Singapore Street Directory** (2004 edition).

Media

Television

The range of programming is diverse and free-to-air television runs for almost 18 hours a day. While local programming has been monopolised for years by Mediacorp, a rival station called Mediaworks was launched in 2000.

There are eight channels, of which **Channel 5**, **Channel i**, **Central** and **Channel NewsAsia** broadcast in English. **Channel 8** and **Channel U** broadcast in Mandarin and **Suria** in both Malay and Tamil. Check the daily papers or 8 Days (a weekly entertainment magazine) for schedules.

Many Singapore homes are wired up and cable-access ready. Pay TV is available through **Singapore Cable Vision** (SCV), which offers almost 40 TV channels to subscribers 24 hours a day. Singapore is a hub for several foreign broadcasters who beam their programmes out of Singapore via satellite to regional and worldwide audiences.

Radio

There are eight English radio entertainment channels. The most popular are the following: **Gold 90FM** (90.5 FM) features adult contemporary music, **Symphony 92.4** (92.4 FM) airs mostly classical and jazz music, **Perfect 10** (98.7 FM) plays contemporary hits and Top 40 music while **Class 95** (95 FM) is easy listening. SAFRA's (Singapore Armed Forces Reservist Association) radio station, **Power 98**, plays the usual mainstream hits.

There is also the 24-hour **BBC World Service** (88.9 FM) to keep you up-to-date on international news events.

Newspapers

The Straits Times and Business Times are good English-language dailies for domestic and foreign news and a very active letters-to-the-editor forum. There is also the tabloid The New Paper, sold in the afternoons. In addition there are two free English daily morning tabloids, *Today* or *Streats*, available free from MRT stations.

A business and investment weekly, *The Edge Singapore* provides in-depth financial-related news on Singapore. For wider coverage of the region, on both politics and business news, pick up a copy of the weekly *Far Eastern Economic Review*.

The *International Herald Tribune* and *Wall Street Journal* are available on the day of publication. American, British, European and Asian newspapers and current affairs magazines are available at hotel newsstands and bookstores such as MPH, Times, Kinokuniya and Borders.

Money

The country's currency is the Singapore dollar (S$). There are no restrictions on the amount and type of currency you can bring into Singapore.

It is divided into 100 cents. Bank notes are available in $1, $2, $5, $10, $20, $50, $100, $500, $1,000 and $10,000. The $1 note, although still in circulation, has largely been replaced by the $1 coin. Other coins are in denominations of 1, 5, 10, 20 and 50 cents.

At the time of press, the Singapore dollar was valued at about $1.70 to the US dollar and $2 to one Euro.

Travellers' Cheques

Singapore is a major financial centre and travellers' cheques can easily be encashed in most of the banks. Many shops also accept travellers' cheques in lieu of cash after conversion at the prevailing rate of exchange.

Credit Cards

Major credit cards are accepted at airline offices, hotels and most restaurants and upmarket stores. Some small travel agencies, camera and electronic goods stores tend to add a sur-

charge of between 2–4 percent. Be sure to ask before making payment.

Amex: 1800-392 2000
Diners: 6294 4222
MasterCard: 800-1100 113
Visa: 800-4481 250

Changing Money

Licensed money changers in shopping malls along Orchard Road (Lucky Plaza) and Scotts Road (Far East Plaza) and North Bridge Road (Peninsula Shopping Centre and Peninsula Plaza) offer better rates than banks. Hotels and department stores offer the least attractive rates.

Money changers trade in most of the world's major currencies and all of the Southeast Asian ones. They are also open for business seven days a week, usually from 9–10am until about 9pm. Exchange rates are not necessarily uniform so don't be bashful in asking for better deals. Generally, you enjoy a better rate if you are changing a large sum of money.

If you are unable to change your leftover Singapore currency before leaving the country, don't despair: you can change it elsewhere in the region as the Singapore dollar is widely accepted.

Emergency Money

Cash advances can also be obtained at banks using major credit cards. Credit cards with a personal identification number and certain bank cards can also be used to withdraw money from automated teller machines (ATMs) found all over the island (at some MRT stations, in shopping centres and outside banks).

Tipping

Hotels, larger restaurants, and many clubs and bars usually levy a 10 percent service charge which is added to your bill along with the standard 5 percent GST and 1 percent cess (tax). There is no need to tip unless the staff have gone out of their way to provide exceptional service.

Porters and bellboys receive S$1 upwards, depending upon the number of bags carried or the complexity of the errand. Beyond that, tipping is the exception rather than the rule. In small local restaurants, food stalls and taxis, there is no service charge and no tipping – a smile with a simple thank you (*terima kasih* in Malay or *xie xie* in Mandarin) is more than sufficient.

P hotography

Never place unexposed film in checked-in luggage as it is subject to multiple X-ray checks. It's safe to leave unexposed film in carry-on luggage when going through airport X-rays unless you are carrying fast film of ASA1000. You can also insist on having your film hand-checked.

In a tropical place like Singapore, it is best to protect camera and film from excessive heat and humidity. Do not leave your camera and your film in the sun or in a hot car. Always use a UV filter to protect your lenses or a polarisation filter in order to reduce glare and to enhance the blue of the sky. Best times for outdoor photography are the earlier part of the day and later in the afternoon when the sun is lower in the sky. Try to avoid photography between 11.30am and 3.30pm.

Film is readily available, and the better shops carry professional and slide film. Processing of colour prints can be done within the hour at any of the hundreds of photo stores. For professional-quality results, go to **RGB Colour**, 01-01 Premier Centre, 103 Beach Road, tel: 6334 6146.

Postal Services

Singapore Post is very efficient and mailboxes can be found at every MRT station. An aerogramme or airmail postcard to anywhere costs just 50 cents. Letters weighing not more than 20 grams to North and South America, Europe, Africa and Middle East countries cost S$1 and to Australia, New Zealand and Japan, it's 70 cents. For all other countries in South-east Asia, it costs 60 cents. The fee for a registered item is S$2 (plus postage).

Apart from postal services, Singapore Post provides other services such as parcel delivery, issuance of travellers' cheques, local and foreign money orders and bank drafts, philatelic sales, post-box mail collection, and a variety of other services.

Singapore Post's main branches are at **Change Alley**, 02-02 Hitachi Tower, 16 Collyer Quay, tel: 6538 6899 (Mon–Fri 8am–9pm; Sat 8am–4pm; closed Sun and public holidays) and at **1 Killiney Road**, tel: 6734 7899 (Mon–Sat 9am–9pm; Sun and public holidays 9am–4.30pm). The Singapore Post branch at **Changi Airport**'s Terminal 2 (tel: 6542 7899) is open 8am–9.30pm daily. Most other branches are open from 8.30am–5pm Monday to Friday (Wed until 8pm) and from 8.30am–1pm on Saturday.

For more information, call 1605 for postal enquiries or check www.singpost.com.

Courier Services

Singapore Post has a courier service called **Speedpost**, which services more than 40 countries at fairly reasonable rates. Call tel: 6222 5777 or check www.speedpost.com.sg for more information and rates.

Several air-cargo carriers including **Federal Express** (tel: 1800-743 2626), **Cargolux** (tel: 6543 0006) and **UPS** (United Parcel Service, tel: 1800-738 3388) all have offices at Changi Airport.

Public Holidays

New Year's Day: 1 Jan
Chinese New Year: Jan/Feb (two days)*
Good Friday: Apr*
Labour Day: 1 May
Vesak Day: May

National Day: 9 Aug
Deepavali: Oct/Nov*
Christmas: 25 Dec
Hari Raya Puasa: *
Hari Raya Haji: *
*Precise dates vary with the lunar calendar, except Good Friday. Check the Singapore Tourist Board (STB) website or any of its Visitor Centres (see page 238).

Public Toilets

When nature calls, you can easily dash into any shopping centre, hotel, bus interchange, or hawker centre, where there are always public toilets available. What may come as a surprise, however, is that the use of such toilets isn't always free. Some public toilets have attendants who charge 10 to 20 cents per entry – which is preposterous considering that some of these toilets are less than hygenic. There are usually one or two toilet stalls which have Asian-style squat toilet bowls– best to be avoided if you have wobbly knees.

R eligious Services

Buddhism and Taoism are most commonly practised by the Chinese, among whom about 17 percent are Christians. Malays are Muslim and Singaporeans of Indian descent are either Hindu, Sikh or Christian. The Eurasians are largely Christians, either Roman Catholic or Anglican.

In multi-racial, multi-religious Singapore, most major religions have their adherents. Call the relevent place of worship directly for prayer times or ask your hotel reception desk.

In the city area, services in English are held at the following churches:

Anglican

St Andrew's Cathedral
11 St Andrew's Road
Tel: 6337 6104
www.livingstreams.org.sg/sac
Sunday services at 7am, 8am, 11am and 5pm.

Roman Catholic

Cathedral of the Good Shepherd
Queen Street
Tel: 6337 2036
www.veritas.org.sg
Saturday sunset mass at 6.30pm; Sunday masses at 8am, 10am and 6pm.

T axes

A **Goods and Services Tax** (GST) of 5 percent is levied. In addition to GST, most hotels, restaurants, bars and nightclubs add a service charge of 10 percent and an additional "cess" (tax) of 1 percent whch goes to fund tourism. As a visitor, you can have the GST refunded on goods purchased through the **Global Refund Tax Free Shopping** scheme (page 224 on Shopping).

If the airport tax has not been incorporated in your air ticket, you'll need to pay S$21 when checking in at Changi Airport.

Telephones

Most hotels rooms have phones that allow you to make **International Direct Dial** (IDD) calls. Charges are reasonable compared to many other countries.
• Singapore's **country code** is 65. There are no area codes.
• To call overseas from Singapre, dial the **international access code** 001 followed by the country code, area code and local telephone number. Alternatively you can dial 013 or 019 for cheaper IDD rates, although the lines may be weaker.
• For **international directory assistance**, operator-assisted, collect or person-to-person calls dial 104.
• For **local directory assistance** dial 100; each inquiry is charged at 63 cents.

Public Phones

There are three types of **public pay phones** commonly found at shopping centres and MRT stations. Coin-operated pay phones for local calls (increasingly rare these days), card phones using phonecards for local and IDD calls, and credit card phones for local and IDD calls.

Phone cards are available in S$3, S$5, S$10, S$20 and S$50 denominations and can be used for both local and overseas calls. Local calls cost 10 cents for the first 3 minutes and 10 cents for every subsequent 3 minutes, up to a maximum of 9 minutes. Phone cards may be purchased from all post offices (*see Postal Services, page 236*) and convenience stores like 7 Eleven shops.

Mobile Phones

Only users of **GSM mobile phones** with global roaming service can connect automatically with Singapore's networks. Check with your service provider at home if not sure, especially if coming from Japan or the US. Mobile phone reception is good to excellent throughout the island including the underground MRT tunnels.

If you're planning to be in Singapore for any length of time, it's more economical to buy a local SIM card from one of the three service providers: Singtel, M1 or Starhub. These cards cost a minimum of S$20 and can be topped up when the value falls. You will be given a local mobile number to use. Note: all local mobile numbers start with a 9.

Contact the following mobile service providers for more information: **SingTel** (tel: 1626 or 6738 0123; www.singtel.com), **M1** (tel: 1627 or 1800-843 8383; www.m1shop.com.sg; and **Starhub** (tel: 1633 or 6825 5000; www.starhub.com).

Time Zones

Singapore is 8 hours ahead of Greenwich Mean Time (GMT).

Tourist Offices

The **Singapore Tourism Board** (STB) is highly respected for the crisp efficiency characteristic of the place it represents. The board also approves tour operators and travel agents and monitors them to make sure their services rank high by international standards.

Head Office

Singapore Tourism Board (STB)
Tourism Court
1 Orchard Spring Lane
Tel: 6736 6622
Fax: 6736 9423
www.visitsingapore.com

STB Visitor Centres

Singapore Visitors Centre @ Orchard
at the junction of Cairnhill Road and Orchard Road
Tel: 1800-736 2000
Open: 8am–10pm daily.
Singapore Visitors Centre @ Liang Court
Level 1, Liang Court Shopping Centre, 177 River Valley Road
Tel: 6336 2888
Open: 10.30am–9.30pm daily.
Singapore Visitors Centre @ Plaza Singapura
1/F Plaza Singapura
68 Orchard Road
Tel: 6332 9298
Open: 10am–10pm daily.
Singapore Visitors Centre @ Changi Airport
Arrival halls, Terminals 1 and 2
Singapore Changi Airport
Open: 6am–2am daily.

STB Offices Overseas

Australia
Sydney
Level 11, AWA Building
47 York Street
Sydney, NSW 2000, Australia
Tel: 61-2 9290 2888
Fax: 61-2 9290 2555
Europe
Frankfurt
Hochstrasse 35-37
60313, Frankfurt, Germany
Tel: 49-69 920 7700
Fax: 49-69 297 8922
London
1st Floor, Carrington House
126-130 Regent Street
London W1B 5JX, United Kingdom
Tel: 44-20 7437 0033

Fax: 44-20 7734 2191
United States
Los Angeles
4929 Wilshire Boulevard
Suite 510, Beverly Hills
CA, 90010, USA
Tel: 1-323 677 0808
Fax: 1-323-677 0801
New York
1156 Avenue of the Americas,
Suite 702, New York
NY 10036 USA
Tel: 1-212 302 4861
Fax: 1-212 302 4801

▥ hat to Bring

There's no reason to fret if you've forgotten any of your daily toiletries and necessities from back home. In fact, you can even arrive here with just your passport and the shirt on your back and not feel lost. From fashion apparel to contact lens solutions, slide film to tampons, you'll find whatever you need in this city.

Websites

food.asia1.com.sg – extensive food and entertainment updates – including restaurant reviews and listings – with links to Singapore's main dailies.
www.makansutra.com – fun and informative site detailing the best in hawker food fare.
www.visitsingapore.com – the Singapore Tourist Board's site providing general tourist information.
www.sg – official government site with facts and figures regarding the Republic of Singapore and useful links to various government offices.
www.talkingcock.com – if you're keen to grasp Singlish, this irreverent site has a comprehensive Singlish dictionary and offers satire, Singapore-style, with its own "news" stories.

Weights & Measures

Most transactions in Singapore are metric, although the old imperial system is still occasionally used at the market.

FURTHER READING

Many books on Singapore have been written, some using Singapore as a setting. If it's fiction you're after, watch out for the works of local writers like Catherine Lim and Hwee Hwee Tan

General

One-Minute Singapore. An online web page detailing vital facts on Singapore by the Ministry of Information, Communications and the Arts (MITA). Access it at www.sg.

Singapore: State of the Art by Ian Lloyd and Joseph R. Yogerst (Weatherhill, 2000). A hard cover book filled with photographs that capture the spirit of Singapore.

History & Culture

From Third World To First: The Singapore Story: 1965 – 2000 by Lee Kuan Yew (HarperCollins, 2000). In this memoir, the man who was responsible for Singapore's miraculous transformation tells his story.

Sinister Twilight: The Fall of Singapore by Noel Barber (Cassell, 2003). Fascinating account of the fall of Singapore.

Singapore Then and Now by Ray Tyers (Landmark Books, 1993). A well written account of Singapore's history.

There is Only One Raffles: the Story of a Grand Hotel by Ilsa Sharp (London Souvenir Press, 1991). Recounts the history of the grand Raffles Hotel.

Fiction

Foreign Bodies by Hwee Hwee Tan (Washington Square Press, 2000). A ripping best seller by homegrown writer. *Asiaweek* hailed it one of the "Best Books of 1999".

The Feng Shui Detective by Nury Vittachi (St Martin's Minotaur, 2004). A quirky and funny crime story set in Singapore.

Raffles Place Ragtime by Philip Jeyaretnam (Times Books Inter-

national, 1996). About love, ambition and social expectations in Singapore.

The Shrimp People by Rex Shelley (Times Books International, 1991). Award-winning, evocative story on Singapore's Eurasians.

The Song of Silver Frond by Catherine Lim (Orion, 2004). A tale of love between a rich old man and a beautiful village girl by a well-known local writer.

Tanamera: A Novel of Singapore by Noel Barber (John Curley & Assoc, 1991). A romantic fiction capturing the splendour of the colonial period.

Walk Like a Dragon by Goh Sin Tub (Flame of the Forest, 2004). A local writer's collection of the personal stories of Singaporeans who relive the bygone years.

Natural History

An excellent series of small handbooks on Singapore has been published by The Singapore Science Centre. Each volume costs just S$5 and the subjects range from Wayside Trees, Ferns and Common Birds to Seashore Life and Freshwater Fish.

Birds: An Illustrated Field Guide to the Birds of Singapore by Lim Kim Seng and Michael Rands (Sun Tree Publishing, 2003). Comprehensive sourcebook for both expert and amateur birdwatchers; filled with nice illustrations.

Birds of Singapore by Christopher Hails and Frank Jarvis (Times Editions, 1987). A comprehensive guide on the subject.

Architecture

Little India, Historic District by Urban Redevelopment Authority (1988). A good reference book

on the various styles of shophouse architecture in Little India.

Pastel Portraits by Gretchen Liu (Weatherhill, 1995). Focuses on Singapore's traditional shophouse architecture. Well-illustrated and filled with lots of interesting details.

Singapore: Architecture of a Global City by Robert Powell, Albert K.S. Lim and Li Lian Chee (Archipelago Press, 2003). Focuses on the city's modern architecture and skyline.

Food

Mrs Lee's Cookbook by Mrs Lee Chin Koon (Eurasia Press, 1999). A delightful introduction to Peranakan cuisine and culture.

Makansutra 2003/4 by K.F. Seetoh (Makansutra Publishing, 2003). A guide to no-frills hawker food in Singapore by Singapore's well-known foodie.

Shiok!: Exciting Tropical Asian Flavours by Terry Tan and Christopher Tan (Periplus Editions, 2002). One of the best books on Singaporean cuisine.

Miscellaneous

Culture Shock! Singapore by JoAnn Meriwether Craig (Graphic Arts Centre Publishing, 2002). The insights to Singapore customs as seen through the eyes of the wife of an expatriate.

The Coxford Singlish Dictionary by TalkingCock.com (Angsana Books, 2002). Can't understand what Singaporeans are saying? This hilarious "dictionary" on Singlish will help.

No Money, No Honey! by David Brazil (Angsana Books, 1998). A photo-journalist's candid insight into Singapore's sex trade.

TRANSPORT

ACCOMMODATION

ACTIVITIES

LAND

ART & PHOTO CREDITS

SINGAPORE STREET ATLAS

The key map shows the area of Singapore covered by the atlas section. An index of street names and places of interest shown on the maps can be found on the following pages. For each entry there is a page number and grid reference.

Map Legend

	Motorway with Junction
	Motorway (under construction)
	Dual Carriageway
	Main Road
	Secondary Road
	Minor road
	Track
	International Boundary
	District Boundary
	National Park/Reserve
✈	Airport
†	Church (ruins)
†	Monastery
🏰	Castle (ruins)
∴	Archaeological Site
∩	Cave
★	Place of Interest
🏠	Mansion/Stately Home
※	Viewpoint
🏳	Beach
	Motorway
	Dual Carriageway
	Main Roads
	Minor Roads
	Footpath
	Railroad
	Pedestrian Area
	Important Building
	Park
⊖	MRT Station
🚌	Bus Station
❶	Tourist Information
✉	Post Office
⊞	Cathedral/Church
☾	Mosque
✡	Synagogue
👤	Statue/Monument
Ⅱ	Tower

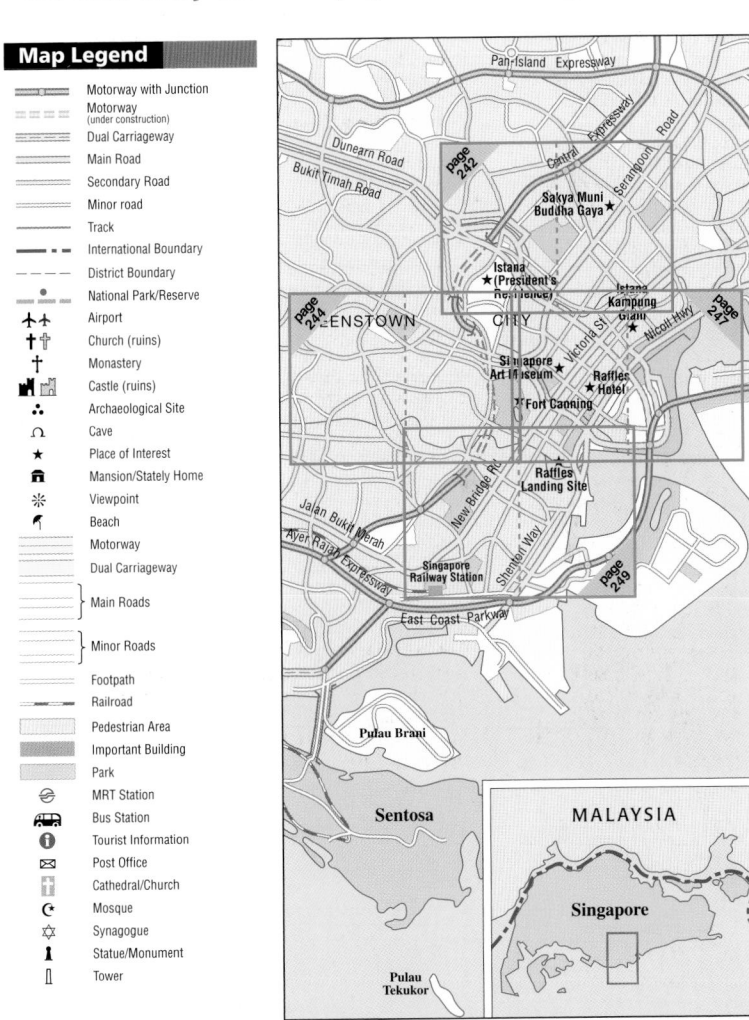

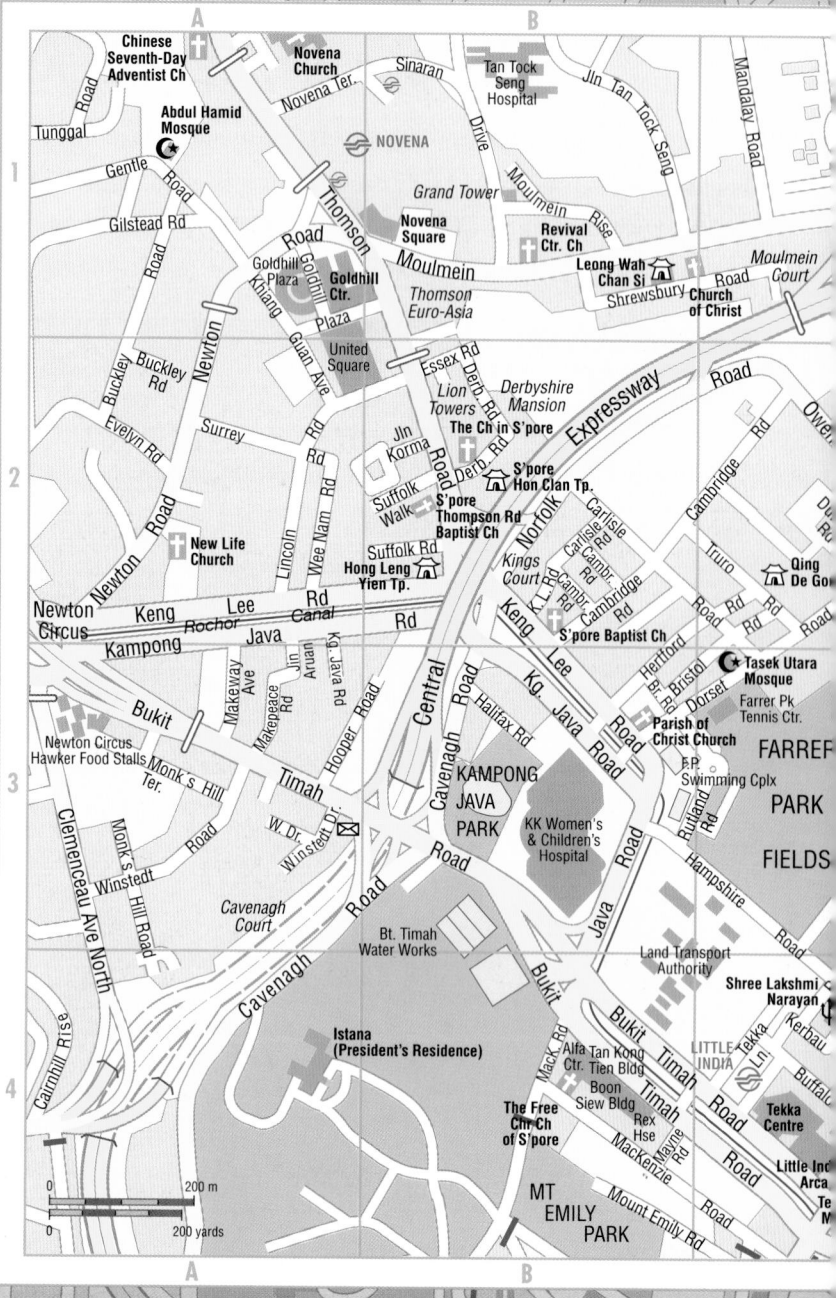

A

B

Chinese
Seventh-Day
Adventist Ch

Novena
Church

Tan Tock
Seng
Hospital

Jln Tan Tock Seng

Mandalay Road

Abdul Hamid
Mosque

Novena Ter.

Sinaran

NOVENA

Moulmein Rise

Tunggal

Road

Gentle

Road

Grand Tower

Drive

Moulmein

1

Gilstead Rd

Thomson

Road

Novena
Square

Moulmein

Revival
Ctr. Ch

Leong Wah
Chan Si

Moulmein
Court

Road

Goldhill
Plaza

Goldhill
Plaza

Goldhill
Ctr.

Thomson
Euro-Asia

Shrewsbury

Church
of Christ

Buckley
Rd

Newton

Road

Khiang

Guan Ave

United
Square

Essex Rd

Derby

Derbyshire
Mansion

Expressway

Road

Owen

Buckley

Lion
Towers

The Ch in S'pore

Rd

2

Evelyn Rd

Road

Surrey

Rd

Jln
Korma

Derby Rd

S'pore
Hon Clan Tp.

Cambridge

Rd

Truro

Du

Rd

New Life
Church

Lincoln

Wee Nam

Suffolk
Walk

S'pore
Thompson Rd
Baptist Ch

Norfolk

Carlisle

Carlisle
Rd

Cambi.

Road

Qing
De Go

Rd

Newton
Circus

Keng

Lee

Rd

Suffolk Rd

Hong Leng
Yien Tp.

Kings
Court

Cambr.
Rd

Cambridge
Rd

Rd

Rd

Rochor

Canal

Rd

K.L.R.

Hertford

Bristol

Tasek Utara
Mosque

Kampong

Java

Keng

Lee

S'pore Baptist Ch

Dorset

Br.

Farrer Pk
Tennis Ctr.

Bukit

Makeway Ave

Jln
Aruan

Kg Java Rd

Hooper

Road

Central

Road

Halifax Rd

Kg Java Road

Parish of
Christ Church

FARRER

Newton Circus
Hawker Food Stalls

Makepeace
Rd

Timah

Monk's Hill
Ter.

Cavenagh

F.P.
Swimming Cplx

Rutland
Rd

PARK

3

Clemenceau Ave North

Monk's Hill Road

Road

W. Dr.

Winstedt Dr.

KAMPONG
JAVA
PARK

KK Women's
& Children's
Hospital

Java

Road

Hampshire

Road

FIELDS

Winstedt

Cavenagh
Court

Road

Bt. Timah
Water Works

Road

Bukit

Land Transport
Authority

Shree Lakshmi
Narayan

Kerbau

Cairnhill Rise

Cavenagh

Road

Istana
(President's Residence)

Alfa
Ctr.

Tan Kong
Tien Bldg

Boon
Siew Bldg

Bukit

Timah

Mack

Rd

LITTLE
INDIA

Tekka

Ln.

Buffalo

4

0   200 m

0   200 yards

The Free
Ch Ch
of S'pore

Rex
Hse

MacKenzie

Mayne
Rd

Road

Tekka
Centre

Little Ind
Arca
Te
M

MT
EMILY
PARK

Mount Emily Rd

Road

Road

A

B

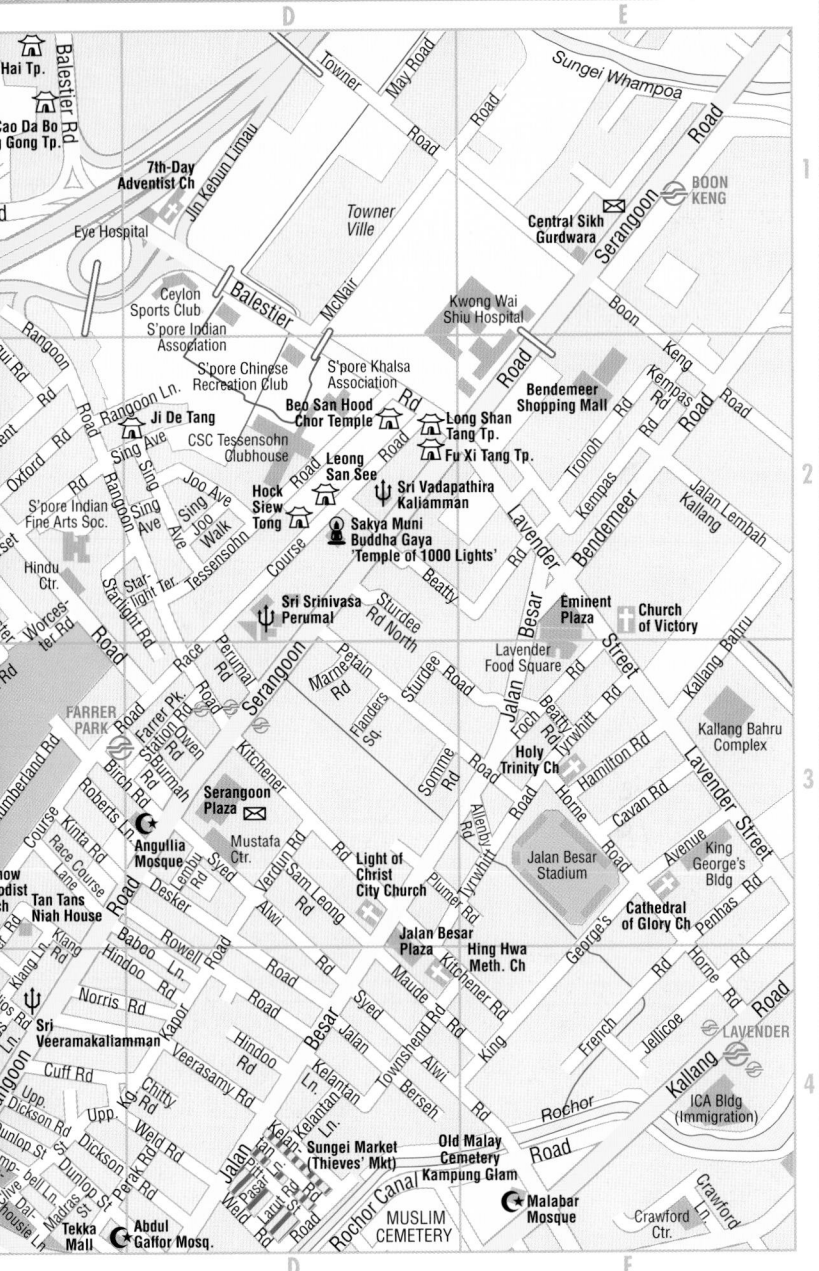

Hai Tp.

Cao Da Bo
g Gong Tp.

**7th-Day
Adventist Ch**

Eye Hospital

Ceylon
Sports Club

S'pore Indian
Association

S'pore Chinese
Recreation Club

Ji De Tang

CSC Tessensohn
Clubhouse

S'pore Indian
Fine Arts Soc.

Hindu
Ctr.

Beo San Hood
Chor Temple

Leong
San See

Hock
Siew
Tong

Balestire Rd.

Towner
Ville

McNair

Balestier

Rangoon Ln.

Sing Ave

Sing Ave

Joo Ave

Joo
Walk

Sing
Ave

Joo Ave

Starlight Ter.

Starlight Rd.

Worces-
ter Rd

Race
Perumal

Tessensohn

Kent Rd

Oxford Rd

gui Rd

Rd

Rangoon

Rangoon

Towner
Road

May Road

Road

S'pore Khalsa
Association

S'pore Indian

Sungei Whampoa

Road

Central Sikh
Gurdwara

Kwong Wai
Shiu Hospital

Rd

Long Shan
Tang Tp.

Fu Xi Tang Tp.

Sri Vadapathira
Kaliamman

Sakya Muni
Buddha Gaya
'Temple of 1000 Lights'

Sri Srinivasa
Perumal

Road

BOON
KENG

Serangoon

Boon

Keng

Kempas Rd

Rd

Tronoh

Kempas

Lembah
Kallang

Bendemeer
Shopping Mall

Bendemeer

Jalan Lembah
Kallang

Lavender

Besar

Eminent
Plaza

Church
of Victory

Beatty

Course

Sturdee
Rd North

FARRER
PARK

Serangoon

Farrer Pk.
Station Rd

Owen Rd

Birch Rd

Roberts Ln.

Kinta Rd

Burmah Rd

Serangoon
Plaza

Angullia
Mosque

Kitchener

Mustafa
Ctr.

Verdun

Sam Leong

Desker

Syed

Rd

Light of
Christ
City Church

Marne
Rd

Petain
Rd

Flander's
Sq.

Somme

Sturdee Road

Lavender
Food Square

Holy
Trinity Ch

Allenby Rd

Plumer Rd

Jalan Besar
Stadium

Jalan

Foch

Horne

Beatty Rd

Tyrwhitt Rd

Hamilton Rd

Cavan Rd

Tyrwhitt

Kallang Bahru

Kallang Bahru
Complex

Lavender Street

King
George's
Bldg

Avenue

Cathedral
of Glory Ch

Penhas Rd

humberland Rd

Course

Race Course
Lane

Tan Tans
Niah House

chow
hodist
ch

Sri
Veeramakalliamman

Klang Ln.

Cuff Rd

Klang

Hindoo

Baboo Ln.

Norris Rd

Kapor

Lembu

Alwi

Rowell Road

Veerasamy Rd

Hindoo
Rd

Chitty
Rd

Weld Rd

Upp.

Upp. KG. Rd

Road

Syed

Besar

Jalan

Kelantan
Ln.

Kelantan

Jalan
Kelantan

Kelantan
Ln.

Maude

Jalan Besar
Plaza

Hing Hwa
Meth. Ch

Kitchener Rd

George's

Rd

Townshend Rd

Alwi

King

Jellicoe Rd

Rd

Horne

Rd

Road

French Rd

LAVENDER

Rochor

Kallang

ICA Bldg
(Immigration)

Upp.

Dickson Rd

Upp.

Dickson Rd

Weld Rd

amp.-

bell Rd

Clive
Dal-

housie Ln.

St.

Dunlop St.

Perak Rd

Madras St.

Tekka
Mall

Abdul
Gaffor Mosq.

Berseh

Jalan

Kelantan

Pasar

Larut
Rd

Weld
Rd

Jalan
Berseh

Sungei Market
(Thieves' Mkt)

Rochor Canal

MUSLIM
CEMETERY

Old Malay
Cemetery
Kampung Glam

Road

Malabar
Mosque

Crawford Ln.

Crawford
Ctr.

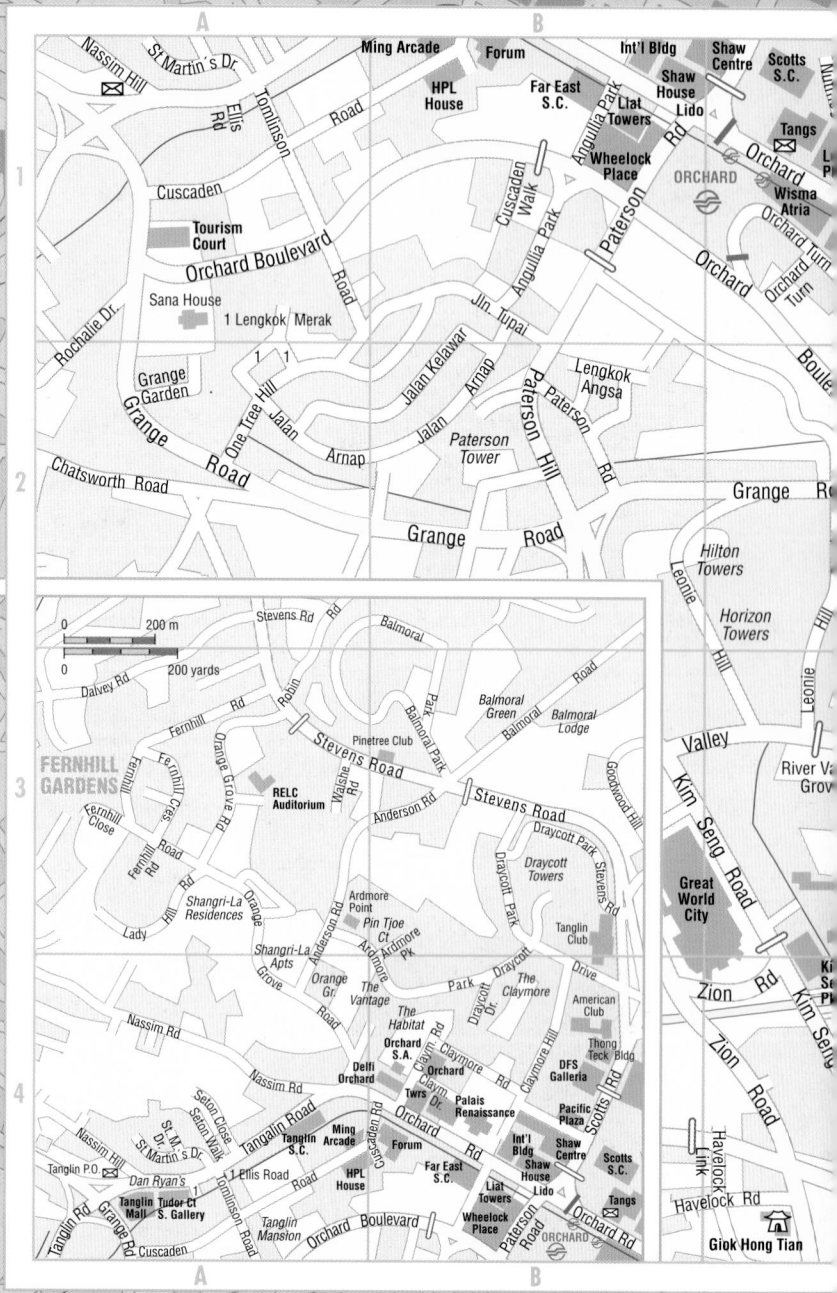

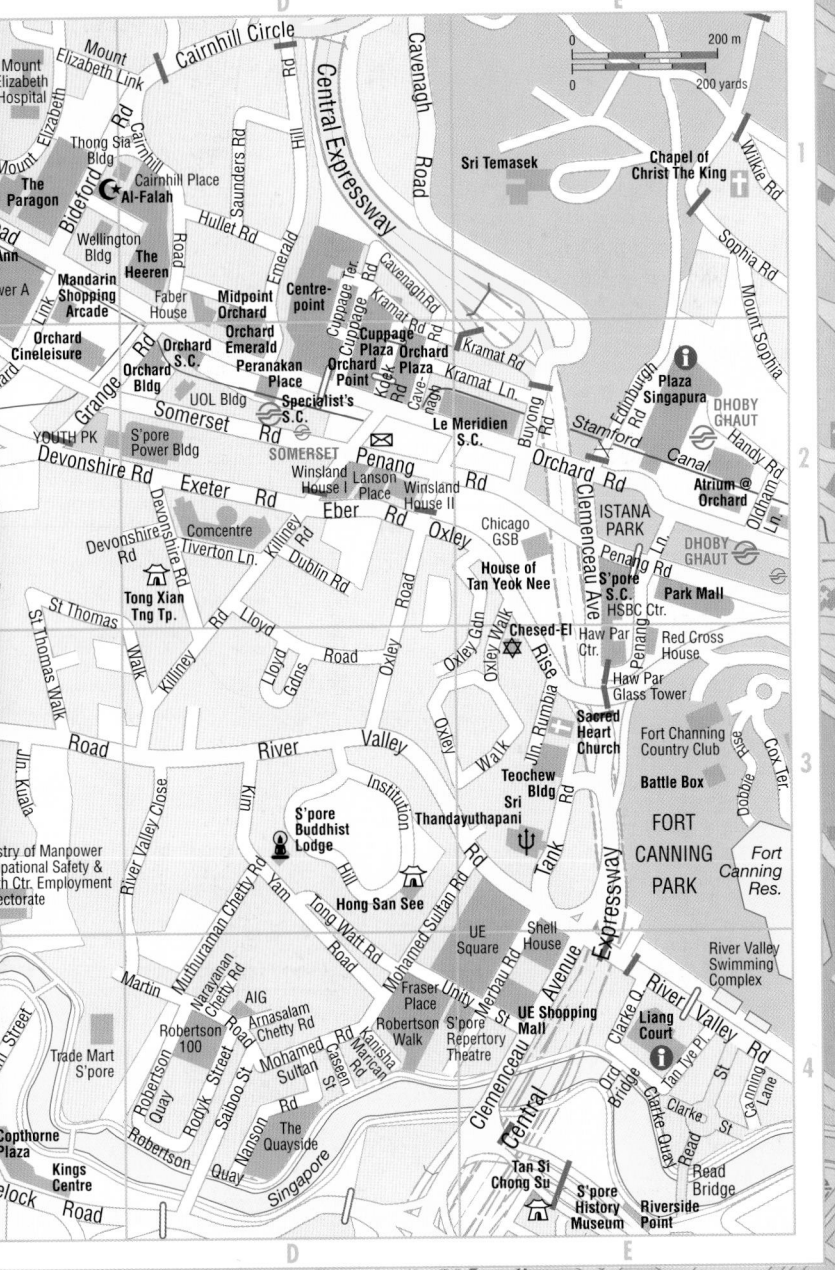

Mount Elizabeth Link
Cairnhill Circle
Central Expressway
Cavenagh Road

Mount Elizabeth Hospital

Sri Temasek

Chapel of Christ The King

Wilkie Rd

Mount Elizabeth Rd
Thong Sia Bldg
The Paragon
Al-Falah
Cairnhill Place
Cairnhill Rd
Saunders Rd
Hullet Rd
Emerald
Hill
Sophia Rd
Mount Sophia

Ann
Wellington Bldg
The Heeren
Faber House
Midpoint Orchard
Centrepoint
Cuppage Ter
Cavenagh Rd
Kramat Rd
Kramat Rd
Plaza Singapura
DHOBY GHAUT

Mandarin Shopping Arcade
Orchard Cineleisure
Orchard S.C.
Orchard Bldg
Grange Rd
Orchard Emerald
Peranakan Place
Specialist's S.C.
UOL Bldg
Cuppage Plaza
Orchard Point
Orchard Plaza
Kramat Ln.
Buyong Rd
Kramat Ln.
Le Meridien S.C.
Stamford
Canal
Handy Rd
Atrium @ Orchard

YOUTH PK
S'pore Power Bldg
Somerset Rd
SOMERSET
Winsland House I
Lanson Place
Penang Rd
Winsland House II
Orchard Rd
Clemenceau Ave
ISTANA PARK
Penang Rd
DHOBY GHAUT

Devonshire Rd
Exeter Rd
Eber Rd
Killiney Rd
Dublin Rd
Chicago GSB
House of Tan Yeok Nee
S'pore S.C.
HSBC Ctr.
Park Mall
Red Cross House

Devonshire Rd
Tiverton Ln.
Tong Xian Tng Tp.
St Thomas
Lloyd
Oxley Rd
Oxley Gdn
Chesed-El
Haw Par Ctr.
Haw Par Glass Tower
Penang

St Thomas Walk
Killiney Rd
Lloyd Gdns
Road
Oxley
Oxley Walk
Jln. Rumbia
Sacred Heart Church
Fort Channing Country Club
Cox Ter.

Jln. Kuala
River Valley Close
Kim
Institution
Teochew Bldg
Sri Thandayuthapani
Tank Rd
Battle Box
FORT CANNING PARK
Dhoby
Fort Canning Res.

istry of Manpower upational Safety & th Ctr. Employment ectorate
River Valley Road
Yam
Hill
S'pore Buddhist Lodge
Hong San See
UE Square
Shell House
Expressway

Street
Trade Mart S'pore
Robertson 100
Martin
Muthuraman Chetty Rd
Narayanan Chetty Rd
AIG
Arnasalam Chetty Rd
Robertson Walk
Fraser Place
Kanisha
Mohamed Sultan Rd
Unity St
S'pore Repertory Theatre
UE Shopping Mall
Clemenceau Avenue
River Valley Swimming Complex
Liang Court
Clarke Q.
River Valley Rd
Tan Tye Pl
Lane

Copthorne Plaza
Kings Centre
Robertson Quay
Rodyk Street
Saiboo St
Mohamed Sultan Rd
Nanson Rd
The Quayside
Singapore
Central
Tan Si Chong Su
S'pore History Museum
Riverside Point
Read
Bridge
Read St
Clarke Quay

lock Road

200 m
200 yards

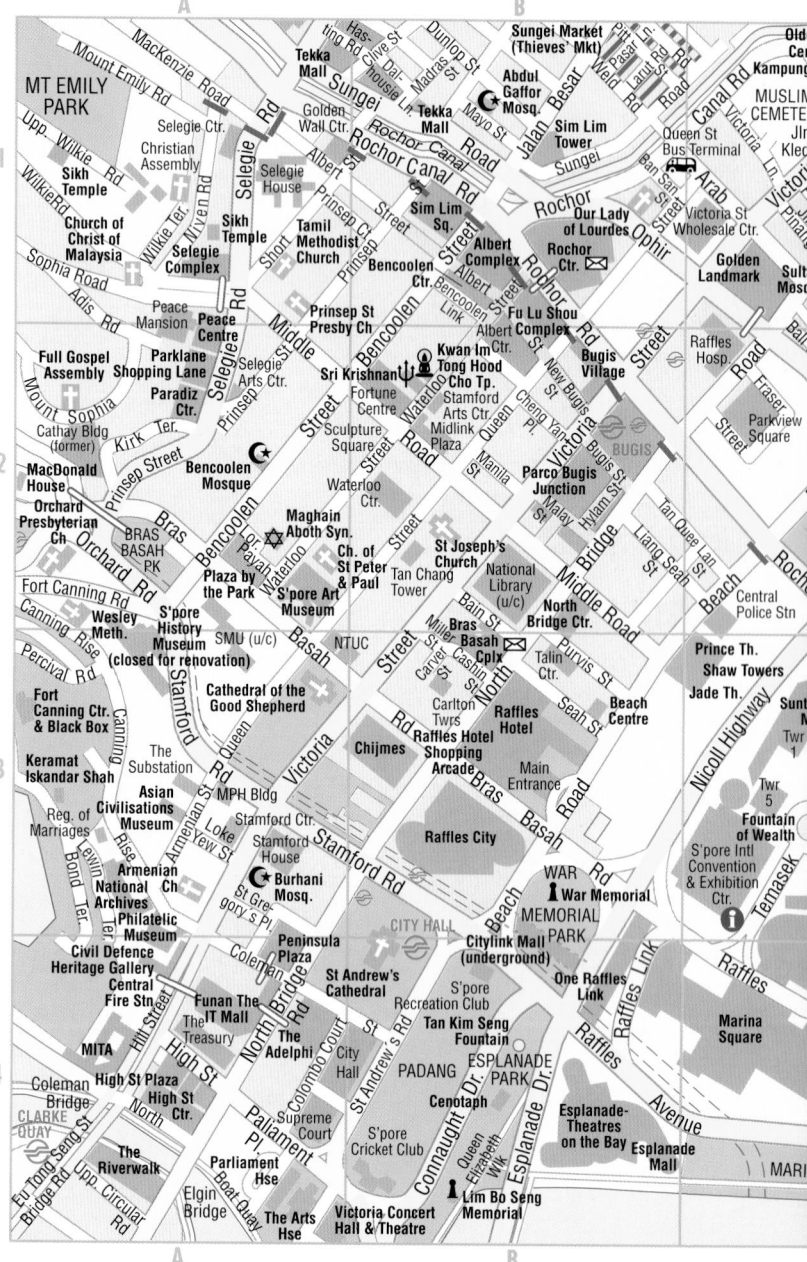

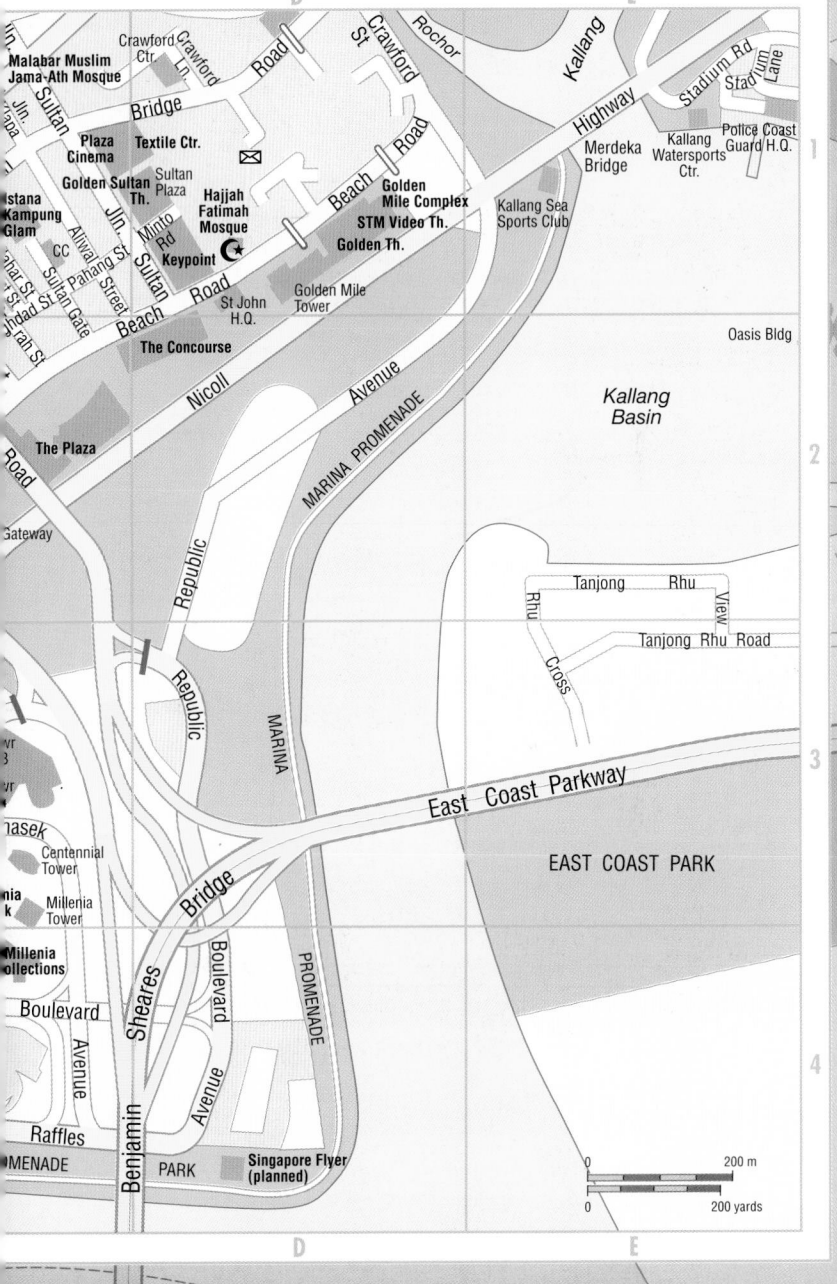

Malabar Muslim
Jama-Ath Mosque

Crawford
Ctr.

Crawford
Ln.

Crawford
Road

Crawford
St

Rochor

Kallang

Bridge

Bridge

Stadium Rd

Stadium

Stadium Lane

Kallang Highway

Plaza
Cinema

Textile Ctr.

Beach Road

Merdeka
Bridge

Kallang
Watersports
Ctr.

Police Coast
Guard H.Q.

Golden Sultan
Th.

Sultan
Plaza

Golden
Mile Complex

Istana
Kampung
Glam

Minto
Rd

Sultan

Hajjah
Fatimah
Mosque

STM Video Th.

Kallang Sea
Sports Club

Pahang Street

CC

Keypoint

Golden Th.

Attwal Street

Sultan

Beach
Road

St John
H.Q.

Golden Mile
Tower

Oasis Bldg

Sultan Gate

The Concourse

Nicoll

Avenue

MARINA PROMENADE

Kallang
Basin

Road

The Plaza

Republic

Gateway

Republic

Tanjong   Rhu

Rhu

Cross

Rhu

View

Tanjong Rhu Road

asek

Centennial
Tower

MARINA

East   Coast   Parkway

EAST COAST PARK

nia
k

Millenia
Tower

Bridge

Millenia
Collections

Boulevard

PROMENADE

Boulevard

Sheares

Avenue

Avenue

Benjamin

Raffles

MENADE

PARK

Singapore Flyer
(planned)

0		200 m

0		200 yards

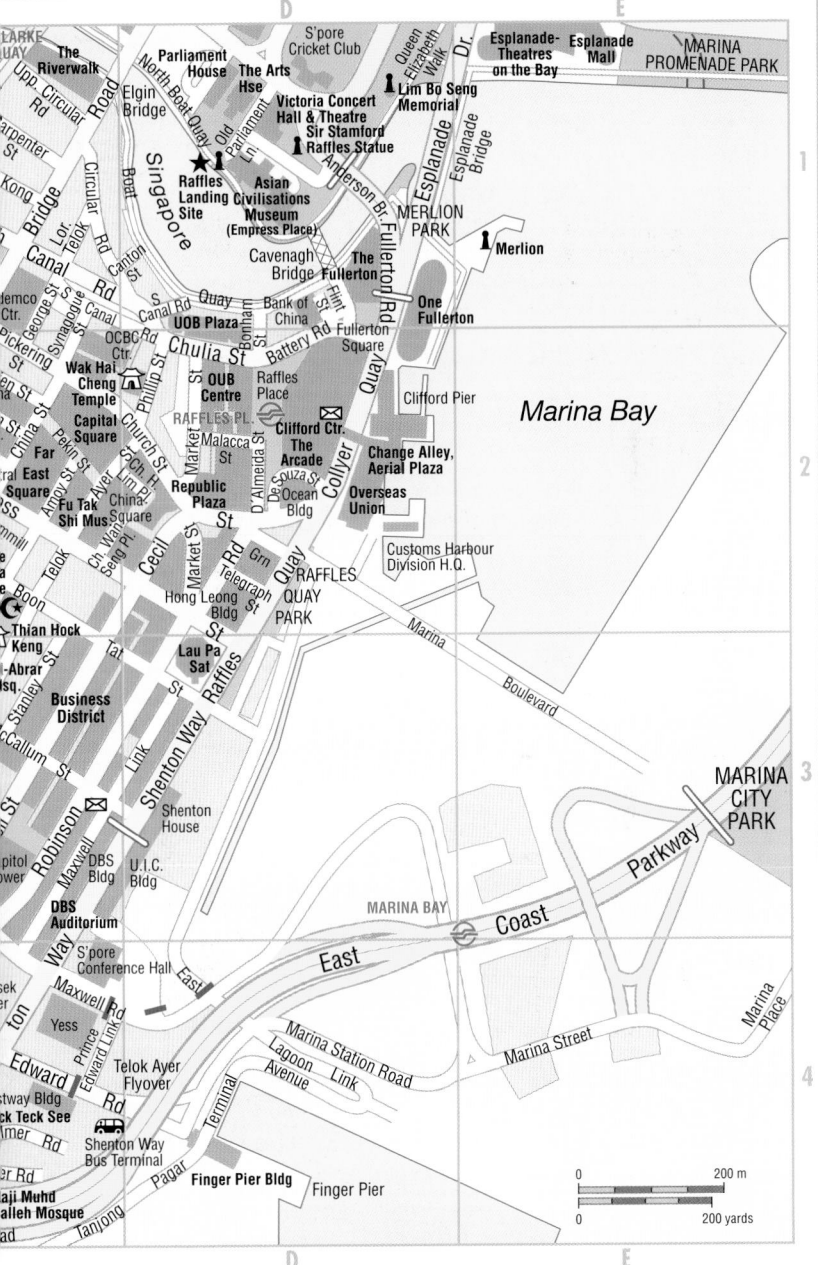

The Riverwalk
Upp. Circular Rd
Elgin Bridge
North Boat Quay
Parliament House
The Arts Hse
Old Parliament Ln
S'pore Cricket Club
Queen Elizabeth Walk
Esplanade Dr
Esplanade-Theatres on the Bay
Esplanade Mall
MARINA PROMENADE PARK

Carpenter St
Kong
Bridge
Canal Rd
Lor. Telok
Canton St
Boat
Singapore
Circular Rd
Raffles Landing Site
Victoria Concert Hall & Theatre
Sir Stamford Raffles Statue
Lim Bo Seng Memorial
Anderson Br.
Esplanade Br.
Esplanade Bridge

Asian Civilisations Museum (Empress Place)
MERLION PARK
Merlion

Lemco Ctr.
George St
Synagogue Canal
Pickering
St
Canal Rd
S Canal Rd
OCBC Ctr.
UOB PLAZA
Chulia St
Cavenagh Bridge
The Fullerton
Bank of China
Bonham St
Flint St
Battery Rd
Fullerton Rd
The Fullerton
One Fullerton

Wak Hai Cheng Temple
Capital Square
Far East Square
Fu Tak Shi Mus
Philip St
Church St
China Square
Seng Pt
OUB Centre
RAFFLES PL.
Market St
Malacca St
Raffles Place
D'Almeida St
De Souza St
Republic Plaza
Clifford Ctr.
The Arcade
Ocean Bldg
Overseas Union
Fullerton Square
Clifford Pier

Marina Bay

Cecil
Telok
Thian Hock Keng
-Abrar
Msq.
Stanley
cCallum St
Tat
St
Hong Leong Bldg
Telegraph St
Grn
Collyer Quay
RAFFLES QUAY PARK
Change Alley, Aerial Plaza
Customs Harbour Division H.Q.

Business District
Lau Pa Sat
Raffles
Shenton Way
Link
St
Marina
Boulevard

Robinson
Maxwell
DBS Bldg
U.I.C. Bldg
Shenton House
MARINA CITY PARK
Parkway

DBS Auditorium
S'pore Conference Hall
MARINA BAY
East
Coast
Marina Place

Maxwell Rd
Yess
Prince
Edward Link
Marina Station Road
Lagoon Link
Marina Street

Edward
Edward Rd
Telok Ayer Flyover
Terminal
Avenue

stway Bldg
ck Teck See
mer Rd
Shenton Way Bus Terminal
Pagar
Finger Pier Bldg
Finger Pier

Tanjong

0   200 m

0   200 yards

STREET INDEX

GENERAL INDEX

MRT System

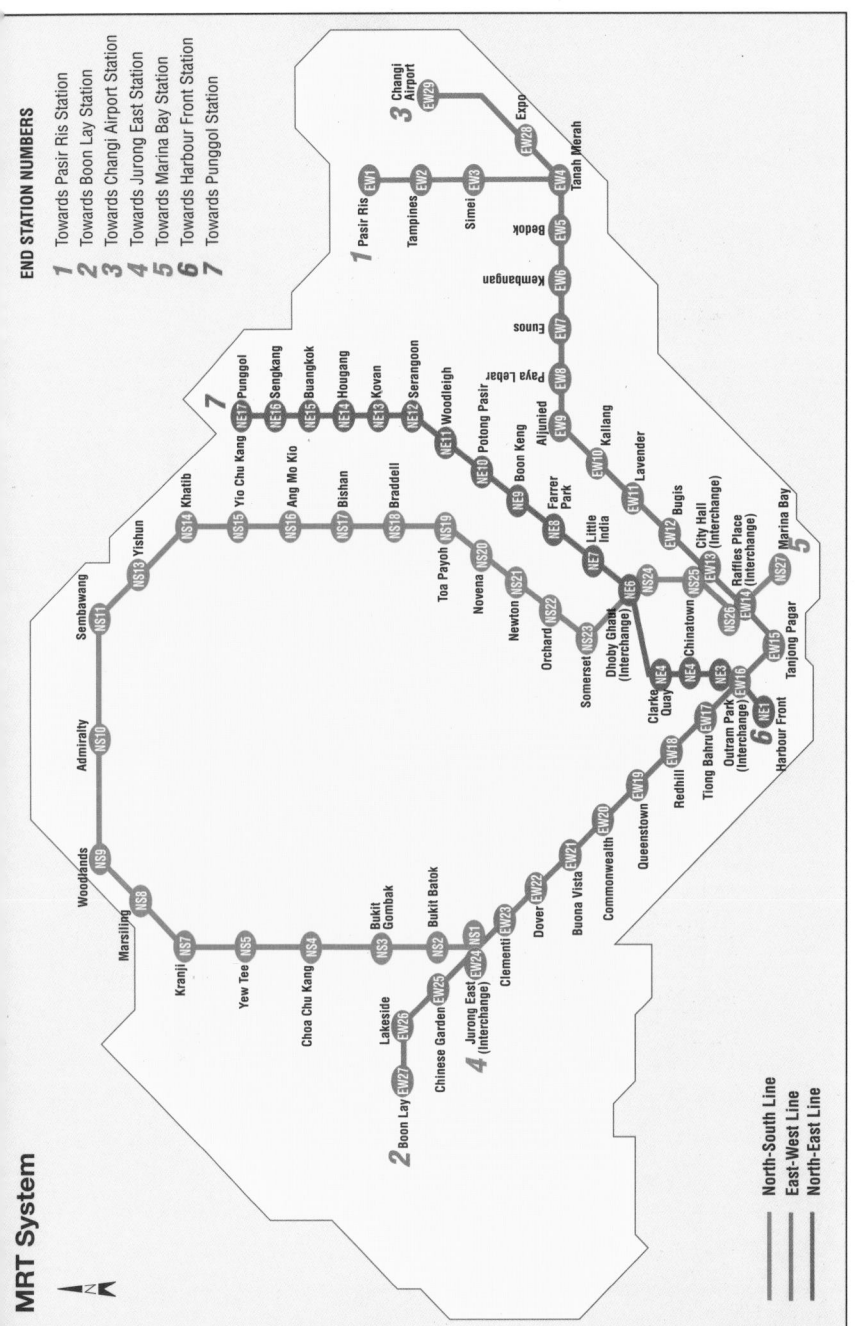

END STATION NUMBERS

1 Towards Pasir Ris Station
2 Towards Boon Lay Station
3 Towards Changi Airport Station
4 Towards Jurong East Station
5 Towards Marina Bay Station
6 Towards Harbour Front Station
7 Towards Punggol Station

North-South Line
East-West Line
North-East Line

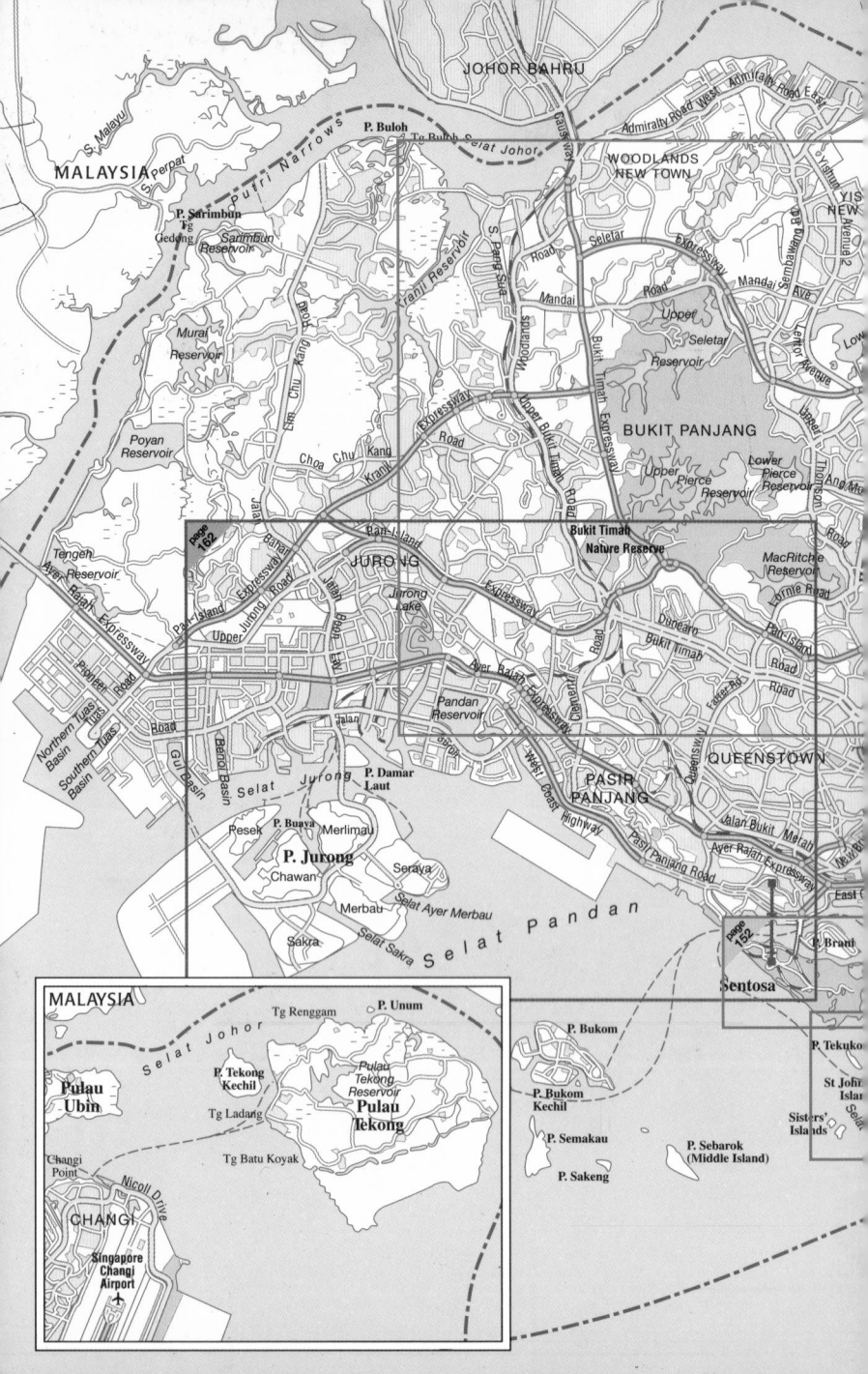